a Ross

THE ORIGINS OF
RHYMES, SONGS AND SAYINGS

THE ORIGINS
OF RHYMES, SONGS
AND SAYINGS

JEAN HARROWVEN

KAYE & WARD · LONDON

GAYLORD
PROFESSIONAL
PUBLICATIONS

TO RON, ROBERT AND RUTH

First published in Great Britain by
Kaye & Ward Ltd
21 New Street, London, EC2M 4NT
1977
Reprinted 1979

This edition published 1979
by Gaylord Bros Inc
TWX 710 545 0232
Box 4901, Syracuse, NY 13221
Box 8489, Stockton, CA 95208
Copyright © Kaye & Ward Ltd 1977

ISBN 0 7182 1123 5 (Great Britain)
ISBN 0-915794-45-4 (USA)

Set in VIP Palatino by S. G. Mason (Chester) Ltd.
Printed in Great Britain by
Biddles of Guildford

CONTENTS

INTRODUCTION   ix

PRE-CHRISTIAN   1
   Lullabies; Moon chants; Water chants; Magic;
Animals; Counting-out rhymes; Counting.

ROMAN   36
   Old King Cole; St. Agnes; Calendars; Numerals;
Biblical; Games; Proverbs; Riddles; Tongue-twisters;
King Arthur.

SAXON   58
   Weather; Nature; Harvests; Festivals; Christmas;
Pancake day; Fortune; St Patrick; St Swithin; St Dunstan;
St Valentine; St David and St Chad; London Bridge.

NORMAN, PLANTAGENET, LANCASTER
AND YORK   91
   Royal rhyme; Norman; Cock Robin; The Wise Men
of Gotham; Spring; The Miller of Dee; Crafts; Doctor
Foster; Bannockburn; St George; Black Douglas;
Robin Hood; Dick Whittington; The Merchants of
London; Baa, baa, black sheep; Witches and
Hallowe'en; Fairies; Domestic; Medical; Fairs.

TUDOR   141

Christopher Columbus; I had a little nut tree; Little
Boy Blue; Jack be nimble; Little Jack Horner; Sing a
song of sixpence; Hark, hark, the dogs do bark;
Oranges and Lemons; St Paul's Cathedral; Three blind
mice; A Scarborough warning; Hey diddle diddle,
the cat and the fiddle; Little bo-peep; Spanish Armada;
Cock a doodle doo; Ride a cock horse to Banbury Cross.

STUART   169

Guy Fawkes; Little Miss Muffet; Humpty Dumpty;
Charles I; General Monk; Charles II; James II; The Old
Pretender; Girls and boys come out to play; Cobbler,
cobbler mend my shoe; Ring-a-ring o' roses; Sir
Christopher Wren; Bessy Bell; Street cries; Rule
Britannia.

HANOVERIAN   209

The Vicar of Bray; Georgian; Social comment; God
save the Queen; The Young Pretender; Auld Lang
Syne; Scottish shanties; Bobby Shafto; Elsie Marley;
The British Grenadiers; Yankee Doodle; Lucy Locket;
Grand old Duke of York; The Marseillaise; Napoleon
and Nelson; Waterloo; Madame Tussaud; Twinkle,
twinkle little star; The Star-Spangled Banner; If I had a
donkey; Sea shanties.

VICTORIAN AND WINDSOR   259

Queen Victoria; Crimea; Annie Laurie; Home
Sweet Home; John Brown's Body; Eton Boating Song;
Boat Race Day; Pop goes the weasel; Nursery rhymes;
George Leybourne; Charles Coburn; For He's a Jolly
Good Fellow; Happy birthday to you; Lily of Laguna;
Blaydon Races; Goodbye Dolly Grey; Edward VII;
Daisy Bell; Don't Dilly Dally on the Way; Policemen
songs; Seaside songs; Twenty-one Today; Hello!
Hello! Who's Your Lady Friend?; Teddy bears; It's a
Long Way to Tipperary; Florrie Forde; Nellie Dean;

Pack Up Your Troubles; World War I; Rhyming slang;
Charlie Chaplin; World War II; Mt Everest; Space
travel; Today.

Acknowledgments   331

Illustration Acknowledgments   332

Bibliography of source material   333

Index of first lines   335

Index of subjects   343

Dear Reader,

       Traditional rhymes, songs and sayings provide links with the past which cannot be matched, and they recall incidents and social conditions in history that may otherwise have been forgotten. In fact, they may be described as the 'poetry of the ages'.

Material things throughout the centuries have crumbled and perished, buildings, books and ideas have lost their identity over the years, but the oral rhyme has thrived, to be repeated over and over again, since time and speech began. The English language as we know it today is made up of many tongues: Celtic, Saxon, Latin and French have combined to produce a complex pattern. The traditional chant has survived these hazards and, because of this, has become a precious part of our inheritance. The recording of old verses was rare. Parchment was scarce and learned people few. Those who could write considered everyday jingles too trivial a subject for record – and where was the need when only a few could read and the rhymes were very strongly represented in the oral collection?

Many of the true meanings of the old verses are lost to us, and they have secrets locked between their lines which can never be told. We repeat them, savouring the lilt and charm which have helped them to survive, but in the main we have no knowledge of the backgrounds from which they sprang. Through reading and research I have collected material which illuminates the origins of some of the rhymes we know so well. Classification has been difficult and, in order to introduce textual continuity, I have endeavoured to group the verses and sayings into the period of history from which it is thought they originated. In doing so, I have tried to provide a brief glimpse into practically every era of British history.

The form of the nursery rhyme is well known and its popularity increases year by year. Many verses have their roots deep in mythology and legend – *Jack and Jill* for example. From supernatural beginnings oral rhymes have multiplied and flourished.

Other nursery jingles that our youngsters chant so joyfully were not originally meant for the amusement of children. They were satires on contemporary political or religious events, popularized perhaps by leading wits and jesters, and sung by strolling minstrels. *Who Killed Cock Robin?*, for instance, has been accepted by many as a parody on the death of William Rufus in the New Forest.

Charms, fortune rituals and weather and nature verses, may not be so familiar to us, but they do reflect the hopes, fears and humour of our ancestors, and give us a deeper understanding of the necessary fight for survival of early man. In a few simple words these doggerels describe the true outlook of primitive folk, and are as fresh and earthy now as when they were first uttered.

Many proverbs, riddles and tongue-twisters are known to be very old and have, therefore, found a place in the opening chapters. Counting-out rhymes – the juvenile code ritual, which precedes numerous children's games – are regarded as having great antiquity also. There are many monuments in Britain today that remind us of our traditional rhymes: Nottingham pays tribute to Robin Hood; London Bridge has been reconstructed yet once more; the remaining *Oranges and Lemons* churches draw sightseers from all over the world.

The working rhymes still have their uses. Lullabies will never fade. Tongue-twisters are valuable to the speech therapist, and proverbs are a necessary part of language. Many of us would feel a little lost if we could not recite *Thirty days hath September*.

More recently, the music hall, now almost obsolete, has provided numerous songs and sayings which have joined the constant stream. This is probably due to the skill and personality of the artistes, who presented the material in such a way that it has remained indelible in the minds of ordinary folk throughout the years. *Daisy Bell* and *Dilly Dally* are just two that have found a place in this collection. These well-loved choruses form the backbone of most branches of community singing in modern times. According to the *Guinness Book of Records* the song that is sung most frequently in the world today is *Happy Birthday To You*.

Together with *For He's A Jolly Good Fellow*, these two simple chants top the popularity poll – and yet both have very different origins.

Our civilization is based on centuries of observation and superstition, and old habits do not die so easily. Charm bracelets are still worn and lucky mascots are popular. Many people will avoid walking under a ladder or will avoid viewing a new moon through glass or trees. Very few people will stand bareheaded in the presence of flying bats. When visiting a well, some people will make a wish and throw money into it. A sudden spine shiver or a stab of fear in the dark cannot be explained. These customs and feelings are relics of former days, and must be accepted as such.

The study of old rhymes and sayings can equip us to understand ourselves more fully and can explain, to a certain extent, the behaviour of humanity as a whole.

It may come to pass that some of my theories will be openly disputed. In this event I shall be well content and will realise that my ambition has been fulfilled – namely, to evoke interest in a subject that has long been neglected.

Whilst this work is based on many years of research and assistance which is borne out in the Bibliography, and list of personal acknowledgements, no one working in this field could possibly omit to acknowledge the pioneer work of Iona and Peter Opie in their 'Oxford Dictionary of Nursery Rhymes' and 'Oxford Nursery Rhyme Book'.

JEAN HARROWVEN

Thorpe St Andrew, Norwich.

'The days of youth are made for glee, and time is on the wing.'

From *The Miller of Dee*

'This subtle Thief of life, this paltry Time,
What will it leave me if it snatch my rhyme?'

Alexander Pope

PRE-CHRISTIAN

LULLABIES

In the beginning there was the lullaby, which must be considered as the germ of all song. It is easy to imagine how mothers of the Stone Age era discovered that soothing, crooning noises and a rocking motion put their babies to sleep. Indeed, even the unmusical tribes that still exist today use the reassuring humming noise of the primitive lullaby when coaxing sleep upon their infants.

It seems logical to assume that from the balanced rhythm of the ancient lullaby stemmed the scanned and rhyming verse, which eventually involved practically every subject known to man. Lullabies are universal and usually follow the same pattern throughout the countries of the world. They contain comforting words and recurring stanzas, set to a rocking rhythm, usually about familiar things; the father, who is often depicted out hunting, other members of the family, sleepy animals, stars shining, and symbols pointing to the realms of sleep. Words often contain bribes to be good and go to sleep: in England *Baby Bunting* is promised a rabbit skin, a Danish baby is promised new shoes with shining buckles, French infants are promised a white bird that will lay a special egg, Greeks are promised a sugar city, Japanese are promised toys, drums and papier maché dogs, and in China a bamboo flute. Mothers in some countries even sing of the bogey man who will take the baby away if he is noisy. In Spain, youngsters are told that a black man will eat babies that cry. In Japan, Hotti (a type of Santa Claus) will not distribute toys and sweets unless children are sleeping. In Germany a black sheep and a white sheep will bite the toes of crying babies.

Rock-a-bye Baby must be one of the oldest known cradle songs. It refers to the ancient custom of hanging babies in rush baskets on branches of trees, to be rocked to sleep by the wind.

> *Rock-a-bye baby on the tree top,*
> *When the wind blows the cradle will rock;*
> *When the bough breaks, the cradle will fall,*
> *Down will come baby, cradle and all.*

An older opening line was 'Rock-a-bye baby on the green boh'. 'Boh' is a Saxon word for bough, and 'bye' is an old English word for sleep. A Scottish version of this song also bears out the theory that cradles were rocked by the wind long ago:

> *I've placed my cradle on yon holly top,*
> *And aye as the wind blew, my cradle did rock;*
> *O hush a ba, baby, O ba lilly loo,*
> *And hee and ba, birdie, my bonny wee dow.*
> > *Hee O! wee O!*
> > *What will I do wi' you.*

An old lady from Wales told me that she always understood that the song *Rock-a-bye* referred to young birds in the nest and was the mother bird's song as she taught them to fly. A bird is mentioned in the above version, so perhaps this is where the idea stems from.

Another old Scottish cradle song connected with birds goes:

> *Hush-a-ba, birdie, croon, croon,*
> > *Hush-a-ba, birdie, croon;*
> *The sheep are gone to the silver wood,*
> > *And the cows are gone to the broom, broom.*
>
> *And it's braw milking the kye, kye,*
> > *It's braw milking the kye;*
> *The birds are singing, the bells are ringing,*
> > *And the wild deer come galloping by.*
>
> *Hush-a-ba, birdie, croon, croon,*
> > *Hush-a-ba, birdie, croon;*
> *The goats are gone to the mountain high,*
> > *And they'll not be home till noon.*

A rhyme little used in modern times uses the intimidation theme once again:

Baby, baby, naughty baby,
Hush you squalling thing, I say.
Peace this moment, peace, or maybe
Bonaparte will pass this way.

Baby, baby, he's a giant,
Tall and black as Rouen steeple,
And he breakfasts, dines, rely on't,
Every day on naughty people.

Baby, baby, if he hears you,
As he gallops past the house,
Limb from limb at once he'll tear you,
Just as pussy tears a mouse.

And he'll beat you, beat you, beat you,
And he'll beat you all to pap,
And he'll eat you, eat you, eat you,
Every morsel snap, snap, snap.

Bonaparte was only one of the 'bogeys' named in this old verse. 'Old Black Knoll' (Oliver Cromwell) was used at one time, 'Tall and black as Lincoln steeple'.

A cradle song which was well-known in days gone by is:

Rock-a-bye baby, thy cradle is green,
Father's a nobleman, Mother's a queen;
And Betty's a lady, and wears a gold ring;
And Johnny's a drummer, and drums for the king.

Perhaps one of the most popular of all secular lullabies is *How Many Miles To Babylon?*:

How many miles to Babylon?
Three score miles and ten.
Can I get there by candle-light?
Yes, and back again.
If your heels are nimble and light,
You may get there by candle-light.

This old rhyme, which may have its roots in a mummer's play dealing with the Crusades, explains with a certain amount of glamour the passageway into the realms of sleep. Babylon has been explained as an incantation of Babyland, but I have always been certain in my own mind that it is a corruption of Bethlehem, linking it with the Crusader background. 'Can I get there by candle-light?' was a saying much used in Elizabethan times.

With the advent of Christianity surely many lullabies must have referred to the birth of Christ, but, because of the turbulent religious history of Great Britain, not many Christian rhymes and songs have survived. *Away In A Manger* is sometimes called *Luther's Cradle Hymn*, but whether in fact Martin Luther did compose it is not known. It is described as an old German folk song, and must be perhaps the most well-known of all Christmas lullabies:

> *Away in a manger, no crib for a bed,*
> *The little Lord Jesus lay down his sweet head;*
> *The stars in the bright sky, looked down where he lay,*
> *The little Lord Jesus, asleep on the hay.*
>
> *The cattle are lowing, the baby awakes;*
> *But little Lord Jesus, no crying he makes;*
> *I love thee Lord Jesus, look down from the sky,*
> *And stay by my side until morning is nigh.*
>
> *Be near me Lord Jesus, I ask thee to stay*
> *Close by me for ever, and love me I pray;*
> *Bless all the dear children in thy tender care,*
> *And fit us for heaven, to live with thee there.*

Another Christmas cradle song of great antiquity is the *Rocking Carol*:

> *Baby Jesus, sweetly sleep,*
> *Do not stir,*
> *We will lend a coat of fur;*
> *We will rock you, rock you, rock you;*
> *We will rock you, rock you, rock you,*
> *We will serve you all we can,*
> *Darling, darling little man.*

Silent Night is considered to be one of the most popular rocking carols in modern times. The story is that it was written by the parish priest of the small church of Arndorf in Austria in 1818.

The church was extremely poor, and the priest and the organist were worried because they felt they had no special music to play for the Midnight Mass. When the organist read the words of *Silent Night* that the priest had written, he was inspired and sat up all night to compose the tune for this carol. It soon became famous and brought prosperity to the church and parish. The organist was Franz Gruber.

> *Silent night, Holy night,*
> *All is calm, all is bright;*
> *Round yon Virgin Mother and Child,*
> *Holy infant so tender and mild,*
> *Sleep in Heavenly peace,*
> *Sleep in Heavenly peace.*
>
> *Silent night, holy night,*
> *Shepherds quake, at the sight,*
> *Glories stream from heaven afar,*
> *Heavenly hosts sing Alleluia;*
> *Christ the Saviour is born,*
> *Christ the Saviour is born.*
>
> *Silent night, holy night,*
> *Son of God, Loves pure light,*
> *Radiant beams from Thy holy face,*
> *With the dawn of redeeming grace,*
> *Jesus, Lord, at Thy birth,*
> *Jesus, Lord, at Thy birth.*

The traditional 6/8 rhythm of the lullaby has been used by many famous composers: Mozart and Schubert wrote the *Wiegenlieder*, and Chopin wrote *Berceuse* for the piano. Here is a verse of a cradle song composed by Lord Tennyson:

> *Sweet and low, sweet and low,*
> *Wind of the western sea.*
> *Low, low, breathe and blow –*
> *Wind of the western sea!*
> *Over the rolling waters go;*
> *Come from the dying moon and blow,*
> *Blow him again to me;*
> *While my little one, while my pretty one, sleeps.*

MOON CHANTS

Many rhymes are very old indeed, having their sources in pre history and originating in folklore and mythology; such is the case concerning rhymes about the man in the Moon. The moon has been an object of wonderment since the evolution of thought and reason. The position of early man was precarious, and his chances of survival were small. He felt insignificant and insecure, and it is not surprising that early stories and superstitions were woven around the moon, as it gave light in the terrifying darkness of the night. Even today children imagine they see 'pictures' or 'faces' on the moon's surface. Primitive man saw these shadows and was convinced that the moon was inhabited. The stories gave him comfort and some sort of mental insurance against the perils of life.

Moon rhymes are repeated in many countries of the world, where they have been passed from generation to generation since the Dark Ages. The Old Testament consists of a collection of legends and stories, which are timeless. In Numbers 15:32-36 we read that Moses came across a man gathering sticks on the sabbath. For working on the holy day, Moses ordered that the man be stoned to death. It is believed that the legend of a man on the moon destined to carry sticks on his back springs from this incident, although moon stories are banned from sacred writings and there is no mention of this punishment in the Bible.

A similar story comes from Germany. A handsome man dressed in his best suit on his way to church met an old labourer hewing sticks. The younger man said, "Do you know that this is Sunday on Earth, when all must rest from their labours?"

"Sunday on Earth or Monday in Heaven, it's all the same to me", replied the woodcutter.

"Then bear your faggot bundle for ever, as you do not value your Sunday on Earth – yours shall be perpetual Moon day in Heaven and be a warning to all Sabbath breakers."

The stranger then vanished, and the old man was whisked away to the moon, where he can still be seen standing with his load of sticks.

1.   Man in the Moon seal, dated 1335.

A writer in the twelfth century, Alexander Nechum, recorded a verse in Latin explaining the shadows on the moon, which in translation says:

> *See the rustic in the Moon,*
> *How his bundle weighs him down;*
> *Thus his sticks the truth reveal,*
> *It never profits man to steal.*

There are many tales from other lands about the man in the moon, and in all cases the man was the wrongdoer, and was banished for eternity on the moon. He had either stolen cabbages or other vegetables, in which case on Christmas Eve he was allowed to turn round once, or he had strewn thorns and brambles on the church path to prevent people from attending Mass.

The old rhyme below refers to this story; it is of German origin:

> *The Man in the Moon was caught in a trap,*
> *For stealing thorns from another man's gap;*
> *If he had gone by, and let the thorns lie,*
> *He'd never have been Man in the Moon so high.*

Shakespeare writes of the man in the moon carrying thorns and a lantern in *A Midsummer Night's Dream*.

From Rantum in north-west Germany we have another interesting explanation of this subject. In this case the man in the moon is a giant who controls the tides. For centuries man has realised that the behaviour of the sea has close connections with the moon's power and the story of the giant simply illustrates this. It is said that, when he stoops and pours water on the Earth, he causes a high tide; when he stands erect and takes his ease, the waters subside and an ebb tide follows.

Other tales say that the man in the moon is accompanied by a woman carrying a butter tub. Her punishment of being there was because she churned butter on a Sunday. Sometimes the moon man has a dog for company.

A curious seal preserved in the Public Record Office in Chancery Lane, London, shows a picture of a man bearing sticks with a dog at his side on the moon. The date on the deed to which the seal is attached is 1335, and the transaction took place during the reign of Edward III. It is a conveyance of buildings and land in the parish of Kingston-on-Thames from Walter de Gredesse, clerk, to his mother, Margaret. The inscription reads, *'Te Waltere docebo, cur spinas phebo gero'* – 'I will teach thee Walter, why I carry thorns in the moon'.

The awe-inspiring presence of the moon has brought forth many superstitions and fortune rhymes stemming from very early days. It is still regarded as lucky to see a new moon. People often bow to it and turn over the money in their pockets. Here are some rhymes which have stood the test of time:

> *I see the moon, and the moon sees me,*
> *God bless the moon, and God bless me.*

Trawlermen's children say:

> *I see the moon and the moon sees me.*
> *God bless the sailors on the sea.*

Yorkshire mothers say:

> *Moon penny bright as silver,*
> *Come and play with little childer.*

A new moon evoked many wishing rhymes:

> *Moon, moon,*
> *Mak' me a pair o' shoon* [shoes]
> *And I'll dance till you be done.*

> *New moon, new moon,*
> *First time I've see'd thee,*
> *Hope before the weeks out*
> *I'll ha' summat gi'ed me.*

Yorkshire rhymes tell us that to see a new moon on a Saturday or a Friday foretells ill luck:

> *A Saturday's Moon,*
> *If it comes once in seven years,*
> *It comes too soon.*

> *Friday's moon*
> *Come when it will, it comes too soon.*

An old Devon rhyme says:

> *Saturday new and Sunday full,*
> *Never was fine, and never was wool.*

Another couplet which connects the moon with rainfall is:

> *A far off brough*
> *Is a storm near enough.*

A 'brough' is a halo round the moon. The next saying has been well proved:

> *Clear moon,*
> *Frost soon.*

During the course of religious and political history the man in the moon has been parodied many times. When Jacobite feeling was running high, many songs were sung and composed to encourage the cause. According to James Hogg, an authority on Jacobite songs, this next verse refers to the Whig parliament which George I set up in 1714; an act which obviously did not please the Jacobites:

There was a man came from the moon,
And landed in our town, sir;
And he swore a solemn oath
That all the knaves must down, sir.
He had an axe into his hand,
A rope around his crap, sir;
And he swore a solemn oath,
That all the rogues must strap, sir.

Another Jacobite verse has a different approach:

The man o' the moon, here's to him;
How few there be that know him!
   But we'll drink to him still
   In a merry cup of ale.
Then man o' the moon, here's to him.

It is not known what is the underlying meaning of this jingle, but it may be assumed that the 'man o' the moon' in this instance refers either to the exiled James Stuart or to his son Charles.

The most well-known and recent moon rhyme is:

The man in the moon came down too soon,
And asked his way to Norwich.
He went to the south, and burnt his mouth,
By eating cold plum porridge!

Plum porridge is a form of plum pudding made in a saucepan in the days before pudding cloths were used, and means, therefore, that this particular verse is at least two hundred years old.

WATER CHANTS

Jack and Jill went up the hill
To fetch a pail of water.
Jack fell down and broke his crown,
And Jill came tumbling after.

Up Jack got and home he did trot,
As fast as he could caper,
He went to bed to mend his head,
With vinegar and brown paper.

Then Jill came in and she did grin,
To see Jack's paper plaster;
Her mother whipped her across her knee,
For laughing at Jack's disaster.

In an original chapbook printed in the early nineteenth century there were fifteen verses to this rhyme. 'Vinegar and brown paper' is an old remedy for a headache. It seems pretty certain that this rhyme has its roots in Scandinavian mythology and is closely connected with moon stories. The legend says that one evening two children, named Hjuki and Bil, had been to the well and were walking home with a full bucket of water suspended on a water pole. Mani, the moon, stole the children and carried them off to heaven (the moon). In Sweden the moon-spots are explained in this way, and the pattern of the two children carrying a bucket and a pole between them is similar perhaps to the man and woman bearing faggots and a butter churn.

'Hjuki' in Norse would be pronounced 'Juki', which would easily become Jack, and Bil, in order to make one of the children feminine, would become Jill. The fall of Jack and the subsequent fall of Jill explains the vanishing of the two moon-spots.

'Hjuki' is derived from the verb *jakka* which means to increase or assemble; Bil is from *bila*, which means to break up or dissolve. Therefore it seems that Hjuki and Bil signify the waxing and waning of the moon, and the water that the children carried represented the rainfall, which is connected with this natural phenomenon, and the ebb and flow of tides, which are also within the moon's power.

People have remarked that it does not seem logical to have a well on a hill as in *Jack and Jill*. Although it is true that castles and fortresses were often built on high ground and must have been served by wells or underground springs, why this particular well was elevated we do not know. Some think that the well had supernatural connections and that the water was heaven-sent.

The superstitions connected with water originated in archaic Nature worship. To our pagan ancestors, Nature and what seems natural to us, was in fact regarded as supernatural by them. All things that lived and moved on the earth or in the sky were thought of as magical, and, therefore, as governed by gods or spirits. The Greeks and Romans dedicated wells and springs to nymphs and goddesses. The Roman goddess of water was called Arnemeza or Aqua Arnemetia. A well in Buxton yielded a much defaced statue from its depths in the seventeenth century. The inhabitants thought that it was a statue of St Ann, but it may well have been an image of the Roman Arnemeza. Thus, every river in Britain had its kelpie, every lake its monster and every spring or well its bogart or banshee. Generally speaking, the spirits of the water were regarded as malignant in pre-Christian times. Sacrifices, often human, were offered to the water gods and it is known that the Druids followed practices of this kind in return for a good supply of pure water.

Rhymes about water date from the very earliest times. The rivers were regarded as 'uncanny' and housed beneath their rippling surfaces dreaded prehistoric animals, who lay in wait for humans to come too near and then dragged them to a watery grave. Two old Scottish rhymes bear this out. The first comes from the Scottish border:

> Tweed said to Till,
> 'What gars ye rin sae still?'
> Till said to Tweed,
> 'Though ye rin wi' speed,
> And I rin slaw,
> Yet whare ye droon ae man,
> I droon twa.'

The second is from Aberdeenshire:

> Bloodthirsty Dee
> Each year needs three;
> But bonny Don,
> She needs none.

A story connected with the Dee rhyme tells us that a basket-maker was crossing the river late one night when his foot slipped off the bridge and he fell into the water, and was drowned by the water sprites. His wife, wishing to find her husband's body, threw his plaid into the spot in the river where it was thought he had drowned. The next morning the corpse was washed up wrapped in his own plaid. People often threw a plaid into the river, hoping that 'Bloodthirsty Dee' would be content with a man's plaid and spare a life. Until the last century, when fishing in the river Tweed, salt was thrown into the water and sprinkled on the nets as an offering to the water spirits in return for a good catch. Two other river rhymes stemming from Yorkshire declare:

> *Wharfe is clear, and Aire is lythe,*
> *Where the Aire drowns one, Wharfe drowns five.*
>
> *The shelvin', slimy river Dun,*
> *Each year a daughter or a son.*

An old ballad from Scotland again tells us that:

> *The side was steep, the bottom deep,*
> *Frae bank to bank the water pouring;*
> *And the bonnie lass did quake for fear,*
> *She heard the water-kelpie roaring.*

In Lancashire a terrible monster called Jenny Greenteeth inhabited certain stagnant pools, or so it was thought. Children were warned not to go too close for fear the water spirit should rise out of the green pool and drag them down to the depths. A water hole near Flamborough, Yorkshire, marks the spot where a young girl, Jenny, committed suicide centuries ago. It is believed by local folk that, if a person should run round the hole nine times, he will see Jenny's spirit rise out of the hole and recite these words:

> *Ah'll tee on my bonnet*
> *An' put on me shoe,*
> *An' if thee's nut off*
> *Ah'll seean catch thoo!*

According to legend, a farmer once rode his horse nine times round the water hole and sure enough Jenny's spirit rose out of the water, and chased after him. The farmer was terrified and spurred his horse to gallop as fast as possible to the nearest village. The spirit followed him to the outskirts, then retreated, but not before it had bitten a piece out of the mare's flank. The horse, so it is said, had a white patch there until her dying day.

Sometimes wells or springs were thought to be inhabited by animals. A pool in the North Esk was the accepted home of a water-horse. This being, so the story goes, was captured by a magic bridle and made to work as a slave, carrying stones for building a castle. One day its bridle was accidently removed and the creature vanished, saying:

Sair back an' sair banes,
Carryin' the Laird o' Morphie's stanes;
The Laird o' Morphie canna thrive
As lang as the kelpy's still alive.

The water kelpie was heard frequently repeating the rhyme in the pool and the fate of the castle and the family who owned it was disastrous from that time onwards.

With the advent of Christianity wells and pools became places of reverence. Many saints adopted prominent wells, blessed them, and banished the malignant water sprites forever. This is why so many wells bear the names of early saints. The water in the wells was then regarded as holy, and used for baptism and many healing purposes. Instead of pagan sacrifices, people would throw in a pebble or coin as payment for the pure water they took. It is thought that the action of the water on stones or metal may well have increased the healing properties or general purity of the water. In early times many pilgrimages were made to important healing or holy wells. Often the pilgrims were told to walk round the well three times, 'deisseil-wise'. This meant clock-wise or sun-wise. It was considered a sign of good luck to do this before partaking of the waters'. If the well was approached anti-clockwise, or 'widdershins' as it was called, bad luck would fall on the person concerned. Only witches or the devil ever walked widdershins.

The merging of paganism and Christianity shows itself in this old rhyme from Portugal, which when translated reads:

St John to see the girls,
Made a fountain of silver;
But the girls were not there,
So St John killed himself.

The ritual of love-making in connection with water is crudely associated here with a saint of the Scriptures.

The medicinal wells and springs at Harrogate in Yorkshire and in the surrounding district were not generally used for commercial purposes until the eighteenth century. However, the locals enjoyed the life-giving waters in comparative peace for centuries before this. Many stories and legends have sprung up concerning the individual wells, some of which have been named after saints. A verse printed in the eighteenth century tells us:

Mythologists might, in this cave lay odds,
That sylvan deities, and water gods,
As dryads, naides, rural nymphs and fawns,
Who haunt the fountains, rivers woods and lawns,
In darkened days, ere learning did appear,
Might be supposed to hold their meetings here.
From whence arose that legendary tale
Of Mother Shipton dwelling in this vale.
Tradition tells and far the mouth of fame
Hath spread the predicts of the Yorkshire Dame;
The boding Sibyl told what would betide;
But Britons hath a true and better guide;
As for her facts we cannot truly tell,
Therefore adieu unto the Dropping Well.

Mother Shipton, as mentioned in the verse, was a well-known character who was born in about 1488, and lived during the reign of Henry VII. She was renowned for her fortune-telling and general healing abilities. It was supposed that she used the waters of the Dropping Well, which was near her cave home, for medicinal purposes. She lived as a 'wild woman', and her unkempt appearance and strange ways contributed to her reputation. Here is an old Yorkshire rhyme which describes her:

Mark well her grot, don't miss this place,
Nor startle at her haggard face;
As you are come to see the well,
Pray take a peep into her Cell.

Mother Shipton, as has been stated, made many prophesies, of which two have been preserved in rhyme:

Between Calder and Aire
Shall be great warfare;
When all the world is aloft,
It shall be called Christ's Croft.

It is thought that 'Christ's Croft' referred to a farmhouse called God's Croft, which lay half-way between Frodsham and Helsby. It was supposed to be the place named by the prophet Nixon, when he was asked where man could seek shelter on Judgement Day.

When lords and ladies stinking water soss,
High brigs o' stean the Nidd sal cross,
An' a toon be built on Harrogate moss.

The verse above in dialect refers to the unpleasant smell of the Harrogate waters, but predicts that, when rich people discover the medicinal properties of the springs, a town will be built on 'Harrogate moss' – all of which came true. Another couplet well-known in Harrogate is:

Said the Devil when flying o'er Harrogate Wells,
I think I an getting near home by the smells.

In Cornwall a well-tried recipe for scalds or burns was to take the water from a holy well and float nine bramble leaves on it. Then the wound was bathed in the holy water, while the nine leaves were passed over the sore place. This charm was recited during the operation:

There came three angels out of the east,
One brought fire, and one brought frost;
Out fire, in frost,
In the Name of the Father, Son and Holy Ghost.

During the times of plague and pestilence, wells that remained pure were naturally revered, as it was thought that the pureness of the drinking water had saved the inhabitants from death. Here is a couplet that bears this out, and alludes to St Olavs' Well in Cruden, Aberdeenshire:

St Olav's Well, low by the sea,
Where pest nor plague shall never be.

Well-dressing is another custom which goes back to ancient times. The Tissington Wells in Derbyshire are famous for this and the ritual is still performed every Ascension day. In *The Well Dressing Guide* by Crichton Porteous, he says that the custom may have developed from 'the age-old fear and worship of water gods and spirits. Into rivers, springs and wells people of countries of the world over have at times cast virgins, children, choice animals and flowers as votive offerings for the gift of water, or as bribes against floods and drought.' The Tissington well-dressing ceremony is widely known and has been traced back to the Black Death of 1348, when the wells remained pure and saved the people in the district from disease. The custom, of course, may be a good deal older than this.

Below are some verses composed only in the last century, but they do record the feelings and gratitude of people for centuries before this:

> *Come visit the fountain adorned with flowers,*
> *Where nature bedecked doth her wonders display,*
> *And science and art, while exerting their powers,*
> *Combined invite you a visit to pay.*

> *The Green Well, the Green Well, this year we adorn,*
> *With flowers that are fragrant and fair as the morn,*
> *From the groves we have brought them all bathed in dew,*
> *And twin'd in a garland, present them to you . . .*

> *Pure as these waters leave their bed*
> *Thy love o'er the earth is spread;*
> *And freed as through the plains they roll,*
> *Thy gifts descend to cheer the soul.*

The last verse is part of a hymn composed for the Tissington well-flowering. On the whole, healing wells have been turned into wishing wells during the last few centuries. In accordance with the ancient custom, coins or pebbles are still thrown into the well before a wish is made. An old rhyme repeated by my grandmother records this:

> *Wishing well, wishing well,*
> *Make my wish come true;*
> *I will throw in a bent pin*
> *To make my wish come true.*

Why the pin had to be bent is a mystery which has remained unsolved. Another Yorkshire verse sets great store by the power of Diana's Well to grant wishes:

> *Whoever eats Hammer nuts,*
> *And drinks Diana's water,*
> *Will never leave Witton town*
> *While he's a rag or tatter.*

Diana's Well or Cast-a-way Well is on the higher slopes of Witton Fell. Pins and other articles are thrown in for luck while the wish is made. Diana's Well at one time supplied drinking water through a pipe in the mouth of a carved stone head nick-named Slaverin' Sal.

At wishing wells the lover's wish has perhaps been the most manifold. An old belief held in Yorkshire is that whoever drops five white stones into the Ouse near the county town, when the minster clock strikes one on a May morning, will see on the surface of the water the face of the loved one.

A certain holy well near Dale Abbey in Derbyshire would grant wishes, it was thought, if the person visited it between the hours of twelve and three on Good Friday, drink the waters thrice, and wish. Here is part of an old Rumanian ballad which records this kind of practice:

> *There, where on Sundays I go alone,*
> *To the old, old well with the milk white stone,*
> *Where by the fence in a nook forgot,*
> *Rises a spring in the daisied grass,*
> *That makes who so drinks of it love – alas!*
> *My Heart's best beloved, he drinks it not.*

MAGIC

Stories about fairies, goblins, elves and pixies have been with us since the Dark Ages. Some of the earliest inhabitants of Europe were small, olive-skinned people, who lived in caves or underground. When taller invaders occupied the land, they fled to the hills, swamps or other inaccessible places. The 'little people', as they were called, were thought to possess supernatural powers. Certainly they were skilled in doctoring their animals and themselves. Also, they probably used poison to kill their enemies. Their small flint-heads can still be found today and are called 'elf arrows'. Legends which said that the 'little people' crept into villages at night and stole human babies, leaving their own, soon developed into the strong belief in fairy changelings.

When the Romans invaded Britain, they brought with them numerous sagas from Roman and Greek mythology, which were integrated with stories of the 'little people', and it is from this source that many traditional fairy stories sprang.

In and out the dusky bluebells,
In and out the dusky bluebells,
In and out the dusky bluebells,
  I am your master.

Tipper-ipper-apper – on your shoulder,
Tipper-ipper-apper – on your shoulder,
Tipper-ipper-apper – on your shoulder,
  I am your master.

In and out the dusky bluebells' is a singing ring game which is probably played all over Britain. It originated in Somerset and was also known in Scotland from an early date. The story goes that in reality it is a fairy or magical song. Certainly, it contains something sinister in the words. Legend has it that bluebells are fairy flowers and, if a child picks them in a wood alone, he will never be seen again. If a grown-up, too gathers the flowers alone then he will be led around by a pixy, until another adult goes into the wood and leads him to safety. Most ring games are known to be very old, originating in Druid customs, and it is not surprising that this particular game is played with a certain amount of suppressed excitement. Norse and Egyptian mythology have also left their mark on fairy rhymes:

The moon shines bright,
The stars give light,
And little Nanny Button-cap,
Will come tomorrow night.

This verse repeated by Yorkshire children has immortalized Nanna, the Norse moon goddess, wife of Baldur, the sun god. 'little Nanny Button-cap' is portrayed as a moon fairy who visits obedient children.

To mention the dead by name was believed, in pagan times, to bring evil upon the household. The ancient Egyptians, however, thought that to speak the name of a dead pharaoh was sufficient to make him live again; this idea is reflected in an old folk rhyme from Scotland:

Gin ye ca' me imp or elf,
I rede ye look weel tae yourself,
Gin ye ca' me fairy,
I'll wark ye muckle tarrie.

Quite often a baby's name was kept secret until after baptism, as it was thought that harm might come to it if its name was mentioned.

> *Hob-hole Hob!*
> *Mah bairn's getten t'kin-cough;*
> *Tak't off – tak't off!*

Hob was a fairy who lived in a cave in Runswick Bay, Yorkshire, or so the story goes. Mothers took their children to see Hob to cure them of whooping-cough. Even today the locals regard the place with superstitious dread and are loathe to pass it at night.

'Find the end of the rainbow, and you'll find a crock of gold' is an old Irish saying which was derived from the Norse legend that the rainbow was in reality Odin's bridge from the realm of man (Midgard) to the home of the gods (Asgard). Many people still look on a rainbow as a 'bridge for souls'. Odin was the chief god of the Scandinavian countries; his name was pronounced 'Woden' by the Anglo-Saxons.

It was thought also by early man that his reflection or shadow represented his soul; therefore care was taken not to step on a human shadow or to break up a reflection in the water by disturbing the surface. Later, when mirrors were invented, it was considered very unlucky to break one, as the soul would be damaged or even killed. This explains the saying 'A broken mirror means seven years bad luck'.

The idea of burning or piercing with pins the effigy of your enemy, while reciting a spell, can be traced back to the Old Stone Age. Many of the cave paintings in Spain, for instance, show the beast which was to be hunted pierced through the heart by an arrow. These early hunters believed that if they made a picture of their ideal then it would surely come true – which, of course, sooner or later it did. Here is an old spell from Scotland, which was repeated while the ceremony of pin-sticking was performed:

> *As you waste away, may she waste away;*
> *As this wounds you, may it wound her.*

The victim was duly told of the ceremony and often wasted away, because she believed in the magical powers of the charm and consequently died of fright.

According to Violet Alford in her book *An Introduction to English Folk-lore,* a Gloucestershire witches curse was found inscribed on a lead tablet more than three foot square behind a cupboard at Wilton Place, Dymock in Gloucestershire in 1892. It is thought to date back to the seventeenth century. At the top is the name Sarah Ellis written backwards, writing or reading backwards was thought to have great magical power. Then come symbols of good and evil spirits of the moon, the mystical number 369 and the words: 'Hasmodet, Acteus, Magalesious, Ormenus, Lisus, Nicon, Mimon, Zeper [which are all evil spirits] make this person to Banish away from this place and country Amen to my desier, Amen'. Poor Sarah Ellis was so terrified by this that she became insane and committed suicide. The story says that she was buried at a crossroads and a stake was driven into the grave to keep her demented spirit from wandering. Suicides were often denied church burials. The legend bears some authenticity as there still exists today a spot called Ellis Crossroads, two miles south of Dymock and the tablet bearing the Dymock curse can still be seen.

The following verse refers to a piece of Scandinavian folklore, the oldest animal superstition known. It tells of a ride by Odin and Baldur the Beautiful. When Baldur's horse slipped and broke its leg, Odin healed it immediately by using a black thread tied in seven knots:

> *Baldur rade, the foal slade [slipped]*
> *He lighted, and he righted,*
> *Set joint to joint and bone to bone,*
> *Sinew to sinew;*
> *Heal in Odin's name.*

The Christian version is:

> *The Lord rade. The foal slade,*
> *Set bone to bone,*
> *Sinew to sinew,*
> *Heal in Holy Ghost's name.*

Black cotton is used even today to cure poisoned thumbs in Cornwall and the proverbial seven knots are still made. Black cotton is often used, too, to tie up puppies' stumps after their tails have been docked.

> *The lion and the unicorn,*
> *Were fighting for the crown;*
> *The lion beat the unicorn*
> *All round the town.*

Some gave them white bread,
And some gave them brown,
And some gave them plum cake,
And drummed them out of town.

It seems that the lion and the unicorn have been rivals since time began. Stories about them appear in many countries in legendary form and they are mentioned in early history books. They have been recognised on ancient Greek coins and on a chequer board which dates from 3500 BC. One story tells us that the unicorn represents the Spring and the lion, Summer, and, naturally, the lion is always the victor.

Hunters and explorers have searched for the unicorn for many centuries and many countries have their own legendary stories about this fabulous beast. It is said to be a most beautiful animal and yet there has never been any factual evidence of its existence. Was it really only a figment of the imagination as were the phoenix and the dragon? The unicorn has been described as a pale bright horse, with a single twisted horn, a solitary beast wishing to communicate with the sky and the stars, and with the moon, under whose special protection it lived. Diana, the moon goddess, was said to be its guardian. It was supposed to be so proud that it would fight to the death, rather than be captured alive. In the early days the unicorn was the symbol of goodness in the world, representing purity of body and mind.

James IV of Scotland, who was the grandfather of Mary Queen of Scots, was so interested in the unicorn and its supposed supernatural powers that he put it on his royal coat of arms. The story goes that he sent a hunter named Philip to travel the world in search of the unicorn and bring back its magic horn to Scotland. Philip travelled hundreds of miles and followed many false trails, for many years, and had almost given up hope of ever finding this elusive animal, when he came to the plains of Tibet. It was a wild land and Philip often risked his life on the perilous journey, until he reached a village high on a plateau. The village chief's daughter who was sixteen, was interested in the old hunter and in his resolution to see the unicorn before he died. One night she pointed to the new moon in the sky. "There is your unicorn", she said. She went on to explain that an old Tibetan legend told of the lion and the unicorn, and of their fight for supremacy of heaven. The lion (the sun) wins at dawn and reigns all day. The unicorn wins at dusk and reigns supreme at night. The new moon, which was likened to the unicorn's horn, drives away all evil in the darkness of the night. The fight goes on eternally, for neither can win the crown of the sky.

Eventually, we are told, Philip was taken to see a real unicorn, after promising not to harm the animal. He witnessed it laying its head in the lap of the young girl – a sight that crowned his life. When he returned home to Scotland, his story was not believed, but, when Mary Queen of Scots' son became James I of England, he included the lion and the unicorn, which were on the Scottish coat of arms, in the royal arms of England – where they have remained ever since.

After the House of Stuart had been replaced by the House of Hanover, the crown was removed from the Scottish coat of arms and strife broke out once more between Scotland and England. This is probably when the nursery rhyme 'The lion and the Unicorn' became popular; another verse referring to the Jacobite wars was added:

> *And when he had beat him out,*
> *He beat him in again;*
> *He beat him three times over,*
> *His power to maintain.*

The better-known second verse, which begins 'Some gave them white bread', is thought to have been added at a much later date.

The horn of the unicorn, known as an 'alicorn', was a prize which was coveted by many in days gone by. It was an essential possession for every wealthy monarch, and its medical powers were said to be miraculous! Even Queen Elizabeth I was reported to have a small cup made of alicorn, and later, in the reign of James I, the horn was removed to the Tower of London and decorated with silver plate. It was estimated to be worth nearly a million pounds sterling by today's standards. The experts said that to test a piece of pure alicorn it must be placed on a scrap of silk on the fire. If the alicorn was true the silk would not burn. As the unicorn is a fictitious animal and always has been, even the 'experts' were deceived by rhinoceros horn.

There was an owl lived in an oak,
The more he heard the less he spoke;
The less he spoke the more he heard,
Oh, if men were all like that wise old bird!

This rhyme appeared in *Punch* in 1875, together with an illustration depicting Punch as the owl. The rhyme, however, is known to have existed in the oral collection long before this. In the Bible the owl is associated with desolation and foreboding, as we read in Isaiah 34. In Roman mythology, too, the owl, like the raven, was regarded as an omen of death. Its solitary habits and its strange unbird-like appearance must have undoubtedly contributed to these myths. Shakespeare wrote of the owl as an omen of death, when depicting a scene of supernatural terror in *A Midsummer Night's Dream,* and in *Macbeth* he wrote: 'It was the owl that shrieked; that fatal bellman, Which giv'st the stern'st goodnight'.

In France also the owl has acquired an evil reputation from an entirely different source. An old French legend tells us that the wren brought down fire from Heaven to Earth and, in doing so, burnt its feathers. All the other birds of the air gave it one feather to replace its lost plumage – all except the owl, who refused, saying it needed all its feathers to keep itself warm during the winter. In Norwich cathedral there is a carved misericord which shows the owl being mobbed by other birds.

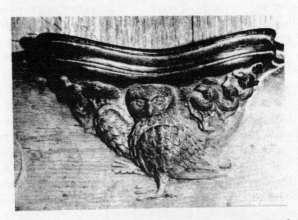

2. The wood carved misericord in Norwich Cathedral illustrates the rhyme which projects the owl, as a symbol of wisdom, teaching other birds. c. 1520.

On the other hand, the owl in Greek mythology was regarded as a symbol of wisdom and became the bird of Pallas Athene (Minerva). The abundance of owls in Athens gave rise to the proverb 'taking owls to Athens', which is matched in Britain by the saying 'taking coals to Newcastle'. Most drachma coins have the head of Minerva on one side and an owl on the other; in fact, coins were nicknamed 'owls'. In more recent times British tradition has favoured the Greek outlook and the owl has again become the emblem of wisdom, because of its judicial appearance. This is a complete fallacy, of course, because owls have no more brain-power than other birds!

> *Snail, snail, come out of your hole,*
> *Or else I'll beat you black as coal.*
> *Snail, snail, put out your horns,*
> *I'll give you bread and barley corns.*

Rhymes about snails are so old that they cannot be reckoned in years, and they can be found in numerous countries in Europe, as well as in Russia and China. The above verse refers to the practice of holding a snail over a candle flame until the creature is forced to vacate its shell. This amusement was popular with children of long ago. They were ignorant of the cruelty involved and regarded the pastime as good sport. The snail was thought to have powers to foretell the future and a quaint ritual performed years ago is recorded in this doggerel:

> *I seiz'd the vermin, home I quickly sped,*
> *And on the hearth the milk-white embers spread.*
> *Slow crawled the snail, and if I right can spell,*
> *In the soft ashes, marked a curious L.*

Snails were put in the ashes of the fire, and the shape of the trail they made was accepted as the initial of a future lover. It was considered lucky if a snail was seen to show its horns and in Scotland this action predicted a fine day:

> *Snailie, snailie, shoot out your horn,*
> *And tell us if it will be a bonny day the morn.*

While in Yorkshire they say:

> *Sneel, sneel, put out yer hoan*
> *Or ah'll kill yer fayther and muther te mean.*

ANIMALS

A swarm of bees in May,
Is worth a load of hay.
A swarm of bees in June,
Is worth a silver spoon.
A swarm of bees in July,
Is not worth a fly.

There is a wealth of myth and superstition concerning the lives of these fascinating creatures. The ancient belief that bees had their origins in the dead bodies of animals stems from the Old Testament. In many European countries it was believed that bees were the messengers of the gods and to 'tell the bees', when someone had died, was to ensure that the news reached the right quarters. The Irish tell their secrets to these insects and believe that bees must never be quarrelled over, for to do so would bring very bad luck.

The wisdom of the bees is widely accepted: 'Ask the wild bee for what the Druids knew' is a saying well-known in Scotland. In Brittany the story goes that bees had their origins in the tears Christ shed on the Cross, while German folklore relates how they were kept to produce wax for church candles. It was thought to be a death omen in England if bees swarmed on your property and it also meant bad news if one died in your house. However, good luck would follow if a bee flew in and out of the home; it foretold the welcome visit of a stranger. Ancient Jewish and Japanese mythology relate how swarms of bees were let loose on enemy armies to sting them to death. Since early times, bee stings have been used as a medicine for rheumatism and neuritis, and the serum is still used today.

Bees can be found in every country of the world, and there are thousands of different species. They have four stages in life; the egg, the grub, the chrysallis, and the adult bee form. The bee's body is usually covered in hairs, which distinguishes it from the wasp. They have always been useful for the pollination of flowers and, of course, for the production of honey. Early man kept swarms of bees in rough hives made out of hollow tree stumps.

Before the honey could be collected, the whole swarm was killed off with poisonous fumes. Nowadays bees are kept in large well-planned hives and the honey is extracted by far less drastic methods. Here is a verse about a bee, published in the early eighteenth century:

> *There's a little short gentleman,*
> *That wears the yellow trews,*
> *A dirk below his doublet,*
> *For sticking of his foes.*
> *Yet in a singing posture,*
> *Where 'er you do him see,*
> *And if you offer violence*
> *He'll stab his dirk in thee.*

> *Ladybird, ladybird, fly away home,*
> *Your house is on fire, and your children are gone –*
> *All but one, and her name is Anne,*
> *And she crept under the porridge pan.*

Legendary stories about the ladybird are timeless. It was thought that the insect had close connections with the Egyptian goddess of magic, Isis. It also has close associations with the Virgin Mary, being called 'Our Lady's Bird'. Other names for the ladybird are 'God's little cow'. 'Mary Gold' and in Norfolk it is affectionately known as 'Bishy Bishy Barnaby'. This verse about the ladybird was popular a century ago:

> *Bless you, bless you, burnie-bee,*
> *Tell me then my wedding day will be;*
> *If it be tomorrow day,*
> *Take your wings and fly away,*
> *Fly to the East, fly to the West;*
> *Fly to him I love the best.*

On finding a ladybird, the usual practice is to set it on the hand, recite a traditional verse, blow once, and invariably it will fly off. The direction in which it flies was thought to be significant in days gone by. The insect has always been treated with respect and care has been taken throughout the years to ensure its safety. It has long been regarded as a fortune omen. In England it was thought the size of the harvest could be estimated by the number of spots on its back. In America there exists an old custom that whoever finds a ladybird in winter shall receive as many dollars as spots on its wings! From Canada comes the superstition that on whatever article of clothing the insect alights the person concerned will receive a new replacement. An old Northumberland rhyme about a ladybird says:

> *Reed reed sodger fly away,*
> *And make the morn a sunny day.*

Further north a Scottish doggerel is still chanted:

> *Lady, Lady, Landers,*
> *Lady, Lady, Landers,*
> *Take up your cloak about your head,*
> *And fly away to Flanders.*
> *Fly over firth and fly over fell,*
> *Fly o'er pool, and running well,*
> *Fly o'er moor and fly o'er mead,*
> *Fly o'er living and fly o'er dead.*
> *Fly o'er corn and fly o'er lea,*
> *Fly o'er river and fly o'er sea,*
> *Fly you east or fly you west,*
> *Fly to him that loves me best.*
>
> *The cuckoo's a fine bird,*
> *He sings as he flies,*
> *He brings us good tidings,*
> *And tells us no lies.*
>
> *He sucks little birds' eggs,*
> *To make his voice clear,*
> *And when he sings 'cuckoo'*
> *The summer is near.*

The cry of the cuckoo was welcomed as a good luck sign in most countries. It was the herald of Spring and brought hope for a new season of growing crops. One old verse goes like this:

> *The cuckoo comes in April,*
> *He sings his song in May,*
> *In the middle of June he changes his tune,*
> *And then he flies away.*

Two other couplets are well-known:

> *If he stays until September,*
> *'Tis as much as the oldest man can remember.*
> *The first cock of hay,*
> *Frights the cuckoo away.*

The first note of the cuckoo's song was supposed to bring good fortune and prosperity to all who heard it. It was considered a good luck sign for marriage, although those who heard the first cry while lying in bed could expect bad luck to befall them. In some countries the cuckoo was regarded as having the form of the devil and that is why the insane are often called 'cuckoo'. This idea may have sprung from the fact that the European cuckoo is a parasite.

The cuckoo's egg is very small for the size of the hen and often varies in colour, so she can lay an egg in practically any bird's nest. She lays approximately twelve eggs in all, one in each nest. She usually flies to a selected nest during the afternoon, lays her egg, and takes one of the original eggs away. This she either destroys or eats. In the verse quoted above, the line 'He sucks little birds' eggs to make his voice clear' refers to this habit. When the baby cuckoo is hatched, he is very strong and manages to tip all other eggs and small birds out of the nest. The mother bird ignores her dead offspring, and concentrates on feeding the monster in the nest. This takes all her time as he grows very big, probably twice the size of the foster mother. The true parents of the cuckoo take no interest in their young and fly off in July or August to warmer climates. The young birds are left to find their own way and often do not leave until September. The male cuckoo has the definite call of 'cuckoo', and both sexes are about one foot long, rather like a sparrow-hawk. They have blue patterned upper parts, and whitish underparts, often striped with black lines. They eat all kinds of insects, even hairy caterpillars which the other birds do not like. The cuckoo is rarely seen in flight, but hides itself in the foliage of trees, observing other birds.

There is an old story that the men of Gotham in Nottinghamshire tried to keep the cuckoo in their village by growing a very high hedge and, in so doing, enjoyed perpetual Spring! The following old folk verse bears this out:

In the month of Averil,
The gawk comes o'er the hill,
   In a shower of rain;
And in the middle of June
He turns his tune again.

'Gawk' means fool or as in this case, foolish bird, ie, the cuckoo.

There were three crows sat on a stone,
Fa, la, la, la, la, la, la, de;
Two flew away, and then there was one,
Fa, la, la, la, la, la, la, de;
The other crow finding himself alone,
Fa, la, la, la, la, la, la, de;
He flew away, and then there were none,
Fa, la, la, la, la, la, la, de.

When travelling along a road, the sight of crows sitting in the path foretold the following:

One crow was bad luck,
Two crows, good luck,
Three crows, a wedding,
Four crows, a burying,
Five crows, speed,
Six crows, very good luck indeed.

The crow family includes the raven, rook, jackdaw, magpie, jay and chough, all of which can be found in the British Isles and in most other parts of the world. The crow may be found singly, in pairs, or in flocks. As its habits are so unpredictable, this may explain why the number of crows seen was so significant in the old fortune rituals. The magpie has been a favourite too:

Magpie, magpie, flutter and flee,
Turn up your tail, and good luck visit me.

and

One for sorrow, two for mirth,
Three for a wedding, four for a birth;
Five for a parson, six for a clerk,
Seven for a babe, buried in the dark.

However, this couplet reflects a different mood:

> Tell-oie-tit,
> *Thy tongue is slit,*
> *An' every dog in the town*
> *Will get a little bit.*

From early times crows have been looked upon with dislike and suspicion. The raven, especially, was considered an ill omen and was often called the 'devil's bird'. Like the vulture, it seems able to sense death and flutters round when it is imminent. Ignorant folk thought that the visit of the raven caused death, when in reality it was only following its instincts. They are carrion birds and feed on dead meat. Perhaps this explains why the ravens first inhabited the lawns of the Tower of London, in the days when public executions were commonplace. Legend has it that the raven was originally a white bird, but turned black when it stayed out of Noah's ark during the flood to feed on the bodies of drowned humans. Positive dislike of the bird, is recorded in this rhyme:

> *Crow, crow, get out of my sight,*
> *Or else I'll eat your liver and lights.*

A legend from Cornwall states that King Arthur still lives in the form of a raven and, therefore, superstitious folk in that part of the country will never kill one of these birds. In China it was believed that, if the voice of the raven was heard between the hours of three and seven in the morning, the hearer would receive gifts. If the voice of the raven was heard between three and seven in the evening, wind and rain would follow. In Japan its croak foretold death, except when heard at six in the morning, which was 'wealth hour', or at noon, which was 'happiness hour'. The raven was the emblem of the Danes in Scandinavian mythology. If in war, they were to be defeated, the bird would droop its wings; if he stood erect, it meant they were to be victorious.

COUNTING-OUT RHYMES

Counting-out rhymes are international. They have no barriers of language, race or creed. They hardly vary at all from country to country, but possess their own special interchangeable code. Children have unconsciously preserved old Church chants and holy phrases in these rhymes that have a characteristic rhythm. They contain a mixture of word fragments stemming from ancient rituals that have been worn smooth through centuries of repetition. Counting-out rhymes are made up of word relics of the following: the Bible, Sanskrit, magic formulas, death rhymes and Druid rites, ancient Freemasons' passwords, Cymric and Celtic numerals and Romany gypsy charms.

What is a counting-out rhyme? It is a formula for finding who is to be 'it' in a group of children playing a certain game. It is the children themselves who have kept these rhymes alive. Adults are not included in this activity and the child who is eventually 'it' does not think to argue, but accepts his role automatically. From early times the child who is 'it' has been called a 'wolf' in Germany, a 'loup' in France, the 'devil' in Japan and, in other countries, a 'leper' or a 'crazy one'. In England I have heard the term 'witch' or 'princess', depending on the game. Here are two rhymes whose words have changed through constant repetition:

> Onery two-ery, six and seven,
> Holy bone, crack a bone, ten and eleven,
> Spit spot, it must be done,
> Twiddle-um twaddle-um twenty-one.

Sometimes 'six and seven' becomes 'ziggery zan' and 'holy bone' can be 'hollow bone', 'hallabone', 'halibo', 'halibut' or 'alibi'. The third line becomes 'spin, span, muskidan'.

> Haley Maley, tipsytee.
> Harley harley, Dominee.
> Hotchy potchy, cotchy notchy,
> Hom pom, tuskee.

'Haley Maley' stems from Hail Mary, while 'Dominee' is a church word. 'Hotchy potchy' comes from hocas pocas, which is a phrase used in the Mass and is also a magic formula.

The most famous counting-out rhyme must surely be:

> *Eena, meena, miny, mo,*
> *Catch a nigger by his toe,*
> *If he hollers, let him go.*
> *Eena, meena, miny, mo.*

The first line is thought to have originated with the Druids. Druidism sprang from the Celts, who conquered Britain before the Roman invasion, and the priests were the most powerful people in the land. They ruled the Celts with barbaric and mysti-cal laws. Archaic Nature worship included many open-air cere-monies. Trees, especially the oak, were revered by the Druids, and the mistletoe on the boughs was thought to bear mystical power and be a gift from the gods. Only a Druid with a golden knife was allowed to cut it down. It is known that these priests of Nature made many sacrifices, both animal and human. The first line of 'Eena meena mina mo' has been credited to the Druids, who may have said it when selecting victims for sacrifice. After the magic charm had been recited, the unlucky prisoners were taken to the Druid island of Mona (Anglesea) where they met a horrible fate in the oak groves. One mode of sacrifice was to burn the victims alive in hanging wicker baskets.

The Roman soldiers under the orders of their leader, Suetonius, killed the Druids and destroyed the sacred groves. The annual Welsh Eisteddfod has sought to revive the dress and some of the nicer customs of Druidism by holding competitions in music, singing, and poetry.

The line 'catch a nigger by his toe' has varied with the years. Before the abolition of black slavery in America, the word 'fiddle' or 'rabbit' was used instead of 'nigger'. When the negroes were being smuggled into Canada after the Slave Act of 1850, the word 'nigger' was introduced into the rhyme. Today, of course, 'nig-ger' is less commonly used, especially in America, and the origi-nal words come into their own once more. In the Second World War, however , American children sang:

> *Eeena, meena, miny, mo,*
> *Catch old Tojo by the toe,*
> *If he hollers, make him say,*
> *'I surrender, U.S.A.'*

Ip, dip,
Sky blue,
Who's 'it'?
Not you.

Ic Dictation,
I'll see you at Thorpe Station,
One two three,
Four five six,
You are out
As sure as sticks.

In the first lines of both these rhymes, which are currently repeated in the playgrounds of Norfolk schools, remnants of ancient numerals can be traced.

COUNTING

A 'shepherd's score' simply means counting in twenties, for in ancient times bare-footed men used both fingers and toes to help them count. Relics of old counting systems still remain today: we still talk about three score years and ten, when reckoning a man's span of life. Fishermen and shepherds used a tally stick when estimating the size of catches or flocks; one notch meant twenty fish or sheep. Women, too, used a similar pattern when counting stitches in knitting.

Other counting systems favoured the quinerary scale (counting in fives). When we study ancient numerals, we see that five-finger counting was the basis, by the pattern and rhythm of the digits. Here is a specimen of Indian counting recorded in Massachussets in 1890:

Een, teen, tuther, futher, fipps,
Suther, luther, uther, duther, dix.
Een-dix, teen-dix, tuther-dix, futher-dix, bumpit;
Anny-bumpit, tanny-bumpit, thuther-bumpit, futher-bumpit,
*   gigit;*
Anny-gigit

At about the same time, and quite independently, this old Lincolnshire shepherd's score counting was recorded:

Yan, tan tethera, pethera, pimp.
Sethera, lethera, hovera, covera, dik.
Yan-a-dik, tan-a-dik, tethera-dik, pethera-dik, bumfit.
Yan-a-bumfit, tan-a-bumfit, tuthera-bumfit, pethera-bumfit,
figgit (twenty).

The similarity of the digits should be noted; no one can really explain why this is so. Both sets of numerals were passed on by word of mouth throughout the centuries, and the only conclusion that we can reach is that at one time these old numerals had a common source. Ancient digits can be divided into roughly three sections:

1.   Welsh counting has been constant and, as the Welsh language is still popular in Wales, the Cymric numerals have been preserved from ancient times. Up to five they read: un, dau, tri, pedwar, pump.

2.   Shepherd's score is still used in Yorkshire and Cumberland, and other sheep-rearing areas, but it is in danger of dying out.

3.   Children's counting-out rhymes only give a jumbled reflection of old digits together with ancient rites and religious phrases. There are many counting rhymes which are in constant use today. In fact the teaching programme surrounding simple numerals would be sadly lacking without old favourites such as 'One, two, buckle my shoe' and 'Ten little nigger boys'. The ancient digits engendered long before the Roman occupation form the basis of numerals used in modern times. It is interesting to note that 'digit' means any one finger, and that any number under ten can also be described as such.

ROMAN

OLD KING COLE

Britain was invaded by Roman troops in AD. 42. After many bitter and bloody battles, most of the land was conquered and the Romans introduced their form of civilization to a hitherto barbarous nation. Roads, temples and houses were built, and an efficient government brought wealth and prosperity. Gradually the Britons learned to live with their new masters and became appreciative of the security that the Roman occupation provided. During the four hundred years of Roman Rule, Britain almost lost her identity and became known as the Roman Island.

When we talk of Roman remains, we naturally think of old coins, pieces of pottery and mosaic patterns, which are the remnants of a wonderful civilization once built on these islands. Old rhymes, too, which are still popular today have their roots in Roman Britain:

> *Old King Cole was a merry old soul,*
> *And a merry old soul was he;*
> *He called for his pipe,*
> *And he called for his bowl,*
> *And he called for his fiddlers three.*

> *And every fiddler had a very fine fiddle,*
> *And a very fine fiddle had he;*
> *Fiddle-diddle-dee went the fiddlers three,*
> *There's none so rare as can compare*
> *With King Cole and his fiddlers three.*

In the third century AD the city of Colchester was said to have been built by Coel, Duke of Britain, who was subject to Roman tribute. According to local records, Coel or Cole was reputed to have had a daughter, Helen, who was a devout Christian and who also possessed a talent for music; she may well have helped to build the character of King Cole as we know him today. Helen married Constantine, who emigrated to Rome, became the first Christian Emperor and was known as Constantine the Great. The Oath Book or Red Parchment Book of Colchester, 1907 contains a curious fourteenth century chronicle entitled *The Legend of King Coel, Helena and Constantine, with other events in the early history of Colchester.* Here is an extract:

AD 219 Coel, Duke of Britons, began to build a city of Colchester then called Kaircoel.

AD 238 Coel, Duke of Colchester, began to reign over Essex and Hertford.

AD 242 Helen, daughter of Coel, is born.

AD290 Coel, Duke of Colchester, Asclepiodotus the tyrant having been slain, reigned over all Britain, subject to the Roman tribute.

AD 297 Coel, the most powerful King of the Britons, died at Colchester, in the second month.

Passage from *Ancient Funeral Monuments* by John Weever (1767 edition) tells us:

'...Yet her inhabitants may brag the burial of Coill, that brave British Prince, who built this their town of Colchester, about one hundred and twenty-four years after the birth of our Saviour Christ. Wherein his son Lucius, Helena and Constantine, the first Christian King, empress and emperor of the world, were born; which made Necham (saith Speed) for Constantine to sing as he did:

> *'From Colchester there rose a starre,*
> *The rayes whereof gave glorious light*
> *Throughout the world, in climates farre,*
> *Great Constantine Rome's emperour bright.'*

Coel is reported to have finished building the city of Kaircoel (Colchester) in the middle of the third century. He lived to a great age and, during his last years, was appointed ruler of the whole of Britain, under Roman law. 'Chester' is the Saxon word for city and so, when at a later date the Saxon hordes overran Britain, Kaircoel was renamed Colchester. Pre-war articles in the *Essex Review* point out that there are still places in Colchester which remind one of the old song: the large gravel pit at Laxden Heath is known as King Cole's Kitchen, and in Balkern there is a site which is called King Cole's Fort; a watering place in Colchester High Street, named King Cole's Pump, could be seen as late as 1933. Although the story of Old King Cole and his connections with Colchester are said to be legendary, various evidence indicates that the events mentioned in the song have a strong element of truth in them.

ST AGNES

An English rhyme, which was popular centuries ago and which also has its roots in Roman times tells of St Agnes, the patron saint of young girls:

> *Sweet Agnes work thy fast,*
> *If ever I be to marry man,*
> *Or even man to marry me –*
> *I hope him this night to see.*

In the reign of Emperor Diocletian, there lived in Rome a girl called Agnes, who, because she was a Christian, refused to marry the pagan son of a Roman official. Although she was only thirteen years old, she was put in a mad-house as punishment, but no one dared to harm her. It was then decided to burn her at the stake, but, when the faggots were lit, they would not ignite. Finally her head was cut off by a Roman soldier and she was buried in a church in Rome, which afterwards bore her name. Her feast day is on 21 January and two lambs are blessed by the Pope (*agnus* is Latin for lamb), and their wool is woven into robes and sent to archbishops as a sign of the authority of the Christian church.

In the north of England it was common practice years ago for a 'dumb cake' to be made by single girls seeking husbands. The cake was made of flour, water, egg and salt, and, after fasting all day, the girls would eat the cake at midnight while reciting the rhyme about St Agnes. It was expected that apparitions of future husbands would then appear and chase the girls upstairs, snatching at their clothes, until they were safely in bed. Then the 'ghosts' would go away. It is recorded in the Denham tracts that one girl saw three apparitions, the last of which had a wooden leg! Apparently it came about that she did have three husbands and the last one had a peg-leg.

CALENDARS

Thirty days hath September
April, June and November,
All the rest have thirty-one,
Excepting February, which has twenty-eight,
And twenty-nine each leap year.

This rhyme has been repeated for hundreds of years and was first recorded in French in the thirteenth century, but the format can be traced back to Julius Caesar. The calendar is, of course, the way in which people measure time for their own convenience – divided into days, weeks, months and years. Early man found that the basic way to do this was to follow the movements of the earth, moon and sun, and thus produce three simple divisions of time – day, month, and year. The day is the time the earth takes to revolve on its axis – approximately 24 hours. The lunar month is the time taken between each new moon – roughly 29½ days, and the solar year is the time taken for the earth to travel round the sun – just over 365 days. The ancient Egyptians were the first people to make a fairly accurate calendar. They measured the year span by the flooding of the Nile every spring, and noticed that the star Sirius rose before sunrise at about the same time.

In the Christian world the birth of Christ marked the beginning of the true calendar, but the Jews, on the other hand, date their calendar from the beginning of the creation of the world, thus, when the Christian year was 1972, the Jewish date was 5730. Julius Caesar laid down the principles of the Christian calendar, namely five months of thirty days, six months of thirty-one and February having twenty-eight days and twenty-nine each leap year, which was every third year in early times. Even then the Julian calendar, named after its founder, was discovered to be eleven minutes too long. These minutes accumulated during the centuries until, in 1582, the calendar was ten days in advance of all church festivities. Pope Gregory decided that ten days should be dropped from that year. Most Catholic countries did this straight away, but Protestant countries were reluctant and it was not until 1753, when Great Britain was eleven days ahead of most other countries, that it was decided to abolish these unwanted days. People rioted in the streets believing that they were being robbed of part of their lives and shouting, "Give us back our eleven days". England was the last country in Europe to change from the Julian to the Gregorian calendar. The reason for this was the adverse feeling towards Catholicism, as this surviving rhyme explains:

> *In seventeen hundred and fifty three,*
> *Our style was changed to Popery,*
> *But that it is liked we don't agree –*
> *Which nobody can deny.*

Even Scotland succumbed in 1600 and a curious story is attached to this, which says that under the auspices of the reformer John Knox, one Michael Scot was sent to Rome to find the lost eleven days!

Under Christianity there are three calendars which are still recognized today; the Gregorian, the Church and the Primitive. The latter is, of course, least favoured being of pagan origin, and it consists, as always, of only two seasons: summer and winter. The coming of summer is celebrated by a fire festival between the 1st and 8th of May called Beltanes, while the approach of winter was celebrated by the slaughter of cattle that could not be fed during the winter at a festival called Martinmas. Beltane time, the first seven days of May, was regarded by the Celts as a highly magical time of the year and this superstition is still retained in the Scottish saying, 'You have the skill of man and beast, if you are born between the Beltanes'. Leap year was changed from every third year to every fourth year by Pope Gregory and has remained stable ever since.

The meanings and origins of the names of the months are as follows:

January   Named after Janus, a Roman god who had two
                   faces and looked two ways – symbolising that

	the first month of the year looks backwards as well as forwards.
February	Named after the Roman god Februs, the god of purification ceremonies.
March	Named after the god Mars, who was responsible for new growth in plants, animals and armies.
April	This may come from the Latin word *aperire*, which means open – symbolising the opening and growth of plants in Spring.
May	Probably named after the Greek goddess Maia, which meant mother or nurse, who was associated with the growing and nurturing of crops.
June	This may have derived from the goddess Juno, who looked after women.
July	Named after Julius Caesar, who established the first calendar.
August	This is named after Augustus Caesar, the first of the Roman Emperors.

September, October, November and December simply mean seventh, eighth, ninth and tenth. Early Roman calendars only had ten months, but we have kept the same names though the numbers do not comply with the present-day order of months.

NUMERALS

Roman numerals were introduced to Britain during the occupation; Here is a rhyme which helps one remember them:

> *X shall stand for playmates Ten;*
> *V for Five stout stalwart men;*
> *I for One, as I'm alive;*
> *C for Hundred, and D for Five;*
> *M for a Thousand soldiers true;*
> *And L for Fifty, I'll tell you.*

As has already been stated, the teachings of Christ reached Britain in Roman times, the passion for architecture took on a new lease of life and Christian temples and shrines were built in abundance on the shores of Britain. A story from the west of

England relates how, after the death of Christ, Joseph of Arimathea came to Britain with his followers and settled in Glastonbury, where he built a small wattle church dedicated to the Virgin Mary. He is reported to have brought with him Christ's crown of thorns, from a twig of which he grew the famous thorn tree of Glastonbury. He is also said to have brought the cup from which Christ drank at the Last Supper and which was used afterwards to collect a few drops of Christ's blood at the crucifixion. The evidence that we have to support this story is that Roman pottery dating back to the first century AD has been found at Glastonbury, but it cannot be identified as having religious connections. However, in other parts of the country definite evidence of Roman Christianity has been found. In Cirencester, for instance, a square of words painted on a plaster wall has been uncovered.

BIBLICAL

ROTAS
OPERA
TENET
AREPO
SATOR

The letters can be arranged to form the word *Paternoster*, which was used in Roman times to denote Christ and can be found in many other parts of Europe, and means the Lord's Prayer.

There must have been numerous verses stemming from the Bible to form a traditional pattern, but the history of religion in this country has been so turbulent and bitter that not many early prayers have survived. However, the charm and memorability of the following prayer were too strong to be broken:

Matthew, Mark, Luke and John,
Bless the bed that I lie on;
Four corners to my bed,
Four angels round my head;
One to watch and one to pray,
And two to bear my soul away.

This verse was often called *The White Paternoster* and this title may well signify its great age. It has been repeated from early times last thing at night as a form of magic spell, ensuring the safety of the occupants of the bed from the evil spirits of the night. It must have been a comforting thought to have the four apostles guarding the four bed posts. On many tombstones, too, the prayer is inscribed and replicas of the saints stand at each corner of the grave, ensuring the deceased a safe journey to heaven.

Another rhyme which is still popular today has its seeds in the New Testament and is mentioned in ancient Jewish history, dating back to the first century AD:

> *If all the world were paper,*
> *And all the sea were ink;*
> *If all the trees were bread and cheese,*
> *What would we have to drink?*

'Hot cross buns' is a nursery jingle that again has Roman roots, for it was the Romans who brought the idea of the sacred, spiced cakes to Britain. They were cooked on special festival days and marked with a cross to show remembrance of the Crucifixion, and aptly named 'quarters'. The rhyme as we know it today was originally a street cry and is dealt with in the Stuart chapter. This stanza which was common in Victorian times reminds us of the original purpose of hot cross buns:

> *Think on this sacred festival,*
> *Think why Cross Buns were given;*
> *Then think of Him who died for all,*
> *To give you right to Heaven.*

Many traditions stemming from early times regarding these spiced cakes still linger in Britain today. In Bedfordshire and the west of England, for instance, it is said that, if a hot cross bun is hung up in the kitchen for a year, it will protect the household from all evil and bring good luck to the occupants.

> *Tid, Mid, Miserae,*
> *Carling, Palm and Paste Egg Day.*

This verse denotes popular names for the Sundays in Lent, while another version goes:

> *Tid, Mid, Miseray,*
> *Carlin, Paum, an' Good Feest Day.*

The first three words are obviously from the old Latin service: *Te Deum*, *Mid Deus* and *Miserere mei*. The other words are explained thus: carlins are grey peas, soaked and boiled and eaten on Care Sunday, before Palm Sunday; Care Sunday and Care Week were so called because it was a period of great religious care and anxiety before the crucifixion of Christ. This custom is very old and peas were used as a substitute for the beans of the heathen. Another rhyme which may have similar roots is:

> *Pease pudding hot, pease pudding cold,*
> *Pease pudding in a pot nine days old.*

The Christian festival of Easter coincided with pagan celebrations to mark the beginning of spring. The giving of eggs on Easter day is a custom which dates back to pre-Christian times, when gift eggs were dyed and decorated and exchanged with rejoicing at the beginning of spring, when the promise of newly-grown crops gave hope of survival for at least a few more months. Before chocolate eggs became popular, eggs were often made out of sweet almond paste.

GAMES

Many children's games and the chants that go with them originated in Roman times, for instance:

> *Rain, rain, go away,*
> *Come again another day.*

This couplet was, in fact, known in the Roman and Greek period, before the birth of Christ, when children chanted a jingle very similar to the one above as a weather charm. It was thought by adults that only children had the power to alter weather conditions and, if it was raining, they were told to recite this magic spell to make the sun reappear once more.

> *I'm the king of the castle,*
> *Get down you dirty rascal.*

Apparently this action game was played equally as happily by Roman children as it is today. Often played on a mound of sand on the shore, the child who succeeds in removing the 'king', then himself becomes 'king'.

'Bucca' was a child's counting game used in Roman times and is recalled in this old English finger-counting chant:

> *Buck, buck,*
> *How many fingers do I hold up?*

The following rhyme shows that the game of ducks and drakes – a form of draughts – and the ever popular hopscotch were both known to children living in the first century AD:

> *A Duck and a Drake,*
> *A nice barley cake,*
> *With a penny to pay the old baker;*
> *A hop and a scotch*
> *Is another notch,*
> *Slitherum, slatherum, take her.*

The last line is reminiscent of a counting-out rhyme.

The game of skimming flat stones on water surfaces was also called Ducks and Drakes

PROVERBS

The origin of the proverb is not clear; it may have had its beginnings in the Bible, in weather lore, in old medical lore or in fables. A proverb can be defined as a lesson learnt from witnessing the same situation many times over and a rhyme or phrase is formulated from observing the repetitious sequence. From the book of Proverbs in the Old Testament, chapter 1, verses 5 and 6, we have these words: 'A wise man will hear, and will increase learning; and a man of understanding shall attain unto wise counsels; To understand a proverb and the interpretation; the words of the wise, and their dark sayings.' Surely the Bible, therefore, must be accepted as the chief source of devious proverbs, and it was with the advent of Christianity in Britain during the Roman occupation that Biblical proverbs were probably first introduced.

Some proverbs can be taken at face value, for instance, 'Rain before seven, fine before eleven'. The majority, however, have a hidden meaning, as in 'Empty vessels make the most sound'. For this reason proverbs and their implications are on the school curriculum. Until a child has mastered proverbs, he is not fully equipped to understand his native language, for they are short-cuts to descriptions of character and place; they act as a form of mental shorthand and take the hard work out of explanation.

The everyday proverbs, such as 'Make hay while the sun shines', are well known so I will not dwell on these. Instead I have collected a few proverbial rhymes which can boast a long life:

> *Birds of a feather flock together,*
> *And so will pigs and swine;*
> *Rats and mice will have their choice,*
> *And so will I have mine.*

This verse above was recorded in Victorian times, but it could be much older.

> *For the want of a nail the shoe was lost,*
> *For the want of the shoe the horse was lost,*
> *For the want of the horse the rider was lost,*
> *For the want of the rider the battle was lost,*
> *For the want of a battle the kingdom was lost,*
> *And all for the want of a horse shoe nail.*

The idea for this rhyme was probably gleaned from an old French military proverb which was used a great deal in the seventeenth century: 'The loss of a nail, the loss of an army.'

> *Jack Spratt could eat no fat,*
> *And his wife could eat no lean,*
> *So between them both and the old black cat,*
> *They licked the platter clean.*

Although the above verse was very popular in the seventeenth century, it may well be a great deal older. Much the same applies to the rhyme below. The first two verses were recorded in 1829 but probably existed in the oral collection long before this. The other verses are later additions.

> *What are little boys made of?*
> *What are little boys made of?*
> *Frogs and snails and puppy dogs' tails,*
> *That's what little boys are made of.*

What are little girls made of?
What are little girls made of?
Sugar and spice and all things nice,
That's what little girls are made of.

What are young men made of?
What are young men made of?
Sighs and leers and crocodile tears,
That's what young men are made of.

What are young women made of?
What are young women made of?
Ribbons and laces and sweet pretty faces,
That's what young women are made of.

What are old women made of?
What are old women made of?
Bushes and thorns and old cows' horns,
That's what old women are made of.

What are our sailors made of?
What are our sailors made of?
Pitch and tar, pigtail and scar,
That's what our sailors are made of.

What are our soldiers made of?
What are our soldiers made of?
Pipe clay and drill, the foeman to kill,
That's what our soldiers are made of.

After dinner rest a while,
After supper walk a mile.

Early to bed and early to rise,
Makes a man healthy, wealthy and wise.

A son's a son till he gets him a wife,
A daughter's a daughter for the rest of her life.

All work and no play makes Jack a dull boy,
All play and no work makes Jack a mere toy.

For every evil under the sun,
There is a remedy or there is none;
If there be one, try and find it,
If there be none, never mind it.

A man of words and not of deeds,
Is like a garden full of weeds;
And when the weeds begin to grow,
It's like a garden full of snow;
And when the snow begins to fall,
It's like a bird upon the wall;
And when the bird away does fly,
It's like an eagle in the sky;
And when the sky begins to roar,
It's like a lion at the door;
And when the door begins to crack,
It's like a stick across your back;
And when your back begins to smart,
It's like a penknife in your heart;
And when your heart begins to bleed,
You're dead, and dead, and dead indeed.

RIDDLES

A riddle has been described as an enigma, a word puzzle or a
metaphor, and may be said to be one of the oldest kinds of
formulated thought. Riddles were very popular with primitive
man, whose taste for comedy seems very childish by adult standards today, for as man became more sophisticated, his idea of
humour changed. During the Tudor and Stuart eras riddles were
used a great deal, but since that time the popularity of the riddle
has steadily declined. Only children nowadays can appreciate
the mirth and wit of a good word puzzle, and we have to thank
the younger generations throughout the centuries for saving it
from absolute extinction.

Riddles are thought to have been used as charms by early man
and were recited during ceremonies and rituals, at certain seasons. At harvest time many riddles were asked of Nature herself –
and the questioners did not know the answers, although their
lives depended on them. The oldest riddles are the nature puzzles. In the Old Testament Samson asked this famous riddle of
the Philistines – one which they could not answer: 'Out of the

eater came forth meat; and out of the strongest came forth sweet-ness' (Judges 14: 14). The answer was a swarm of bees that had made honey inside the carcass of a dead lion. Here is a collection of old nature riddles:

> *On yonder hill there is a red deer,*
> *The more you shoot, the more you may;*
> *You cannot drive that deer away.*
> Answer: The rising sun.

> *I have an apple I can't cut,*
> *A blanket I can't fold,*
> *And so much money that I can't count it.*

This riddle describes the moon, sky and stars – images that have been used for countless generations.

> *The more you feed it,*
> *The more it'll grow high;*
> *But if you give it water*
> *It'll go and die.* Answer: fire

I washed my face in water
That neither rained nor run,
I dried my face on a towel,
That was neither woven nor spun. Answer: dew and sun.

> *Four stiff standers,*
> *Four dilly-danders,*
> *Two lookers,*
> *Two crookers,*
> *And a wig-wag.* Answer: a cow.

In early times, riddles were asked at weddings and the couple had to find the solution together, as a rehearsal for the many problems they would have to share in their future life. Turkish girls asked their fiancés tough riddles to test their intelligence and commonsense – puzzles like this perhaps:

> *My first is in apple and also in pear,*
> *My second's in desperate and also in dare,*
> *My third is in sparrow and also in lark,*
> *My fourth is in cashier and also in clerk,*
> *My fifth is in seven and also in ten,*
> *My whole is a blessing indeed unto men.*
> Answer: peace.

Or this:

> Two legs sat upon three legs
> With one leg on his knee,
> In comes four legs
> And runs away with one leg;
> Up jumps two legs,
> Throws it after four legs,
> And makes him bring back one leg.
>   Answer: a three-legged stool.

Rhymes about legs are very old indeed, and it is thought that this particular riddle may be one of the oldest in existence.

> Elizabeth, Elspeth, Betsy and Bess,
> They all went together to seek a bird's nest;
> They found a bird's nest with five eggs in it,
> They all took one, and left four in it.
>   Answer: only one girl,
>   Elizabeth, took a bird's egg.
>   The other three names are
>   diminutives of Elizabeth.

> As I was a-walking on Westminster Bridge,
> I met with a Westminster scholar;
> He pulled off his cap, an' drew off his gloves,
> Now what was the name of this scholar?
>   Answer: Andrew

> As round as an apple,
> As deep as a pail;
> It never cries out
> Till it's caught by the tail.
>   Answer: a bell

> Little bird of paradise,
> She works her work both neat and nice;
> She pleases God, she pleases man,
> She does the work that no man can.
>   Answer: a bee.

The following riddle is so old that its original setting has been forgotten and, although we are told the answer, it does not explain the mystery of its origin:

White bird featherless
Flew from Paradise,
Pitched on the castle wall;
Along came Lord Landless,
Took it up handless,
And rode away horseless,
To the King's white hall. Answer: snowflakes.

Little Nancy Etticoat
With a white petticoat,
And a red nose;
She has no feet or hands,
The longer she stands
The shorter she grows. Answer: a candle.

What God never sees,
What the king seldom sees,
What we see every day;
Read me my riddle, I pray. Answer: an equal.

In modern times the practice of solving riddles by adults is confined to Christmas-time, when the crackers have been pulled. Over the debris of fancy hats and colourful cracker paper, grown-ups for once indulge themselves in solving cracker puzzles. This benign state of affairs lingers on during the afternoon, when the old habit of cracking riddles, and nuts also, is revived. The modern riddle consists of a straight question and answer, and the rhyming riddle is not often used. Here are a few examples

Which travels faster, heat or cold?
Heat, because you often catch cold.

What goes between London and Glasgow without moving?
The railway line.

What can a blind man see?
A good joke.

Can a boy jump higher than a lamp post?
Yes, because a lamp post cannot jump.

Why did the beetroot blush?
Because it saw the salad dressing.

What is the most difficult riddle?
Life, because we all have to give it up.

TONGUE-TWISTERS

As language developed, it is easy to imagine how early man began to experiment with words and eventually invented the tongue-twister. It has been described as a tricky word rhyme, which has deep-rooted origins. It is difficult to pinpoint exactly when the first tongue-twister was invented, but I am including it in the Roman section together with proverbs and riddles, because it seems likely to have begun in this period.

The tongue-twister is a popular form of folklore using alliteration, which makes correct pronunciation difficult. The childish humour of primitive man must have been easily satisfied by these 'words cramps', as they are called in America, and it could not have been long before it was realized that these hard-to-say rhymes had other uses. If they were repeated with concentration, they helped to establish clear speech. Many have been used throughout the ages to correct lisping, stuttering, and other forms of speech impediment. One of the oldest tongue-twisters ever recorded is:

> *Amidst the mists and coldest frosts,*
> *With barest wrists and stoutest boasts,*
> *He thrusts his fists against the posts,*
> *And still insists he sees the ghosts.*

It is entitled *The Drunken Sayler* and presents somewhat of mystery as the words and original meaning have never been understood fully.

It was only in the last century that tongue-twisters were written down; until that time they existed only in the oral collection and, even now, there must be hundreds which have never been seen in print. The original of *The Ragged Rascal* is said to be:

> *Robert Rutter dreamed a dream,*
> *He dreamt he saw a raging bear,*
> *Rush from the rugged rocks,*
> *And around the rugged rocks*
> *The ragged rascal ran.*

Another tongue-twister that is very old is:

> *Three grey geese in the green grass grazing,*
> *Grey were the geese, and green was the grazing.*

Some tongue-twisters were used as a cure for the hiccups:

> *Three crooked cripples went through Cripplegate.*
> *And through Cripplegate went three crooked cripples.*

> *Hickup, snickup, rise up, right up.*
> *Three drops in the cup are good for the hiccups.*

It was generally thought that if *Peter Piper* was recited correctly, without taking a breath, then the hiccups would go:

> *Peter Piper picked a peck of pickled pepper,*
> *If Peter Piper picked a peck of pickled pepper,*
> *Then where is the peck of pickled pepper, that Peter Piper picked?*

Many a judge long ago has asked a man to repeat a 'twister' to find out if he was drunk! Today tongue-twisters still have their uses. They are a necessary part of the speech therapist's programme and such rhymes as the following are practised frequently:

> *The big black bug bit a big black bear,*
> *Made the big black bear bleed blood.*
> *As round the rough and rugged rocks,*
> *The ragged rascal ran.*

> *The rat ran over the roof of the house,*
> *With a lump of raw liver in its mouth.*

> *She seldom sells shellfish.*

Dentists often request their patients to recite a tongue-twister to test a new plate or set of dentures: 'The sea ceaseth and it sufficeth us' or 'She sells sea shells on the sea shore'. Actors and announcers are often asked to repeat tongue-twisters as a test of elocution, for example 'Shave a cedar shingle thin' or 'Pure food for poor mules'. The following are tongue-twisters which have been recorded during the last hundred years:

> *My dame hath a lame tame crane.*
> *My dame hath a crane that is lame.*
> *Pray gentle Jane let my dame's tame crane,*
> *Feed and come home again.*

A thatcher of Thatchwood went to Thatchet a-thatching.
Did a thatcher of Thatchwood go to Thatchet a-thatching?
If a thatcher of Thatchwood went to Thatchet a-thatching
Where's the thatching the thatcher of Thatchwood has thatched?

Moses supposes his toeses are roses,
But Moses supposes erroneously;
For nobody's toeses are posies of roses
As Moses supposes his toeses to be.

The Leith police dismisseth us,
I'm thankful, sir, to say;
The Leith police dismisseth us,
They thought we sought to stay.
The Leith police dismisseth us,
We both sighed sighs apiece,
And the sigh that we sighed as we said goodbye
Was the size of the Leith police.

My grandmother sent me a new fashioned three-cornered
cambric country-cut handkerchief,
Not an old-fashioned three-cornered cambric country-cut
handkerchief,
But a new-fashioned three-cornered cambric country-cut
handkerchief.

Swim son, swim, show me you're a swimmer,
Swim just how the swans swim — you know how the swans swim.
Six sharp sharks are come to swipe your limb,
So swim as swiftly as you can, and swim son, swim.

Betty Botter bought some butter,
But she said this butter's bitter;
If I put it in my batter,
It will make my batter bitter.
But a bit of better butter,
That would make my batter better.
So she bought a bit of butter
Better than her bitter butter,
And she put it in her batter,
And the batter was not bitter.
So 'twas better Betty Botter
Bought a bit of better butter.

The above rhyme is a good example of how some tongue-twisters
mix up similar sounding consonants as well as using alliteration

to make correct repetition very difficult. This next rhyme appropriately completes the 'twister' section:

When a Twister a-twisting will twist him a twist,
For the twisting of his twist, he three twines doth intwist;
But if one of the twines of the twist do untwist,
The twine that untwisteth, untwisteth the twist.

KING ARTHUR

When good King Arthur ruled this land,
He was a goodly king;
He stole three pecks of barley-meal
To make a bag pudding.

We cannot pretend that this and other verses have survived word for word from early times. Perhaps the first line is a remnant of a long forgotten ballad but, nevertheless, memories of incidents in early history have been kept alive in verse form. After the fall of Rome and the subsequent collapse of the Roman Empire, the Roman legions left Britain and returned to the Continent. The country was then in a very vulnerable state and the Britons, not used to fending for, organizing or protecting themselves, were at a loss to know how to cope with the new dangers that faced them. In addition to the constant attacks by the Scots from Ireland and by the Picts from the North, other barbarous tribes from the Continent frequently raided the South and East coasts. The Angles from Denmark and the Saxons from Germany coveted the rich Roman island, and, when Britain lay unprotected, they launched a full-scale invasion. Having no leader and very little knowledge of warfare, the Britons in the South and East were quickly overrun. But in the West it was a different story. A great warrior emerges out of the mists of time to remind us that Britons do not give up without a fight. Yes, it was Arthur, 'Roman Britain's last champion' as he was called by Beram Saklatvala in his delightful book on the life of Arthur.

When the cobweb fantasies concerning King Arthur and his knights of the round table have been brushed aside, we find that the true Arthur was a Christian soldier. Together with a small band of trusted men, he united many of the warring tribes of the West to fight the common Saxon foe. For approximately twenty years he succeeded and gave Britain the breathing space she needed. The Romans had used cavalry to render their armies more mobile during the last years of occupation and Arthur's army, too, used horses. The early image of the knight develops from this.

Arthur was known to have close associations with Glaston-bury. It is thought by many that the Holy Grail, which he sought, was in reality the sacred cup belonging to Christ. It was stolen many times in those early years and was soon lost for ever. Arthur adopted the Virgin Mary as his standard, which links him with Glastonbury church, also. His right-hand man, Sir Galahad, is reported to have been a descendant of Joseph of Arimathea.

Arthur was in his sixties when he was killed in a civil war, fighting against a warring tribe from the North. Mordred, his nephew, led an army against Arthur, for he wanted to succeed his uncle and become leader of the free West. After the death of the great warrior in AD 537, the rest of the country was overrun and surviving Britons escaped to Wales, where the Saxons did not venture. The country was at this point renamed England.

Many writers throughout history have romanticised about King Arthur and his gallant knights. Sir Thomas Malory wrote *Morte d' Arthur* in the fifteenth century and it was first printed by Caxton. Mallory believed that the true Camelot was Winchester and wrote this verse:

> *And so great Arthur's seat ould Winchester prefers,*
> *Whose ould round table yet she vaunteth to be hers.*

The round table can still be seen today in Winchester castle, but it is now known to be of a much later date.

In Scotland there are many natural monuments bearing Arthur's name and it is known that he had relations living in that part of the British Isles, so the connections may well be genuine. This verse is well-known in Scotland and is considered to be a reference to the great leader:

Arthur O'Bower has broken his band
And he comes roaring up the land;
The King of Scots with all his power,
Cannot stop Arthur of the Bower.

In the North, too, there are many ballads about King Arthur, although there is no evidence that he ever lived in Carlisle:

King Arthur lives in merry Carlisle,
And seemly is to see;
And there with him Queen Guenever
That bride so bright of blee.

In Wales King Arthur's name is widely known and there are many places that bear his name, but, as I said earlier, the remaining Britons fled to that country after the Saxon victory and probably named parts of their new land after their great national hero.

Although Tintagel castle in Cornwall is commonly thought to have close connections with Arthur, it is in reality a Norman castle, though this does not rule out the possiblity that Arthur was brought up in this part of the country. The story of Arthur and his knights presents something of an enigma. It is now accepted by most historians that he was indeed a great warrior and champion of the Britons, but the actual archeological proof of his existence is very scarce. In this case, like so many others, it has been left to the oral rhyme to preserve the memory of this great man.

SAXON

WEATHER

After the first flush of victory, when the Saxons had tired of looting, burning and killing, they took stock of the land that they had captured. They were a pagan people to whom nothing was sacred: temples and homes alike lay in ruins, and they had no thought for or understanding of the civilization that they had destroyed. Not without justification were the Saxon warriors called 'the men of the long knives'. However, they were essentially a farming people who soon substituted farm implements for their weapons of war, and began the fight for survival in the only manner they knew. They brought many new ideas for farming to England, including a hand plough, which improved cultivation considerably. It is from this era that many of our weather and nature rhymes probably stem. The behaviour of the elements was very important, and the size of the harvest was weighed against the length and severity of the winter. A poor harvest meant starvation, pestilence and death. The rhymes included in this section are the result of centuries of observation and surely must bear serious consideration even in these sophisticated days:

> A red sky in the morning,
> Is a shepherd's warning.
> A red sky at night,
> Is a shepherd's delight.
>
> Rain before seven,
> Fine before eleven.
>
> If a rainbow comes at night,
> The rain will be gone quite.

> *Mackerel sky,*
> *Not long dry.*

This last couplet must be universal. A mackerel sky is usually accepted as referring to cirrocumulus cloud formation, which is high, thin cloud patterned in flakes or ripples. Another cloud rhyme says:

> *When clouds appear like rocks and towers,*
> *The earth's refreshed by frequent showers.*

Early man thought that storms were sent by weather demons and bells were often rung during a storm to frighten away evil spirits, while charms and spells were recited. Here is a verse that has survived:

> *Beware of the oak, it draws the stroke,*
> *Avoid the ash, it courts the flash,*
> *Creep under a thorn, it can save you from harm.*

The behaviour of plants and animals too was thought to be very important as regards the weather in days gone by. A good crop of wild berries, for instance, foretold a long, hard winter:

> *Holly berries shining red,*
> *Mean a long winter, 'tis said.*

Also from Scotland we have the saying, 'Many haws, many snaws'. This means that, if there is a large number of haws on the hedge rows, there will be a hard winter with plenty of snow. An old Yorkshire folk rhyme tells us:

> *Snaw, snaw, come faster,*
> *White as allybaster;*
> *Poor owd women pickin' geese,*
> *Sendin' the feathers down to Leeds.*

The idea that snow is in reality goose feathers is very old.

> *In Yorkshire ancient people say*
> *If February's second day*
> *Be very fair and clear,*
> *It doth portend a scanty year*
> *For hay and grass, but if it rains*
> *They never then perplex their brains.*

The general feeling seemed to be that if the weather was sunny on

Candlemas day then a bad crop year would follow. If the weather
was not good, it foretold a good harvest:

> *When Candlemas day is cloudy and black,*
> *It always hugs winter away on its back.*

Fog and mist brought forth rhymes as well:

> *For every fog in March,*
> *There'll be a frost in May.*
> *A northern harr, [mist] brings*
> *Fine weather from afar.*

> *When the mist comes from the hill,*
> *Then good weather it doth spill;*
> *When the mist comes from the sea,*
> *Then good weather it will be.*

The first leaves on the trees were accepted as having significance:

> *Oak before ash, all wet and splash;*
> *Ash before oak, all fire and smoke.*

Before a storm cows were said to lie down in the fields, and
donkeys to bray. This old Yorkshire saying refers to the fact that
seagulls fly inland during rough weather:

> *Seagull, seagull, get thi on t' sand,*
> *It'll never be fine while thou'rt on t' land.*

Bees and crows and their habits were thought to be important
too:

> *If bees stay at home,*
> *Rain will soon come;*
> *If they fly away,*
> *Fine will be the day.*

> *On the first of March*
> *The crows begin to search;*
> *By the first of April*
> *They are sitting still;*
> *By the first of May*
> *They've all flown away,*
> *Coming greedy back again,*
> *With October's wind and rain.*

The livelihood of fishermen is especially dependent on the

vagaries of the weather. Here are some old rhymes passed down from parent to child by fishermen throughout the ages:

> *A spraggy cod'll grow no fatter*
> *Till it gits a sup o' new May water.*

> *A north-west breeze as big as a sheet,*
> *And the sails'll take no harm to-night.*

> *When the wind goes opposite the sun,*
> *Trust it not for back it'll come.*

> *When the wind is in the east,*
> *'Tis neither good for man nor beast;*
> *When the wind is in the north,*
> *The skilful fisher goes not forth;*
> *When the wind is in the south,*
> *It blows the bait in the fish's mouth;*
> *When the wind is in the west,*
> *Then 'tis at the very best.*

NATURE

According to Norse mythology, the first man on Earth was Askr, who was created from an ash tree by the gods, which is why the ash became so significant in folklore. Numerous verses are still repeated in many parts of Britain and elsewhere dealing with fortune and romance:

> *Even ash I do thee pluck,*
> *Hoping thus to meet good luck.*
> *If no luck I get from thee,*
> *I shall wish thee on the tree.*

Another rhyme from Yorkshire goes like this:

> *Even ash, even ash, I pluck thee,*
> *This night my own true love to see,*
> *Neither in his rick nor in his rare,*
> *But in his clothes he does everyday wear.*

An ash leaf that had an equal number of divisions on either side was thought to be lucky – rather like a four-leaved clover. A failure of the crop of ash-keys foretold a death in the royal family, or so it was thought centuries ago. There was such a failure, we are told, in 1648 and in January 1649 Charles I was executed. If a twig of ash was worn, it was believed it protected the wearer from snakes. The ash was also thought to possess magical medicinal properties, and it featured in many herb remedies (see Medical section).

A local rhyme from Norfolk tells us of the good fortune entailed by finding a 'two-leaved clover':

> *A clover, a clover of two, put it in your right shoe,*
> *The first young man you meet, in field, street or lane,*
> *You'll have him, or one of his name.*

The tradition that it is unlucky to leave Christmas decoration up after Twelfth Night (Candlemas) can be traced back to a rhyme recorded by Robert Herrick, a chronicler who lived during the late Saxon era:

> *Down with the Rosemary and so,*
> *Down with the Baise and Mistletoe;*
> *Down with the Holly, Ivie, all*
> *Wherewith ye drest the Christmas Hall.*

It was feared that these trimmings would attract goblins and thus bring unnecessary bad luck on the household, if they were not removed by Candlemas.

Ivy was regarded as a 'benevolent' plant in ancient times: as a Christmas decoration it bestowed good luck on women-folk. If grown in the house, it protected the household from witches and other evils. A garland of ivy hanging outside a tavern denoted that wine was sold there. An ivy leaf placed in water on New Year's Eve and left until Twelfth Night foretold a good healthy year if it remained fresh and green. If, however, it showed black spots, it foreboded illness and death in the family. An old Oxfordshire rhyme goes:

> *Ivy, Ivy, I love you,*
> *In my bosom I put you,*
> *The first young man who speaks to me*
> *My future husband he will be.*

Girls wishing to find a husband picked an ivy leaf and held it against their hearts while repeating this rhyme.

Apples provided a wealth of superstitions and sayings, for

example, if blossom appeared on the tree in Autumn, the family could expect a death:

> *A bloom on the tree when the apples are ripe,*
> *Is a sure termination of somebody's life.*

It was also considered to be a death omen if an apple was left on the tree during the winter months.

Fortune games with apples were very popular with young people centuries ago. An apple was peeled whole and the peel thrown over the left shoulder, because it was thought the shape of the peel when it lay on the ground would signify the initial of the future wife or husband. Apple pips were sometimes pressed on a girl's cheek while she recited a list of possible mates and the pip that stuck the longest denoted the future husband. Apple pips, too, were often placed on the bars of the fire while this charm was recited:

> *If you love me, bounce and fly,*
> *If you hate me, lie and die.*

If the pip spurted, it meant the lover was true but, if it burnt quietly away, it meant that he was false. A couplet from Yorkshire is self-explanatory:

> *Apple pie without the cheese,*
> *Is like a kiss without the squeeze.*

Robbing birds' nests of eggs was considered wrong, even in early times:

> *Robin takker, robin takker,*
> *Sin, sin, sin.*
>
> *Rob a robin,*
> *Go a-sobbing.*
>
> *The robin and the redbreast,*
> *If ye take from their nest*
> *Ye'll never thrive agen.*
>
> *The robin and the red-breast,*
> *The martin and the swallow*
> *If ye touch one o' their eggs,*
> *Ill luck will surely follow.*

Being such nutritious vegetables, the sowing and picking of peas and beans were considered important:

> *Sow peas and beans on David and Chad,*
> *Whether the weather be good or bad.*

The 1st and 2nd of March are the festival days of St David and St
Chad.

> *Be it weal or be it woe,*
> *Beans should blow before May go.*

Even the onion and its skin was thought to be important:

> *Onion skin,*
> *Very thin,*
> *Mild weather coming in;*
> *Onion skin thick and tough*
> *Coming winter cold and rough.*

The seasons were summed up thus:

> *Spring: Slippy, drippy, nippy!*
> *Summer: Showery, flowery, bowery;*
> *Autumn: Hoppy, croppy, poppy;*
> *Winter: Wheezy, sneezy, breezy.*

HARVEST

Christianity soon became a part of the lives of the Saxons. Not
only did they learn about it from the descendants of those
Romanised Christians who had escaped slaughter during the
invasion, but priests from Rome were also spreading the word of
God throughout most European countries. The power of Rome
was being felt once again – not as a military force, but in a much
more subtle and stronger way. The Roman Catholic faith offered
all men equality and immortality after death, and in return asked
for allegience to God and the Pope. The famous story by Adam
Bede, who lived from A.D. 673 to 735 in his *Ecclesiastical History of
the English Nation* is believed to be true. Pope Gregory the Great
saw some fair-haired children in the slave market in Rome. He
was so struck by their unusual colouring that he inquired from
whence they had come and, when told they were Angles from
England, he replied, 'Not Angles, but Angels'; he then sent St
Augustine to convert Britain to Christianity. The new religion
appealed to all men, especially those born into slavery. It gave
them new hope and lifted their spirits above the miserable

earth-bound existence to which they were accustomed. It also brought rest days, when all were commanded to cease their labours and pay homage to the Christian church. These occasional holidays were treasured by the labouring folk and an old North country couplet reflects this:

> On Good Friday rest thy plough,
> Start nowt, end nowt, that's enough.

Festivals were marked by many traditional songs and rhymes. Whether they were pagan or Christian, the festivals of the seasons were celebrated in connection with the cycle of life, of which the Harvest Festival was the most important. Many old harvest customs such as the bringing in of the last wagon of corn from the fields, called the 'Horkey' wagon, would have been forgotten but for surviving rhymes:

> Home came the jovial Horkey load,
> Last of the whole year's crop,
> And Grace amongst the green boughs rode,
> Right plump upon the top.
>
> The boughs do shake, and the bells do ring,
> So merrily comes our harvest in,
> Our harvest in, our harvest in.
> We've ploughed, we've sowed,
> We've reaped, we've mowed,
> We've got our harvest in.

Another old verse reminds us that a tithe was imposed on all harvest produce and was usually paid to the Church:

> We've cheated the Parson, we'll cheat him again,
> Why should the Vicar have one in ten?
> One in ten, one in ten,
> Why should the Vicar have one in ten?

After the 'horkey' cart had been duly welcomed into the barn, every labourer would be invited to a harvest supper given by the farmer's wife in her large kitchen. Free beer would flow, and there would be singing and rejoicing for many hours. Wages were paid, and it is feared that much of the hard-earned cash was spent in the local taverns, and wives and children suffered accordingly. Later the farmer invited whole families to partake of the harvest supper. This idea developed into Harvest Festivals

being held by the Church and the produce was divided among
deserving cases. Other harvest rhymes are remembered in Yorkshire:

> *Blest be the day that Christ was born,*
> *For we've getten the mell of the farmer's corn.*
> *It's weel bun but better shorn.*

> *Weel bun' an' better shorn,*
> *Is Mister Readhead's corn;*
> *We hev her, we hev her,*
> *As fast as a feather;*
> > *Hip, hip, hip,*
> > *Hurrah! hurrah! hurrah!*

The custom of shouting 'Hip, hip hurrah' is obviously very old.

The lot of the farm labourer was very hard and it was not until
the last century that substantial improvements were made. For
centuries he worked for a starvation wage and probably only
tasted meat at Harvest and Christmas times:

> *Bread and cheese, work at your ease,*
> *Beef and pudden, work like a good 'un.*

Another verse that has survived from ancient times tells of the
plight of the plough boy:

> *Good Master and good Mistress,*
> *As you sit by the fire,*
> *Remember us poor Plough lads*
> *That run through the mire.*

This was part of the *Plough Play*, the oldest known English
mummers' play.

The Christmas ceremony to bless the apple harvest is thought
to be very old and was performed on Twelfth Night, usually in
Sussex and the West country – it was called Apple Wassailing. At
dusk all the folk who worked on the farm would go to the apple
orchard and select one tree to represent the others. They carried
handbells, trays , pots and other articles capable of making a
noise. Quantities of cider or mead were drunk and some was
thrown over the roots of the tree. Three men bowed low three
times, imitating the laden tree. Then much noise and clatter was
made by the company to drive away all evil and harmful spirits
that might have been lurking in the orchard. After this, all the

people present joined hands round the tree and sang the a-wassailing song, entitled *Hail To Thee Old Apple Tree*:

> *Stand fast root,*
> *Bear well top;*
> *Pray God send us a good howling crop.*
>
> *Every twig, apples big;*
> *Every bough, apples enow;*
> *Hats full, caps full,*
> *Full quarter sacks full.*
> *Holla boys, holla, huzzah!*

Another couplet regarding fruit goes:

> *September blow soft,*
> *Till the fruit's in the loft.*

The fruit harvest was summed up by:

> *A cherry year,*
> *A merry year;*
> *A pear year,*
> *A dear year;*
> *A plum year,*
> *A dumb year.*

Animal foodstuffs were remembered by this little rhyme:

> *Hay is for horses,*
> *Straw is for cows,*
> *Milk is for little pigs,*
> *And wash for old sows.*

Thistles and groundsel, too, were mentioned in verse:

> *Cut thistles in May,*
> *They grow in a day;*
> *Cut them in June,*
> *That is too soon;*
> *Cut them in July,*
> *Then they will die.*
>
> *Through storm and wind,*
> *Sunshine and shower,*
> *Still you will find*
> *Groundsel in flower.*

FESTIVALS

Robert Herrick supplies us once again with a clear picture of the lighter side of life in Saxon times:

> *I tell of Christmas mummings, New Year's day,*
> *Of Twelfth Night, King and Queen and children's play;*
> *I tell of Valentines and true love's knots,*
> *Of omens, cunning men and drawing lots;*
> *I tell of Maypoles, hock carts, wassails, wakes ...*

No single community celebrated all the festivals on the calendar. Some were more popular than others and have, therefore, survived in many places throughout the country. Other quaint festivals were only known to special villages and many of these have died out as communities changed during the course of history. Mothering Sunday has certainly not disappeared and is perhaps made more of in modern times than when it was first celebrated. It is the fourth Sunday in Lent, and in the olden days mothers were visited and given simple presents of tea, flowers or a Simnel cake. An old rhyme recalls this:

> *I'll to thee a Simnel bring,*
> *'Gainst thou go'st a mothering.*

CHRISTMAS

The tradition of carol singing and collecting money at Christmas time may have its roots in the North country custom of a group of musicians called 'waits' parading the streets at night playing and entertaining. Originally these musicians were watchmen and sentinels, who begged for Christmas money in return for entertainment. An old tower in Newcastle was formerly called 'Waits' Tower, because this was their meeting place. An old rhyme reminds us of these minstrels:

> *Good morning Mister Capstick,*
> *Good morning Mrs Capstick,*
> *And all the little Capsticks;*
> *It's five o'clock and a frosty mornin'.*

This verse was sung by labourers' children before Christmas:

> *I wish you a merry Christmas and a happy New Year,*
> *A pocketful of money and a barrelful of beer;*
> *Good luck to your feather-fowl, fere;*
> *And please will you give me my Christmas-box!*

The *Cleveland Vessell Cups' Song* is better known to us as 'God rest you merry, gentlemen:

> *God rest you merry, gentlemen,*
> *Let nothing you dismay;*
> *Remember Christ our Saviour*
> *Was born on Christmas day,*
> *To save our souls from Satan's power;*
> *Long time we've been astray,*
> *This brings tidings of comfort and joy.*

There are two more similar verses. A verse chanted by children towards the end of the year was:

> *Bounce buckram, velvet's dear,*
> *Christmas comes but once a year.*

> *And when it comes it brings good cheer,*
> *But when it's gone it's never near.*

Another verse reminds us that the goose was much more popular years ago at festive seasons than it is today:

> *Christmas is coming and the goose is getting fat,*
> *Please put a penny in the old man's hat;*
> *If you haven't a penny, a halfpenny will do,*
> *If you haven't a halfpenny, God bless you!*

The rhyme above of course refers to the old monetary system.

> *Dame get up and bake your pies*
> *On Christmas day in the morning.*

The custom of baking pies for Christmas is very old. Although we still call our traditional pies mince-pies, they no longer contain meat. In ancient recipe books the general.rule was to add minced meat to the currants, apples and spices.

PANCAKE DAY

Pancake day, Pancake day,
If you don't give us a holiday,
We'll all run away!

School children still chant this in some parts of the country, but they have to be content with pancakes and forgo the holiday. Shrove Tuesday is the last day before the commencement of Lent on Ash Wednesday. People were summoned to church centuries ago by the Pancake Bell to confess their sins in preparation for the forty days of fasting and denial that lay before them. Collop Monday preceded Shrove Tuesday, and on that day large quantities of collops and bacon were consumed: 'Pit-a-pat, the pan's hot, I be come a-shroving'. Many pancakes were made and eaten on Shrove Tuesday as it was the last chance before Lent for merrymaking and feasting. Many places had pancake-eating contests and in Cheshire the first bell of the day was called Guttit Bell for this reason. In Yorkshire children chant:

When the pancake bell begins to ring,
All Halifax lads begin to sing.

At Olney in Buckinghamshire a race for housewives carrying frying-pans and tossing pancakes has been staged for many centuries. Other places in England and America, too, have taken up this old custom. Westminster School holds a 'pancake greeze' on Shrove Tuesday. The chef tosses a large pancake into the play area, and the boys scramble for it. The one who gets the largest piece is rewarded with a guinea by the Dean of Westminster.

Ash Wednesday is so called after the ancient custom of sprinkling ashes on the heads of penitents.

April noddy's past and gone,
You're a fool and I'm none.

The old name for April Fools' Day was All Fools' Day. No one really knows why the custom of playing practical jokes on 1st April sprang up. One theory is that it marked the last day of celebrations of the Spring equinox, when the sun's rays fall vertically on the equator and day and night are of equal length all over the world. The rhyme refers, of course, to the rule that after midday the one who still plays practical jokes is himself the fool.

Bede said that the word 'easter' was derived from 'Eostre', an Anglo-Saxon word meaning the coming of Spring. Again this pagan ritual was merged with the important Christian event of Christ's death on the cross and the resurrection. Eggs were regarded as the symbol of life the world over and it is not surprising that the giving of eggs has survived until this day. Children and the poor begged for eggs at Easter time, and were called 'pace-egger's':

> *'Although I am ragged and not so well dressed,*
> *I can carry a pace-egg as well as the rest.'*

This couplet is still recited in the North, where children used to roll their coloured eggs about until they were broken. The word 'pace' is derived from an old mummer's play called the *Pascal* or *Pace Play*.

FORTUNE

Fortune rhymes, like the weather and nature jingles, were regarded as a form of oral education by simple folk. It was the only logical way of passing on to their children the knowledge accumulated over the years, the essential knowledge that was vital, as they thought, to the survival of the race. Children learned the simple verses automatically and naturally believed in their philosophy.

The three great events in human life – birth, marriage and death – feature prominently in the fortune jingles. The mystery and wonderment of birth has never ceased to intrigue man. In early times the survival of babies and young children was precarious, and many superstitions and charms were repeated and adhered to in the first few years of life, for instance, if a child was born at three, six, nine or twelve o'clock, it was thought that he would have a keen perception of life and would be invulnerable to the evil influence of witches. If he was born with a caul, he could never be drowned, and sailors often bought cauls from midwives to take to sea as good luck tokens.

To rock an empty cradle was thought to be unlucky, but, in East

Anglia where babies were many and wages few, the old rhyme says:

> *Rock cradle empty, rock in plenty.*

The day on which the child was born was considered important, and an old rhyme, which is still very popular today, goes:

> *Monday's child is fair of face,*
> *Tuesday's child is full of grace,*
> *Wednesday's child is full of woe,*
> *Thursday's child has far to go.*
> *Friday's child is loving and giving;*
> *Saturday's child works hard for a living.*
> *And the child that is born on the Sabbath day,*
> *Is bonny and blithe, and good and gay.*

To cut the baby's nails before he was a year old was thought to make the child light-fingered. And indeed, even today, some mothers and nurses still bite the nails of young children. Even after a year, it was considered very important which day was nail-pairing day – Friday was thought to be a black day and Sunday was worse! In Durham they say:

> *Better a child had ne'er been born,*
> *Than to cut his nails on the Sabbath morn.*

A verse that is still well-known in other parts of Great Britain goes:

> *Cut them on Monday, cut them for health,*
> *Cut them on Tuesday, cut them for wealth,*
> *Cut them on Wednesday, cut them for news.*
> *Cut them on Thursday for a pair of new shoes,*
> *Cut them on Friday, cut them for sorrow,*
> *Cut them on Saturday, see your true love tomorrow.*
> *Cut them on Sunday, and the devil will be with you all the week.*

Small white specks on the nails were thought to be a sure sign of good fortune and we still say:

> *A gift on the thumb is sure to come;*
> *A gift on the finger is sure to linger.*

Another rhyme says, commencing with the thumb:

> *Friend, foe, letter, lover, journey to go.*

The colour and form of human hair was thought to indicate character in early days: lank hair showed a cunning nature, while curly hair denoted inner serenity and a cheerful disposition; red hair was regarded with suspicion and this belief probably dates back to the time when red-haired Danish pirates raided British coasts. Red hair was thought to signify a terrible temper and unfaithfulness. This rhyme has survived from early times:

> *Beware of that man,*
> *Be he friend or brother,*
> *Whose hair is one colour*
> *And moustache another.*

Like nail-pairing, the day on which hair was cut was considered important:

> *Best never been born if Sunday shorn*
> *And likewise leave out Monday.*
> *Cut Thursday and Saturday and you'll never grow rich;*
> *But live long if cut on a Tuesday.*
> *Shear a beast on a Wednesday morn,*
> *And mankind on a Friday.*

Hair clippings, when thrown on the fire promised a long life if they burned brightly, but if they smouldered then misfortune could be expected.

Tickling rhymes are of great antiquity and are still firm favourites with children today:

> *Tickle, tickle, on the knee,*
> *If you laugh then you don't love me.*

> *If you're the lady as I take you to be,*
> *You will neither laugh nor smile when I tickle your knee.*
> *Old maid, old maid, you'll surely be,*
> *If you laugh or you smile when I tickle your knee.*

The saying 'Better the last smile than the first laughter' is a proverb with ancient roots and probably gave rise to 'He that laughs last, laughs longest'. An old rhyme explains this:

> *If you sing before breakfast,*
> *You'll cry before night.*

Yorkshire is rich in local rhymes, as we have seen – here is a 'dimple' verse:

A dimple on your cheek
Your living to seek;
A dimple on your chin
You'll have your living brought in.

Sneezing rhymes were often quoted. In fact, a sneeze was treated with respect and regarded as a small explosion in the head, coming from the gods. Nowadays people still say, 'God bless you' and after a sneeze in days gone by the correct procedure was to doff the hat at the same time. A sneeze before breakfast predicted a present in the week. Here is a common sneezing verse used years ago:

Monday for danger, Tuesday kiss a stranger,
Wednesday for a letter, Thursday something better,
Friday for sorrow, Saturday meet your lover tomorrow.

From Cornwall comes this couplet:

Sneeze on Sunday morning fasting,
Enjoy your true love everlasting.

Another goes like this:

One for a kiss, two for a wish,
Three for a letter, four for a better,
Five for a silver, six for gold,
Seven for a secret never to be told.

In Scotland, it was thought that a new baby was not safe from the fairies until it had sneezed, and this was also thought to prove that it was mentally normal, for it was generally accepted that idiots could not sneeze! If you sneezed to the right, it was regarded as lucky and promised a long safe journey, but, if you sneezed to the left or near a grave, it was an ill omen.

Burning cheeks, itching palms and feet, were all thought to bear significant tidings: an itching elbow foretold another bed mate; itching hands meant a gift of money, and itching feet a walk on new ground. Even today we still believe that burning cheeks and ears denote that we are being talked about. An 'ear' couplet says:

Right for spite,
Left for love.

Centuries ago, this charm would be recited to protect the victim who suffered from burning cheeks:

> *Right cheek, left cheek, why do you burn?*
> *Cursed be she that doth me harm;*
> *If it be a maid, let she be slayed,*
> *If it be a wife, let her lose her life,*
> *And if it be a widow, long let her mourn,*
> *But if it be my own true love, burn cheek, burn.*

Courtship and marriage were, and still are, regarded as two of the most important events in human life. It was thought that the month in which you married had great bearing on your future happiness. When Mary Queen of Scots married James Hepburn, Earl of Bothwell, on 15th May 1567, it boded ill for her, or so people said who quoted this old rhyme:

> *The people say,*
> *That only wantons marry*
> *In the month of May.*

The day of the week that you chose to get wed was thought to be important also:

Monday for wealth – lucky in most parts of the country;
Tuesday for health – lucky in most parts too;
Wednesday the best of all, especially in the English Midlands;
Thursday for losses – particularly those in Britain, Holland, and Switzerland, but good in Shropshire;
Friday for crosses – bad for Christians but good for Norsemen;
And Saturday no luck at all – most popular day of all.

Later, an act of Parliament forbade marriage between certain dates: 27 November – 13 January, 6 February – 18 April and 16 May – 6 June. Here is a rhyme taken from a register of St Mary's in Beverley, Yorkshire:

> *When Advent comes do thou refraine,*
> *Till Hillary set ye free again;*
> *Next Sepiugesima saith thee nay,*
> *But when Lowe Sunday comes thou may;*
> *But at Rogation thou must tarry,*
> *Till Trinitie shall bid thee marry.*

A couplet which refers to these marriage rhymes warns:

> *If you marry in Lent,*
> *You will live to repent.*

Another quaint superstition is preserved in the following:

> *To change the name and not the letter,*
> *Is a change for the worse, and not for the better.*

This meant that misfortune would befall you if the man you married possessed the same initial in his surname as yours, for example Brown and Black. It was also thought unlucky to marry during Harvest time:

> *They that wive between sickle and scythe,*
> *Shall ne'er survive.*

On the other hand, good fortune would come if you married during a leap year:

> *Happy they'll be that wed and wive*
> *Within Leap Year; they're sure to thrive.*

Another wedding rhyme says:

> *A weddin', a woo, a clog an' a shoe,*
> *A pot full o' porridge an' away they go.*

In some parts of the country children still chant this doggerel as the couple drive away after the marriage feast. They pretend to take off their shoes and throw them after the bride and groom. The custom was known as 'trashing' in early times, and an old shoe is still called a 'trash'.

It was considered in the North to be very unlucky to wear green and white together:

> *Green and white,*
> *Forsaken quite.*

On the other hand, it was thought essential to wear the following when taking the marriage vows:

> *Something old, something new,*
> *Something borrowed, something blue.*

This saying is very old too:

> *Happy is the bride the sun shines on,*
> *Blessed is the corpse the rain falls on.*

The following rhyme was often chanted at weddings years ago:

> *The bridegroom's health we all will sing,*
> *In spite of Turk or Spanish king;*
> *The bride's good health we will not pass,*
> *But put them both into one glass.*
> *See, see, see that he drink it all,*
> *See, see, that he let none fall,*
> *Or if he do, he shall drink two,*
> *And so shall the rest of the company do.*
> *When I doe ring, God's praises syng,*
> *When I doe tole, pray heart and souls.*

This old couplet, denoting the power of the church bell over folk of long ago, was inscribed on the bell of St Mary's in Hornby, during the reign of Henry VII. Although bells were not cast until the twelfth century, they had before then been fashioned by hand and were in use thousands of years before Christ. As the above rhyme explains, bells acted as messengers bearing glad or sad news to the community. Another verse says:

> *I rang for the living, I tolled for the dead,*
> *I gave the first greetings to those who were wed;*
> *And still in God's house I stand by the door,*
> *To open the portals to rich and to poor.*

Many people still believe that the tolling of the church bell at times of death, called the 'passing bell', is done in order to drive away evil spirits and give the deceased a safe passage to heaven.

> *When the bell begins to toll,*
> *Lord have mercy upon the soul.*

> *When thou dost hear a toll or knell,*
> *Then think upon thy passing bell.*

The passing bell was tolled nine times for a man, six for a woman and three for a child. It was the signal for all the people of the village to pray for the departed and also for them to reflect for a while on their own 'passing', which was sure to come sooner or later. The Venerable Bede was the first to record this custom, whereas the custom of posting the name of the deceased on the door of the manor house has long been forgotten by most people.

More information about bells is to be found in the section on 'Oranges and Lemons'.

Horseshoes have always been considered lucky and, therefore, have close connections with fortune rhymes. Many buildings in both town and country still follow the custom of nailing horseshoes over doors and arches to bring good luck. It was reported that Admiral Nelson even nailed a horseshoe to the mast of his ship. Horseshoes have obvious connections with the mystic powers of fire and iron, and perhaps the following rhyme will help to explain the superstition concerning them:

> Nail horseshoe over door, saying,
> 'Father, Son, and Holy Ghost;
> Nail the devil to this post,
> Thrice I smites with Holy Crook,
> With this mell I thrice do knock,
> One for God, and one for Wod[en]
> And one for Lok[i]'.

'Woden', as previously mentioned, was the Saxon word for Odin, the King of the Norse gods, while Loki was the Norse god of fire. This rhyme is a good example of confusion between pagan and Christian worship, the like of which must have been very common in the Saxon era. The story goes that St Dunstan, of whom there is more later, once caught the devil, nailed a horseshoe to one of his hooves and fastened him to a wall. He refused to free him until the devil had promised never to enter a place where a horseshoe is on view. Perhaps this is why horseshoes are prevalent at weddings – to protect the newlyweds from the devil's power.

Another old rhyme, from Shropshire this time, reflects the custom that it is considered lucky to find a horseshoe:

> Pick 'en up 'e 'orse shoe, and spatter en wi' spittle,
> Make a wish fully quick, and throw en o'ert shoother
> [shoulder],
> Walk on by, an' ne'er glance back.

The memory of the protection of man by another saint is kept alive in this old couplet:

> Within the sound of the great bell,
> No snake or adder o'er shall dwell.

A curious tradition is attached to the tenor bell in the Abbey Church at Dorchester-on-Thames: it is said that snakes cannot abide its tone. Dorchester is only a small village nowadays, but in the seventh century it was the cathedral city of St Berin, who was the apostle of Wessex that died of a snake bite and was buried in the church in AD 650. Ever since then, it has been believed that St Berin has protected the people in the village by the power of the bell. The existing bell was cast in the fourteenth century and has an inscription in Latin on it describing the protection of the saint.

ST PATRICK

The hymn to St. Patrick, often called *St Patrick's Breastplate*, is very old and is accepted by most experts as being composed by the saint himself. The song is well-known in Ireland and other parts of the world, and is still repeated as a charm and protection against all forms of evil. Here is part of the hymn as presented by James Henthorn Todd in his book *St Patrick, Apostle of Ireland*:

I bind myself today,
The strong power of an invocation of the Trinity,
The faith of the Trinity in Unity,
The Creator of the elements.

I bind myself today,
The power of the incarnation of Christ, with that of his Baptism,
The power of the Crucifixion, with that of his burial,
The power of the Resurrection, with the Ascension,
The power to the coming to the Sentence of Judgement

> *I bind myself today,*
> *The power of Heaven,*
> *The light of the Sun,*
> *The whiteness of Snow,*
> *The force of Fire,*
> *The flashing of Lightning,*
> *The velocity of Wind,*
> *The depth of the Sea,*
> *The stability of the Earth,*
> *The hardness of Rocks.*

I bind to myself today,
The Power of God to guide me,
The Might of God to uphold me,
The Wisdom of God to teach me,
The Eye of God to watch over me,
The Ear of God to hear me,
The Word of God to give me speech,
The Hand of God to protect me,
The Way of God to prevent me,
The Shield of God to shelter me,
The Host of God to defend me,
   Against the snares and demons,
   Against the temptations of vices,
   Against the lusts of nature,
   Against every man who meditates injury to me,
      Whether far or near,
      With few or with many.

I have set around me all these powers
Against every hostile savage power,
Directed against my body and my soul,
Against the incantations of false prophets,
Against the black laws of heathenism,
Against the false laws of heresy,
Against the deceits of idolatry,
Against the spells of women and smiths, and druids,
Against all knowledge which binds the soul of man.

   Christ protect me today
   Against poison, against burning,
   Against drowning, against wound,
   That I may receive abundant reward.

   Christ with me, Christ before me,
   Christ behind me, Christ within me,
   Christ beneath me, Christ above me,
   Christ at my right, Christ at my left,
   Christ in the fort,
   Christ in the chariot-seat
   Christ in the poop.

The last three lines mean in effect: Christ protect me at home, and
when travelling by land or sea.

Patrick (AD 389-461) was the son of a Christian official, who lived in South Wales. When he was about sixteen, he was captured by Irish raiders and taken to Ireland as slave labour. He spent six years as a shepherd boy and endured much hardship and cruelty, which his Christian training helped him to bear. At the age of twenty-one he escaped on a trading boat to France, where he entered a monastery to train as a missionary. After some years, he returned to Wales to see his family and, of course, they were overjoyed to see their lost son once again. Soon he realized that his calling lay in Ireland, where paganism abounded. He went back to a French monastery for further training, before setting out again with a small band of monks to bring Christianity to Ireland. At first the people were very suspicious, but they were gradually won over by his doctrine and teaching. A chieftain named Dichu lent him a barn where he could hold meetings and convert people to Christ. The town of Saul on the river Slaney in Ireland still commemorates this, for the name Saul is the Celtic word for barn. Patrick often had to combat Druids, who were fearful that he would diminish their power. Many miracles were performed by him – one being that he collected all the snakes in Ireland, put them in a box and threw them into the sea. The story goes that this is why no snakes are to be found in Ireland and why the Irish sea is so rough – due to the writhing snakes trying to escape from their box!

Patrick was made Bishop of Ireland in 432 and from then on Ireland was converted to the Catholic faith. He introduced Latin as a basis for Church literature, and brought a new culture and education to a hitherto barbarous nation.

The hymn to St Patrick was written in Old Irish and was originally called *The Instruction of the Deer* to commemorate the time when Patrick and his followers escaped the wrath of the pagan king Laoghaire by changing themselves into deer and running into the forest. The verse that mentions protection against 'women, smiths and druids', adds to the general belief that St Patrick actually wrote this hymn. Old women, blacksmiths and Druids were thought to have evil magic powers, and this belief was a pagan superstition that was intermingled with early Christian beliefs.

St Patrick is said to have used the three-leafed shamrock to explain the Trinity and this is why it is the emblem of Ireland. His death on 17th March 461 is remembered all over the world as St Patrick's Day and is the greatest of all the Irish feast days.

ST SWITHIN

Other rhymes which must have originated in the Saxon era also concerns saints. Some people believe, even today, that, if it rains on St Swithin's Day (15 July), it will rain for forty days and nights. This belief stems from a story about St Swithin, who lived in the ninth century:

> *St Swithin's Day, if thou dost rain,*
> *For forty days it will remain.*
> *St Swithin's Day, if thou be fair,*
> *For forty days 'twill rain no mair.*

St Swithin was the spiritual adviser of Egbert, King of Wessex and he became Bishop of Winchester in AD 852. Winchester was regarded as the most important city in England at that time. While St Swithin lay dying, ten years later, he expressed a wish to be buried outside Winchester Cathedral and under 'the feet of the passer-by'. A century later the current Bishop of Winchester decided that it would be more fitting if St Swithin's remains were to be placed inside the Cathedral. On the day set for the removal of the coffin, 15 July, it poured with rain and the ceremony had to be postponed. It rained for forty days and forty nights, and ordinary folk said that this was because St Swithin was annoyed at having his wishes disobeyed.

ST DUNSTAN

> *St Dunstan as the story goes,*
> *Once pulled the devil by his nose*
> *With red hot tongs, which made him roar,*
> *That could be heard ten miles or more.*

St Dunstan, one of the better known English saints, lived from AD 909 to 988. He was a clever man for, as well as writing and

3. St. Dunstan as represented in a window in Wells Cathedral

painting beautiful religious texts, he was musical and composed many hymns and chants used in the abbey of Glastonbury, where he resided. He also delighted in making many useful things for the abbey such as hand bells, organs and other musical instruments. He is sometimes referred to as the patron saint of goldsmiths. The 'red hot tongs' mentioned in the rhyme refer to the fact that he was a skilled metalworker.

St Dunstan was Bishop of London and Worcester, before becoming Archbishop of Canterbury. At the coronation of King Edgar, St Dunstan introduced certain rituals into the coronation service that are still performed today. The investiture with the sword, sceptre and rod of justice, the playing of a traditional anthem, the Archbishop's consecration and anointing, and the shout of recognition from the assembled lords are all rituals which are still carried out in present times. The idea of patriotism was introduced for the first time into the crowning of the king – his followers saw their leader as a national figure.

ST VALENTINE

St Valentine's Day is another example of the merging of Christian and pagan customs. The feast of Lupercalia was celebrated in pre-Christian Rome by a mating ritual. The names or tokens of all young girls of marriageable age were put into a love urn, and the local lads each took a name and paired off with the appropriate girl. The date of this event was 15 February. St Valentine was a priest in Rome, who was martyred for his faith on 14 February. Pope Julius I commemorated the saint by building a church in his memory and allotting him a saint day.

When Christianity reached Britain it was decided tactfully to move the mating ritual day back one day and share it with St Valentine. Many verses were repeated on St Valentine's Day and presents were given by the man to the woman of his choice. Old rhymes record these customs:

> *Good morning to you Valentine;*
> *Curl your locks as I do mine,*
> *One before and two behind,*
> *Good morning to you Valentine.*

The men concerned were known as valentines. The gift of a pair of gloves symbolized a lasting love:

> *Roses are red and violets are blue,*
> *Carnations are sweet and so are you.*
> *Thou art my love, and I art thine,*
> *I draw thee for my Valentine.*

> *The rose is red, the violet blue, Gillies are sweet, and so are you;*
> *These are the words you bade me say,*
> *For a pair of new gloves on Valentine's day.*

When cards became the fashion, many valentines were sent and this custom reached its peak during the Victorian era. It is still not known, however, why the cards must be anonymous. Perhaps it is to recapture some of the excitement felt by the young people drawing lots from the love urn thousands of years ago. Another old verse mentioning St Valentine is:

> *If she be a good goose, her dame well to pay,*
> *She will lay two eggs before Valentine's Day.*

ST DAVID AND ST CHAD

A couplet on a similar theme to the one about St Valentine tells
us:

> *Before St Chad*
> *Every goose lays both good and bad.*

The sowing of peas and beans before the saint days of David and
Chad – the 1st and 2nd of March, has been mentioned previously in the section on nature (p.64). St David is the patron saint
of Wales, but very few facts are known about him. He was born in
approximately AD 500 and lived to be nearly a hundred years old.
He was head of the Church in South Wales and later moved the
seat of Church government to Monmouthshire, to Menevia,
which is now known as St David's, a cathedral city. It became a
popular shrine for pilgrims. David was much revered and many
churches in Wales and Ireland were dedicated to him. At the
request of Henry I, Pope Calixtus II made him a saint in 1120.

The name of St Chad is to be found in many local nature
rhymes, although his history is obscure. He died in AD 672 and
was the first Bishop of Lichfield. He and his brother, St Cedd,
were both educated in Lichfield under St Aiden. His first bishoprick was at Lastingham, but while the then Bishop of Northumbria, whose See was at York, was away in France, King Oswy
appointed Chad to take his place. When Bishop Wilfrid returned
from the Continent, Chad humbly resigned the position and
King Oswy gave him Lichfield instead. St Chad was said to have
founded a monastery at Barrow as well.

LONDON BRIDGE

> *London Bridge is broken down,*
>   *Dance over my Lady Lee,*
> *London Bridge is broken down,*
>   *With a gay lady.*
>
> *How shall we build it up again?*
>   *Dance over, etc.*

Build it up with mud and clay,
   Dance over, etc.

Mud and clay will wash away,
   Dance over, etc.

Build it up with iron and steel,
   Dance over, etc.

Iron and steel will bend and bow,
   Dance over, etc.

Build it up with silver and gold,
   Dance over, etc.

Silver and gold will be stolen away,
   Dance over, etc.

Build it up with stone so strong,
   Dance over my Lady Lee,
Hurrah, 'twill last for ages long,
   With a gay lady.

Bridges have been in existence for thousands of years – the first being perhaps a log laid across a stream or a slab of stone over marshy ground. It was the Romans who first built successful bridges – in fact, in Portugal there exists a Roman arched bridge, the Alcantara, over the river Tagus, which is still used. When the Romans invaded Britain in AD 43, they searched along the marshy ground that flanked the Thames until they came to a slight elevation, later known as Cornhill, which corresponded with a narrow stretch of water. It was here that the Thames was successfully bridged for the first time by the first London bridge which, because of its position and stability, gave birth to the first settlement of London that later became a stronghold fortress.

Although it was the Romans who built the first wooden London bridge, this well-known nursery song is included in the Saxon section because it is from this era that the song about broken bridges originated. The collapse of a bridge in early times meant, so people thought, that the water spirits were displeased at having their privacy disturbed. There have been many stories of humans, especially children, being walled up alive into the bridge construction to act as sacrifices to the evil spirits of the water. Only in the last century, when an old bridge in Bremen was dismantled, the skeleton of a child was found in the foundations.

When London Bridge was being built or repaired, it was the custom to set a night watchman to guard against evil spirits. An additional verse which is sometimes sung at the end of the song bears this out ;

> *Then we'll set a man to watch,*
> *Dance over my Lady Lee,*
> *Then we'll set a man to watch,*
> *With a gay lady.*

During the Saxon era, England was subject to numerous attacks by raiding tribesmen – the Danes were the most troublesome. King Alfred, who was by far the greatest of all the Saxon kings, made peace with the intruders and taught them to live with the people they had fought. He was the first leader to build ships to protect our shores and consequently he has been known ever since as 'the father of the English navy'. However, on one Viking raid in the year 1014, in the time of King Ethelred, Olaf the Norseman sailed up the river with his fleet to destroy the bridge. At first they were unsuccessful, but, having managed to protect the boats sufficiently at last, they were able to tie ropes round the supporting piles. The Vikings then rowed their boats downstream as hard as they could and tore the timbers of the bridge from the foundations, thus destroying it completely. This event is recorded in one of the old Norse sagas by Ottar Svarte entitled *Heimskringla:*

> *London Bridge is broken down,*
> *Gold is won and bright renown,*
> *Shields resounding,*
> *War-horns sounding,*
> *Hildur shouting in the din.*
> *Arrows singing,*
> *Mailcoats ringing,*
> *Odin makes our Olaf win!*

Odin, as mentioned before, was the King of the Norse gods and was also the god of war.

The building of old London Bridge pictured in most nursery rhyme books was begun in 1176 by a French monk, Peter de Colechurch. It was situated approximately thirty yards down-

4. Old London Bridge

stream from the site of the present bridge, and touched the bank on the City side opposite the church of St Magnus Mary. Until the middle of the eighteenth century it remained the only bridge to ford the Thames in the London area. Therefore, the fate of the bridge – its tendency to fall down or catch fire must have worried a good many people concerned with commerce, not to mention the folk who actually worked and lived on it. The design using masonry piers was the first of its kind used in a tidal river and from old prints we can see the numerous buttresses that were included in the construction. Navigating through the bridge in those days was a dangerous business. On the upstream side of the river was fairly calm, but through the arches the water swirled at a great rate and only skilled watermen could accomplish the tricky task of taking a boat through safely. This was called 'shooting the bridge' and gave rise to the old proverb: 'London Bridge was made for wise men to go over, and fools to go under'.

Water mills worked from the bridge and the noise of these and the rush of water must have been quite deafening. Many people were drowned in those days when they fell into the river because their cries for help were never heard. The bridge spanned the river like a street; houses and shops were crowded together, often strutted overhead to stop them falling down. Shakespeare must have visited it, for in his time it was a well-known literary quarter, having many bookshops and publishers. From time to time buildings either collapsed or were destroyed by fire, and as fashion changed it became, later, a well-known tailoring and dressmaking centre. When coaches became popular, the traffic jams on the bridge were numerous, for at one point the road was only twelve feet wide. The heads of traitors were often spiked upon the top of the Great Stone Gate and served to remind all visitors to the City of the drastic consequences of displeasing the ruling monarch. Such sights were commonplace in those days, and the public probably took no notice.

At the beginning of the nineteenth century the old London Bridge was dismantled. It has been said that the fifteen tons of iron which had clad the piers were bought by a cutler in the Strand and he reported that it made the best cutlery that he had ever known! The stone went to build Ingress Abbey near Greenhithe. Thousands of snuff boxes and other knick-knacks were made from the old elm, and two shelters taken from the bridge can still be seen today in Victoria Park, Hackney, by St Augustine's Gate. The shelters are semi-octagonal in shape and are built in white stone. The inscription above the timber seats is faint, but the first sentence says, 'This alcove which stood on Old London Bridge was presented to her majesty by Benjamin Dixon Esq. J.P., for the use of the public 1860.'

The New London Bridge with only four piers was designed by John Rennie in 1822 and in 1831 the bridge was officially opened by King William IV. It survived for more than a hundred years, carrying the burden of London's ever increasing traffic on its back and allowing safe passage to river craft. Even the blitz during the Second World War did not shake it and it was not till 1967 that demolition began. An American firm bought the facing stone of the old bridge for $2,460,000. As each section was dismantled, it was marked and coded, and shipped across to America. When all the stone had reached its destination, at Lake Havasu, Arizona, the bridge was reconstructed as a tourist attraction. The present London Bridge is supported on two piers, which provide a clear central span of 330 feet across the main shipping channel. The eddies and currents are reduced, and the buttresses are much slimmer, all of which makes for easier navigation. It is interesting to trace the changing structure of London Bridge throughout the ages. The number of piers has decreased with each new design, which shows clearly how bridge building techniques have gradually become more sophisticated.

> *London Bridge is broken down,*
> *Broken down, broken down,*
> *London Bridge is broken down,*
> *My fair lady.*

The popularity of the nursery song has not changed over the years. With its gay tune and unforgettable words, it is still in constant use in play groups and schools. The good skipping metre lends itself to many action games and community dances, and serves to remind us of the traditions that lie behind bridge building throughout the centuries.

Royal Rhyme

First William the Norman,
Then William his son;
Henry, Stephen and Henry,
Then Richard and John;
Next Henry the third,
Edwards one two and three,
And again after Richard
Three Henrys we see.
Two Edwards, third Richard,
If rightly I guess;
Two Henrys, Sixth Edward,
Queen Mary, Queen Bess,
Then Jamie the Scotchman,
Then Charles whom they slew,
Yet received after Cromwell
Another Charles too.

Next James the second
Ascended the throne;
Then good William and Mary
Together came on.
Till Anne, Georges four,
And fourth William all past,
Came the reign of Victoria
Which longest did last.
Then Edward the Peacemaker,
He was her son,
And fifth of the Georges
Was next in the run;
Edward the eighth
Gave the crown to his brother,
Now God's sent Elizabeth –
All of us love her.

NORMAN, PLANTAGENET, LANCASTER AND YORK

NORMAN

William the Conquerer 1066
Played on the Saxons oft cruel tricks.

As we have seen, England was the object of many attacks during the Saxon era. In 1066 William from Normandy overthrew the Saxon army, and for the last time Britain was conquered by a foreign power. King Harold was well aware of the Norman plans to attack and had himself previously visited Normandy, in fact, many of the French nobles were related to him due to former marriages into Saxon stock. The French invasion was well timed – it took place a few days after the Vikings from Norway had landed on the East coast, where Harold and his army had defeated them in a glorious battle at Stamford Bridge. By this decisive victory, Harold gained the support of many English lords, who pledged allegiance to him. On hearing that William had landed at Pevensey, Harold did not wait for reinforcements, to hear good advice or to rest his weary men. He turned his army about and marched with all haste to the south.

William's army was not large, although they were hand-picked, and he was waiting for reinforcements. Harold, still flushed with the victory over the Vikings and over confident, made the mistake that altered the history of England. Historians agree that, had Harold waited to raise a bigger and fresher army, the Normans would undoubtedly have been defeated. However, Harold arrived at Hastings after a forced march and entrenched his troops at Battle. On Saturday 14 October, the two armies met in combat. By evening both Harold and his two brothers had been killed, and the English army routed. William then marched to London, devastating the countryside as he went, and the ruthlessness of his methods soon dissipated any resistance. He was crowned King of England on Christmas Day 1066 in Westminster Abbey.

The conquerer had no mercy for the opposition and soon the Saxon hierarchy was almost non-existent. The rich lands and property of England were divided amongst the greedy Norman lords. 'Oft cruel tricks' were indeed played on the Saxons, who lost all power and wealth. On the other hand, William I did many things which laid the foundation for a strong, well-organised country: he built numerous castles, many of which can still be seen today; being a religious man, he strengthened the power of the Church; he instigated work on the *Domesday Book*, which was an inventory of population and industry in Britain at that time; and he abolished slavery and developed the feudal system, in which land was given in return for loyalty to the king. The remaining Saxons were employed as servants and farm workers in the feudal demesnes, and the bondage remained for many centuries.

On his death-bed William pronounced a wish that his second son, William Rufus, should succeed him, for his eldest son, Robert, had displeased him and had, therefore, lost his right to the throne of England.

COCK ROBIN

William II had the same thick-set build and red face of his father, and it is thought by many that he had red hair – all of which led to his being called Rufus. He was an unpopular king and was disliked by many of the barons, because they thought that his elder brother was the rightful heir to the throne. He was an irreligious man and was therefore disliked by the clergy, as he only used the Church as a source of wealth. He was disliked by the common people because he lived extravagantly and was a bachelor – an unnatural state of affairs for the King of England. He also bore the stigma of delving into black magic and witchcraft, but to his friends he was generous and was considered by them to be a good and trusty soldier.

His death in the New Forest has remained one of the unsolved mysteries of English history. The textbooks relate that he died when a stray arrow hit him whilst hunting. There have been many theories as to why this happened, but none have been substantiated; the only thing that is certain is that the accidental death of William Rufus was very convenient for his younger brother, Henry, who was also in the hunting party. Henry seized the English throne a few days after the event. There is a strong belief, especially in the West country, that the nursery song 'Who killed Cock Robin?' is a direct dramatization of the death of William Rufus.

Who killed Cock Robin?
I said the Sparrow,
With my bow and arrow,
I killed Cock Robin.

Who saw him die?
I, said the Fly,
With my little eye,
I saw him die.

Who caught his blood?
I, said the Fish,
With my little dish,
I caught his blood.

Who'll make the shroud?
I, said the Beetle,
With my thread and needle,
I'll make the shroud.

Who'll dig his grave?
I, said the Owl,
With my pick and shovel,
I'll dig his grave.

Who'll be the parson?
I, said the Rook,
With my little book,
I'll be the parson.

Who'll be the clerk?
I, said the Lark,
If it's not in the dark,
I'll be the clerk.

Who'll carry the link?
I, said the Linnet,
I'll fetch it in a minute,
I'll carry the link.

Who'll be chief mourner?
I, said the Dove,
I mourn for love,
I'll be chief mourner.

Who'll carry the coffin?
I, said the Kite,
If it's not through the night,
I'll carry the coffin.

Who'll bear the pall?
We said the Wren,
Both the cock and the hen,
We'll bear the pall.

Who'll sing the psalm?
I, said the Thrush,
As she sat on a bush,
I'll sing the psalm.

Who'll toll the bell?
I, said the Bull,
Because I can pull,
I'll toll the bell.

All the birds of the air,
Fell a-sighing and a-sobbing,
When they heard of the death of poor Cock Robin,
When they heard of the death of poor Cock Robin.

The song is known to be of great antiquity and there is no justifiable reason to doubt its association with William Rufus.

The fate of Cock Robin is thought by many to be linked with Buckland Rectory in Gloucestershire. The rectory has some fine diamond-paned windows, with paintings of birds upon them. Some birds are pierced with arrows, one is admiring a peacock's feather, and one is sitting on a throne holding a sword – a symbol of sovereignty. However, contrary to popular belief these birds are not robins, but blackcocks, which are a type of grouse.

The vicar of Buckland Rectory, the Reverend Bland, says that in medieval times the blackcock was thought to be evil, because of its peculiar mating dance and the way it spreads its tail to attract the female bird. It was suspected of witchcraft and was hunted and killed until it became almost extinct in southern England. This probably accounts for the paintings of birds killed with arrows on the rectory windows although the birds redeem themselves, as is fitting for a rectory, by being shown as uttering 'In Noie jhu' – 'In the name of Jesus'. The link, therefore, between the song Cock Robin and the painted windows in Buckland Rectory seems rather remote, to say the least.

Perhaps a robin was chosen to represent the King in the ballad because of its solitary habits – the robin has its own distinct territory – or perhaps there is a connection between the ruddy countenance of William Rufus and the red breast of the robin. It has been recorded by chroniclers of the time that the King was brought from the forest on a hand barrow and his chest was soaked in blood, thus providing yet another link. It is interesting to note, also, that a bird exists in northern Europe, which, though not strictly a robin, is called a Rufus Bush Robin.

Some historians believe that William Rufus was a pagan and that he was killed deliberately, as the sacred king who had to be sacrificed on Lammastide. There was a strong group of people in England at that time who followed the pagan customs of holding ceremonies known as fertility rites. At these gatherings a sacrifice of a 'sacred king' was made and his blood spread over the land to ensure fertile soil for the next crop. Lammastide was one of the four great festivals of this pagan order, and has been stated before, William probably had red hair, which fitted him for this role. Even today some primitive tribes still follow this practice of sacrificing a sacred king to ensure the richness of future crops.

THE WISE MEN OF GOTHAM

A fairly well-known rhyme pertaining to the county of Notting-hamshire is *The Wise Men of Gotham!*

> *Three wise men of Gotham,*
> *They went to sea in a bowl;*
> *If the bowl had been stronger,*
> *My song had been longer.*

This nonsense jingle dates from the reign of King John. The castles in the west of England and Wales were a source of pride to King John, and he spent much of his time travelling from one to another. On one such cross-country journey the King's party wished to pass through the small village of Gotham. In those days whichever path the King took, automatically became a public highway. The inhabitants of Gotham feared this and prevented the advance guard of the King's cavalry from passing through the village. When John heard of the incident, he became very angry and sent messengers to find out the reason. Meanwhile the villagers, fearing the reprisals that were sure to come, decided to pretend to be idiots, and the King's men retreated hastily to report what they had seen. The story goes that the people of Gotham were never troubled again and the legend of the 'village of fools' has lasted over the centuries in the form of the nursery rhyme above.

As previously mentioned, another story connected with Gotham, describes how the inhabitants once tried to keep the cuckoo, which is the symbol of spring, in their parish by growing a very high hedge round it. They thought that by forcing the bird to stay they would ensure everlasting spring! This too enhanced the reputation of 'the village of fools'.

SPRING

> *Summer is icumen in*
> *Loud sing cuckoo!*
> *Groweth seed and bloweth mead*
> *And springeth the wood now –*
>   *Sing Cuckoo!*

The unknown poet who wrote these immortal words in the thirteenth century reflected the joyous feeling of the community, when the cry of the cuckoo was first heard as a sure sign of spring. The 1st of May has been a public holiday for many centuries. In the olden days it was spent in rejoicing, people rising with the sun to collect May tree branches or to wash their faces in the dew!

> *Oh, we've been rambling all this night,*
> *And some time of this day;*
> *And now returning home again*
> *We bring you in the May.*

Young men stuck branches of may into the ground outside their sweetheart's house, and garlands of birch and other greenery hung over every doorway. It is not known when the maypole was first introduced into Britain as a symbol of fertility and merry making, but it is known that poles were used in southern Europe and France for many celebrations throughout the year, when they were danced round. The English maypole was usually just a birch trunk, decorated with garlands of May and other spring flowers. It is interesting to note that the ritual of plaiting the ribbons of the maypole and the dance that goes with it were not introduced to England until the end of the nineteenth century, when a school mistress at Whitelands College introduced the plaiting ceremony and the dance that went with it. Before this, maypole dancing was confined to ring or country dances and the dance closely connected to it is called Sellenger's Round:

> *They never can be half so merry as we*
> *When we are a-dancing of Sellenger's Round.*

After the Civil War, the Puritans banned all celebrations and maypoles were dismantled. However, with the return of the monarchy in the form of Charles II, merrymaking was again permitted and a huge maypole, 134 feet high, was erected in the Strand. It was allowed to stay as a permanent fixture. May revels were very popular during the Middle Ages and Tudor times, but later they were regarded by many as just 'lewd sports'. However, May Day celebrations, including the crowning of the May Queen and dancing round the maypole, have been revived in many places in Britain today.

> *To the Maypole haste away,*
> *For it is a holiday.*

THE MILLER OF DEE

The Norman's flair for engineering did not stop at castle building – many canals and waterways were built across Britain in the twelfth century, improving communications and industry. The great canal builder Hugh Lupus built a dam across the river Dee, thus taming the waters and using their power to turn mills for grinding corn and spinning cloth:

> *There was a jolly miller once,*
> *Lived on the River Dee;*
> *He worked and sang from morn till night,*
> *No lark more blithe than he.*
> *And this the burden of his song*
> *Forever used to be,*
> *I care for nobody, no! not I,*
> *If nobody cares for me.*

According to local records, the Dee mills (there were more than one) were first built at the beginning of the twelfth century, just above the ford near Chester. This project was considered to be one of the greatest engineering feats of the time and the Dee mills were soon famous for their industry, not only in Britain but on the Continent also.

The legend of the solitary miller is one that cannot be attached to one particular person. At first the mills belonged to the Earl of

5.   The old Dee Bridge and Mills in 1837.

Chester and his serfs, and all the people of the neighbourhood were forced to bring their grain to be ground at the Dee mills. The Earl cheated them in every way he could by giving short measure or doubling the legal tariff for grinding corn. The mills were looked upon as a symbol of tyranny in those days, and were often stormed by peasants, who regarded the forbidding, prison-like buildings as a kind of Bastille.

Chaucer wrote of the Dee miller, 'Well coude he stelen corn, and tollen thryes' The song *The Miller of Dee* has it that nobody 'cared' for the miller. This was surely an understatement, for millers were the subject of derision centuries ago in rather the same way as taxmen and traffic wardens are today.

It has been said that all the millers of Dee came under the spell of the mills. Although much of their revenue was gained unlawfully, they were masters of their craft and Chaucer described the miller as having 'a thombe of gold'. Chaucer meant that his success partly depended on his skill in judging the work his millstones were doing by rubbing the grains between finger and thumb, a technique aptly described in *Chester* by Francis Duckworth (1910): 'Again, it is a life to develop a man's latent sensibilities. The noise of churned waters, the regular pulsations of the machine, the quick response to his hand on the levers, the brightness and clean savour of the fresh-ground meal, all this must have its influence even if he were unconscious, making him say that his mill was "as parent, child and wife".'

Later, the mills became the property of the King, who in his turn leased them out to those who could afford the uncommonly high rent. In the time of Edward I the mills were leased to 'Richard the Engineer', who was employed by the King as a foreman and master mason, and supervised castle-building in Wales. His special assignments were the fortifications of Rhuddlan and Flint, though the actual design of the castles was done by Edward, who followed the tradition of the Norman kings. 'Richard the Engineer' provided the materials and the workmen and under his personal supervision, his business prospered and he invested his money in the Dee mills, renting them from the King for £200 per annum. When he retired, he resided at the mills and lived up to the lines of the song: he kept himself to himself, letting the satisfaction of the work done on the premises fill his whole life. Although I have stated that the legend of the jolly miller of Dee cannot be applied to any one person, 'Richard the Engineer' could well have served as a model. He apparently found the work at the mills totally absorbing and wished for no other interest in life. The hum of the machinery, the swish of the water, the satisfying smell of freshly ground grain are said to have turned him into a self-sufficient and contented man.

There is an old saying in Chester expressing great extravagance: 'If you had the rent of the Dee mills, you would spend it'. This could not have been applied to 'Richard the Engineer', for there is a story which shows how jealously he guarded his investment. One day he went out for a walk and met a man by the name of William Fox, who was bringing a cartload of stale bread from Worcester into the city of Chester. Richard ordered the bread to be confiscated by his men and stated that no one in Chester might eat bread unless it was made with meal that had been ground at his mills.

However black the reputation of the Dee miller was in the Middle Ages, by the eighteenth century he seems to have redeemed himself. This is shown in two differing versions of the miller's song. According to Egerton Leigh's *Ballads and Legends of Cheshire,* published in 1867, the earliest known version was written on the fly-leaf of a volume of Dryden's poems published in 1716:

> There was a jolly Miller once, etc.

> The reason why he was so blithe
> He once did thus unfold:
> The bread I eat my hands have earned;
> I covet no man's gold;
> I do not fear next quarter day,
> In debt to none I be,
> I care for nobody, etc.

> A coin or two I've in my purse
> To help a needy friend;
> A little I can give the poor,
> And still have some to spend.
> Though I may fail, yet I rejoice
> Another's goodhap to see,
> I care for nobody, etc.

So let us his example take,
And be from malice free;
Let everyone his neighbour serve
As served he'd like to be;
And merrily push the can about
And drink and sing with glee.
If nobody cares a doit for us,
Why not a doit care we.

The second version is taken from Convivial Songster, 1782:

There was a jolly miller, etc.

I live by my mill, God bless her; she's kindred, child and wife.
I would not change my station for any other life.
No lawyer, surgeon, or doctor e'er had a grout from me.
I care for nobody, no, not I, if nobody cares for me!

When spring begins its merry career, oh how his heart goes gay!
No summer's drought alarms his fears, nor winter's sad decay;
No foresight mars the miller's joy, who's wont to sing and say,
Let others toil from year to year, I live from day to day.

Thus like the miller, bold and free, let us rejoice and sing;
The days of youth are made for glee, and time is on the wing,
This song shall pass from me to thee along this jovial ring;
Let heart and voice and all agree to say 'Long live the king'.

Both versions use the tune that we know today called *The Bedgeon, It is a Delicate Trade*, which is known to be a good deal older than the words.

The Dee mills were often destroyed by fire – four times in the last two centuries. The last fire was in 1895 and they were never rebuilt, as the miller had died the year before. Today, a great hydro-electric power station stands on the site and it is good to know that the power of the water of the river Dee is still being utilized – true to tradition.

The Miller of Dee has been used as a children's ring game for many centuries and this fact probably explains the continued popularity of the old song. The words sung in the game are:

There was a jolly miller and he lived by himself,
As the mill went round he gained his wealth;
One hand in the hopper and the other in the bag,
As the mill went round, he made his grab.

As with all ring games, this particular game is played with much suppressed excitment. The miller is portrayed as a greedy man, who makes his 'grab' at the circle of children at the right moment, and reflects the early image of the miller as seen by the rest of the community. At the end of the game this verse is sung:

> *Sandy he belongs to the mill,*
> *And the mill belongs to Sandy still,*
> *And the mill belongs to Sandy.*

Other dialect verses from Yorkshire enhance the opinion that most millers were greedy and grew rich on the heavy charges they imposed when grinding corn for the community:

> *Miller, miller, mooter poke*
> *Take a laid and steal a stroke.*

'Mooter' means a toll, so a 'mooter poke' is a toll-gate.

> *Down in yon lum we have a mill,*
> *If they send more grist we'll grind more still,*
> *With her broad arm and mighty fist,*
> *She rams it into the mooter-chist.*

A miller near Rotherham in Yorkshire gained the reputation for taking too much 'toll' for the corn he ground. First he charged tolls, then his son charged them and Big Betty, his wife, did too – and lastly he tolled the corn all over again. When the miller had a new parlour built on to the mill, a local wit called it a 'pinch-poke-parlour' and wrote the above verse.

CRAFTS

The work of craftsmen, some long forgotton, is recorded in old rhymes. The home weaver, for instance, operating on a hand loom, is the subject of this verse:

> *There's meat hung down afore the fire to roast,*
> *There's the puddin' on the brandree afore it to toast,*
> *Potatoes top o' the hob, they'll be done enough soon,*
> *But I think yee can weave a few more bobbins by noon.*

Before the invention of the flying shuttle in the eighteenth century, the home weaver was comfortably off and not lacking in food or warmth, as recorded in the rhyme. In fact, many agricultural workers turned to weaving when employment was hard to come by. However this cottage industry died a slow death when cloth could be produced by machinery in the mills, at a much lower price.

The thatcher, too, was in much demand centuries ago, as two jingles record:

> *Thatcher, thatcher, thatch a span,*
> *Come off yer ladder and hang yer man.*

> *When my master has thatched all his straw,*
> *He will then come down and hang him that says so.*

Another rhyme which recalls an old cottage industry is the *Dent Knitters' Song*:

> *Sally an' I, Sally an' I,*
> *For a good pudding pye*
> *One half wheat and the other half rye,*
> *Sally an' I for a good pudding pye.*

DOCTOR FOSTER

> *Doctor Foster went to Gloucester,*
> *In a shower of rain;*
> *He stepped in a puddle*
> *Right up to his middle,*
> *And never went there again.*

A popular explanation of this rhyme in the West country is that the original Doctor Foster was Edward I. Often remembered as 'the castle builder', Edward established many fortifications, especially in Wales. It is said that, during a particularly rainy spell, the King visited the city of Gloucester and his horse floundered in the deep mud of the main thoroughfare. The King's horse became well and truly stuck and the monarch felt himself to be in a very undignified situation. It took many men, together with planks of wood and ropes, to free the animal. Edward I was so distressed by the incident that he vowed that he would never visit Gloucester again and he kept his word.

> *Kyng Edward,*
> *When thu havest Beric,*
> *Pike thee!*
> *When thu havest geton,*
> *Dike thee!*

This old rhyme is remembered in Scotland and stems from the time when Edward I and his army besieged Berwick – it was a taunt which the King did not take lightly!

BANNOCKBURN

The following verse, according to Robert Fabyan, the chronicler, was sung with joy in Scotland after the victory at Bannockburn in 1314:

> *Maydens of Englonde, sore maye ye morne,*
> *For your lemmans ye haue loste at Bannockisborne,*
> *With heue a lowe.*
> *What wenth the kynge of Englonde,*
> *So soon to haue wonne Scotland*
> *With rumbylowe.*

The curious word 'rumbylowe' in the last line is known to be an old seafaring word meaning 'yo-heave-o'. Some historians take the use of this word to be a direct reference to the fact that, after the disastrous battle of Bannockburn, Edward II made his escape from Dunbar in a small skiff.

Although Edward I conquered Scotland in 1291, the Scots managed to rebel successfully against their English overlords and by the time Edward II became king, the Scots had driven the English from their country, except for one fortress – Stirling Castle. The chief of the castle sent to Edward II for help, which arrived in the form of a large well-equipped English army to break the siege. The canny Scots, however, dug pits and covered them with branches, so that, when the English cavalry charged into the valley of Bannockburn, they floundered in the traps and were quickly slain or routed by the Scots, as were the foot soldiers who followed. Thus Scotland achieved home rule once again, and Robert Fabyan wrote that the above verse 'was after many dayes sungyn, in daunces, in carolis of the maydens and mynstrellys of Scotlande'.

ST GEORGE

One of the versions of the St George's mummer's play, recorded in 1738, contains the lines:

> *Oh! here comes I St George,*
> *A man of courage bold,*
> *And with my spear I winn'd,*
> *Three Crowns of Gold,*
> *I slew the dragon,*
> *And brought him to Slaughter,*
> *And by that very means,*
> *I married Sabra, the beauteous King of Egypt's daughter.*

These words reflect the legend of St George as told by the Palestinians, to the crusaders from England, who were fighting in the Holy Wars. The story so stirred the imagination of the crusaders that, when they returned to England, they told it to their king, Edward III. This is the gist of the story: long ago a fearful dragon in Asia Minor ruled the land and demanded a human sacrifice every day for food. Each day someone was chosen for this terrible end, until one day it came to be the turn of the King's daughter. While she was waiting for the dragon, a Christian knight appeared, riding his charger. After hearing about the fate awaiting the maiden, George, for that was his name, vowed that he would kill the dragon. He made the sign of the cross and, when the dragon appeared, he ran it through with his sword. He then told the girl to tie her gold silk girdle round the dragon's neck and lead it to the nearest market place. This she did and, in front of a crowd of excited people, George cut off the dragon's head, and so released the land from the awful curse.

Edward III thought that this story was one of the best he had ever heard and so he made St George the patron saint of England. In doing so, he immortalized the feeling of good triumphing over evil reflected in the conduct of Christian knights in their battles with the heathens during the crusades. St George was also made a patron of the Order of the Garter, a new order of knighthood created by the same king. Later, St George's banner was flown for the first time by Richard I. It is of course a red cross on a white background and now forms part of the Union Jack.

The famous St George soon became a leading character in mummer's plays and later had a play named after him. St George and the dragon were also portrayed in carnivals and processions. For many the dragon proved far too difficult to imitate, but a human character repeated these 'dragon' lines in a ferocious way:

> *My head is made of iron,*
> *My body is made of steel,*
> *My fingers are made of beaten brass,*
> *No man can make me feel!*

The dragon in fact was described as wearing the very best armour, as worn by knights of the period! A play called *St George and The Dragon,* which is performed annually in Norwich can be traced back to the year 1408, and a dragon called Snap was paraded in this city until as late as 1834. Throughout the years, in various mummer's plays St George has become King George or even King William, and, like everything else, the character has changed with the times. St George and the dragon medallions were sold as good luck charms to sailors at London docks, a custom which probably dated back to the Middle Ages.

Very little factual evidence is known about the true St. George, but it appears that, like St Valentine, he was martyred for his faith at Diospolis (Lydda) in Palestine, probably by Diocletian, in the third century, but he was not created a saint until some two hundred years later. St Georges' Day in England is 23 April, and St George is also the patron saint of Portugal, Greece, Aragon and Germany. He is revered in the East as the patron saint of soldiers and the avenger of women.

BLACK DOUGLAS

Although the verse below was used as a lullaby, it has been included at this point because of its strong historical connections:

Hush you, hush you,
Little pet you,
Hush you, hush you,
Dinna fret you,
The Black Douglas,
Shall not get you.

According to Fraser in his work *The Douglas Book* Black Douglas was Sir James Douglas, a Scottish knight born in 1286, who was well-versed in military strategy and regarded by many as equal in the art of war to Robert the Bruce himself. He was known in Scotland as 'good Sir James' and became his country's national hero when he helped Robert the Bruce defeat the English at the battle of Bannockburn. 'Good Sir James' was said to have been engaged in over seventy battles, of which only thirteen were lost. In England he was dreaded and mothers were known to quieten their children by threats of the Black Douglas.

In 1329 Robert the Bruce died of leprosy and Sir James promised to carry out the dying King's last request, namely to go on a crusade to the Holy Land, carrying the embalmed heart of his king in a golden casket. This he did. Later he was involved in another European war, for in 1330 he offered his services to Alfonso, King of Castile, who was at war with the Saracen King of Granada. In a battle on the plains of Andalusia, victory was gained for Alfonso, but Sir James Douglas died in the fighting. His body was brought back to Scotland and buried in the church of St Bride at Douglas in Lanarkshire.

ROBIN HOOD

Robin Hood, Robin Hood,
Is in the mickle wood;
Little John, Little John,
He to the town has gone.

Robin Hood, Robin Hood,
Is telling his beads,
All in the greenwood,
Among the green weeds.

Little John, Little John,
If he comes no more,
Robin Hood, Robin Hood
He will fret full sore.

The legend of Robin Hood has been widely known in England for nearly eight hundred years. He was born of a good family in the county of Nottinghamshire in approximately 1160. During the early years of his life, Henry II, the first of the Plantagenet kings, was on the throne of England. After the weak rule of King Stephen, when near anarchy raged throughout the land, Henry had a hard task to restore law and order. It took years to rid the country of the thieving barons who commandeered money and property whenever it suited them. Such was the case with Robin Hood, who was also known as Robin Fitzooth and Robin of Barnesdale. At an early age his lands and property were confiscated and he was forced to live as an outlaw in Sherwood Forest where he soon collected a band of trusted 'merry men'. Many romantic stories and poems have been written about this gallant hero, who robbed the rich to give to the poor. He was the champion of the underdog and said to be a good sportsman and a superb marksman.

When Henry II died, his son, Richard I, became King of England. He was a good man but was more interested in fighting in the crusades than in governing the country. Nevertheless, Robin Hood soon established his loyalty to the new King and, when Richard returned one time from a crusade, he sought out Robin.

As a reward for loyal service in his absence, the King pardoned Robin Hood and his men, and restored their rights as free citizens. In addition, Robin was reimbursed with his land and property, and for sixteen years he lived in peace with Maid Marion.

After Richard's death, his brother John seized the throne. It is common knowledge what kind of man the new King was: weak, cruel, untrustworthy and extravagant; he did nothing to improve conditions in England. John's soldiers destroyed Robin's castle of Malaset and killed Maid Marion. Thus, Robin was forced to return to the forests and, of course, he gathered his band of trusted followers together once more. Owing to his daring escapades, Robin Hood soon made many enemies among the nobles and a large reward was offered for his capture, dead or alive. Sir Roger of Doncaster swore to trap him, after an incident in which Robin had outwitted him. The outlaw often visited Kirklees nunnery for treatment for a wound, because his cousin Ursula was the Abbess and she used to bleed him to reduce the fever, as was the custom in those days. Roger of Doncaster knew of this, so he bribed the Abbess with thirty acres of corn land for the nunnery and a pair of gold candlesticks – all she had to do was to cut Robin's vein deeply and let him bleed to death under the power of a sleeping draught. Fearing reprisals, she agreed to do this, but the potion was not strong enough and Robin awoke and was able to blow a note on his horn, summoning his outlaws to come to his aid. Little John came running into the chamber with his men, only to find his leader dying. Little John drew a knife to kill Ursula for her treachery, but Robin restrained him, chivalrous to the end, saying that he had vowed never to kill a woman. With his last remaining strength he shot an arrow through the window, with the request that he should be buried where it fell.

Robin Hood was said to be approaching seventy when he died. There has never been anything to contradict the story of his death and of his burial place, although the location of his grave has now been lost. Today tales of Robin Hood have been translated into many languages and are famous all over the world. Many films and plays have been produced using his image, and the lines 'Robin Hood, Robin Hood, riding through the glen' are well known. He is, indeed, an important character in English literature.

His kinsmen – Little John, Friar Tuck, Will Scarlet, Alan-a-Dale, and others – feature in many local traditional May games and early plays in Nottinghamshire, which surely proves that they were not fictitious.

In modern times Sherwood Forest has almost dwindled to nothingness, yet there are some trees left which could have sheltered the outlaws; one is a dilapidated oak called the Shambles or Robin Hood's Larder, where it is said that he hung his venison. Another, named the Great Major Oak, is thirty feet in circumference and still stands, although hollow, near the village of Edwinstowe, where Robin is traditionally supposed to have married Maid Marion. Many places in Nottinghamshire can be linked with this legendary character: at Papplewick there is a cave known as Robin Hood's Stable, and near Kirby-in-Ashfield are Robin Hood Hills and Robin Hood's Chair. There are also many wells bearing his name, one of which is concealed in a wood near Beauvale Priory. Modern Nottingham has not forgotten its history, for the clock in the market square is called Little John and, although the market itself has been moved to a more convenient site, the memory of the time when Robin Hood defeated a potter and sold his pots in the market at a cut price still lingers on.

DICK WHITTINGTON

The royal houses of Lancaster and York lasted from 1399 until 1485. During the period 1455-1485 the throne of England seemed almost constantly to be in jeopardy from the fourteen battles that constituted the Wars of the Roses. The old rhyme about Dick Whittington reflects in its historical background many facts relating to this era:

> Turn again, Whittington,
> Whittington, turn again;
> Turn again Whittington,
> Lord Mayor of London.

Richard Whittington was a rich mercer (draper), who became Lord Mayor of London four times – the first time being in 1397. He came from a wealthy family and never knew poverty. After he married Alice Fitzwarren, daughter of a Dorset knight, they went to live in London where his business flourished – he often lent large sums of money to Henry IV and his son, who became Henry V. Whittington was a charitable man, who did much to alleviate the suffering of the poor and when he died, he left his money to charity. Much of his fortune was used to rebuild Newgate prison, for Whittington had been shocked at the conditions there; some other money went to repair St Bartholomew's Hospital, and the residue was spent in building a college at the church of St Michael Paternoster, where he was buried.

The story of the poor boy who made his fortune with the help of his cat is well-known in many countries. In Britain the pantomime story of Dick Whittington was first performed in 1605 and has been a firm favourite ever since. In the fairy tale Dick is portrayed as a poor orphan who obtained work as a scullion in the kitchen of Hugh Fitzwarren, a rich merchant. It was the custom of the household for each occupant to contribute something to the master's ship when it sailed to foreign lands, because the gift was thought to bring luck to the vessel. Dick therefore gave his cat – his most treasured possession – and the ship reached a part of Africa which was overrun with vermin, where the King bought the cat for a fabulous sum.

Meanwhile, Dick despairing of ever making his fortune, had left his employment and was trudging out of London. He stopped to rest in the evening sunlight, on the top of Highgate Hill, and listened to the sound of Bow bells, which seemed to be pealing out a message for him – 'Turn again Whittington, Lord Mayor of London' – over and over again. At last Dick was compelled to obey the message of the bells and he returned to the Fitzwarren household. When he arrived, he was greeted with great excitement and praise, for the ship had docked and his cat had brought him a fortune. Later, he married Alice Fitzwarren, his master's daughter, and in time became Lord Mayor of London.

It is not known how the pantomime story came to be about Richard Whittington, the rich merchant – perhaps he was immortalized in this way because of his compassion for the poor.

According to custom the Lord Mayor of London and the Lord Mayor of York are the two leading mayors in the country – London having precedence. They should both be addressed as the 'Right Honourable', whereas the other mayors are addressed as 'Lord Mayor' or 'His Worship the Mayor'.

> *Lincoln was, London is, but Yorke shall be,*
> *The greatest city of the three.*
>
> *Yorke, Yorke, for my monie;*
> *Of all the citties that I ever see,*
> *For merry pastime and companie,*
> *Except the cittie of London.*

These two rhymes have yet to be proved. The custom that a Lord

Mayor only retains his title for a year, but that his wife enjoys the title of Lady for the rest of her life, is the subject of this doggerel:

> *He is lord for a year and day,*
> *But she is a lady for ever and aye.*

THE MERCHANTS OF LONDON

> *Hey diddle dinkety, poppety pet,*
> *The merchants of London they wear scarlet;*
> *Silk in the collar and gold in the hem,*
> *So merrily march the merchant men.*

This jingle conjures up very vividly a picture of the rich merchants and their expensive clothes during the trade boom of this era. Scarlet was the colour worn by the richest group and the other colours were worn according to income. The merchants of London had every cause to be merry! Another common fortune jingle lists some of the professions and occupations of the time:

6. Sheep shearing.

> *Tinker, tailor,*
> *Soldier, sailor,*
> *Rich man, poor man,*
> *Beggar man, thief.*

William Caxton was the first man to bring a printing press to England and, what is more important, he is credited with being the first man to print books in English. In addition he wrote a book called *The Game and Playe of the Chesse*, in which each pawn represents a trade or profession – the eight individuals represented were a smith, a merchant, a guard, a ribald, a taverner, a labourer, a physician and a clerk. Some historians think it is possible that our well-known fruit stone chant above stems from this source.

BAA, BAA, BLACK SHEEP

During the Middle Ages, there were many social problems, and the rhyme 'Baa, baa, black sheep' reminds us of the plight of the agricultural worker:

> *Baa, baa, black sheep,*
> *Have you any wool?*
> *Yes sir, yes sir,*
> *Three bags full;*
> *One for the master,*
> *And one for the dame,*
> *And one for the little boy,*
> *Who cries down the lane.*

This rhyme has survived word for word in the oral nursery collection for at least six hundred years and is thought to be an innovation of the wool trade in the fourteenth or fifteenth century. Nearly all the available land was turned into sheep walks at this time and the agricultural labourer often found himself out of work for it took many men to grow produce on arable land, but only one shepherd was required to look after a flock of sheep. There was no organized relief for the unemployed and many became vagrants and thieves, wandering about the country gaining food and shelter by any means that lay open to them.

Wool was gathered in great quantities and sent to London, where it was exchanged for silks, salt, spices and jewels from other lands. While the wool merchants grew richer, the common people grew poorer and there were many revolts against the greedy nobility: in Exeter ten thousand men formed a besieging party, and in Norwich Walter Kett, the tanner, gathered a great band of followers and held council under an oak tree called the Oak of Reformation. For a while his actions were ignored, for he maintained that he was a loyal subject of the King and only asked for a better deal for the working people. At last, however, an army was gathered in the King's name and a great battle was fought on Kett's Hill. The rebels were defeated and all of them were put to death, including Walter Kett and his brother. Kett's Hill is still a famous landmark in Norwich today.

It is thought by some that the phrases 'my master' and 'my dame' included in the 'Baa, baa, black sheep' rhyme referred to the King and the wool merchants, and that 'the little boy who cries down the lane' referred to the common people, who always were given the scant third allotted to them and had their cries of protest muffled by the executioner. The line 'three bags full' may have been a reference to the tax on wool, introduced at about this time. The verse is sung to a very old French tune called *Ah Vous Dirai Je*.

In 1397 Richard II sold Blackwell Hall to the City of London and it became 'the greatest woollen cloth-market in the world'. The English wool merchants and cloth manufacturers became increasingly rich, and during the next five centuries England's exports of woollen cloth reached incredible proportions. It is fitting that the highest dignitary in the British Parliament sits on a woolsack. John Dyer's poem *The Fleece* published in 1757, reflected the nation's pride in the wool industry.

> *For ev'ry realm, the careful factors meet,*
> *Whisp'ring each other. In long ranks the bales,*
> *Like war's bright files, beyond the sight extend.*
>   *Pursue,*
> *Ye sons of Albion, with unyielding heart,*
> *Your hardy labours; let the sounding loom*
> *Mix with the melody of ev'ry vale*

WITCHES AND HALLOWE'EN

From the very beginning we have seen that night was a frightening time for most folk. During the Middle Ages there was real danger from robbers and vagrants, who roamed the countryside and attacked outlying cottages and farms or loan travellers, but the dark held even more terrifying dangers, or so the simple folk thought who lived in this era: evil spirits, pagan sprites and even the devil himself reigned during the black hours. These terrors were the enemies of Christianity and were, therefore, thought to have supernatural powers like the Druids in the pre-Christian era. There have always existed pockets of people who did not accept the Christian faith and continued to worship pagan gods as before. It is probably from these groups that the image of the witch, as we know her today, emerged. At first she was the wise woman of the village, who performed medical cures or gave advice where needed. When things went wrong the wise woman was blamed and punished, and the reputation of the evil witch evolved from this. Those delving in black magic developed a cult which is still practised today in remote parts. The god of the witches was usually depicted as an animal with horns like a goat, stag or bull, which may explain why the devil himself is often portrayed as having horns and a shaggy countenance.

It seems very likely that the word 'witch' was derived from 'wit' or knowledge possessed by certain people. These special humans, it was thought, had the power of the 'evil eye', that is, they had the power to bewitch ordinary folk, usually by reciting certain spells or charms engendered by the devil.

The word 'magic' can be traced back to the Persian word 'magnus', meaning a wise man or soothsayer; the plural is 'magi' and the three wise men of the East who visited Christ were described thus. Two 'magic' phrases that are still used today are 'open sesame', found in the story of Ali Baba and the Forty Thieves, and 'Abracadabra', which was first recorded in the writings of the personal physician to the Roman Emperor Septimus Severus in the second century AD and was thought to have the power to cure fevers and other illnesses.

This surviving charm describes how witches changed themselves into hares at night:

> *I shall goe into an hare*
> *With sorrow and such and much care,*
> *I shall goe in the devil's name,*
> *Until I come home again.*

In the Isle of Man and along the Welsh border witches were thought to transform themselves into bats at night and enter houses in that form. The old superstition that, if a bat entangles itself in your hair, it cannot be freed also stems from this part of the country. This idea was disproved in 1959, when the Earl of Cranbrook put three different types of bat into three young women's hair, with their consent, of course. The bats all escaped quite easily. In Oxfordshire it was considered a death omen if a bat flew round the house three times and children were taught to recite the following rhyme when they saw a bat:

> *Black bat, bear away, fly over here away,*
> *And come again another day, black bat, bear away.*
> *Airy mouse, airy mouse, fly over my head,*
> *And you shall have a crust of bread;*
> *And when I brew and when I bake,*
> *You shall have a piece of my wedding cake.*

Witches were also thought to have the power to strengthen or abate the wind as the mood took them. It was believed that a witch could stir the wind to full force by beating a wet rag on a stone, while reciting the following rhyme:

> *I knock this rag upon this stane,*
> *To raise the wind in the devil's name.*
> *It shall not lie until I please again.*

The wind would die down when the rag was completely dry.

Butter churning was a long and arduous task and, if the butter was slow in 'coming', it was thought to be under the evil influence of a witch's spell. It was believed that witches had the power to enchant the cream or essence of the butter from a distance, drawing it away, and making it impossible to produce butter. As a protection, charms were continually repeated during the work:

> *Churn butter dash,*
> *Cows gone t'marsh,*
> *Peter stands at the toll gate*
> *Begging butter for his cake,*
> *Come butter, come.*

In the Midlands they used to say:

> *Come butter, churn,*
> *Come butter, come,*
> *The Great Bull of Banbury,*
> *Shan't have none.*

'The Great Bull of Banbury' may well signify the image of the god of the witches – mentioned before.

Salt was believed to bring good luck if thrown on the fire during churning and the butter churn was often made of rowan· wood, as it was thought that witches had no power over the rowan tree. A red-hot poker thrust into the cream was supposed to burn the witches and it certainly altered the temperature, which was effective in producing butter. Three white hairs from a black cat's tail or a silver coin thrown into the mixture was thought to be helpful too while churning.

Hallowe'en, 31 October, is as the name implies, the evening before All Hallow's Day or the Feast of All Saints, as it is some-times called. 'Hallow' is an old word for holy and the feast is sometimes called Nutcrack Night, when the harvested nuts were roasted before huge fires. Hallowe'en is also the last of the four pagan festivals in the calendar year and was thought to be the night of the witches and other evil spirits, and those who believed in black magic years ago did not venture out after dark on this particular night.

> *Hallowe'en, Hallowe'en,*
> *Witches, witches, can be seen.*

In Scotland too Hallowe'en was made much of in days gone by as rhymes bear this out:

> *Hey-how for Hallowe'en!*
> *All the witches to be seen,*
> *Some in black and some in green,*
> *Hey-how for Hallowe'en!*

Hallowe'en was also a time for wishing:

> *This is Hallowe'en,*
> *And the morn's Hallowday;*
> *If you want a true love,*
> *It's time you were away*
> *Tally on the window board*
> *Tally on the green*
> *Tally on the window board*
> *The morn's Hallowe'en.*

A charm sometimes recited at Hallowe'en was supposed to protect innocent people from the curses of black magic. Haly is a shortened version of Hail Mary and gave added protection:

> *Haly on a cabbage stalk,*
> *Haly on a bean,*
> *Haly on a cabbage stalk,*
> *The morn's Hallowe'en.*

Another supernatural creature is described this way:

> *O, Pearlin Jean!*
> *O, Pearlin Jean!*
> *She haunts the house,*
> *She haunts the green,*
> *And glowers on me*
> *With her wild-cat e'en.*

> *If your whip stock's made of rowan,*
> *Your nag may ride through any town.*

As mentioned before, rowan wood was believed to give protection against witches and all forms of black magic.

An old story from the North tells of a plough boy who was confronted in the middle of a field that he was ploughing by a witch. He was amply prepared having a whipstock of rowan, with which he touched his horses and broke the spell. The witch then let out this curse:

> *Dam the lad,*
> *With the rowan tree gad.*

A 'gad' is a wooden rod or handle. Two other witches' charms have been recorded:

Fire come, fire go, curlin' smoke keep out o' pan;
There's a toad in the fire, and a frog on the hob,
Here's the heart from a crimson ask,
Here's the tooth from the head,
From one who is dead,
And never got through his task.
  It boils, Thoo'll drink,
  He'll speak, Thoo'll think,
  It boils Thoo'll see,
  He'll speak, Thoo'll dee.

Take two that's red and one that's black,
Of poison berries three,
Three fresh-culled blooms of Devil's glut,
And a sprig of rosemary;
Take henbane, bullace, bumm'llkite,
And fluff from a dead bullrush,
Nine berries shake from a rowan tree,
And nine from the bottery bush.

Hallowe'en, All Soul's Day and All Saints' Day, namely 31 October, 1 and 2 November, were regarded as a period of time with great magical potential. Within these three days the girl that was anxious to know who her future lover would be went into the garden after dark and sprinkled hempseed, reciting these words:

  Hempseed I sow,
  Hempseed I throw,
  Let him who be my true love
  Come after me and mow.

She then glanced over her shoulder and expected to see the shape of her husband to be, or maybe she would see his reflection in a looking glass or water.

The custom of making lanterns from hollowed out turnips or pumpkins and candles has been revived by school children in recent years. In Norfolk, for example, hollow turnips are used on Hallowe'en, which usually have faces that glow weirdly when the candles are lit. In Somerset, in the little village of St George the last Thursday in October was called Punkie Night, because scooped-out mangolds were cut in intricate designs to show houses, trees and scenes in general. Candles were lit and placed inside them, then everyone with a 'punkie' joined a procession through the village after dark singing:

> *It's Punkie Night tonight,*
> *It's Punkie Night tonight,*
> *Give us a candle, give us a light,*
> *It's Punkie Night tonight.*

This was regarded as the time when the spirits of the dead returned to visit their families. Punkies were, in fact, representations of the dead and a positive invitation to spirits to revisit their habitat on earth, which is basically a pagan custom. Nowadays it is thought better taste to visit graveyards and place flowers on family graves, or perhaps honour the dead with a peal of church bells.

'Souling' or 'Soul cake' is again a fusion of pagan and Christian ritual. In Cheshire on All Souls' Day children still sing this 'souling song', which begs for a 'soul cake' to be given to the dead:

> *A soul cake, a soul cake,*
> *Please good mistress a soul cake;*
> *One for Peter and one for Paul,*
> *And one for the Lord who made us all.*

Not very long ago tables laid with food could be seen around this time of year through cottage doorways, awaiting the arrival of the hungry departed souls.

FAIRIES

Unlike witches, fairies are not mentioned a great deal in old rhymes concerned with folklore. They are always present of course in fairy tales, but they were not regarded with superstition by many ordinary folk, perhaps because on the whole their image was not regarded as a malignant one. There is a story about a boy called Tamlin, who was stolen by the Fairy Queen while sleeping underneath an apple tree. He thought that 'fairy land was a pleasant place' but he was finally rescued by his true human love on Hallowe'en:

> *Just at the mirk and the midnight hour,*
> *The fairy folk did ride.*

Green was believed in England to be a fairy colour, while in France it symbolized true love and was worn when couples eloped, 'the maydens wore a kirtle of green'. Ladies of the Court also wore fashionable green, as our old song *Greensleeves* relates.

The word 'fairy' is derived from the Latin *fatum* which means fate or destiny, or possessing mystical powers. The image of the fairy has been changed over the centuries, mainly due to the writing of William Shakespeare, who introduced a new type of fairy in his play *A Midsummer Night's Dream*. It is from this source that the modern image of a fairy with a crown and silver wings was developed. An old couplet tells us:

> *Fairies small, two feet tall,*
> *With caps of red upon their heads.*

DOMESTIC

Living conditions became more civilized in Britain after the Norman Conquest, as houses became more stable and the furniture in them more elaborate. It is probably from this period, therefore, that superstitions recorded in traditional rhymes about household effects became popular. The bed, no longer a straw mattress, became the most important piece of furniture in the house. There was usually only one big bed in the home in which all the family slept. The order in which the family retired to bed was thought important hence the following verse:

> *Go to bed first, a golden purse;*
> *Go to bed second, a golden pheasant;*
> *Go to bed third, a golden bird.*

The head of the household usually lay at the stock, which was considered the place of honour and was by the outer edge of the bed rail, as the following rhyme records:

> *He that lies at the stock,*
> *Shall have a gold rock;*
> *He that lies at the wall,*
> *Shall have a gold ball;*
> *He that lies in the middle,*
> *Shall have a gold fiddle.*

It was considered unlucky to turn beds or mattresses on certain days of the week: if turned on a Sunday, the sleeper would suffer nightmares, if turned on a Friday, the ships at sea would be lost. To enter the bed on one side and leave it in the morning from the other forebode ill tidings. People still say to someone suffering from a bad temper 'You must have got out of bed on the wrong side'. It was also thought significant which way the bed pointed, i.e. north to south, or east to west, and this custom is still observed by some people. An old Oxfordshire couplet says:

> *If one day you would be wed,*
> *Turn your bed from foot to head.*

The common pin was the subject of much superstition centuries ago. As metal was very scarce, pins were treasured possessions and to find one about the house was considered a lucky omen:

> *See a pin and pick it up,*
> *All the day you'll have good luck.*
> *See a pin, and let it lay,*
> *And you'll rue it all the day.*

Pins were stuck in door posts and kept in bottles under the floor boards to guard the house against witches. Many of these bottles have been found in old houses. It was thought important to remove all pins from a bride's wedding dress before her wedding night, for to overlook one might bring misfortune, and all pins used in making the shroud for a corpse were always buried with the dead person.

It is still regarded by some people as unlucky to give a gift of pins to a friend as this would probably terminate the friendship. Also, sailors did not welcome pins aboard ship, as it was thought that their presence might induce a leak. Twelve new pins thrown on the fire at midnight, while the following charm was recited, was a sure way of recalling a loved one, or so it was thought, in days gone by:

> *'Tis no these pins I wish to burn,*
> *But – – – –'s heart I wish to turn;*
> *May he neither sleep nor rest,*
> *'Till he has granted my request.*

Pricking a candle through the wick with a pin, while reciting theverse, would have the same effect, it was thought. In the same way that pins were thrown into wishing wells as payment for a wish, so too they were used as payment for other things:

> *A pin to look in*
> *A very fine thing.*
>
> *A pinnet a piece to look at a show,*
> *All the fine ladies sat in a row,*
> *Blackbirds with blue feet,*
> *Walking up a new street;*
> *One behind and one before,*
> *And one beknocking at the barber's door.*

The two above rhymes refer to the peep shows that children used to make, which often consisted of pressed flowers arranged on glass to form a picture; a piece of paper covered the 'show', leaving only a small peep hole for the person who was prepared to pay a pin to look through it. An old Scottish rhyme records that pins were given in payment for entertainment:

> *A pin to see a puppet show,*
> *A pin to see a die,*
> *A pin to see an old man*
> *Climbing to the sky.*

The busy housewife has been the subject of many sayings and so too have her chores – apparently the days on which clothes were washed had significance:

> *They that wash on Monday*
> *Have a whole week to dry;*
> *They that wash on Tuesday*
> *Are not so much awry;*
> *They that wash on Wednesday,*
> *May get their clothes clean;*
> *They that wash on Thursday,*
> *Are not so much too mean;*
> *They that wash on Friday*
> *Wash for their need;*
> *They that wash on Saturday*
> *Are clarty-paps indeed.*

May was considered an unreliable month as regards weather, for:

> *You must not wash blankets in May,*
> *Or else you'll wash your soul away.*

and:

> *Don't cast a clout*
> *Till May is out.*

This meant that one should keep all winter clothes on until the end of May.

Friday was considered the 'black' day of the week and still is for some people, especially Friday the 13th:

> *Don't on a Friday buy yer ring,*
> *On Friday don't put the spurrins' in;*
> *Don't wed on Friday. Think on this,*
> *Neither blue nor green must match her dress.*

Another saying commonly known by women of long ago was:

> *Friday flits,*
> *Have not long sits.*

A large, lively fire was said to predict a quarrel:

> *Stir up the fire, and make it low,*
> *Or in this house, there'll be a row.*

Talkative women are immortalized in this proverb:

> *That house doth everyday more wretched grow,*
> *Where the hen louder than the cock doth crow.*

Whistling women, too, have not gone unnoticed and it was thought in Cornwall unlucky for a woman to whistle:

> *A whistling woman and a crowing hen,*
> *Are two of the unluckiest things under the sun.*

This needs no explanation:

> *A garthful of geese and no turds,*
> *A houseful of women and no words.*

It was considered unlucky to meet on the stairs and the old saying goes, 'Meet on the stairs, and you won't meet in Heaven'. To fall upstairs was considered lucky and to fall down unlucky – which, after all, is very sensible! If a picture or ornament fell down of its own accord, it was regarded as an ill omen and foretold a death in the family:

> *When a picture leaves the wall,*
> *Someone then receives a call.*

MEDICAL

Other verses that originated in this era give an insight into the social problems of the day; ideas on health and medical treatment, for instance, differed considerably from the modern practice of the National Health Service! In the event of a haemorrhage or a deep wound, it was the custom to call in a blood charmer, who would repeat 'magical' charms until the bleeding stopped. These two verses are remnants of this ritual:

> *In the blood of Adam death was taken,*
> *In the blood of Christ it was all to-shaken;*
> *And by the same blood I do thee charge,*
> *That thou do run no longer at large.*

> *As I was going to Jordan wood,*
> *There was the blood, and there it stood,*
> *So shall thy blood stay in thy body;*
> *I do bless thee in the name of the Father, Son and Holy Ghost.*

A Highland charm, which could only be used once on the patient, had to be repeated in a loud voice, with the speaker's arms outstretched, by a man to a woman, then by a woman to man, and so on until the bleeding ceased:

> *The charm of God the Great,*
> *The free gift of Mary,*
> *The free gift of God.*
> *The free gift of every Priest and Churchman,*
> *The free gift of Michael the strong,*
> *That would put strength in the sun.*

Another way to terminate bleeding which dates back to the Middle Ages was to lay a black cobweb across the wound and then place a puff-ball in it.

Before the general use of false teeth and anaesthetics, teeth and the pain they caused were constant worry to our ancestors. Many superstitions grew up regarding this subject, some of which are recorded in ancient doggerels. Here are two charms which were repeated when an old tooth was sprinkled with salt and thrown on the fire:

> *Good tooth, bad tooth,*
> *Pray God send me a good tooth.*
> *Fire burn, burn tooth,*
> *And give me another,*
> *Not a cruck's one*
> *But a straight one.*

It was considered unlucky to lose a tooth, because a witch or an animal might find it. If an animal inadvertedly swallowed a human tooth then the person concerned could be expected to grow a tooth the shape of that animal. There is a humorous story related in the Denham tracts, that a woman accidently threw one of her husband's teeth in the pig's swill and after a few months her husband grew a large hog's tooth! Mice teeth were much admired for their shape and sharpness, and from Germany comes the rhyme which bears out the belief that humans grew the teeth of the animal that took the discarded ones. Children were encouraged to throw their teeth in a dark corner of the room and chant these lines:

> *Mouse! Here I give thee a tooth of bone,*
> *But you give me an iron one.*

Later, written charms were carried to protect the owner from toothache, such as:

> *Peter was sitting on a marble stone,*
> *And Jesus passed by;*
> *And Peter said, 'My Lord, My God*
> *How my tooth doth ache'.*
> *Jesus said, 'Peter art whole*
> *And whosoever keeps these words for my sake,*
> *Shall never have toothache'.*

Powdered worms were used as an antidote for toothache many years ago, while later, in Georgian times, teeth were branded with a red hot poker to kill the nerve and molten lead was poured into aching cavities – all, of course, without pain killers. The charms and herb remedies, ineffectual though they were, must surely have been more popular than the rough and ready methods of the black-smith dentist!

The following rhyme repeated thrice was said to be a certain cure for the hiccups:

> *Hick-up snick-up look-up right-up,*
> *Three drops in a cup*
> *Is good for the hiccup.*

While another said:

> *Hiccup, hiccup, go away,*
> *Come again another day!*
> *Hiccup, hiccup, when I bake,*
> *I'll give you a butter cake!*

Frogs and toads were thought to have magic healing properties centuries ago and they feature in many medical recipes. To cure a lovesick girl, a live frog was caught and pinned in a box until it died, and left until it withered. The small key-shaped bone was then removed and attached to the coat of the unwitting sweetheart, while these words were chanted:

> *I do not want to hurt thee frog,*
> *But my true lover's heart to turn,*
> *Wishing that he no rest may find,*
> *'Till he come and speak his mind.*

It was then expected that the man whom the girl loved would propose!

A sure cure for whooping cough was to take a spider, preferably black, and hold it over the head of the child in question saying:

> *Spider as you waste away,*
> *Whooping cough no longer stay.*

The spider was then put into a bag and hung over the mantle-piece until it had perished.

The age-old belief that the juice of a dock leaf cured nettle stings is apparent from this jingle:

> *Out nettle, in dock,*
> *Dock shall have a new smock,*
> *But nettle shan't have none.*

There have been many charms and cures for warts, two of

which are still practised. The first method is for the person who is
desirous of losing warts to cut a notch in a stick from an ash tree
and throw it over the left shoulder, repeating:

> *Ash tree, Ashen tree,*
> *Pray buy this wart of me.*

If the person concerned did not look at the stick again, the warts
would disappear. The second method is still used by Mr J.
Symons, who lives in Devon and has cured warts and ringworm
in humans and cattle for over fifty years. The charm has to be
repeated three times in succession and must be passed on from
male to female, and from female to male throughout the generations to ensure its effectiveness:

> *In the name of the Lord,*
> *I viggi, viggi, viggi thee.*

Viggi may have been derived from an old Norse word meaning
begone.

FAIRS

Fairs can be traced back to Roman times, when they were held
principally to barter slaves and dogs usually greyhounds. The
Saxons developed this, and fairs to exchange local produce,
usually on a saint's day, were organised by the local monastery.
Most of these fairs were held on consecrated ground such as
churchyards, and some semblance of order had to be introduced,
so the Saxon king or lord of the manor would often send his glove
or gauntlet as a symbol of authority. The glove was attached to a
long pole and, when erected, it was a signal for the fair to begin;
when it was taken down, the gathering was expected to disperse.
Chester Fair has a long history dating back to pre-Norman times
and the tradition of the Chester Glove or Hand is well known.
The ancient token is a carved wooden replica of a hand, measur-
ing roughly 12" by 6" at the wrist. It has been painted many times
and now belongs to the corporation of Liverpool. On the hand are
the words 'Hugo comes Cestria' and 'Guilda De Civit Mercat
MCLIX' which, being translated, reads 'Hugh Earl of Chester,
Guild Merchant of the City, 1159'. It is thought that the date given

is not authentic, but that the hand is a replica of the original probably dating back to the seventeenth century.

The Lammas Fair at Exeter in Devon is opened with a parade, in which a large, stuffed glove, decorated with ribbons and garlands, is carried attached to a long pole. It is then placed on the guildhall roof while the fair is officially declared open. The town crier at Honiton in Devon, dressed in an old-world costume, carries a pole decorated with flowers and surmounted by a large gilt model of a gloved hand, and he publicly announces the opening of the fair by saying:

> *Oyez! Oyez! Oyez!*
> *The Fair's begun, the glove is up.*
> *No man can be arrested until the glove is taken down.*

At Southampton, Portsmouth and Penzance, all in the south of England similar rituals are observed.

It was not until after the Norman Conquest that fairs became really organized and were recognized by the authorities as important events. The Normans were anxious to develop trade and because of this, they encouraged the introduction of as many fairs and markets as possible. Numerous charters were granted and merchants from overseas were welcome to bring their produce to Britain. Consequently silks, furs, spices and goods such as ebony, ivory and precious jewels were at last for sale in English towns. In return, woollen cloth and tin were exported. It is from this period, therefore, that the majority of our fair rhymes and songs sprang. The most famous fairs during the Middle Ages were the ones held near a river, because there was access for foreign ships – Sturbridge in Cambridgeshire, Winchester in Hampshire and St Bartholemew's in London were the most successful.

There was a curious custom that has been preserved in verse form which took place at Sturbridge Fair. New visitors would be introduced to other merchants by an initiation ceremony, which took place at the Robin Hood Inn, usually on the eve of the horse fair. The newcomer was placed on a chair with his head covered and his shoes off. After some preliminary questions the person officiating, who was dressed in a Cambridge University graduation gown and cap, would ring a hand bell and chant:

> *Over thy head I ring this bell,*
> *Because thou art an infidel,*
> *And I know thee for thy smell –*
> *With a hoorius proxiux mandamus*
> *Let now vengeance light on him,*
> *And so call upon him.*

The newcomer would then be named by one of his sponsors, probably by a slang name such as Nimble Heels. Then the officials and the newcomer would drink a full bumper of punch and the organiser would recite:

> *Nimble Heels henceforward shall be his name,*
> *Which to confess let him not feel shame*
> *Whether 'fore master, miss or dame.*

> *This child first having paid his due,*
> *Is welcome then to put on his shoes,*
> *And sing a song or tell a merry tale,*
> *As he may choose.*

This practice was known for hundreds of years before the dissolution of Sturbridge Fair in the nineteenth century.

The Bartholomew Fair was initiated by Rahere, the jester to Henry I, who founded the Hospital and Church of St Barthmolomew at the same time. Rahere became Lord of the Fair and a judge at the Court of Pie Powder, of which we shall say more later. With the dissolution of the monasteries in the time of Henry VIII, the fair was held as a secular event on a piece of ground called Smithfield and was, of course, the forerunner of the present Smithfield meat market. Apart from its fame for the sale of woollen and linen cloth, and other sundry commodities, the fair had a wide variety of sideshows. Wrestling was a great attraction and, during the Stuart era, it became the tradition for leading actors from London's theatres to give performances at the fair. Here is a verse, published in 1682, which describes its many attractions:

> *Here's that will challenge all the fair,*
> *Come buy my nuts and damsons and Barbary pears,*
> *Here's the Woman of Babylon, the Devil, and the Pope*
> *And here's the little girl just going on the rope.*

Here's Dives and Lazarus and the World's Creation,
Here's the Tall Dutch Woman, the like's not in the nation.
Here is the Booth where the high Dutch maid is,
Here are the Bears that dance like any Ladies, -
Tat, tat, tat, says little penny Trumpet,
Here's Jacob's Halls, that does so jump it, jump it;
Sound, Trumpet, sound, for silver spoon and fork,
Come, here's your dainty Pig and Pork.

Ben Jonson was so taken with the fun and atmosphere of the fair that he wrote his celebrated comedy *Bartholomew Fair*. In the nineteenth century a Victorian purge of many fairs throughout the country took place because they were thought to be dens of iniquity that encouraged immorality. The last traditional fair of St Bartholomew's was held in 1855.

Most verses describing old fairs are anonymous, for their author's names have disappeared in the mists of time, as have many of the fairs described.

Another London fair, which is remembered now only as a name, was May Fair (Mayfair), which contained the usual sideshows and trading stalls, but one interesting feature was Tiddy Doll, a well-known trader who sold ginger-bread. He was always dressed as one of the gentry, wearing fine laces and velvets, white stockings and a white apron. He would attract his customers with this piece of drollery:

Mary, Mary, where are you now Mary?
I live when I'm at home at the second house in Bethel Street,
Two steps under ground, with a wiscum, riscum and a why-not.
Walk in Ladies and Gentlemen,
My shop is on the second floor,
With a brass knocker on the door,
Here is your nice ginger bread,
Your spice ginger bread,
It will melt in your mouth like a red hot arrow,
And rumble in your inside like Punch and his wheelbarrow.
Ti-tiddy, ti-ti, Ti-tiddy, ti-ti,
Ti-tiddy, ti-tiddy, ti-ti,
Tiddy diddy dol-lol,
Tiddy ti, tiddy ti ti,
Tiddy tiddy, dol.

The May Fair was dissolved in approximately 1764, because the space was needed for building expansion.

Gingerbread was sold in such large quantities years ago that some fairs were called gingerbread fairs – there were two at Birmingham and one in Enfield, Middlesex. Here is a rhyme which tells of the cry of the gingerbread stallholder:

Smiling girls and rosy boys,
Come and buy my little toys;
Monkeys made of gingerbread,
And sugar horses painted red.

Gingerbread was often made into attractive shapes, such as miniature men and women, and covered in gold or silver paper.

Fairlop Fair was founded by one Daniel Day who was born in 1683 near Wapping, not far from the famous Fairlop Oak, which was said to date back to the Christian era. This tree stood in Hainault Forest, three miles from Ilford and was reported to have a girth of sixty feet. Daniel Day was a great benefactor of the parish of St Mary Overy, in which he lived, and donoted a bell to the new church in 1760. He was an engineer by trade, making engines and pumps, and, although he was not a rich man, he devoted his life and money to needy charities. On the first Friday in July he would go to the old oak and distribute beans and bacon to his friends and neighbours. This picnic became so famous that soon numerous booths were erected and many strangers attended, and so Fairlop was born. Here are stanzas which describe this famous fair:

Come my boys with hearty glee,
Of Fairlop Fair bear chorus with me,
Held in Hainault Forest which many can tell,
For many a year as bore the belle.
Let the song round, and the music sound,
We'll dance on the ground and be merry I'll be bound,
And booze it away and old care we'll defy,
And be merry on the first Friday in July.

As over Hainault Forest Queen Ann did ride,
She behold a beautiful oak at her side,
And after viewing it from bottom to top
She said to her courtiers it was Fairlop.

It is eight fathoms found, shades an acre of ground,
They have plastered each wound to make the tree sound.
So we'll booze it away and old care we'll defy,
And be merry on the first Friday in July.

Near a century ago, as I have heard say,
This fair was began by old Daniel Day,
As hearty a fellow as ever could be,
His coffin was made from a limb of the tree.
He made his men merry with black-strap and sherry,
Old care did they bury with brandy and perry.
And booze it away and all sorrow defy,
And we're happy on the first Friday in July.

On 25 June 1805 the famous oak was caught in a forest fire and part of its trunk was consumed. High winds in 1820 brought the huge tree to the ground and so it was taken away. The remains were purchased by the builder of St Pancreas Church, Mr Seabrook, who arranged that the pulpits of that church be made out of the wood. They can, of course, still be seen today and in the church, too, is a drawing of Fairlop oak dated 1800. Fairlop Fair was abolished in 1853 by an order of the Commissioners of the Woods and Forests.

In comely sort their foreheads did adorne,
With goodly coronets of hardy horne.

Another London fair with a curious custom attached to it was the Charlton Horn Fair. Tradition has it that King John was riding through Charlton after hunting on Shooter's Hill and Blackheath. He stopped at the house of a certain miller and the only occupant at the time was the miller's wife, who was very young and beautiful. King John was attracted to her and was just going to venture a kiss, when the miller returned and caught them. He drew his dagger and attacked the King, whereupon John revealed his true identity. The miller was then full of apologies. King John graciously bestowed upon him all the land visible from Charlton to the bank of the river near Rotherhide, where a pair of horns were strapped to a pole. In return the King asked pardon for himself and the miller's wife for their breach of conduct. The miller was also given the privilege of an annual fair on 18 October, which was the supposed date of the incident. The miller was to preside over the fair as lord of the manor.

The Horn Fair was held at Charlton for many centuries after this. It was the custom to dress as kings, queens and millers, all with a pair of horns attached to the head-dress. Men would often disguise themselves as women and it was the practice to arrive by boat, sailing up the river. This was at its height during the reign of Charles II, but it was discontinued in the last century. This is part of a traditional doggerel which reminds us of this once famous fair, entitled *The Merry Humour of Horn Fair*:

> It was on the eighteenth of October,
> As over Blackheath I did repair,
> To tell the truth I was not sober,
> So straight I tripit to Horn Fair.

> The king, the miller and the beggar,
> No distinction, all were horn'd;
> Some on foot and some on horseback,
> And thro' the streets they went in form.

Frost fairs were very popular centuries ago and the most well-known ones were held on the river Thames in London. The first record we have of a Thames Frost Fair was in 1608, but there may have been many before this. At this particular time the ice was so thick that horses and carriages crossed the river on it; booths were put up, and many entertainments from London were soon in full swing. At the 1684 Fair a printing press was set up on the ice and the printer earned up to £5 per day printing the names of the visitors attending the fair – a great novelty in those days. Fires were lit and braziers cooked hot chestnuts and other foods. That year the winter was so severe that hundreds of people perished from the cold and even the seas were frozen. An excerpt from an old poem tells us of some of the attractions of London Frost Fairs:

> Behold the wonder of this present age,
> A famous river now becomes a stage;
> The Thames is now both fair and market too,
> And many thousands daily do resort
> There to behold the pastime and the sport.
> And there the quaking watermen will stand ye,
> Kind master drink your ale or beer or brandy?
> Walk in kind sir, this booth it is the chief,
> We'll entertain you with a slice of beef.

Another cries, "Here Master", they do but scoff ye,
Here is a dish of famous new made coffee.
There may you also this hard frosty winter
See on the ice a working printer.
There is bull-baiting and bear-baiting too;
That no man living yet e're found so true;
And football play is there so common grown,
That on the Thames before was never known.

Roundabouts and swings were present at the last Frost Fair held in 1813, when after many weeks, a sudden shower of rain brought a quick thaw, and numerous booths and much equipment sank into the icy waters. In the nineteenth century, locks and canals built on the Thames ensured a more rapid flow of water, and the Frost Fairs could no longer be held.

Other markets and fairs held in London long ago are named in this old stanza:

At Islington a fair they hold,
Where cakes and ales are to be sold.
At Highgate and Holloway,
The like is kept here every day.
At To'nam Court and Kentish town,
And all these places up and down.

The places named were all country villages years ago, but are now parts of London.

The gipsies wandered about the country in their horse-drawn caravans visiting most of the larger fairs and markets. Their livelihood depended to some extent on goods sold at these gatherings. If gipsies were banned from a prosperous fair, they probably suffered real hardship as a result. The following poem records the protest of the gipsies when they were denied entrance to St Giles' Fair in Oxfordshire more than a hundred years ago:

O Mr Mayor, O Mr Mayor:
What have we Gipsies done or said
That you should drive us from the Fair
And rob us of our 'customed bread?

Dread not the name, good Mr Mayor,
No more the witches power we claim;
But still we are the Muses care,
And Oxford poets guard our fame.

You welcome Lions to the Fair,
Tigers and Monkeys, Punch and Fool;
Then suffer us another Year,
To hold there our Gymnastic School.

Meanwhile, farewell good Mr Mayor,
Your frowns dismiss, resume your smiles;
We'll leave off cheating – take to prayer,
And claim thy patronage – St Giles!

St Giles' Fair is still held today and is one of the largest pleasure
fairs in the Midlands. Another Oxfordshire fair has been immortalized in the nursery collection:

As I was going to Banbury,
Upon a summer's day,
My dame had butter, eggs and fruit,
And I had corn and hay!
Joe drove the ox, and Tom the swine,
Dick took the foal and mare,
I sold them all – then home to dine,
From famous Banbury Fair.

A charter was granted by Mary I for a fair to be held in Banbury
and from then onwards many fairs were held in the vicinity.
Banbury was famed for its hiring fair, at which unemployed
workers would seek new jobs. There were many of these 'mop'
fairs, in fact, a fair at Stratford-on-Avon is still so called.

Today only one fair, Michaelmas Fair, is still held in Banbury.
In the centre of the town booths and stalls are erected by show
people who have attended Banbury Fair for generations, and the
traffic is diverted for two days while the fair is open.

Bury St Edmunds, which was named in memory of the martyred Saxon king, Edmund, who was buried in one of its
churches, can boast of the existence of a fair since Norman times
and probably before. Cloth was the most important commodity
sold at the fair in early days and merchants would come from
London to buy great quantities. Even the kings of England wore

gowns made from Bury cloth. Here are some verses from *Edmundsbury Fair*, which tell of past delights:

O, Suffolk is a noble county, full of lovely views, miss,
And full of gallant gentlemen for you to pick and choose, miss,
But search the town all around, there's nothing can compare, miss,
In measurement of merriment with Edmundsbury Fair, miss;
Then sing to Bury, merry town and Bury's merry mayor too,
I know no place in all the world old Bury can compare to.

Sir Edmundsbury Godfrey was martyr represented;
Our only Godfrey now is he who the cordial invented;
Saint Edmund's martyrdom, the Danes, the wolf and other passages
Of his life were once discussed. We now discuss the sausages
That in Bailies' booth so nicely fry, when Pie Poudre court and Mayor
With beadles and with criers come to open Bury Fair.

There are two things worthy of comment in this doggerel: firstly, the introduction of sausages in this county caused quite a stir and they soon became very popular; secondly, the mention of 'Pie Poudre Court', or Pie Powder Court as it is called in some other places, reminds us of a condition attached to most fair charters granted by the monarch. This condition ensured that a Court of Justice should be present at every fair held to keep law and order, and as a guarantee of fair trading. The name is rather unusual and probably comes from the French *pied poudré*, which means dusty feet. The courts at the fairs in France were often called the courts of the dusty feet, as people travelled many miles on foot to be present at a fair. The only fairs held at Bury St Edmunds in present times are the cattle and sheep markets.

'Twas Goose Fair cracked the merriest wheeze
Where Babel's babble filled the breeze;
Glad Goose Fair's gambols oft would cheer
The country side throughout the year.

Nottingham is rich in verses pertaining to its famous Goose Fair, which can be traced back to Norman times, though it did not gain the title of Goose Fair until some centuries later, due to the increasing numbers of geese driven to market from the stubble. A story involving the naming of the fair, well-known locally, gives an amusing version of events as follows. Once there was a certain yeoman of good repute, whose wife died when her son was born.

The father vowed that he would bring up his son in ignorance of the opposite sex, so that no temptation should befall him until the age of twenty-one. This he succeeded in doing and on the boy's coming of age he took him for an outing to Nottingham Fair. When the lad saw a pretty girl in a feathered hat, he asked his father what it was, to which his father replied rather brusquely that it was a goose. Many more attractive females were sighted, of course, during the day and the father explained that they were all just geese, and tried to interest his son in other more educational and worthy things on show. At the end of the day, he asked his son what he would like to purchase at the fair to take home. The son cried without hesitation, "A goose, father, buy me a goose"! From that day the fair gained the title of Goose Fair. Another old stanza gives us a plain description of the fair:

> *Goose Fair comes and Goose Fair goes,*
> *With its roundabouts and shows,*
> *Vendours ply their gaudy toys,*
> *Organs grind discordant noise,*
> *Showmen yell until they're hoarse,*
> *Each show 'best of all' of course;*
> *Young and old do congregate*
> *For the time at any rate;*
> *Thrown confetti strews the place,*
> *'Ticklers' wiz around your face,*
> *Crowds are happy in the fun,*
> *Others thankful when it's done.*

Perhaps the most famous English fair is Widdecombe Fair in Devon, a fact which is due almost entirely to the enormous popularity of the song:

Tom Pearce, Tom Pearce, lend me your grey mare,
All along, down along, out along lee,
For I want for to go to Widdecombe Fair,
Wi' Bill Brewer, Jan Stewer, Peter Gurney, Peter Davy, Dan'l
  Whiddon, Harry Hawk, and old Uncle Tom Cobley and all,
Old Uncle Tom Cobbley and all.

And when shall I see again my grey mare?
All along, down along, out along lee,
By Friday soon, or Saturday noon,
Wi' Bill Brewer, etc.

Then Friday came, and Saturday noon,
All along, down along, out along lee,
But Tom Pearce's old mare hath not trotted home,
Wi' Bill Brewer, etc.

So Tom Pearce he got up to the top of the hill,
All along, down along, out along lee,
And he seed his old mare down a-making her will,
Wi' Bill Brewer, etc.

So Tom Pearce's old mare, her took sick and died,
All along, down along, out along lee,
And Tom he sat down on a stone, and he cried
Wi' Bill Brewer, etc.

But this isn't the end of this shocking affair,
All along, down along, out along lee,
Nor, though they be dead of the horrid career
Of Bill Brewer, etc.

When the wind whistles cold on the moor of a night,
All along, down along, out along lee,
Tom Pearce's old mare doth appear, gashly white,
Wi' Bill Brewer, etc.

And all the long night be heard skirling and groans,
All along, down along, out along lee,
From Tom Pearce's old mare in her rattling bones,
And from Bill Brewer, Jan Stewer, Peter Gurney, Peter Davy, Dan'l
*   Whiddon , Harry Hawk, Old Uncle Tom Cobbley and all,*
Old Uncle Tom Cobbley and all.

The first recorded date of Widdecombe Fair was 1850, but this
does not mean to say that it did not exist long before and the song
is thought to be based on an older folk song. Church records
show that a Tom Cobbley was baptised at the Crediton parish
church in the late seventeenth century, and in the same register
are the names of Pearce, Stuer, Davy and Hawke, which seems to
suggest that this was the birth place of not only Uncle Tom but of
his friends also.

Sprayton is another Devon village which has strong ties with
Uncle Tom Cobbley, for in the churchyard there can be seen a
tombstone of one Tom Cobbley, who died in 1784 aged 96. In an
old manuscript we can read an interesting account of how Tom

Cobbley made his will, being very particular as to whom he left his money: he had a large collection of rightful heirs, but only a few were in his favour. He was a well-to-do yeoman, who owned various properties and a small but valuable fortune. Before his death Tom Cobbley became increasingly suspicious of the people in charge of drawing up his will – he even mistrusted his solicitors and in those days he probably had good cause. It is said that he was very hard of hearing and had poor eye-sight, so it took many drafts of the will before he was satisfied that it carried out his wishes, and bequeathed his property and money to the appropriate relatives.

Years ago Widdecombe Fair was primarily a horse and cattle fair held in September, but in modern times, due mainly to the fame of the old song, the fair has become much larger and caters for the thousands of tourists who visit it each year. The tradition of Old Uncle Tom Cobbley is recalled by locals who dress the part and re-enact the song with appropriate actions, much to the amusement of the many sightseers.

TUDOR

CHRISTOPHER COLUMBUS

Henry Tudor, who belonged to the House of Lancaster, defeated Richard III and the Yorkists at the Battle of Bosworth Field in 1485, thus ending the Wars of the Roses. Within a matter of hours Henry Tudor was crowned Henry VII of England and a new era of British history began:

> *In fourteen hundred and ninety two,*
> *Columbus sailed the ocean blue.*

The Tudor period marked a new age of adventure and discovery. With the invention of the marine compass, sailors gained more confidence to sail out into 'the green sea of darkness', as they called the Atlantic Ocean. An Italian named Christopher Columbus gained financial support from Queen Isabella of Spain and set sail from Portugal in August 1492. He commanded three ships: the Santa Maria of one hundred tons and two smaller vessels, the Nina and the Pinta, whose crews were mostly convicts. Columbus believed that, if he sailed a straight course due west, he would reach India and Japan. After a stormy journey, the small fleet reached an island which he named San Salvadour, now called Watling Island. Columbus thought that he had reached India and that is why this group of islands is called the West Indies, and their original inhabitants known as Indians. While visiting other islands, the Santa Maria hit a rock and sank, so Columbus transferred to the Nina, leaving his crew to garrison a fort at Haiti, where they were slaughtered by natives. The small ship Nina returned to Portugal in March 1493 – the Pinta having been sunk on the homeward journey.

Columbus was treated with great honour by Queen Isabella, but not rewarded financially. He made other sea-going expeditions to the west, but owing to the jealousy of many of his contemporaries, he died in poverty and obscurity in 1506. The tomb of Columbus can be seen in Seville, but his body travelled across the Atlantic and back before it was finally decided on the permanent resting place.

I HAD A LITTLE NUT TREE

I had a little nut tree,
Nothing would it bear
But a silver nutmeg and a golden pear;
The king of Spain's daughter
Came to visit me,
And all for the sake of my little nut tree.

Many people believe that this well-known verse contains a direct reference to an incident which took place during the reign of Henry VII. The King was anxious to make an alliance with Spain and had successfully married his son Arthur to Catherine of Aragon, but unfortunately Arthur died when only a young man. Henry then betrothed his son Henry to Catherine, but agreed that his second son was too young for marriage at that time. The following year Henry's wife, Queen Elizabeth, died and after a suitable period of time Henry decided to offer his own hand in marriage to Juanna of Castille, daughter of Queen Isabella and King Ferdinand of Spain. Juanna had suffered the recent death of her husband, when she first visited the English court, and it soon became obvious that she was not in her right mind. Henry had heard rumours before but had chosen to ignore them. He would not admit for some time that the Spanish princess was insane and clung to the belief that, even if she was, it did not matter as long as she could bear healthy children. (Juanna had borne six normal children by her first husband.) However, at last the king had to agree that such a match would be repulsive, unpopular with his subjects, and an embarrassment in diplomatic circles.

LITTLE BOY BLUE

Little Boy Blue, come blow up your horn,
The sheep's in the meadow, the cow's in the corn,
Where is the boy who looks after the sheep?
He's under the haystack fast asleep.
Who will wake him, no not I,
For if I do he's sure to cry.

It has often been said that this rhyme is a parody on the life of Cardinal Wolsey. This may be so, as Wolsey was the son of an Ipswich butcher and might well have been used to looking after animals in his early days, for many butchers kept their own flocks and herds at that time.

Wolsey was a brilliant child and was sent to college at Oxford, where he obtained his degree at the age of fifteen. He then entered the Church. Henry VII recognised him to be an exceptionally clever man and made Wolsey his personal chaplain. When the King died and his son succeeded him as Henry VIII, Wolsey was at the peak of his power; he was made Archbishop of York and Lord Chancellor, and became almost as rich as the king himself. He had many years of prosperity, though he was a man who loved pomp and splendour, and lived very extravagantly. It made no difference to him if the common people were taxed to starvation level, providing he could live in luxury. Because Cardinal Wolsey proved himself to be a very efficient diplomat in foreign affairs, he became the King's chief adviser in these matters.

After nearly twenty years of married life with Catherine of Aragon, the King grew tired of her and wished to marry Anne Boleyn. Not only did Wolsey dislike Anne, but he tried to persuade the King not to break up his marriage for political reasons. When Wolsey realized that the King would not be moved, he tried to secure permission from the Pope for a royal divorce. He was not successful in this and was consequently banished from the Court. The King married Anne Boleyn, who succeeded in turning him against Wolsey.

In an effort to appease him, Wolsey presented the King with a new palace at Hampton Court, but although the King accepted the gift, he remained very bitter towards the Cardinal. As a result

of the King's feelings, many of Wolsey's titles and other properties were confiscated, and Wolsey retired to York, where he was
still Archbishop. He had made many enemies during his life and
they eventually evolved a plot which resulted in Wolsey being
accused of treason. Although failing in health, he was summoned to London for trial and did not survive the journey. He
died at Leicester Abbey with these words on his lips, 'If I had
served God as diligently as I have done the King, he would not
have given me over in my grey hairs.'

JACK BE NIMBLE

Jack be nimble,
Jack be quick,
Jack jump over the candlestick!

A long history of lace-making lies behind this well-known
rhyme. The candlestick has played an important part in the lace
craft of Buckinghamshire and other Midland counties, including
west Suffolk, which was formerly a lace-making centre.

When Catherine of Aragon was banished from the court of
Henry VIII with her daughter Mary, they lived in the Dower
House of Ampthill Park in Bedfordshire. Being of Spanish descent, the ex-queen had the knowledge and tradition of lace-
making at her command, and she soon busied herself teaching
the local inhabitants this intricate art, thus establishing a cottage
industry which thrived for many centuries. A pattern named
after her is still well known. The cottagers were delighted with
this new art, which brought an unexpected prosperity to the
districts concerned.

St Catherine of Alexandria, who was tortured on a wheel in AD
307, is the patron saint of spinners and the lace-makers of Europe
adopted her as their own. St Catherine's Day or Catterns as it was
called by some was celebrated in England on 25 November. It was
one of the great holidays of the lace workers and was celebrated
with feasting on special cakes and a delicious beverage called 'hot
pot'.

One of the fortune rituals played on these feast days was a
game called Jack be Nimble, in which the workers stood in a ring

and took turns to jump the candle. If the flame was extinguished, ill luck would befall the unfortunate person throughout the coming year. As the candlestick was over two feet high and about three inches higher with the flame, it was quite a difficult feat for a girl dressed in long skirts to jump over it. In Ireland the aim of the game was to put out the flame with the toe while jumping and not topple the candle. At other lace schools the boys and girls danced in a ring round the candlestick singing:

> *Wallflowers, wallflowers, growing up so high,*
> *All young maidens surely have to die;*
> *Excepting Emma Caudrey, she's the best of all,*
> *She can dance and she can skip,*
> *And she can jump the candlestick.*
> *Turn, turn, turn your face to the wall.*

Each participant had a turn at jumping the candlestick, while the others faced the outside of the ring.

The intricate lace patterns were made on a 'lace pillow' with many bobbins, which was an extremely skilled craft. In the lace-making villages every five weeks was Cut Off Day, when the lace was removed from the 'pillow' and taken to the lace markets to be sold. The people who lived near Bedford took their products to one Thomas Lester, who owned the draper's shop. If the lace was poorly done, he would pinch the girl's fingers in a drawer but if the work was well done, the girl would receive a reward of a bobbin bearing the words 'Thomas Lester'. Owing to the shortage of small change in those days, the laceworkers were often paid in tokens, which were coins with the name of a certain shop stamped on them. It seems that payment was more often in kind than in money and the system certainly did not encourage savers.

Today the craft of making lace has almost withered away and only one or two skilled workers remain.

LITTLE JACK HORNER

> *Little Jack Horner sat in a corner,*
> *Eating his Christmas pie,*
> *He put in his thumb and pulled out a plum,*
> *And said what a good boy am I!*

The origin of this rhyme lies in an event which took place during the reign of Henry VIII. After his marriage to Anne Boleyn and consequent break with the Catholic Church, the King established the Church of England. Catholics were dismissed from all official positions, and their lands and properties were confiscated. Monasteries were ransacked and burned, and the monks either killed or ejected by force.

The Abbot of Glastonbury in Somerset, Richard Whiting, was a man of good character and although he was the head of one of the richest monasteries in England, he was a generous man, who served his tenants well. In 1535 he had an extensive kitchen built onto the monastery, which was so costly that the news reached the King's ears. He was told that the building was bigger and better than his own kitchen, and this of course enraged him. Fearing royal displeasure, the Abbot sent a large pie to London as a Christmas present for his majesty and under the crust were the title deeds of twelve Somerset manors.

John Horner, who was steward to the Abbot at that time, was entrusted with the valuable pie and instructed to make the journey to London in a rough wagon. The story goes that, while sitting in the corner of the wagon, he pulled a plum from the pie – the title deeds of the Manor of Mells – and kept them himself. When John Horner returned home, he told the Abbot that the King had given him the title deeds of the manor as a reward for safely delivering such a coveted prize and the Abbot believed him, as it was common practice to reward a messenger who brought good tidings. A rhyme known to local Somerset people goes:

> *Little Jack Horner*
> *Sat in the corner*
> *Eying his Christmas pie,*
> *He put in his thumb,*
> *And pulled out a plum*
> *Saying, What a brave boy am I.*

Perhaps the steward was wiser than the Abbot and, seeing the futility of the gifts, took what he could while he had the opportunity. In 1539 the King requisitioned the monastery and other church properties in the area, and Richard Whiting was hung, drawn and quartered, as an example to remaining abbots of what could happen if they did not sign the Act of Supremacy.

The Horner family, on the other hand, have consistently denied this story. They say that it was Thomas Horner and not John who first possessed Mells, and that the jingle had nothing to do with the events which took place in Henry VIII's time. Another verse, popular at the time, declares:

> *Jack Horner was a pretty lad,*
> *Near London he did dwell,*
> *And in the corner he would sit,*
> *In the Christmas Holidays.*

This verse sprang from a much earlier ballad entitled *The Basyn*, which told of the wonderful adventures of a boy called Jack and his magic basin. It is from this source, the Horner family claims, that the jingle as we know it today first originated. After the King had acquired the Church properties, negotiations were made to sell individual houses and it is reported that Thomas Horner bought the manor for cash, and the family say there still exists a bill of sale to prove it.

It is known, however, that Horner was on the jury that tried Richard Whiting for his life and a local couplet says:

> *Wyndham, Horner, Popham and Thynne,*
> *When the abbots came out, they came in.*

The evidence of the Somerset rhymes and the nationally-known one is so strong that it is likely that the story behind *Little Jack Horner* was true – this at least is the feeling of most local people. It is reported that Thomas Horner paid cash for Mells, but where would a steward come by such a large amount of money? In addition, the fact that the jury men received material reward after the condemnation of Richard Whiting seems to establish the true origin of the rhyme.

SING A SONG OF SIXPENCE

> *Sing a song of sixpence,*
> *A pocket full of rye;*
> *Four and twenty black birds*
> *Baked in a pie.*

When the pie was opened,
The birds began to sing;
Wasn't that a dainty dish
To set before the king?

The king was in his counting house
Counting out his money;
The queen was in the parlour,
Eating bread and honey.

The maid was in the garden,
Hanging out the clothes,
Along came a black-bird,
And pecked off her nose.

There are various stories attempting to explain the background to this well-loved jingle and almost all of them allude to Henry VIII and the dissolution of the monasteries. One theory is that the blackbirds were twenty-four title deeds hidden under the pastry, while another suggests that the birds represented the choirs of the monasteries about to be liquidated, that the queen was Catherine of Aragon, and that the maid was Anne Boleyn, waiting to take her place.

An interesting Italian recipe dating from the sixteenth century described how to make pies, so that when the crust was cut the birds would fly out alive – a trick that was often done when the host wanted to add excitement to his party. The birds would fly out of the pie and flutter straight to the candles, as moths do, and snuff out the flames, leaving the guests in total darkness!

An old lady from Wales wrote to me insisting that this rhyme was of Chinese origin, but how she knew this she could not say. She also gave me another explanation of the rhyme, as she had always known it. It symbolized, she said, the passing of night and day: the twenty-four blackbirds represented the number of hours in a full day, the king was the sun and the queen was the moon, when the pie crust was cut it was the sign of the dawning of another day, freeing the birds (hours) to run their course; the coins that the king counted represented the sunbeams, and the bread and honey that the queen ate were the moonbeams; the washing on the line symbolized the clouds in the sky. This hitherto oral explanation of the rhyme has never been recorded before, to my knowledge.

HARK, HARK, THE DOGS DO BARK

Har, hark, the dogs do bark,
The beggars are come to town,
Some in rags and some in tags,
And one in a velvet gown.

The number of unemployed people reached alarming figures during the Tudor era. As mentioned earlier, the agricultural labourer found it difficult to gain employment because of the many sheep walks on agricultural land. The dissolution of the monasteries brought added hardship to the poor and needy, as the one source of help had now been denied them. Many people could not pay the heavy taxes imposed on them by King Henry VIII to pay for his foreign wars, and so were forced out of their homes. Out of a population of under five million, it is estimated that in Tudor times there were more than ten thousand people unemployed.

The Poor Law Act of 1495 divided the unemployed into two categories: the impotent poor, which included orphans, cripples, sick people, lepers, wounded soldiers and shipwrecked sailors, and the valiant beggars, which included all able-bodied men and women. The impotent poor were sent back to the place of their birth and provision was made to care for them within their own parish, while the valiant beggars were subjected to harsh treatment. Under the Vagrancy Law beggars caught wandering the streets were whipped and tortured. Stocks and pillories were introduced at about this time.

Punishment, of course did not alleviate the situation and nothing was done for the unfortunate vagabonds. They continued to roam the countryside in large bands, raiding lonely cottages and farms. The velvet gown mentioned in the verse was most probably stolen property. An unlicensed beggar was described by a contemporary writer of the time as a 'caterpillar of the commonwealth, who licks the sweat from the labourer's brow'.

During the reign of Elizabeth I further Poor Laws instructed each parish to erect alms and work houses for the destitute, providing some means of employment for the persons concerned. 'Beggars can't be choosers' and 'If wishes were horses, beggars would ride' are two proverbial sayings which no doubt date from this period.

ORANGES AND LEMONS

Oranges and lemons,
Say the bells of St Clement's.

You owe me five farthings,
Say the bells of St Martin's.

When will you pay me?
Say the bells of Old Bailey.

When I grow rich,
Say the bells of Shoreditch.

When will that be?
Say the bells of Stepney.

I'm sure I don't know,
Says the great bell of Bow.

Here comes a candle to light you to bed,
Here comes a chopper to chop off your head.
Chop, chop, chop, chop, last man's head.

Throughout the ages bells have played an important part in the lives of the common people. They have served to call people to church and acted as messengers, bringing good or bad tidings to the community.

'What the bells say' has been a popular pastime with people since they were first rung. The clear notes and rhythmic repetitious chimes have inspired the composition of many verses and songs throughout the world. *Oranges and Lemons* tells of old churches which would have been long forgotton but for the song; it tells of the churches of today, in London, that still exist and are proud to be associated with the rhyme; it tells stories of grim traditions, when, before being publicly executed, the victims were paraded in the streets to the toll of the bells. Some say it is a parody on the fate of two of Henry VIII's wives – Anne Boleyn and Catherine Howard, who were executed in the City – and it is for this reason that *Oranges and Lemons* has been included in the Tudor section.

Above all it must be regarded as the most popular children's game ever played. No young children's party is complete without the arches, the line of children chanting the rhyme in its entirety, the gathering climax on the 'chop, chop, chop, chop, last man's head', the indecision as to whether to be an orange or a lemon, and, best of all, the exciting tug-of-war between the two fruits, which invariably ends with a rough and tumble on the floor!

Apparently there are three versions of the rhyme: the standard version, the long version, going from east to west, and the City version, which relates to the City churches. The standard version is the most well known, although in some cases there is doubt about which church is referred to, for instance the church which says 'Oranges and lemons' may be St Clement Danes or St Clement's in Eastcheap, which was situated near the docks at London Bridge. Until the mid-eighteenth century London Bridge was the only one to cross the Thames in the area and, therefore, trading ships from many parts of the world sailed right up to the bridge unloading their cargoes on the wharves nearby. The citrous fruit berth was near St Clement's Eastcheap.

This theory is contradicted, however, by the old legend sent to me by the vicar of St Martin-in-the-Fields. It relates how in the Middle Ages a poor foreigner living in the parish of St Clement Danes was saved from taking his own life, on hearing the bells of St Clement Danes and St Martin's ringing *Oranges and Lemons*. They reminded him of the orange and lemon groves in Italy and of the bells on the hillside, and gave him a new purpose for living. There is of course another St Martin's Church in St Martin's Lane, so the legend may refer to either church. Here are some additional couplets to the song:

> *Bulls eyes and targets,*
> *Say the bells of St Margaret's.*
>
> *Poker and tongs,*
> *Say the bells of St John's.*
>
> *Pancakes and fritters,*
> *Say the bells of St Peter's.*

Two sticks and an apple,
Say the bells of Whitechapel.

Old Father Baldpate,
Say the slow bells of Aldgate.

Maids in white aprons,
Say the bells of St Catherine's.

Brickbats and tiles,
Say the bells of St Giles'.

Kettles and tongs,
Say the bells of St Anne's.

There are, however, two churches which have definite links with the standard version of the song, these are St Sepulchre's, whose bells ring for the Old Bailey, and St Mary-Le-Bow, which provides the 'big bell of Bow'. The Central Criminal Court, erected in 1902, stands on the site of the old Newgate Prison in Old Bailey Court and does not possess a bell. It was the bells of St Sepulchre's that represented the Old Bailey in the nursery rhyme and the church stands opposite. The tower is 150 feet high and contains a peal of ten bells responsible for the line 'When will you pay me?' Most of the bells date from the eighteenth century, but nowadays all but two are silent, until the money can be found for their renovation. In this tower, too, hung the Great Bell that was rung when prisoners at Newgate were about to be executed. It is also known that this bell was used for ringing the curfew in the City of London in 1345. In 1605 Robert Dowe was given £50 for the ringing of the Great Bell on the mornings of executions at the prison and also for 'other services concerning condemned prisoners'. In the church a hand bell is displayed under a glass case, which was known as the 'execution bell', and serves as a grim reminder of days gone by. The bellman, under the direction of Robert Dowe, passed through an underground passage that ran from the church to the prison and rang his bell at midnight outside the condemned cell, reciting:

All you that in the condemned hole do lie,
Prepare you, for tomorrow you shall die.
Watch all and pray; the hour is drawing near
That you before the Almighty must appear.

Examine well yourselves, in time repent,
That you may not to eternal flames be sent,
And when St Sepulchre's bell in the morning tolls
The Lord have mercy on your souls.

The passage entrance can still be seen in the church wall.

The history of St Mary-Le-Bow Church is long and interesting. The first known church was built in Norman times and was called St Mary Newchurch, probably because it was built on a demolished Saxon building. The church was soon renamed St Mary of the Bow or Arches, because it was built over an arched crypt, hence Bow Church. Kings and Queens and other officials watched tournaments and pageants from its tower, which over-looked Cheap market, and the church also gave sanctuary to those who needed it. At first the church possessed only the curfew bell of Bow itself, which rang at 9 pm to close shops and clear streets, and again at 5.45 am to awaken the City. In the early Middle Ages the City was only perhaps a mile square and the sound of Bow bell defined the boundaries – and today it is still accepted that a true Londoner, a Cockney, is one that has been born within the sound of Bow bells. As mentioned previously, Dick Whittington is said to have retraced his steps into London on hearing the peal of the Bow curfew bell from Highgate Hill, which would have been quite possible on a quiet evening.

This old verse signifies a very human error by the bell-ringer in early days!:

Clerk of Bow bell with the yellow locks,
For thy late ringing thy head shall have knocks.
Children of Cheap, hold you all still,
For you shall have Bow bell rung at your will.

Since William the Conquerer, the church of Bow bells has been damaged or completely destroyed by fire many times, but, like the phoenix, it has always managed to rise again from the ashes. After the Great Fire of 1666, Sir Christopher Wren completely rebuilt the church, designing the belfry to take a peal of twelve bells and the first bell to be cast was the Great Bell of Bow, in 1669. However, it was not until two hundred years after the restoration of the church that the belfry contained the intended twelve bells. The steeple of this famous church was regarded as one of Wren's greatest creations and the weather vane on the pinnacle was a golden dragon, which had been a special feature of the church since early times. Although the church was bombed in 1941, it has since been completely restored.

Oranges and Lemons has been linked, as mentioned earlier, with the fate of two of Henry VIII's wives, but the fortune of all six has been summarised by the couplet:

> *Divorced, beheaded, died,*
> *Divorced, beheaded, survived.*

Catherine of Aragon was divorced, Anne Boleyn was beheaded, Jane Seymour died, Anne of Cleves was divorced, Catherine Howard was beheaded and Catherine Parr lived to survive the King.

ST PAUL'S CATHEDRAL

> *Upon Paul's steeple stands a tree,*
> *As full of apples as it may be;*
> *The little boys of London town*
> *They run with hooks to pull them down,*
> *And then they go from hedge to hedge*
> *Until they come to London Bridge.*

Many public buildings and churches were in a dilapidated condition in the sixteenth century. St Paul's was a great Gothic cathedral in those days, and it was a common sight to see trees and grass growing within its walls. The steeple, however, was destroyed by fire in 1561 and so the rhyme must pre-date this. Inigo Jones, the London architect of this time, patched up the cathedral, but lack of funds prevented him from doing a satisfactory renovation.

THREE BLIND MICE

Henry VIII died in 1547 and his nine-year-old son, Edward, succeeded him, but he was a sickly boy and died when he was

7. Mary Tudor 1553 – 1558.

fifteen. It was then the turn of Mary, daughter of Catherine of Aragon, to take the throne. Mary had spent much of her life in the country, with her mother, and her childhood had not been a happy one, for she had never enjoyed good health. It has been said that Mary grew up into a grim and humourless woman – a devout Catholic who abhorred the new religion of the Protestant Church, which had been introduced to Britain by her father.

> *Three blind mice, three blind mice,*
> *See how they run, see how they run,*
> *They all ran after the farmer's wife*
> *Who cut off their tails with the carving knife,*
> *Did you ever see such a thing in your life,*
> *As three blind mice?*

There are many theories as to the underlying meaning of this well-known jingle, which has been sung since 1609, the most

popular theory points to events that happened in the reign of
Mary. The new Queen was determined to re-establish the
Catholic Church in Britain, so she commanded that the land and
property confiscated during her father's reign be returned to their
previous owners where possible and, because of this, she was
often referred to as the 'farmer's wife'. Meanwhile Protestants
were hunted, persecuted and killed.

In 1554 Mary married the Catholic Philip II of Spain, who lived
in England in a lavish and extravagant fashion. Commoners
objected to him and would not accept him as the Queen's husband, so Philip, finding that he was not to be crowned king of
England, returned to Spain. Mary was brokenhearted, for she
really loved her husband, and in her unhappiness she redoubled
her persecution of the Church of England. The prominent Protestants tried to frustrate her plans and reverse the proceedings.
Archbishop Cranmer and Bishops Ridley and Latimer proved
themselves to be 'blind mice', who had their tails cut off, when
Mary sent her lords to persuade these leaders of the Church to
renounce their faith. After their recantations, they were burnt at
the stake together with nearly three hundred other Protestants at
Smithfield in London and at Oxford. The excuse was that by
burning the Protestants their souls would be purged by fire.

The death of the martyrs, who 'when the fire was flaming
about their ears did sing psalms', did more to convert Tudor
Englishmen to Protestantism than any other policy. Bishop
Latimer's last words as he perished at Oxford were 'Be of good
cheer Master Ridley, we shall this day light such a candle by
God's grace, as I trust shall never be put out'. Archbishop
Cranmer had signed a recantation of his beliefs, but when he was
on the stake he said that the hand that wrote such a treacherous
thing should be burned first. The rhyme of *Three Blind Mice* has
been sung as a round since 1609.

During the unhappy reign of Mary I, foreign policy, too, was
not at its best. Calais was the only remaining English port on the
Continent and was very valuable as a trading post between the
wool town of Flanders and English ports. It was recaptured by
the French in 1558, which was a sorry blow to all discerning
Englishmen. Mary felt the loss deeply and told her courtiers that
when she died they would find the word 'Calais' engraved on her
heart.

A SCARBOROUGH WARNING

A Scarborough warning
A word and a blow,
But the blow first.

This saying has an interesting story behind it dating back to 1557, when, during the reign of Mary I, a certain Thomas Stafford with a small band of men seized and overcame Scarborough Castle, without any warning of his intentions. However, within six days, a rival party headed by Lord Westmorland liberated the castle and Stafford and his company were taken to London, where they were beheaded. Thus, to this day, 'a Scarborough warning' means no warning at all, but a sudden surprise. The modern saying runs, 'If you do that much longer I will give you a Scarborough warning'.

HEY DIDDLE DIDDLE, THE CAT AND THE FIDDLE

Elizabeth I, daughter of Anne Boleyn and Henry VIII, ascended the throne on the death of Mary. She favoured the Protestant Church, but did not believe in religious persecution. The Protestants had accepted her mother's marriage to Henry VIII as legal and so recognized Elizabeth as the rightful heir to the throne, though the Catholics believed that Mary Queen of Scots, Elizabeth's cousin, had a stronger claim, as she was a direct descendant of Henry's elder sister and was a fervent Catholic. However, the majority of the population welcomed the new Queen, who was so tolerant in her outlook. After the bitter experiences of events in Mary's reign, the country was able to relax and enjoy the comparative freedom of the Elizabethan era.

Hey diddle diddle, the cat and the fiddle,
The cow jumped over the moon;
The little dog laughed to see such sport,
And the dish ran away with the spoon.

This nonsense rhyme is thought to have originated in the reign of Queen Elizabeth I and indeed there are many public houses dating back to this era named The Cat and Fiddle. It is believed that the verse referred to the jovial merrymaking that took place at the official residence of the Queen, Whitehall Palace. She was gaily dubbed the 'cat', who danced with gay abandon to the fiddler's tune throughout her long and successful reign. Even at the stately age of 48 she was to be seen dancing happily to the tune of the fiddler in her apartments.

She not only had the power and bearing of a monarch of England, but she also played with her Cabinet as if her ministers were so many mice.

8.   Elizabeth I 1558 – 1603.

Elizabeth is said to have possessed a charming personality and a quick wit, and she sought to use these attributes when dealing with foreign affairs. She soon had the attention of every important statesman in Europe, and many royal suitors, including Philip of Spain, hoped to gain her hand in marriage, but, in spite of many pressures, she remained a spinster. In her coronation speech she pledged her life to serve the people of England and this was a promise that she kept.

The 'moon' in the rhyme is thought to symbolize the Earl of Walsingham, one of her favourites, and the 'dog' the Earl of Leicester, who was jeered at in the line 'The little dog laughed to see such sport', because he sulked at the Queen's flirtatious behaviour and asked to leave the Court to take up a post in France.

Elizabeth did much to combine the two leading religious sects in England. She ordered that the Prayer Book be so worded that the Communion Service could be used by both and for the first time that the church services should be conducted in English, so that the commoner could understand what was being said. Everyone was expected to attend church and the penalty for not so doing was one shilling. Ordinary folk were delighted that at last they could understand the religious rituals, which for centuries had been a mystery to them. It is from this time also that chained bibles were introduced in churches for the benefit of all. The Queen summarized the carefully defined religion of her time with these words:

> *His was the Word that spake it;*
> *He took the bread and brake it;*
> *And what that word did make it;*
> *I do believe and take it.*

This grace was popular in Elizabethan times:

> *God bless our meat,*
> *God guide our ways,*
> *God give us grace,*
> *Our Lord to please.*
> *Lord, long preserve in peace and health,*
> *Our gracious Queen Elizabeth.*

A well-made wedding cake was considered to be important to the future of the marriage, as witnessed by this rhyme, which dates back to the Elizabethan era:

> *Today, my Julia, thee must make,*
> *For mistress bride an wedding cake,*
> *Kneade but the dow and it will be,*
> *Turned to prosperitie by thee;*
> *And now the paste of almonds fine,*
> *Assures a broode o' childer nine.*

LITTLE BO-PEEP

Little Bo-Peep has lost her sheep,
And doesn't know where to find them;
Leave them alone, and they'll come home,
Bringing their tails behind them.

Fragments of this rhyme have been traced back to Elizabethan times, and up to a century ago the rest of the jingle was often quoted:

Little Bo-Peep fell fast asleep,
And dreamt she had heard them bleating;
But when she awoke, she found it a joke,
For still they were all fleeting.

Then she took her little crook,
Determined for to find them;
She found them, indeed, but it made her heart bleed
For they'd left their tails behind them.

It happened one day, as Bo-Peep did stray
Along the meadow hard by;
There she espied their tails side by side,
All hung up on a tree to dry.

She heaved a sigh and wiped her eye,
And ran o'er hill and dale, O
And tried what she could, as a shepherdess should,
To tack to each sheep its tail, O.

From this rhyme may well have sprung the tradition of calling catkins 'lamb's tails'.

There is a strong belief held by some people that the rhyme is a direct parody on the life of Mary Queen of Scots. Mary was born in 1542 and was the cousin of Elizabeth I. She became Queen of Scotland on the death of her father, when she was only a young baby. Her mother was French and, when she was five, Mary was betrothed to the Dauphin, so she spent most of her childhood in France and was brought up in the Catholic faith. In 1558 she married the Dauphin, but the young French King died two years later.

9. Mary, Queen of Scots.

Mary therefore returned to Scotland as the rightful Queen, but she was not well received, as many Scotsmen had been converted to the Protestant faith under the strong leadership of John Knox. Soon after her husband's death she married Lord Darnley, but, being a very beautiful and high-spirited woman, she also had other affairs – one being with her secretary who was an Italian named David Rizzio. The puritanical Scots mistrusted her and Rizzio was murdered in her presence in 1566, possibly on the orders of her husband.

Not long after her son was born, Lord Darnley was murdered and Mary married the Earl of Bothwell almost immediately. The Protestants became increasingly dissatisfied with affairs at the Scottish Court and believed that Mary was responsible for her second husband's demise – Mary was indeed losing her sheep. Protestant nobles took her prisoner and forced her to give up the Scottish throne in favour of her son, who later became James I of England.

Later she escaped from the Castle Island in Loch Leven, Kinrosshire, and went to England, where the Catholics welcomed her and did their best by various means to restore her to the throne of Scotland. They even planned to overthrow Elizabeth and establish Mary on the throne of England. The English Cabinet was well aware of the situation and Mary was not allowed to reside in any one place for long, so for nineteen years she was moved from castle to castle and was treated as an alien prisoner. Eventually a plot was discovered in which Elizabeth was to be murdered, and Mary was arrested, tried and found guilty of treason.

Elizabeth refused to sign her death warrant for many months, but at last, under the pressure of her ministers, she consented and Mary was executed on 8 February 1587 at Fotheringay Castle in Northamptonshire – a queen to the end. Her body was buried in Peterborough Cathedral and was later removed to Westminster Abbey.

Another well-known verse believed to be directly related to the life of Mary Queen of Scots is:

> *Mary, Mary, quite contrary,*
> *How does your garden grow?*
> *With silver bells, and cockle shells,*
> *And pretty maids all in a row.*

The pretty maids were said to be the ladies-in-waiting, who were four in number and were also named Mary. The cockle shells are believed to have been part of the decoration on an expensive dress given to Mary by the Dauphin. The general tone of the rhyme suggests derision at her flirtatious behaviour.

THE SPANISH ARMADA

> *The Spanish Armada met its fate,*
> *In fifteen hundred and eighty-eight.*

This couplet reminds us of the power of the English navy in Elizabethan times. Under the direction of men such as Sir Francis Drake, Sir Martin Frobisher and Sir John Hawkins, the coasts of the British Isles were well guarded. It is interesting to note that the navy in those days included such ships as the Revenge, the Ark Royal and the Victory.

After his proposal of marriage to Elizabeth had been rejected, Philip II of Spain sought to conquer Britain in a less subtle way and Spain prepared a huge armada of large and cumbersome ships. The Spanish fleet sailed for England on 12 July 1588, with the formal blessing of the Pope Sixtus V. On board were thousands of heavily armed soldiers, as well as many instruments of torture intended for use on British citizens. These included whips 'to stripe the backs of English women' and branding irons for the foreheads of those who resisted, which would mark them for perpetual slavery.

The armada was sighted off the Lizzard in Cornwall on 19 July and the traditional story that Drake was playing bowls in Plymouth at the time may indeed be true, for the English navy was taken unawares. As soon as the armada was sighted bonfires were lit on high ground and soon news of the imminent invasion spread throughout the land. The English warships, however, were soon ready and, as the Spanish fleet sailed up the English Channel, they crept out of the secluded ports under the cover of darkness, and sank or crippled the enemy galleons one by one. The armada took refuge at Calais which was the neutral port. Many ships had been lost or damaged and the soldiers on board had proved nothing but a hindrance. Many had been killed or wounded, and nearly all were sea-sick, as they had never been trained for sea warfare.

Taking advantage of the tide and the wind, the English then sent eight fire ships into Calais harbour. Crammed with faggots and pitch, these blazing infernos sent the Spanish commanders into a blind panic – they cut the cables and allowed their large and vulnerable fleet to drift out into the open channel. This was their undoing. The battle raged all day and the fleeing Spanish ships sailed northwards to skirt Scotland and Ireland, before returning home to Spain. The English navy had to abandon the chase at this stage because of shortage of ammunition. However, the elements were against the Spanish and the enemy ran into terrible storms. Many ships were wrecked and the survivors were killed by the barbarous tribes of Scotland and Ireland. In all, Spain was said to have lost over ten thousand men and countless ships, while English losses amounted to less than one hundred men and only one ship. When victory was assured Queen Elizabeth is reported to have said 'God blew and they were scattered', while on hearing news of defeat Philip is said to have remarked philosophically, 'God's will be done. I sent you forth to fight with men and not against the elements.'

COCK A DOODLE DOO!

An event which took place during the Elizabethan era has been immortalized in the lines of the following nursery rhyme:

> *Cock a doodle doo!*
> *My dame has lost her shoe,*
> *My master's lost his fiddling stick,*
> *And doesn't know what to do.*

A rich yeoman, Anthony James, and his wife Elizabeth lived in Essex as respectable citizens with their two children, a girl of eight and a boy of seven. One evening the servants were given some time off to visit a local fair. A party of thieves – nine men and a women – broke into the house, bound the parents and held the children, while they ransacked the property for gold and valuables. Then the parents were murdered and their bodies were taken out and buried in a nearby wood. For some unknown reason, the children were put in two panniers and taken on horse- back to an inn in Hatfield. The thieves gave gold to the inn- keeper's wife, Anis Dell, on the understanding that she and her son, George, would dispose of the children. During the evening there was merrymaking and drinking at the inn, and the boy, who was called Anthony after his father, wandered out into the street. A tailor who was passing noticed the good cut of his green coat and managed to procure a rough pattern of it for his future work. During the night the boy was murdered by Anis Dell and the girl's tongue cut out, so that she could not tell what she had seen. A weight was tied to Anthony's body and he was thrown into a pond, a few yards from the inn. A passing beggar was given some money to take the girl away, but he took her to a wood and left her. She crawled into a hollow tree for shelter, where she was later found. Afterwards it seems that the child wandered about begging, having no home or guardian.

Meanwhile, after some weeks, the boy's body was found and, because of his red hair and fine coat, was identified by the tailor as the child who had stayed at the Dell's inn. The coat was dried and cleaned, and hung up in the market place in case someone should recognize it and come forward with more information. The Dells were arrested on suspicion of murder and were held for approximately four years.

One day the girl, Elizabeth, wandered into Hatfield and became agitated at the sight of the Dell's house. The Justices of the town thought that she might be the murdered boy's sister and did a series of tests on her. When they eventually showed her her brother's coat, she became so passionate that their suspicions were confirmed. She was given the coat to wear and was entrusted to a suitable family for safe keeping. Elizabeth thrived on good food, affection and security. One day while playing with her friends in King's Park, Hatfield, the children began to 'mock the cocks', as was the custom in those days, chanting 'Cock a doddle doo, Peggy hath lost her shoe'. One child urged the dumb girl to say it and to everyone's amazement Elizabeth opened her mouth and repeated the rhyme, very similar to the one known today.

The news that the dumb girl had regained the power of speech travelled fast, and people journeyed from far and wide to hear her, and to look into her mouth that had no tongue. She repeated all she knew of her brother's murder to an incredulous audience and was then again cross-examined by the Justices. One of Sir Henry Boteler's men performed a peculiar test on the girl. He dressed up as the devil, with mask and horns, and jumped out from a bush to frighten Bess, as she was called. He told her that she must tell the truth about the Dells or he, as the devil, would tear her to pieces. She replied, 'Good gaffer devil, do not hurt me; I speak nothing but the truth, and what the thing within me instructeth me to speak.' This piece of evidence was accepted and the Dells were tried and subsequently executed. It is not known whether the original miscreants were ever caught.

It is worthwhile considering that medical records show that in some cases tongueless people have been known to speak after the wound has healed. They have more chance of regaining the power of speech if the tongue was not professionally removed, i.e. not cut out by the roots. In the case of Elizabeth James it is thought that her tongue was not wholly extracted, and that also the luxury of a home after much hardship might have helped her regain her speech. This story is known locally as 'The Hertfordshire miracle'.

RIDE A COCK-HORSE TO BANBURY CROSS

Ride a cock-horse to Banbury Cross,
To see a fine lady ride on a white horse.
With rings on her fingers and bells on her toes,
She shall have music where ever she goes.

It is very difficult to pin-point the origin of this popular verse, but, because of the line containing 'and bells on her toes', it has been included here in the Tudor section, as the wearing of toe bells was fashionable at this time.

There are varying explanations of this rhyme. One lady who lives in Natal, South Africa, is convinced that she is a descendant of the fine lady mentioned in the second line. She relates that there exists a traditional story in her family that has been passed down through the generations. Her grandmother it seems was descended from the Norman line of Fiennes. Long ago a nobleman of the house of Fiennes married a Spanish lady and carried her off to his castle near Banbury (probably Broughton Castle). The lady with her dark beauty and strange exotic clothes would only ride a white horse – a fact that soon singled her out for comment among the locals, thus the line 'To see a fine (Fiennes) lady ride on a white horse'. The correspondent adds that although fairness is a family trait, her grandmother was dark-eyed and olive-skinned, and so is her cousin – colouring inherited, she likes to think, from the original Fiennes lady.

Another story pertaining to this verse was sent to me by an old lady who resided in Aberystwyth. She stated that her grandmother told her that the 'lady on the white horse' was in fact Lady

10.   The original Cake shop, Banbury.

Godiva, who rode naked through the streets on her horse in protest against the extremely high taxes imposed upon the people by her husband. To warn people of her approach she carried a hand bell and fastened bells to the stirrups, hence 'bells on her toes'. She asked the citizens to retire to their houses, draw the blinds and bolt the doors. This they did, so it is said, except for one man who was 'evil' enough to raise the curtain as she went by, for which action God immediately struck him dead! He was known as the original 'peeping Tom'. Tradition has it that Lady Godiva was associated with Coventry, so how she became connected with Banbury is not known.

The original Banbury Cross referred to in the nursery rhyme was destroyed by Puritans in 1602, when religious feeling was running high against the Catholics. The stone of the cross was so defaced that it was impossible to restore it. The present hexagonal, neo-Gothic cross was erected in 1860. Another rhyme about this town refers to the well-known Banbury cakes:

> *Ride a cock horse to Banbury Cross,*
> *To see what Tommy can buy.*
> *A penny white loaf, a penny white cake,*
> *And a two penny apple pie.*

The spiced cakes of Banbury were first introduced in approximately 1608, but did not find much public favour until thirty years later. The original cake shop, which was situated in Parson Street, was alas, demolished in 1968.

There are many nursery rhymes about Banbury, due to a bookseller and printer called J. G. Rusher, who lived in the town during the nineteenth century. He realized the need for literature, especially children's books, and published many chapbooks selling for a penny to the residents of Banbury. He also engaged pedlars to sell his works further afield. Most of his early chapbooks were undated, but the earliest must have been published around the year 1810. The illustrations followed the Bewick tradition and the same engravings or wood cuts must have been used repeatedly. Rusher also saw the great potential in advertising and he often composed verses for this purpose, and printed them on chapbook covers. On the front of the *Famous History of John Gilpin* it says:

> At Rusher's fam'd Warehouse,
> Books, Pictures and Toys,
> Are selling to please all
> The good girls and boys.
>
> For youths of all ages
> There's plenty in store,
> Amusement, instruction,
> For rich and for poor.

Some of these original chapbooks have been reprinted and they make fascinating reading. Many have been reprinted by Anne and Peter Stockham, and on the back of *Death and Burial of Cock Robin*, Rusher added this verse:

> Ride on a horse,
> To Banbury Cross,
> To Cock Robin's grave,
> On a galloping horse.

STUART

GUY FAWKES

When Queen Elizabeth died in 1603, James VI of Scotland, the son of Mary Queen of Scots, was invited to become James I of England. The Scottish parliament had been weak and James had been used to having his own way, however, handling the English government was a very different matter. James believed in the Divine Right of Kings, but the English parliament opposed this theory. The new king was a Protestant and many Catholics feared renewed persecution. Robert Catesby and Thomas Percy were among a group of leading Catholics who conceived a plot to rid the country of its king and parliament, but they needed the help of someone who knew how to obtain and handle gunpowder.

> *Remember, remember the fifth of November,*
> *Gunpowder, treason and plot;*
> *I see no reason why gunpowder treason,*
> *Should ever be forgot.*

Through this rhyme we have kept alive an event which happened over 350 years ago. The man who was responsible for the traditional bonfire and firework night on 5 November was, of course, Guy Fawkes. He was born in 1570 in York and was brought up in the Protestant faith, but when his lawyer father died, Guy Fawkes became a Catholic. At the age of twenty-three he joined the army and fought with the Spanish forces in Flanders, as Spain ruled Belgium at that time. Fawkes was a good soldier and he soon gained a reputation for bravery and loyalty. It was while he was in the army that he learned about the properties of gunpowder.

The Catholic plotters in England were favourably impressed by the career of Guy Fawkes and sent word to him of their plans. He agreed to help them and crossed to England in 1604. Thomas Percy rented a house next to the Houses of Parliament and later managed to gain access to the room directly underneath the House of Lords. How Guy Fawkes managed to smuggle a ton and a half of gunpowder in barrels into the building, without arousing suspicion, still remains a mystery. He covered the barrels in the cellar with firewood and coal, and was elected the man to light the fuse – a quick way of escape being left open to him. It was planned that he should use special 'slow' matches to light the fuse.

11.   The 'dark' lantern belonging to Guy Fawkes.

At the eleventh hour one of the plotters, probably Lord Tresham, wrote a letter to his brother-in-law, Lord Mounteagle, warning him not to attend the opening of Parliament: 'Though there be no appearance of any stir, yet I say they shall receive a terrible blow, the Parliament, and yet they shall not see what hurts them'. The letter was shown to other members of the Government, and the buildings were consequently searched.

Fawkes was discovered and taken to the Tower of London, where he was ill-treated and tortured to force him to betray the other conspirators. Although under great pressure, he never gave way. However, the rest of the traitors revealed themselves, when they tried to raise an armed rebellion against the King. Seven others and Fawkes were tried, found guilty of treason and sentenced to death. Guy Fawkes was taken from the Tower on 31 January 1606 and executed opposite the buildings that he had tried to destroy.

After the executions, further plans were discovered in which Spain had promised to support the new Catholic government set up in England, if the Gunpowder Plot had succeeded in ridding the country of the English King and his Parliament. Since 1605, before the opening of each new Parliament, the buildings are searched to ascertain the safety of the Government.

The following rhyme was chanted by children long ago, in London and was recorded in 1818. The habit of making a guy and exhibiting it in order to collect money probably stems from the seventeenth or eighteenth century:

> *Who comes riding thither as black as coal,*
> *With matches and old tinder box,*
> *And holding his lantern, a figure so droll?*
> *'Tis nobody less than Guy Fawkes.*

The dark deeds of Guy Fawkes and his companions are also immortalized in the following rhyme:

> *Guy Fawkes and his companions did contrive*
> *To blow the House of Parliament up alive*
> *With three score barrels of powder down below,*
> *To prove Old England's wicked otherthrow;*
> *But by God's mercy all of them got catched,*
> *With their dark lantern and their lighted match.*
> *Ladies and gentlemen sitting by the fire,*
> *Please put hands in pockets and give us our desire;*
> *While you can drink one glass, we can drink two,*
> *The better for we, and none the worse for you.*
> > *Rumour, rumour, pump a derry,*
> > *Prick his heart and burn his body,*
> > *And send his soul to purgatory.*

The history of the 'dark lantern' is convincing enough to suppose that it was the actual lamp used by Guy Fawkes. Prior to 1887, the lantern was housed in the Bodleian Library, Oxford, having been given by Robert Heywood of Brasenose College in 1641. He became the proctor of the University in 1639, and his father was the Justice of the Peace who arrested Guy Fawkes.

Yorkshire has its own collection of rhymes and sayings referring to Guy Fawkes. A certain patriotic feeling is apparent in:

> *A stick and a stake*
> *For King James' sake;*
> *Please give us a coil, a coil.*

This rhyme shows rather more imagination:

> *Awd Grimey sits upon yon hill,*
> *As black as any awd crow.*
> *He's gitten on his long grey coat*
> *With buttons down afore,*
> *He's gitten on his long grey coat*
> *With buttons down afore.*

The next rhyme also exhorts us to remember Guy Fawkes' Day:

> *Gunpowder Plot*
> *Shall ne'er be forgot,*
> *As long as Bella Brown*
> *Sells tom-trot.*

In some parts of the north of England, the making and selling of tom-trot, a sticky sweetmeat of half-baked treacle, was more important to the locals than the traditional burning of the guy on 5 November. Another lady famous for her tom-trot is immortalized in rhyme:

> *Gunpowder Plot will never be forgot,*
> *So long as Jenny Dunn sells good tom-trot.*

An alternative word for 'tom-trot' is 'parkin'.

The practice of lighting fires early in November is a great deal older than the story of Guy Fawkes. This ritual dates from pagan times, when the month of November was considered the month of the dead, when evil spirits roamed the land spreading death and misery. Bonfires were lit on 1 November to rid the neighbourhood of these dreaded happenings.

LITTLE MISS MUFFET

James I was a man of learning and was one of the few monarchs of England to write at length. Among his books was one entitled *The True Law of a Free Monarch*, in which he set out his ideas of how a country should be governed, though his theories were never accepted by his subjects. He possessed very little commonsense and a French writer of the time described him as 'the wisest fool in Christendom'. Although James wrote with austerity, his own behaviour and, consequently, the behaviour of his court, was far from moral. He once told the Venetian ambassador that if he executed everyone who defrauded the state, as was the custom in Venice, then he would have no subjects left!

James' wife died young and the king in later years became almost completely homosexual – his love for the Duke of Buckingham was well-known. A topical couplet describes his character:

> Who. kept a brace of painted creatures to be hand,
> And to be drunk in a new tavern, till he not be able to stand.

However, there were many noted scholars of the period who were regarded as being both knowledgeable and wise. The following verse, which must be one of the most popular of all nursery rhymes, probably had its roots in this era:

> Little Miss Muffet
> Sat on her tuffet,
> Eating her curds and whey;
> There came a big spider
> And sat down beside her,
> And frightened Miss Muffet away.

It is thought to be a parody on the life and work of Thomas Muffet. As well as being a doctor of medicine, he was also an expert on insect life, a subject which had not been studied in great detail up to that time. During his stay in Spain, he became interested in the silk worm and consequently wrote a poem about this creature and its habits entitled *The Silk Worme and its Flies*. Later, he compiled a more serious study of insects, spiders and lesser creatures, which was written in Latin and dedicated to James I. Thomas Muffet died in 1604 and the work was not published until 1643. Later, it was translated into English under the title *The Theater of Insects and Lesser Living Creatures*. Dr Muffet had one daughter by his first marriage named Patience and it is thought likely that she may have been the original Miss Muffet. A 'tuffet' means a tuft of grass and the practice of sitting on a tuffet of soft grass, waiting for something exciting to happen, can be traced back to the Dark Ages.

HUMPTY DUMPTY

James I died in 1625 and his eldest son, Charles, succeeded him. Charles I was a small man – only five feet tall – and he had an impediment of speech. He did not enjoy good health and his legs were so weak that he preferred to ride on horseback whenever possible. These disabilities did not improve his character and he was considered by most to lack the qualities needed for a monarch. He, like his father, believed in the Divine Right of Kings and severe disagreements occurred between him and the English parliament, which eventually led to the Civil War between Royalists and Roundheads. Charles I stated that he was fighting for the cause of the Church, while the rebels said they were fighting for the rights of the people.

The King rode out of London with his wife and family in 1642 and he rode in again for his trial in 1648. His wife, Henrietta Maria, returned to London in 1660 – an old woman.

> *Humpty Dumpty sat on a wall,*
> *Humpty Dumpty had a great fall.*
> *All the king's horses and all the king's men,*
> *Couldn't put Humpty together again.*

The origin of this old rhyme, which has become so popular over the years, has puzzled historians for centuries. Recently new information has come to light regarding its source. Richard Rodney Bennett's children's opera *All The King's Men* is based on an incident which took place during the Civil War. Charles I and his men were garrisoned at Oxford, and a certain Dr Chillingworth was employed to invent effective war machines to surprise the enemy. Such tactics were already very popular on the Continent. The Roundheads at that time were commanded by young Colonel Massey and their headquarters were at Gloucester. The Royalist army arrived outside the walls of Gloucester and the King asked Dr Chillingworth to think of a plan to take the city without much loss of life.

The inventor planned a huge war machine which would roll down the steep slope on wheels, bridge the river Severn and provide a covered way over the walls of the city, enabling the King's men to enter without undue casualties. It was modelled on a similar machine used by the Romans called a 'tortoise'. Troops on both sides christened this invention 'Humpty Dumpty'.

The citizens of Gloucester were informed of the plan long before it was put into operation, however, and took steps to widen the river. The huge war machine was launched with hundreds of troops packed inside, but it did not reach the far bank and collapsed in mid-stream, drowning a large number of soldiers. The following verse is sung in the opera and is the forerunner of the one we know today:

> *Humpty Dumpty lay in the beck,*
> *With all his sinews around his neck;*
> *All the king's surgeons, and all the king's wrights,*
> *Could not put Humpty Dumpty to rights.*

The King's army despondently marched away, not knowing that Colonel Massey had only three barrels of gunpowder left for the defence of the city.

Humpty Dumpty has its counterpart in many countries, perhaps because the story of the unsuccessful machine was retold by soldiers serving on the Continent, and the story was handed down from one generation to the next. An old definition of a Humpty Dumpty explains that it was an egg and brandy drink. Also a plump person was often called by that name years ago.

CHARLES I

After many battles, the King finally surrendered and in June 1646 the royalist garrison at Oxford capitulated.

> As I was going by Charing Cross,
> I saw a black man upon a black horse;
> They told me it was Charles the First;
> O dear, my heart was ready to burst.

This verse, dating back to the Stuart era, most probably refers to Charles I's ride into London after his surrender, for it is known that he wore black after his defeat as a sign of mourning for his cause and also, of course, he had black hair and beard – all of which earned him the description of 'a black man'.

During his trial and imprisonment, the King conducted himself with a bearing of which any royal personage would be proud. He had never lacked physical courage and his steadfastness stirred not only the English people, but also foreigners:

> King Charles the First walked and talked,
> Half an hour after his head was cut off.

Although this couplet is used primarily as a lesson in punctuation, it also serves to remind us of the fate of this unhappy king. Before his death, the King told Elizabeth, one of his daughters, that he would die a martyr and he doubted not but the Lord would settle the throne upon his son, and that the country would be happier than could have been expected if he had lived. The Queen, Henrietta Maria, was safely in France together with Charles, Prince of Wales, and this fact, above all others, enabled Charles I to face his death with equanimity. He refused to utter the usual words of forgiveness to the executioner, because he said that only God could forgive the slaying of his anointed.

Another traditional song that is still well-known today refers to the Civil War and may have been a marching song of the Cavaliers, 'Here's a health unto his Majesty':

> Here's a health unto his Majesty,
> With a fal lal la la la la la!
> Confusion to his enemies
> With a fal lal la la la la la!

> And he that will not drink his health,
> I wish him neither wit nor wealth,
> Nor yet a rope to hang himself,
> With a fal lal la la la la la la la la,
> With a fal lal la la la la la!

All Cavaliers will please combine,
With a fal lal la la la la la!
To drink this loyal toast of mine
With a fal lal la la la la la!

If anyone should answer 'No'
I only wish that he would go
With Roundhead rogues to Jericho,
With a fal lal la la la la la!

GENERAL MONK

Oliver Cromwell was never accepted by the English people as the rightful head of state, though during his term of office numerous rigid laws were introduced and a puritanical regime was enforced. The following traditional poem dates back to the Reformation, when numerous revels and country customs were forbidden, thus allowing many ancient rituals and feasts to be forgotton forever. The maypole, for example, and all that it stood for, was abolished at this time, and it is only in recent years that maypole dancing has been revived:

In London thirty years ago,
When pretty milkmaids went about,
It was a goodly sight to see,
Their May Day pageant all drawn out.

Themselves in comely colours dresst,
Their shining garland in the middle,
A pipe and tabor on before
Or else a foot inspiring fiddle.

They stoppt at houses, where it was
Their custom to cry 'Milk below!'
And while the music played with smiles
Join'd hands and pointed toe to toe.

Thus they tripp'd on, till – from the door
The hop'd for annual present sent –
A signal came to curtsey low,
And at that door cease merriment.

Such scenes and sounds once blest my eyes,
And charmed my ears, but all have vanish'd.
On May Day now no garlands go,
For milkmaids and their dance are banish'd.

The purpose of the milkmaids' dance seems to have been to collect presents of tips from the houses where they delivered the milk.

It can be said, however, that Oliver Cromwell, who was a good soldier, was the first military leader to realize that a reliable army needed trained men, regular pay, billets and uniforms – his soldiers were dressed in red. He formed his Ironsides and later developed the New Model Army. This was the beginning of regiments as we know them today:

Little General Monk sat upon a trunk
Eating a crust of bread.
There fell a hot coal,
And in his clothes burnt a hole,
And now little General Monk is dead.

After the death of Cromwell and the realization that his son Richard was unfit for leadership, the country found itself without a figurehead and the gentry decided that they wanted the monarchy to return. General Monk was one of Cromwell's most intelligent and influential commanders, and was ruler of Scotland at the time of Cromwell's death. He sent word to Charles II, who was living in Holland, that there was a likelihood of his being made King of England – he had already been crowned King of Scotland. Charles was advised to write to the English parliament promising pardon for all, if he were invited to become King. Charles did this and his suggestions were welcomed thankfully by the government, so on 8 May 1660 Charles II was proclaimed King even before he had reached England.

Meanwhile, General Monk recruited fresh troops from Coldstream on the Scottish border for the New Model Army. When all was ready, he marched south and arrived in London to welcome the new King. Charles and his brothers landed on English soil on 23 May and entered London in triumph on the 29th – his birthday. General Monk assembled his army on Tower Hill and, as the King passed by, he ordered the men to lay down their arms as Cromwell's Commonwealth and take them up again as His

Majesty's Regiment of Foot Guards. The regiment has been known ever since as the Coldstream Guards.

The First Foot Guards had been the body guard of Charles II while in exile and were renamed the Grenadier Guards. Other early regiments named at the time were the 1st and 2nd Life Guards and the Horse Guards. The following verse records the joyful anticipation of the common folk at this particular moment in history:

> High diddle ding,
> Did you hear the bells ring?
> The parliament soldiers are gone to the King!
> Some they did laugh, some they did cry,
> To see the parliament soldiers pass by.

Parliament ordered that 29 May, being the birthday of King Charles II and also the day when he entered London in triumph, should thereafter be kept as a day of thanksgiving and rejoicing; in fact, a national holiday was proclaimed:

> Royal Oak Day,
> Royal Oak Day,
> The twenty-ninth of May,
> If you don't give us a holiday,
> We'll all run away!

This verse has been chanted by schoolboys from that date. Royal Oak Day was observed by people wearing oak leaves in their hats, and horses wore them on their bridles. Oak leaves were chosen to keep alive the memory that it was in an oak tree that Charles hid at Bosobel in Shropshire, when fleeing from his enemies during the Civil War. An extract from Pepys' Diary states: 'Parliament had ordered the 29th of May, the King's birthday, to be for ever kept as a day of thanksgiving for our redemption from tyranny and the King's return to his Government, he entering London on that day.'

Dryden in a poem commemorating the *Happy Restoration and return of His Sacred Majesty, Charles II* wrote:

> How shall I speak of that triumphant day,
> When you renewed th'expiring pomp of May!
> (A month that owns an interest in your name:
> You and the flowers are its peculiar claim.)

General Monk enjoyed prosperity to the end of his days, as a reward for helping to re-establish the English monarchy. He lived through the Great Plague and the Fire of London in 1666, and died in 1669. It is possible that the last lines of the jingle about him refer to the Great Fire.

CHARLES II

Charles II was apparently a disappointment to many people. True, his escapades with women on the continent had not gone unnoticed, but public opinion hoped that, once crowned King of England, Charles would reform his ways. Alas, this did not happen, hence the verse:

> *Rowley, Powley, puddin' and pie,*
> *Kiss'd the girls and made them cry.*
> *When the boys came out to play,*
> *Rowley powley ran away.*

'Old Rowley' was the nickname for Charles II, and this verse is an earlier version of *Georgey Porgey*. Unfortunately, Charles' wife was barren, but by his many mistresses he had at least fourteen illegitimate children. The Duke of Monmouth was his eldest son and, after his father's death, he led a rebellion aimed at claiming the throne:

> *See saw, sack-a-day;*
> *Monmouth is a pretie boy,*
> *Richmond is another,*
> *Graften is my onely joy;*
> *And why should I these three destroy,*
> *To please a pious brother!*

According to Andrew Lang this jingle is a direct reference to three of the King's sons, who, if they had been born in wedlock, would have been heirs to the throne, but, as it was, the throne went to James II, Duke of York, when Charles died.

This lampoon was sung openly during the reign of Charles II:

> *We have a pretty witty king,*
> *Whose word no man relies on;*
> *He never said a foolish thing,*
> *And never did a wise one.*

The King's traditional reply to this was: 'That is very true, for my words are my own – my actions are my ministers'.

Nell Gwyn was perhaps the most well-known and popular of all Charles' mistresses. When she was a child, she sold oranges in the streets of London. Later, she became an actress and, when she was fourteen, she starred in John Dryden's play *The Indian Emperor* at Drury Lane. The King saw the play and invited her to Court. Samuel Pepys described her as 'pretty witty Nell' and she soon became a favourite with the British public. The fact that she was of the Protestant faith stood her in good stead. Nell was described as not being particularly good looking, but very gay, possessing a quantity of auburn hair, which was her crowning glory. It is thought likely that it was Nell Gwyn who persuaded the King to establish the Royal Chelsea Hospital as a home for aged and disabled soldiers. Before Charles died, he said, "Let not poor Nellie starve" and consequently, she was given a country estate called Bestwood Park, near Nottingham. She was buried in the church of St Martin-in-the-Fields.

JAMES II

Continuing the Elizabethan tradition, the playwrights and authors of the Stuart era created many plays and entertainments of a high standard, but, on the whole, the audiences were ill-behaved and forced many reputable theatres to close. The following couplet, often repeated in those days, bears this out:

> *One half the play they spend in noise and brawl,*
> *Sleep out the rest, then wake and damn it all.*

After the death of Charles II, his brother succeeded him as James II of England. By his first marriage James had two daughters, Mary and Anne:

> *What is the rhyme for porringer?*
> *What is the rhyme for porringer?*
> *The King he had a daughter fair,*
> *And gave the Prince of Orange her.*

This verse refers to the marriage between Mary and William of Orange, who was a grandson of Charles I.

In later life James remarried and his second wife was a beautiful Italian princess, Mary of Modena. It was thought very unlikely that James would have any more children, so it had been arranged that on his death William and Mary should succeed to the throne and rule jointly. Anne, too, was considered in line to the throne. When Mary of Modena gave birth to a son, called James Francis Edward, it certainly upset the well-laid plans, for under English law a king's son takes precedence over his older sisters when inheriting the throne. The Queen was a firm Catholic and it is probably for this reason that her son never became King of England. The Act of Settlement passed in Parliament in 1689 forbade anyone of the Catholic faith to sit on the throne of England.

James II was ageing fast and more than ever needed the comfort and support of his daughters, but they deserted him in his hour of need and he was forced to flee to France, for he justifiably feared assassination. The Queen and her baby son fearing reprisals, also left the country. The way was then clear for William and Mary to claim the throne. A Scottish nursery rhyme echoes and develops the English version:

> *O what's the rhyme to porringer?*
> *Ken you the rhyme to porringer?*
> *King James the seventh had a daughter,*
> *And gave her to an Oranger.*
>
> *Ken you how she requited him?*
> *Ken you how she requited him?*
> *The lad has into England come,*
> *And taken the crown in spite of him.*
>
> *The dog, he shall not keep it long,*
> *To flinch we'll make him fain again;*
> *We'll hang him high upon a tree,*
> *And James shall have his ain again.*

As has already been mentioned, King James II of England was James VII of Scotland.

THE OLD PRETENDER

James II's daughter Anne was married to Prince George of Denmark and the turbulent events of the time are recorded in the following verse:

> *William and Mary, George and Anne,*
> *Four such children had never a man;*
> *They put their father to flight and shame,*
> *And called their brother a shocking bad name.*

The last line of the jingle probably refers to the 'warming pan' story, which Mary and Anne circulated at the time of the birth of their step-brother. They said, in effect, that the Queen had not given birth to a baby at all and that James Francis Edward was no other than a 'varlet's brat', smuggled into the royal household in a warming pan. However, this piece of fabrication was finally openly disputed, and rejected.

Though Anne gave birth to seventeen children, she survived them all, and towards the end of her reign the problem arose as to who would succeed her. If James 'III' could have changed his faith and become Protestant then he might well have been invited to become the next monarch. By this time the Jacobite movement was well established and there existed in England many Jacobites ready to swear allegiance to the rightful heir, the Prince of Wales, when the opportunity arose. A fair number of Jacobite songs and verses were engendered during the eighteenth century to remind us of the hopes and fears of this strong political party.

However the Act of Settlement was adhered to and the English Parliament looked for a Protestant successor. George of Hanover, a German, who could speak no English, was eventually invited to become King of England, because he was related to the English royal line. The Jacobites, on the other hand, were firmly convinced that the throne should go to the 'Old Pretender', James 'III', and they circulated a medal or badge with his head engraved upon it. A popular Jacobite ballad recorded at the end of Anne's reign defines the situation thus:

> *Let's joy in the Medal with James III's Face*
> *And the Advocates that pleaded for him;*
> *Tho' the Nation Renounces the Popish Race*
> *Great Louis of France will restore him.*

Let Schismaticks Pine, let Republicans Wine,
And henceforth abandon these nations,
With Louis rejoyce, and cry with one Voice
Obedience without Limitations.

Let the Whigs that love Trade, the South Seas invade,
And there we will give 'em Debentures,
For the Money they're lent, till the whole Sum be spent,
And a Sponge wipe out all their Adventures.

They shall have for Director, their German Elector,
Who certainly will not play Booty,
He's too much in the Stock, the Project to Shock,
Good Princess Sophia, Adieu Eye.

To which the Whigs replied with another ballad, sung to the tune
of Lilliburlero:

A plot's now on foot, look about, English boys,
Blow up the plotters as soon as you can;
A plot which our Hanover's title destroys,
And shakes the high throne of our glorious Queen Anne.
    Over, over, Hanover, over,
    Haste and assist our Queen and our State;
    Haste over Hanover, fast as you can over,
    And put in your claim before 'tis too late.

A bargain our Queen made with her good friends
The States to uphold the Protestant line;
If the plot does succeed, that bargain then ends,
As well as her majesty's gallant design.
    Over, over, etc.

A creature there is that goes by more names
Than ever an honest man could, should or would;
And I wish we don't find him an arrant King James,
Whenever he peeps out from under his hood.
    Over, over, etc.

Let's fill up a bumper with brave racy wine,
To Princess Sophia, th' elector and all
The Protestant princes of that noble line,
Before 'em may Popery and Tyranny fall.
    Over, over, etc.

During the Hanoverian period we shall see how Jacobite songs recorded the history of the time, as no other history book has done.

It is very likely that the following nonsense verse refers to the fight for the English throne between the Old Pretender and George I:

> *Jim and George were two great lords,*
> *They fought all in a churn;*
> *And when that Jim got George by the nose,*
> *Then George began to girn.*

This was just wishful thinking by the Scottish author! Another traditional verse says:

> *Of all the days that's in the year,*
> *The Tenth of June to me's most dear,*
> *When our White Roses will appear*
> *To welcome Jamie the Rover.*

James 'III' was born on 10 June.

GIRLS AND BOYS COME OUT TO PLAY

> *Girls and boys come out to play,*
> *The moon doth shine as bright as day,*
> *Leave your supper and leave your sleep,*
> *And join your playfellows in the street;*
> *Come with a hoop, come with a call,*
> *Come and be merry or not at all,*
>   *Up the ladder and over the wall,*
>   *A half penny loaf will serve us all.*

The content and meaning of this rhyme has often puzzled people. To modern thinkers it seems unnatural for children to play by moonlight, when they should be in bed asleep. However, in the seventeenth century, children were treated like miniature adults. They were forced to work or study very long hours and it was not considered necessary to let them out to play. A tract written in Stuart times describes how children, when the moon was bright, gathered in the churchyard for fun and games. The church was a communal centre for secular as well as religious matters, and markets and entertainments were often held on consecrated ground. The urge to play overcame the urge to sleep, and often it was past ten o'clock at night before the youngsters returned home.

COBBLER, COBBLER, MEND MY SHOE

Cobbler, cobbler, mend my shoe,
Get it done by half past two;
Half past two is much too late,
Get it done by half past eight.

There was a large number of cobblers in proportion to the population at this time and, like many other craftsmen, they were divided into grades according to skill. Those who could afford to pay high prices went to the skilled shoemaker, who ran a made-to-measure shop, where the complete shoe was made on the premises. Lower down the scale was the less skilled operator working in one room, using leather which had already been cut out for him by the leather cutter. He was what could be classed as an out-worker. At the bottom of the hierarchy was the 'translator', whose job was to renovate second-hand shoes for the poor. The rhyme probably refers to the latter.

From ancient times there has been a wealth of superstition surrounding the subject of shoes. It was deemed unlucky to place a pair of shoes on a table, as this action was said to foretell a death in the family or a new child within a year. Death by hanging was connected with shoes and the phrase 'to die with one's boots on' was probably derived from this tradition. A person's character was judged by the way his shoes or boots wore down, as is witnessed by this suffolk rhyme:

Tip at the toe, live to see woe,
Wear at the side, live to be a bride,
Wear at the ball, live to spend all;
Wear at the heel, live to save a deal.

Creaking shoes denoted that the shoemaker had not been paid. It was considered unlucky to leave shoes in the form of a cross at night, but left in the form of T or soles uppermost was believed to prevent cramp, nightmares and rheumatism. Nerve pains in the foot were said to be cured by making the form of a cross on the shoe. The smell of burning shoes was thought to ward off demons, serpents and plague epidemics.

The use of old shoes as a sign of authority or good luck dates from pagan times. At Anglo-Saxon weddings the father transferred his authority over his daughter to her husband by giving his son-in-law one of the bride's old shoes. The husband would then touch his wife's head with it, symbolizing that he was the new master. Shoes were often thrown after ships putting to sea as a sign of good luck, and this may well have been the origin of old shoes being thrown at the newly-wed couple after the wedding ceremony. This custom is still observed, when shoes are tied to the couple's car.

It is interesting to note that it was only old shoes that were used in all these customs. To use a new pair of shoes was thought to invite ill luck. An old riddle about shoes which cannot be measured in years goes:

> *Two brothers we are*
> *Great burdens we bear*
> *On which we are bitterly pressed;*
> *The truth is to say,*
> *We are full all the day,*
> *And empty when we go to rest.*

RING-A-RING O' ROSES

> *Ring-a-ring o' roses,*
> *A pocket full of posies;*
> *Atishoo, atishoo, we all fall down.*

It is accepted by many people that this little jingle which our youngsters chant so joyfully had gruesome beginnings. It seems likely that it was a skit on the Great Plague which hit Britain in approximately 1664. The 'ring-a-roses' was the mark on the skin which indicated a victim of the dreaded disease. The 'pocket full

of posies' were the 'magic' herbs that were carried in the pocket to
ward off the virus. 'Atishoo, atishoo' referred to a cold, which
was one of the symptoms, and 'we all fall down' meant that the
person had either collapsed being very ill, or was dead!

The plague was the most dangerous of all the diseases which
affected our ancestors, as very few who caught it survived.
Daniel Defoe records that many died in the streets, not knowing
that they were victims, so quickly did it strike. The disease swept
across Europe to British ports and spread through dirty streets
and houses, and open sewers. We know now, of course, that it
was the flea-bearing rat that carried the virus, but in Stuart times
it was thought that cats, dogs and other domestic animals were
the cause of the trouble. During an epidemic all domestic animals
caught wandering in the streets were killed, thus removing the
only possible deterrents of the disease, while the rats were
allowed to go free and multiply in the ramshackled houses.

Here is a charm recited by North country people to rid their
houses of vermin:

> Ratton and mouse,
> Lea' the puir woman's house,
> Gang aw' over t'mill,
> And there ye'll get y're fill.

The 'magic' herbs were often carried in a pomander and consisted of rue, elder leaves, cloves, cinnamon, nutmeg, onions and
the proverbial unicorn's horn. The infection was thought to be
kept at bay by chewing rhubarb, lovage or tobacco. Herbal
recipes were believed to cure all ills and even doctors practised
cures involving magic, for instance, the wearing of an Eastern
hyacinth stone was thought to be protective. The way to reduce
fever was to apply the half of a pigeon to the soles of the feet! The
colour red was believed to give protection against disease and
especially in times of the plague people slept in red beds, with
curtains and covers to match, and surrounded themselves with
as many red objects as possible! This is probably the origin of 'red
flannel'.

The planting of box hedges was considered a safe way to keep
infection at bay. In Dorset today certain box hedges can still be
seen, which were planted in haste in the sixteenth and seventeenth centuries in an effort to keep away the plague.

At first, people in London did not take much notice of the disease, for they were used to small outbreaks and protected themselves as they had been taught. However, as the weather grew warmer, it was evident that this illness could wipe out whole cities. Those who could left the big towns, thus probably spreading the disease. At one time a thousand people a day died in London alone. In certain cases a member of a family suffering from the plague was left with his family inside their house and the door nailed up from the outside. They were left to die or survive within their own home. If they did not die of the disease then they probably starved to death, for no organized relief was available. The dead cart came along the streets each day, and the dead were piled into the cart, to be taken to a communal burial ground outside the City wall. There was a law which said that no one who died of this disease could be buried on consecrated ground.

The King and his Court, of course, left London in times of plague. In fact, in the Stuart era the royal party spent most of the time away from London, only returning for civic functions. Theatres and coffee houses were closed, sometimes for over a year when disease was rife.

Cornish children sing another verse of 'Ring-a-ring o' roses':

> *Ashes in the river,*
> *Ashes in the sea;*
> *We all jump up,*
> *In a one, two, three.*

This most certainly refers to the Great Fire of London in 1666. Although the fire was very frightening and much valuable property and many works of art were lost, it had its beneficial aspect in that it destroyed the last traces of the plague. The wooden houses burned so fiercely that people were at a loss to know how to check the flames. There was no fire brigade, so, after a while, buildings were pulled down adjacent to the fire, in order to create a gap.

The fire started in Pudding Lane, near London Bridge and at first people did not attempt to put it out, because they were used to small fires and took it for granted that it would die out quickly by itself. However this was not to be the case. Soon it had spread beyond all control and the fire raged for four days, a gusty wind spreading flames and sparks at an alarming rate. At last the King

12. The Fire of London – burning of old St Paul's and Newgate.

and his brother took charge of operations, and gunpowder was used to blow up buildings near the flames. Although many buildings, including the old St Paul's Cathedral and four hundred streets had been lost, only six people were killed.

Samuel Pepys wrote in his diary about the fire: 'Everybody endeavouring to remove their goods, and flinging them into the river, or bringing them into lighters that lay off; poor people staying in their houses as long as till the very fire touched them, and then running into boats, or clambouring from one pair of stairs to another. And among other things the poor pigeons... were loathe to leave their houses, but hovered about the windows, and balconies till they... burned their wings and fell down.'

To commemorate the Great Fire a monument was built close to Pudding Lane, where it was supposed to have started. The Monument is a pillar 202 feet high with golden 'flames' coming out of a bowl at the top, designed by Sir Christopher Wren. Another couplet which reminds us of this catastrophe is:

> *In sixteen hundred and sixty-six,*
> *London burnt like rotten sticks.*

SIR CHRISTOPHER WREN

After the Great Fire, Sir Christopher Wren (1632-1728) was given the tremendous task of planning and rebuilding the whole City of London. He was a learned man, having been educated at Westminster and Oxford, and was a Professor of Astronomy at the age of twenty-four. He possessed so many attributes and interests that he was over thirty before he began disigning buildings. His plan of a domed St Paul's Cathedral caused much comment and interest at the time, and the building itself was described as a work of genius:

> *Sir Christopher Wren*
> *Said 'I am going to dine with some men,*
> *If anybody calls –*
> *Say I am designing St Paul's.*

The dome of St Paul's is in fact made up of two domes – one inside and one outside. In between there is a brick cone which takes the weight. The structural work is hidden on all sides by a clever design and there is an iron chain girding the bottom of the dome to prevent the structure from spreading outwards. It is recorded that Wren was so interested in the building of the dome that he was hauled up in a basket three or four times a week to watch progress. He was thirty-six years old when work first started on the cathedral, and seventy-eight when the last stone was laid. Wren was buried in St Paul's and his memorial tablet has an inscription in Latin, which in translation reads: 'If you seek his monument, look about you.'

BESSY BELL

> *Bessy Bell and Mary Gray.*
> *They were two bonny lassies;*
> *They built their house upon the lea,*
> *And covered it with rushes.*

This rhyme has its roots in events that happened during the Great Plague. Scottish people will perhaps know the verse well and the story behind it. It tells of two friends who fled in 1645 from the plague that had broken out in Perth, seven miles from their home. It was the custom in those days to avoid outbreaks of disease by leaving the big cities and taking refuge in the country. Mary Gray was the daughter of the Laird of Lednock and local records substantiate this, but Bessie Bell is not so easy to trace and may have been a traditional name. The two girls built themselves a bower or shelter in a pleasant spot called Beaky Burn, just before the stream flows into the river Almond at Dronach-haugh. A sweetheart of Mary Gray brought them food each day and the story goes that one day he brought a rich handkerchief and a pearl necklace as gifts. He had purchased them from a Jew, who in his turn had stolen them from a person dying of the plague. Soon Mary and Bessie contracted the disease, and died in their bower, as did the boyfriend too. Here is the Scottish ballad that relates all the facts:

> *Oh Bessie Bell an' Mary Gray,*
> *They were two bonnie lasses,*
> *They biggit a bower on yon burn-brae,*
> *And theekit it owre wi' rashes.*

> *They theekit it owre wi' rashes green,*
> *The happit it roun' wi' heather;*
> *But the pest cam' frae the burrows-toun*
> *An' slew them baith tegither.*

> *They thocht to lie in Methven kirk*
> *Beside their gentle kin;*
> *But they maun lie in Dron-haugh*
> *An' beik forment the sin* [sun].

> *Oh Bessie Bell an' Mary Gray,*
> *They were two bonnie lassies,*
> *They biggit a bower on yon burn-brae,*
> *And theekit owre wi' rashes.*

The plague raged over Perth and the surrounding countryside, destroying practically everyone. The few who survived became immune and were called the 'cleansers', because the job of burying the dead and tending the stricken fell to them. As in most places, people who died from the 'pest', as it was called in Scotland, were not buried on consecrated ground, so the banks of the river Almond served as a communal burial place. The site of the grave of the two girls was marked with a heap of stones. Over a hundred years later a laird of Lednock removed all rubbish and enclosed the grave within a wall, laying a double gravestone with the names of the two girls engraved upon it. He planted flowering shrubs and created a beautiful memorial on the small area of 'classic ground'. Another laird, probably in the Victorian era, placed a large stone slab over the graves with the inscription 'They lived, they loved, they died'. He then surrounded the spot with heavy iron railings and yew trees. It can still be seen today.

STREET CRIES

Come buy my gudgeons fine and new,
Old cloaths to change for earthenware.

The idea of exchange and mart must go back to primitive times, and barter was a sure way of increasing the range of goods available to small communities. The pedlar was a familiar and welcome figure on the horizon to people living in isolated homesteads. Non-perishable goods such as salt, spices, buttons, threads and ivory trickled through the country by means of wandering vendors in Roman and Saxon times. Craftsmen, too, such as tinkers and potters travelled from one village to another providing a repair service to those who needed it. There were, of course, markets and fairs held in the towns, but the roads were poor, and robbers and beggars desperate for food and clothing lurked in many areas. It was safer and easier for ordinary folk to wait until the hawker visited them.

Each vendor had his own special cry to arouse interest in his wares. We cannot pin-point exactly when any particular street call came into being, in the same way that we cannot say for sure when many of the older traditional rhymes were first used. We can only assume that they originated during a certain period of history.

London became the hub of wandering pedlars during the Middle Ages and, as the city increased in population, more and more street vendors flocked to it to seek their fortune. By the Stuart era the lanes of London echoed and re-echoed with the melodious calls of hawkers selling a variety of goods. In fact a writer of the times went so far as to describe the streets of London as 'Bedlam let loose'. The nature of the goods sold, dates the cry to a certain extent and obviously many of the street cries remembered today must be a good deal older than the Stuart period. Others, of course, were not used until a later date. This cry, recorded in the early part of the nineteenth century, by J. Rusher, a printer and bookseller of Banbury as mentioned earlier, could be very old indeed:

> *Here oranges sweet,*
> *From China they come,*
> *Here apples and pears,*
> *And sweet orline plum.*

Nell Gwyn was once an orange vendor, and it may have been a chant similar to this that she used to advertise her wares. We know that oranges were grown in China before the birth of Christ and that they were not grown in Europe (Italy) until the sixteenth century. Apples were cultivated from wild crab apples and the Romans brought several different species to Britain during the occupation. Another apple cry went:

> *Here are fine golden pippins,*
> *Who'll buy them, who'll buy?*
> *Nobody in London sells better than I,*
> *Who'll buy them, who'll buy?*

Pippins, Pearmains and Costards were some of the species introduced by the Romans. The costermonger was originally called a costardmonger, which meant he was an apple vendor.

Pears also have been cultivated from early times in this country and the plum probably came from the sloe, the bitter black fruit of the black thorn. Cherry plums were first found in the Caucasus mountains, and the damson originated in Damascus, Syria. Other fruits such as strawberries and gooseberries became favourites with the public later:

> *Buy ripe Strawberries, fine Strawberries*
> *Ripe Strawberries, ripe Strawberries, O!*
> *In lovely beds, by nature taught,*
> *The Strawberries are displayed,*
> *And hence for us, to market brought,*
> *By this industrious maid.*

Although wild strawberries have grown in Europe since prehistoric times and were cultivated in France from the fourteenth century, it was not until the nineteenth century that the juicy fruit as we know it today was produced. The fruit was called hautbois and street-sellers used to call out 'hotboys'

> Here strawberries, the best,
> Nice Hautboys fresh and fine;
> With cream by all confest,
> Delicious vespertine.

> Buy my fine Gooseberries, fine Gooseberries,
> Threepence a quart, ripe Gooseberries:
> Ripe Gooseberries in town you'll buy,
> As cheap as can be!
> Of many sorts you hear the cry;
> Pray purchase, Sir, of me!

Gooseberries are so named because a sauce made from the fruit was eaten with roast goose centuries ago. The fruit was cultivated in England during Tudor times and became great favourites with the cottage gardener during the eighteenth century. In fact, in Lancashire many gooseberry clubs were formed, and competitions were organised to ascertain the largest fruit in the vicinity. One trick used to produce a large gooseberry was to feed the plant with sugar solution through a slit in the stalk.

This poem written by Christina Rossetti has immortalized the cherry vendor as observed in the streets many decades ago:

> 'Cherries, ripe cherries', the old woman cried,
> In her snowy apron and basket beside,
> And the little boys came, eyes shining, cheeks red,
> To buy bags of cherries to eat with their bread.

The cry of the vegetable lady went:

> Potatoes and apples
> And peas, the fat marrow,
> Dame Durgin can sell you,
> From her well-stored barrow.

Peas and apples were commonly eaten in Roman times and before, but potatoes, surprisingly enough, were not introduced to Britain until Elizabethan times and were not widely eaten until the seventeenth century, although they were welcomed in Ireland in the previous century. During the industrial revolution and after, a cheap and easily-prepared food had to be found to feed the workers, and it is from this time that the potato took the place of bread as a staple of the British diet.

Fish and meat, unless dried and salted, were commodities that relied on quick sales. Boats bringing fish sailed up the river Thames and fishermen sold their catch quite often straight from the decks. This is how Billingsgate Fish Market originated. Fish vendors often sold their wares whilst they were still alive to ensure complete freshness:

> *Sprats alive oh!*
> *Buy my sprats alive!*
> *Dame Dolly's Shrill cry*
> *Repeated by brats*
> *Kind customers buy*
> *Dame Dolly's live sprats.*

Oysters are another delicacy which have been eaten and enjoyed since ancient times. Many oyster shells have been found buried in Roman camps and it is a well-known fact that, when Julius Ceasar invaded Britain, one of his first pleasures was to hunt for pearls obtained from the freshwater variety found round the shores of Britain. Here are two cries used by oyster sellers:

> *Buy my Oysters, live Oysters, O!*
> *Twelve pence a pack, Oysters, O!*
> *My fine Native Oysters,*
> *Fresh and fine are the best,*
> *For court and for cloisters,*
> *For yourselves or your guest.*

This verse describes the oyster vendor:

> *From Billingsgate industrious Will,*
> *Brings Oysters from the town,*
> *Thro' frost and rain he feels no ill,*
> *But cries them up and down.*

Cooked meat encased in piecrust has been a popular food commodity from early times. Simple Simon tried to purchase a pie without any cash, Jack Horner found the contents of his pie very rewarding and the pie in Sing a Song of Sixpence contained a very strange filling, too.

The 'pig pye man' was a familiar hawker in days gone by. He,
like many other street sellers, was a disabled serviceman, who
took up street vending when the army had no more use for him.
He sold pastry pigs filled with sugar and currants to tempt hungry children. The unfortunate Tom the Piper's son, who 'stole a
pig and away did run', took his pig from the pig pye man's tray. It
certainly explains the mystery of how a boy could eat a live pig, as
we had all been led to believe! Here is one of the pig pye man's
chants:

> *A long tail'd pig,*
> *Or a short tail'd pig,*
> *Or a pig without any tail;*
>> *A sow pig,*
>> *Or a boar pig,*
>> *Or a pig with a curly tail.*
> *Take hold of the tail*
> *And eat off his head,*
> *And then you'll be sure*
> *The pig hog is dead.*

Similarly, the man who cried:

> *Young lambs to sell, young lambs to sell,*
> *If I had as much money as I could tell,*
> *I never would cry young lambs to sell.*

was not in fact selling live lambs, but toys made out of cotton-
wool, horn and glue.

Hot cross buns, as mentioned in the Roman section, is now a
firmly established nursery rhyme and was a street cry years ago:

> *Hot cross buns, hot cross buns,*
> *One a penny, two a penny, hot cross buns.*
> *If you have no daughters, give them to your sons,*
> *One a penny, two a penny, hot cross buns.*

Another couplet which was sung in the last century and before
went:

> *If you have none of these pretty little elves,*
> *Then you can do no better than to eat them yourselves.*

A street cry recorded in 1733 also mentions these spiced cakes:

> *Good Friday comes this month, the old woman runs;*
> *With one a penny, two a penny, hot cross buns.*

Gingerbread was a sweetmeat that was in much demand years ago, and probably became popular when ginger and other spices first became available in England. As mentioned in the section on fairs, gingerbread markets were held in Birmingham and London, and this charming cry is reminiscent of those times:

> *Smiling girls, rosy boys,*
> *Come and buy my little toys;*
> *Monkeys made of gingerbread,*
> *And sugar horses painted red.*

The muffin man was a familiar sight in the streets of London until World War I. Francis Grose, the historian, described them in the eighteenth century as traders with an ancient past. Muffins are spongy, round cakes, eaten toasted or warmed with butter. A tray of hot muffins covered with a baize cloth was carried by the muffin man on his head, leaving a hand free to ring a bell. Then he would call:

> *My bell I keep ringing,*
> *And walk about merrily singing,*
> *My muffins, my muffins.*

Today, of course, the muffin man can no longer be found in London, but muffins can still be bought in winter at bakers and supermarkets. All that is left to remind us of the muffin man are verses still chanted by children:

> *Have you seen the muffin man,*
> *The muffin man, the muffin man,*
> *Have you seen the muffin man,*
> *That lives in Drury Lane?*
>
> *Yes, I've seen the muffin man,*
> *The muffin man, the muffin man,*
> *Yes, I've seen the muffin man,*
> *Who lives in Drury Lane.*

The meat and fur of the rabbit was in great demand centuries ago, and the poor folk relied on this animal to eke out their meagre fare. Rabbits were introduced to Britain in approximately the twelfth century and soon became pests to the farmer, and a boon to the labourer. Here are two street cries of the rabbit man:

Here I am with my rabbits
Hanging on my pole,
The finest Hampshire rabbits
That e'er crept from a hole.

Here rabbits wild and tame,
Here rabbits great and small,
From warren-royal came,
I wish to please you all.

Milk has been used by man since the Stone Age and the milk vendor must have been a familiar sight for centuries past. It was not until the mid-nineteenth century that it was discovered that pasteurization killed bacteria in milk, which had hitherto given rise to many diseases, the most prevalent being tuberculosis. This street cry was recorded by J. G. Rusher in his book *Cries of Banbury and London* and the milk was sold from pails carried on a yoke, and had not been treated in any way:

The milk-woman's here,
With pails to avow,
Her cream and her milk
Are fresh from the cow.

Herbs were in much demand and although they were grown in cottage gardens, the street vendor provided many varieties. They were used for flavouring food, scenting clothes, medical potions or as lucky charms to ward off disease – hence the proverbial 'pocket full of posies'. The call of the lavender seller must be one of the best remembered. Set to a melodious refrain the cry:

Who'll buy my lavender, fresh lavender,
Sweet blooming lavender, who'll buy?

was once heard frequently in the quiet squares of western and central London. Mitcham in Surrey, the traditional home of lavender, has probably been growing this commodity for four hundred years or more and has, therefore, developed special cries:

Who'll buy my Mitcham lavender?
It makes your handkerchief so nice,
Who'll buy my blooming lavender,
Sixteen branches for a penny.

Come all you young ladies and make no delay,
I gathered my lavender fresh from Mitcham today.

Will you buy my sweet blooming lavender?
There are sixteen dark blue branches a penny.

You buy it once, you buy it twice;
It will make your clothes smell sweet and nice.

Who'll buy my sweet blooming lavender?
Sixteen full branches for a penny.

Lavender grows wild in Mediterranean areas and other parts of Europe. It has been used for its oil as well as its scent for many centuries. Even today the oil from some species is used in the painting of porcelain and as a medicine for the treatment of animals.

The girl who cried, 'Sweet Lilies of the Valley', was probably not selling her wares for decoration. According to John Gerard's book, *The Herbal or General Historie of Plantes* (1597) this plant grew wild on the heaths around London – Hampstead and Bushey in particular. The flowers of the lily of the valley were used in distilled wine to ease gout, dumb palsy and a failing memory. Also, it was said that, if the flowers were bottled in water and left on an ant hill for one month, the water applied externally took away the pain of gout!

The herbs mentioned in this next traditional rhyme are of special interest:

Here's fine rosemary, sage and thyme,
Come buy my ground ivy.
Here's feverfew, gilliflowers and rue,
Come buy my knotted marjoram ho!
Come buy my mint, my fine green mint.
Here's lavender for your clothes,
Here's parsley and winter savoury,
And heartsease which all do choose,
Here's balm, and hissop and cinquefoil
Let none despise the merry cries
Of famous London Town.

Here's penny royal and marygolds
Come buy my sage of virtue O!
Come buy my wormwood and mugwort.
Here's fine herbs of every sort,
And southern wood that's very good,
Dandelion and horseleek,
Here's Dragon's tongue and horehound;
Let none despise the merry cries
Of famous London Town.

Rosemary, a sweet smelling plant, was in great demand years ago. Not only was it used to sweeten clothes, as was lavender, but it was also thought to bring comfort to those who were mentally fatigued, to restore speech to those stricken with the 'dumb palsie' and above all to strengthen the memory, which is why rosemary is often called 'remembrance'. The crushed flowers of the plant taken in distilled water early in the morning was a guaranteed cure for all these ills.

Sage was another commodity that was very popular, not so much because of its flavour as it is today, but for its marvellous medical powers! It was said to be good for the head and brain, quickening the senses and curing shaking and trembling. Used as snuff it was effective for drawing phlegm 'out of the head' and it was also taken for spitting of blood, serpents' bites and pains in the side.

Thyme, as far as can be ascertained, was only used for food flavouring, and so was winter savoury, which belongs to the same plant group.

Ground ivy, celandine and daisies, stamped and strained and mixed with rose water, gave relief to smarting eyes if a few drops were applied. Feverfew, a weed that grows on waste ground, dried and ground to powder and taken with honey and sweet wine, was thought to cure vertigo and general fainting fits, and was also good for melancholy! I have a suspicion that the wine and honey would have been just as effective if taken neat!

Rue, like feverfew, is a bitter herb and was only used for medicinal purposes. Pickled rue was eaten in order to improve the sight and also, dropped into the ears, to cure ear ache.

Sweet marjoram was a herb which, it seems, had many uses. It was effective against rheumatism if boiled in water and the concoction drunk. It was also supposed to cure cramps, convulsions, toothache, and the leaves dried and mingled with honey, made a healing ointment for sores and bruises.

Heartsease, a form of wild pansy, was a small flower usually blue, yellow or white and was the forerunner of the cultivated garden pansy that is grown today. True to its name, it was supposed to cure all complaints of the heart.

Balm or bawme had many uses. It grew wild or in cultivation and was said to delight bees, which produced much honey from it. The hives, if rubbed on the outside with the leaves, would keep the bees together and prevent swarming. The leaves, too, if drunk with wine would prevent melancholy, and if applied externally would cure snake bites or bites from mad dogs; also they were very effective in stemming blood from a wound if pressed to it.

Cinquefoil is a type of five-leaved clover, and was used as a lucky charm. Penny-royal is a grass which grows wild and in great quantities on English soil. The leaves dried and cast into unclean water were thought to purify it. Also, garlands of this weed worn round the head prevented giddiness and fainting, it was thought.

The common garden marigold as we know it today was regarded as very useful. The yellow petals were dried and frequently added to broths for flavouring. The French marigold, however, was regarded as a poisonous plant and was never used for medicinal purposes or as flavouring for food.

Nettle tops were and still are used in winemaking, and water-cress was grown, as now, for its nutritious value.

Wormwood and mugwort were both names given to the same plant used for medicinal cures. Dandelion leaves were used in salads and winemaking, as today. The dandelion took its name from the Normans who called it *dent de lion,* because its leaves were indented and jagged like a row of lion's teeth.

Dragon's tongue is a plant with a bitter juice that was used in medicine, and horseleek or horsetail is a plant with bristling leaves that was used for scouring pans by housewives, which is why it is sometimes known as pewterwort. Horehound is another plant with bitter juices that was used as a cough medicine.

Broom, which grows wild on commons and heaths in Britain, has a long and useful history. The bush, not to be confused with gorse, can grow as high as five feet. The Latin name is *scoparius*, which means twig-broom. Sweeping brooms made out of the green stems of the bush have been in use for centuries and the word 'broom' comes from this. Here is a version of the *Broom Squire's Song*:

> *Here's a large one for the lady,*
> *Here's a small one for the baby;*
> *Come buy my pretty lady,*
> *Come buy o' me a broom.*

King Henry II threaded the yellow flowers of broom through his helmet when he went into battle, so that he could be easily recognised by his men. The flower was named *planta genista*, from which the royal house of Plantagenet derived its name. King Henry VIII drank broom tea to cure his indigestion, and even today a powerful heart tonic is extracted from the young shoots of the plant.

Many commodities sold by the wandering pedlar have interesting origins. The button seller, for instance, is an ancient figure and here is his cry, as recorded in the nineteenth century:

> *Buttons a farthing a pair,*
> *Come, who will buy them of me?*
> *They are round and sound and pretty*
> *And fit for the girls of the city.*
> *Come, who will buy them of me?*
> *Buttons a farthing a pair.*

Buttons have been used since prehistoric times and we know that the Beaker people who lived in Britain in 1800 BC had buttons of jet, bone and sandstone. Later, the Romans fastened their garments with brooches, and buttons were not generally used until the eleventh century. They were then made of precious materials, such as gold, silvergilt, coral, bronze and crystal, and were used to fasten shoes as well as clothes, and were also ornamental. Only men wore buttons, for it was not until the mid-nineteenth century that women took up the fashion. From then onwards the button industry flourished to an even greater extent, as the fourth line of the verse bears out. British buttons have been exported since Elizabethan times, since which time they have been renowned for their quality.

Another hawker selling much sought-after wares was the haberdasher. Each commodity was treated with respect and used with care. To lose a needle, for example, centuries ago was regarded as a major misfortune:

> Here, ladies, are cotton,
> Combs, needles and laces;
> For gentlemen razors,
> And shoestrings and braces.

Cotton was not commonly used in Britain until after the industrial revolution. Before this, linen and wool thread were used. Combs made out of bone or tortoiseshell were considered a luxury, and it was only the moderately rich who could afford one. Needles with eyes have been used since the Stone Age and were made out of polished bone or crude metal. Monks took up needle-making in medieval times, and needles were made in monasteries, the most well-known of which was near Redditch in Worcestershire. Today Redditch is still famous for its needle industry.

Razors, too, have a long history – they were used before the time of Christ and were fashioned from flint or metal. Lace was a rare luxury before Tudor times, as it came chiefly from Spain. Catherine of Aragon, when divorced by Henry VIII, spent much of her leisure-time teaching the art of lace-making to cottage workers in Bedfordshire (see page 144). Consequently, English lace was available to the public at a reasonable price from this time onwards.

Shoelaces made out of crude twine or leather thonging have existed since the first shoe was made, but trouser braces were not generally worn in Britain until the nineteenth century. At first they were made of leather or twine, and later of elasticated material.

Ready-made new clothes were a luxury that not many of the poorer classes could afford, therefore the cry of the Old Clothes' Man was welcomed by many:

> This man cries Old Clothes!
> To buy or to sell;
> Hats, coats, shoes and hose,
> What more I can't tell.

Clothes were often exchanged, which was a particularly

unhygienic method, as it often transmitted disease from one family to another.

The sand man who cried:

> *White sand, grey sand,*
> *Who'll buy my white sand,*
> *Who'll buy my grey sand?*
> *Come buy, come buy!*

reminds us that, before blotting paper was used to dry ink, sand was sprinkled over manuscripts and letters for this purpose.

As previously mentioned, many wandering pedlars provided repair services, which were welcomed by the community. The chair mender, for instance, repaired all kinds of wicker and rush furniture:

> *Old Chairs to mend, Old Chairs to mend;*
> *If I had as much money as I could spend,*
> *I would never cry 'Old Chairs to mend'.*

The wheelwright, too, must have offered a valuable service, especially to farmers:

> *The wheelwright makes his wheel*
> *For carriage strong and good;*
> *Of iron, or wood or steel,*
> *To gain a livelihood.*

The shoeblack, usually seen in towns, provided a service which was very welcome to the gentry. Leather shoes have been cleaned and protected against weather conditions for generations. Beeswax or animal fat was generally used as 'blacking':

> *Here's Finiky Hawkes,*
> *As busy as any;*
> *Will well black your shoes,*
> *And charge but a penny.*

The courier or messenger became the postman early in the nineteenth century, and mail was delivered regularly. The word 'post' means a position of trust and this is why the courier was originally called the postman:

> *The postman hurries forth to bring your daily news;*
> *From east, west, south or north,*
> *To instruct and to amuse.*

In the early days postmen travelled on foot and carried a horn, which he blew when entering a community, so that citizens could come and claim their mail. This practice is reminiscent of the town crier, who rang a bell and cried 'Oh Yez, Oh Yez' before shouting the daily news.

In most large towns refuse collection was organized by the nineteenth century, but it was usual to pay the dustman for his services on every visit:

> *Now the dustman's arrived,*
> *To earn him a crust, O!*
> *To take off your refuse,*
> *So down with the dust, O!*

In those early days the dustmen or refuse collectors wore hats with a large back piece attached, which protected their heads and shoulders from the dust and dirt. It was not until much later that the service became automatic, with householders paying for the service out of the rates.

The role of the busker and street entertainer is an ancient one, as the three cries below bear witness:

> *The tumbler's expert,*
> *On feet or on hands;*
> *Turns summersets, vaults,*
> *Or on his head stands.*

> *The drummer goes round*
> *T' entice if he can,*
> *Young master and miss*
> *To his caravan.*

These two cries like many others presented in this section can be found in Rusher's publication. The third advertisement for entertainment can be found in 'The Oxford Nursery Rhyme Book'.

> *Punch and Judy*
> *Fought for a pie;*
> *Punch gave Judy*
> *A knock in the eye.*
> *Says Punch to Judy,*
> *Will you have any more?*
> *Says Judy to Punch,*
> *My eye is too sore.*

The character of Punch was based on a roguish Italian actor named Pulcinella who lived in the sixteenth century. He was so popular that by the seventeenth century puppet showmen all over Europe had taken up the role he had played and portrayed it in puppet form. Charles II was a great admirer of Mr Punch and his cast. It is not known exactly when Punch and Judy, and other characters such as Toby, the dog and the hangman, came into being, but by the Victorian era this children's show, as we know it today, was very popular.

Wandering pedlars were often homeless, hungry and desperate, despite their cheerful faces and melodious songs. Although it is beneficial to treasure and remember street cries as such, the community as a whole must be thankful that the demand for travelling vendors has more or less ceased. The cry of the beggar heard centuries ago endorses this sentiment:

> *Pity a poor old man,*
> *Who trembles at your door*
> *His days the shortest span,*
> *Relieve and bless your store.*

The one street vendor very much in evidence, in modern times, whether we like it or not, is the ice cream man. His van and music-box chimes can be heard and seen daily in almost every street. Italian ice cream sellers made an appearance on the streets early in this century. Their gaily coloured barrows were usually stationary and many of us will remember the cry of 'Stop me and buy one', heard before the last war.

RULE BRITANNIA

Rule Britannia is another traditional song which originated in the Stuart period. In 1707 Scotland and England were united under one monarch, namely Queen Anne. A Scottish poet, James Thompson, helped to establish Britannia as a symbol of unity in the United Kingdom by his song *Rule Britannia*, which appeared in a masque called *Alfred* performed in London in 1740. Afterwards the song was published separately and was received with such enthusiasm that it almost became a second national anthem.

The figure of Britannia, which appeared on old British pennies, is an emblem of Britain. She is a graceful woman wearing a helmet, and holding a trident to show she rules the waves and a shield with a Union Jack on it. Britannia was the name given to Romanized Britain during the Roman occupation and the Roman coin used in Britain at that time had the same symbol engraved upon it. The idea was not used again until Charles II's reign, when the womanly figure was engraved on coins once more. Today, the figure of Britannia can be seen on a fifty pence piece and on the backs of paper money.

Dr Arne is credited with the revival of this national song and he may have re-arranged the words:

> *When Britain first at Heaven's command,*
> *Arose from out the azure main,*
> *Arose from out the azure main,*
> *This was the charter, the charter of the land,*
> *And guardian angels sang this strain:*
>   *'Rule Britannia! Britannia rule the waves;*
>   *Britons never, never, never will be slaves'.*
>
> *The nations not so blest as thee,*
> *Must in their turns to tyrants fall,*
> *Must in their turns to tyrants fall,*
> *While thou shalt flourish, shall flourish great and free,*
> *The dread and envy of them all.*
>   *'Rule Britannia, etc.*
>
> *Still more majestic shalt thou rise,*
> *More dreadful from each foreign stroke,*
> *More dreadful from each foreign stroke,*
> *As the loud blast, the loud blast that tears the skies,*
> *Serves but to root thy native oak.*
>   *'Rule Britannia, etc.*

These are the first three stanzas of the song, which contains six verses in all.

HANOVERIAN

THE VICAR OF BRAY

Queen Anne died in 1714 and George of Hanover was invited to become George I of England. From the words of the following song, *The Vicar of Bray*, we can trace the fluctuations of the monarchy as regards religion and politics from Charles I's reign:

In good King Charles' golden days
When loyalty no harm meant,
A furious High-Church Man I was
And so I gained Preferment,
Unto my flock I daily preached,
Kings are of God appointed
And damn'd are those who dare resist
Or touch the Lord's Anointed.

And this is Law, I will maintain
Until my dying day, Sir,
That whatsoever King shall reign
I will be the Vicar of Bray, Sir.

When Royal James Possest the Crown
And Popery grew in fashion,
The Penal Law I hunted down
And read the Declaration;
The Church of Rome I found would fit,
Full well my Constitution
And I had been a Jesuit,
But for the Revolution.

And this is Law, etc.

When William our Deliverer came
To heal the Nation's Grievance,
I turned the Cat in Pan again
And swore to him allegiance;
Old Principles I did remove,
Set conscience at a distance,
Passive Obedience is a Joke,
A jest is Non-resistance.

And this is Law, etc.

When glorious Anne became our Queen,
The Church of England's Glory,
Another face of things was seen
And I became a Tory;
Occasional Conformists base
I damn'd and Moderation,
And thought the Church in danger was
From such Prevarication.

And this is Law, etc.

When George in Pudding time cam' o'er
And moderate Men looked big, Sir,
My Principles I chang'd once more
And so became a Whig, Sir;
And thus Preferment I procur'd
From our Faith's Great Defender,
And almost every day abjur'd
The Pope and the Pretender.

And this is Law, etc.

The Illustrious House of Hanover
And Protestant Succession,
To these I lustily will swear,
Whilst they can keep possession;
For in my Faith and Loyalty
I never once will falter,
But George my Lawful King shall be,
Except the Times should alter.

And this is Law, etc.

This well-known song is generally thought to be anonymous, but there is a theory that it was written by an army officer in the reign of George I. It was based on an earlier ballad entitled *The Religious Turncoat*. The original Vicar of Bray, whose determination to keep his appointment became proverbial, was said to be Simon Aleyn, who lived in Tudor times and was Vicar of Bray between 1538 and 1565. He intended to keep his position and changed his religion to suit the official faith in favour at the time. He was 'taxed for an inconstant changeling' and his reply to this was that he had always kept true to his principle – to live and die Vicar of Bray.

GEORGIAN

Here lies Fred,
Who was alive and is dead.
If it had been his father,
I would much rather;
If it had been his brother,
Still better than another;
If it had been his sister,
No one would have missed her;
If it had been the whole generation,
So much better for the nation,
But as it's only Fred,
Who was alive and is dead,
Why there is no more to be said!

Frederick was a son of George I, who was hit accidentally by a cricket ball and subsequently died. The author of the above verse was obviously a Jacobite with a sense of humour. Another well-known song having strong Jacobite connections is *Tom he was a Piper's son*:

Tom he was a Piper's son,
He learnt to play when he was young,
The only tune that he could play,
Was 'over the hills and far away,
Over the hills and great way off,
The wind shall blow my top knot off'

The phrase 'over the hills and far away' has been used for many centuries and is a good deal older than this period. The tune, also, is considered to be of great antiquity. In 1719 a plot was evolved to overthrow the English government with the help of Spain, in favour of James, the Old Pretender. However, this plot came to nothing, and it is said that Scottish pipers played this older version as a disappointed dirge:

> There was a wind, it came to me
> Over the south and over the sea,
> And it has blown my corn and hay
> Over the hills and far away.
> But, though it has left me bare indeed
> And blew my bonnet off my head,
> There's something hid in Highland Brae,
> It has not blown my sword away.
> Then o'er the hills and over dales,
> Over all England and thro' Wales,
> The broadsword yet shall bear the sway,
> Over the hills and far away!

SOCIAL COMMENT

One poet in particular at the beginning of the eighteenth century was responsible for many well-known proverbial sayings. Alexander Pope was the man who made famous such lines as 'A little learning is a dangerous thing', 'For fools rush in where angels fear to tread', 'Hope springs eternal in the human breast', and a line which describes the calibre of Pope's work adequately, 'What oft was thought, but ne'er so well expressed'.

During this period, in spite of many wars, the English gentry flourished and grew rich, while the fate of the poor and unemployed grew steadily worse. Thompson, the creator of *Rule Britannia*, wrote:

> The Country teems with Wealth,
> And property assures the Swain,
> Pleas'd and unwearied in his guarded toil.

An anonymous satirist of the day elucidated the attitude of the governing rich towards the toiling poor:

> *Shall those who drudge from morn till night*
> *Pretend to talk of wrong and right?*
> *No, no, the sweat that toil produces,*
> *Exhausts the intellectual juices!*

Pope, also, had a very clear message:

> *God cannot love (says Blunt with tearless eyes)*
> *The wretch he starves' – and piously denies.*
> *But the good Bishop, with a meeker air,*
> *Admits, and leaves them, Providence's care.*

Some attempts were made to provide shelter and work for the unemployed and homeless. Institutions which were pleasant enough places to begin with, were set up in the West country and in Norfolk, but, as time went by, enthusiasm and money supplies waned and these workhouses became places to dread. Here is part of *The Village: Village Life* by George Crabbe which illustrates this:

> *There children dwell who know no Parent's care;*
> *Parents, who know no Children's love, dwell there;*
> *Heartbroken Matrons on their joyless bed,*
> *Foresaken Wives and Mothers never wed,*
> *Dejected Widows with unheeded tears,*
> *And crippled Age with more than childhood fears;*
> *The Lame, the Blind, and far the happiest they!*
> *The moping Idiot and the Madman gay. .*

After the Great Fire, London increased in size every year, as can be seen from this verse of *Time's Changes* by James Bramston, published in 1729:

> *Where's Troy, and where's the Maypole in the Strand?*
> *Pease, cabbages and turnips once grew where*
> *Now stands New Bond Street and a newer Square;*
> *Such piles of buildings now rise up and down,*
> *London itself seems going out of Town.*
> *Our fathers crossed from Fulham in a Wherry,*
> *Their sons enjoy a Bridge at Putney Ferry.*

England's capital was notorious for vices of all sorts, and law and order were almost non-existent: robbers roamed the streets, press gangs and slave labour kidnappers lurked in dark alleys, drunkeness was commonplace, and there was an abundance of brothels. John Gay in his poem *Trivia* described Drury Lane thus:

> *O may thy virtue guard thee thro' the roads*
> *Of Drury's mazy courts and dark abodes!*
> *The harlot's guileful paths who nightly stand*
> *Where Catherine Street descends into the Strand.*

Even George II was accosted by a thief, while walking alone in the garden of Kensington Palace. He lost his watch, money and shoe buckles.

Most people turned a blind eye to the shocking state of the prisons in this era. The debtor's prisons were in fact places of iniquity, filth and death, and the warders were usually cruel, depraved men, who were only helpful when they were bribed. Here is an excerpt from a poem by John Thompson, written when at least one human 'monster' was punished for his treatment of prisoners:

> *Drag forth the legal monsters into light,*
> *Wrench from their hands oppression's iron rod,*
> *And bid the cruel feel the pains they give.*

The infamous Bambridge, jailer of Fleet Street prison, was dismissed from his post together with 'his murderous subordinates'.

THE YOUNG PRETENDER

The word 'Jacobite' comes from the Latin *Jacobus* which is the equivalent of the name James. The Jacobite movement began when James II was deposed in 1688 and was strengthened considerably when James's son by his second wife was born, because he was in fact the rightful heir to the English throne. James III, as he was called, was a Catholic and could not be accepted as a British monarch because of acts of Parliament passed at the end of the seventeenth century forbidding a reigning Catholic king (see page 182).

The Jacobite movement featured strongly in the first half of the eighteenth century in British history. Many songs and verses were composed to commemorate those turbulent times. They echo and record the hopes and hardships of the brave Scotsmen who fought for the cause that they held so dear. In the words of a Scottish lawyer about the traditional songs and airs of Scotland,

'Suffer us to make the songs of our country, and do you make its laws'.

James III, the Old Pretender, lived a long life on the Continent. In 1715 he landed in Scotland in order to raise a rebellion to place himself on the throne of England and depose George I. This failed and, although many plots were made, it was not until 1745 that another real danger to the English throne presented itself. Bonny Prince Charlie, (the 'Young Pretender'), the son of James, landed in Scotland and was proclaimed king of that country in his father's name. Although the promised help from France was not forthcoming, Charles's army gathered strength and courage, and began the march south from Edinburgh on 31 October 1745.

'Charlie is my darling' was a popular Scottish marching song at the time and must have been sung frequently by the Scottish Jacobite army. Here is the popular version, as written by James Hogg, based on an older song:

> *'Twas on a Monday morning,*
> > *Right early in the year,*
> *That Charlie came to our town,*
> > *The young Chevalier,*
> *And Charlie he's my darling,*
> > *My darling, my darling,*
> *And Charlie he's my darling,*
> > *The young Chevalier.*
>
> *As Charlie he came up the gate,*
> > *His face shone like day;*
> *I grat to see the lad come back,*
> > *That has been lang away.*
> *And Charlie he's my darling, etc.*
>
> *And ilka bonny lassie sang,*
> > *As to the door she ran,*
> *Our king shall hae his ain again,*
> > *And Charlie is the man,*
> *And Charlie he's my darling, etc.*
>
> *Out-owre yon moory mountains,*
> > *And down yon craigy glen,*
> *O nothing else our lassies sing,*
> > *But Charlie and his men.*
> *And Charlie he's my darling, etc.*

Our Highland hearts are true and leal,
  And glow without a stain;
Our highland swords are metal keen,
  And Charlie is our ain.
And Charlie he's my darling, etc.

James Hogg, known as the Ettric Shepherd, spent most of his life (1770-1835) collecting and recording Jacobite songs. In his book *The Jacobite Relics of Scotland*, which was published after his death in 1874, mentions that the above song was a particular favourite of the ladies at the time. James Hogg was born in a small village called Ettrick Bridge in Selkirkshire, Scotland, and came from a long line of sheep farmers, which explains the origins of his *nom de plume*.

When Prince Charles and his army of Scottish clans reached Derby without much resistance en route, they set up camp, rested and talked of future plans.

The English generals were amazingly slow to attack the Scotsmen. General Wade, who had done much soldiering in Scotland and had disarmed the Highlands, was content to stay in Newcastle and threaten the Scottish flank. Wade was an old man and did not relish moving out of comfortable barracks, especially as the weather was unusually severe for the time of year. Although the Prince felt that an attack on London would bring victory, his advisers were pessimistic. They felt insecure and vulnerable in a strange land, and voted to retreat. They did not know that a large army was marching from Wales to support them and they did not realise that English Jacobites were waiting to make themselves known in London, when the time was ripe to support the rightful heir. They did not know that hundreds of leaflets advertising the Jacobite cause were posted on London walls at night and that the English banks were prepared for the take-over. George II even had a ship waiting to take him and his family to the safety of the Continent, should the need arise.

Communications were difficult, partly due to bad weather and it was this fact, plus the lack of enthusiasm on the part of his advisers, that doomed the bid that Charles made, when success was within his grasp. Historians agree that the course of British history would have been changed yet once again if Charles had followed his instinct and marched on London. As it was, the

Scottish army turned tail and made its weary way back to Scotland.

These events gave birth to the British National Anthem, which appeared in the first instance as a patriotic poem of four verses in *Gentlemen's Magazine* in October 1745. It was entitled 'God Save Great George Our King'. Here are the first three verses; the words have not altered a great deal from the original:

> God save our gracious King,
> Long live our noble King,
>   God save the King.
> Send him victorious,
> Happy and glorious,
> Long to reign over us,
>   God save the King.

> O Lord our God arise,
> Scatter his enemies,
>   And make them fall;
> Confound their politics,
> Frustrate their knavish tricks,
> On thee our hopes we fix,
>   God save us all.

> The choice gifts in store,
> On him be pleased to pour,
>   Long may he reign.
> May he defend our laws,
> And ever give us cause,
> With hearts and voice to sing,
>   God save the King.

The last verse as presented in the original poem is not used nowadays:

> Lord grant that Marshall Wade,
> May by Thy Mighty Aid,
>   Victory bring.
> May he Sedition hush,
> And like a Torrent rush,
> Rebellious Scots to crush,
>   God save the King.

It is not known for certain who wrote the words to the National Anthem, but it may well have been Dr Arne. The tune was either composed by John Bull or Henry Purcell in the seventeenth century. The anthem soon became a very popular song and was adopted in various forms in many other countries of the world, including America.

When the news of the Scottish retreat reached the English camps, the surprised generals then became well-organised and full of military strategy! General Wade followed the Scots in hot pursuit, but it was not until 1746 at the battle of Culloden Moor that the Jacobite cause was finally lost. At about the same time as the National Anthem was published in England, the same air with different words was being sung by Jacobite opponents. Entitled *The King's Anthem*, it has been said that this song has changed sides as many times as some Jacobites and many Whigs and Tories, when the occasion suited:

> *God bless our lord the King!*
> *God save our lord the King,*
> *God save the King!*
> *Make him victorious,*
> *Happy and glorious,*
> *Long to reign over us;*
> *God save the King!*
>
> *God send a royal heir!*
> *God bless the royal pair,*
> *Both King and Queen;*
> *That from them we may see,*
> *A royal progeny,*
> *To all posterity*
> *Ever to reign!*
>
> *God bless the Prince, I pray,*
> *God bless the Prince, I pray,*
> *Charlie I mean;*
> *That Scotland we may see,*
> *Freed from vile Presbyt'ry,*
> *Both George and his Feckie,*
> *Even so, Amen.*

God bless the happy hour!
Make the Almighty Power,
  Make all things well;
That the whole progeny,
Who are in Italy,
May soon and suddenly
  Come to Whitehall.

God bless the church, I pray,
God bless the church, I pray,
  Pure to remain.
Free frem all Whiggery,
And Whig's hypocrisy,
Who strive maliciously,
  Her to defame.

Here's to the subjects all,
God send them great and small,
  Firmly to stand.
That would call home the king,
Whose is the right to reign,
This is the only thing,
  Can save the land.

Two verses of the Jacobite version of the National Anthem containing slightly different words are engraved on a Jacobite 'Amen' wine glass, which is now to be seen in the National Museum of Antiquities of Scotland and is dated c. 1720-50. It is also engraved with a crown and the royal cipher 'JR8', signifying James VIII of Scotland (the Old Pretender).

On bleak Culloden Moor in Inverness, one of the bloodiest battles in British history was fought in April 1746. The Scots under Bonnie Prince Charlie were routed by the English under the Duke of Cumberland, who was commonly known as 'Butcher' Cumberland.

Over a hundred years later, in 1881, Duncan Forbes erected a Memorial Cairn twenty feet high to mark the spot where the fiercest fighting took place. The graves of the dead of both sides can still be distinguished beside the road. Near this monument can be seen the Well of the Dead and Old Leanach Farmhouse. Here is part of a ballad entitled *Culloden Day* translated from the Gaelic:

Fair lady mourn the memory of all our Scottish fame;
   Fair lady mourn the memory,
Ev'n of Scottish name!
   How proud we were of our young Prince,
And of his native sway!
   But all our hopes are past and gone,
Upon Culloden Day.

There was no lack of bravery there,
   No spare of blood or breath,
For one to two, our foes we dar'd,
   For freedom or for death.
The bitterness of grief is past,
   Of terror and dismay;
The die was risked and foully cast,
   Upon Culloden Day.

A foreign and fanatic sway,
   Our Southern foes may fall;
The cup is fill'd, they yet shall drink
   And they deserve it all,
But there is nought for us or ours,
   In which to hope or trust,
But hide us in our fathers' graves,
   Amid our fathers' dust.

Following this decisive defeat, Bonnie Prince Charlie went into hiding with a few of his trusted men. The rest of the surviving army were either killed or captured, and many atrocities were perpetrated on the Scottish people: numerous soldiers were deported for slave labour, civilians were killed and their homes looted and burned by English soldiers. There was famine and death in Scotland after the failure of the '45 rebellion.

Although a large reward amounting to £30,000 was offered for the Prince, not one Scotsman betrayed him. The loyal folk of Scotland hid and helped their leader whenever possible, and many suffered imprisonment, torture and death because they refused to betray him.

Over the water and over the lea,
And over the water to Charlie,
Charlie loves good ale and wine,
And Charlie loves good brandy.
  And Charlie loves a pretty girl,
  As sweet as sugar candy.

This nursery song echoes another Jacobite air pertaining to the movements of Bonny Prince Charlie. The reference to alcohol in the verse is interesting, for it was well-known that Charles, especially in his later years, was addicted to the bottle. Here is the original ditty:

Come boat me o'er, come row me o'er,
Come boat me o'er to Charlie;
  I'll gie John Ross anither bawbee
  To ferry me o'er to Charlie.

We'll o'er the water, we'll o'er the sea,
We'll o'er the water to Charlie;
  Come weel, come wo, we'll gather and go,
  And live or die, wi' Charlie.

It's weel I lo'e my Charlie's name,
Though some there be abhor him;
  But O to see Auld Nick gaun hame,
  And Charlie's faes before him!

We'll o'er the water, etc.

I swear by moon and stars sae bright,
And sun that glances early,
  If I had twenty thousand lives,
  I'd gie them a' for Charlie.

We'll o'er the water etc.

I aunce had sons, but now hae nane;
I bred them toiling sairly;
  And I wad bear them a' again,
  And lose them a' for Charlie.

We'll o'er the water etc.

This is another song which found much favour with the ladies of Scotland around the mid-eighteenth century.

Of all the people who helped Charles to escape, the most famous must undoubtedly be young Flora MacDonald, who was an educated woman and a great admirer of the Jacobite cause. Her step-father was the commanding officer in charge of troops hunting down the Scottish Prince. Flora was asked to assist in Charles' escape from the mainland to the Island of Skye. The plan was that she and another man, a friend of the Prince, and a servant woman, Betty Burke, should make the journey to Skye in a small boat. The servant woman was, of course, the Prince dressed in woman's clothing. Many a jocular remark was passed referring to the clumsy gait of Betty Burke! The Prince, it seems, enjoyed his role and in his usual devil-may-care way made the most of a light-hearted situation. After many narrow escapes, the Prince reached a French boat chartered to carry him to the safety of France. Here is part of an old ballad which reflects this story, entitled *The Lament of Flora MacDonald*:

> *Far o'er yon hills of the heather so green,*
> *And down by the correi that sings to the sea,*
> *The bonny young Flora sat sighing her lane,*
> > *The dew on her plaid and the tear in her e'en.*
> > *She looked at a boat with the breezes that swung.*

> *Away on the wave, like a bird of the main;*
> *And aye as it lessen'd, she sighed and she sung,*
> *'Fareweel to the lad I shall ne'er see again!*
> > *Fareweel to my hero, the gallant and young!*
> > *Fareweel to the lad I shall ne'er see again'.*

Flora was arrested soon after the Prince's escape and was taken to Edinburgh, where she was kept prisoner on a ship in Leith Roads for a year. She was then taken to London, but was later liberated without any charge being made. She returned to Scotland and in 1750 married Kingsburgh's son. Later, Flora entertained Dr Johnson, who described her as 'of middle stature, soft featured, gentle manners and elegant presence'.

After a while she and her husband emigrated to North Carolina, where there was a large Highland colony. When the American War of Independence broke out, the MacDonalds thought it fit to return to Scotland. Flora was the mother of seven children and lived until 1790. She died two years after Prince Charlie. Although popular feeling created romance between Charlie and

Flora, there was never any indication of this in contemporary literature. Another song which recalls the alliance between Flora and Charles is *Speed Bonny Boat*.

While Prince Charles was plotting to gain the English throne, his father, the Old Pretender, was living out his days quietly in Italy. Of the two men, it is accepted by most historians that James possessed the stronger character: in the face of constant disappointment and adversity James did not flounder. He resorted to none of the vices that his son developed and showed himself to be a man of integrity to the end. It is generally agreed that James might have made a first-class King of England. James died in 1766 and was buried in St Peter's in Rome with full regal honours. Here is an anonymous passage which illustrates the feeling of the people for James – and his son:

> *Red roses under the sun,*
> *For the King who is lord of the lands,*
> *But he dies when his day is done,*
> *For his memory careth none,*
> *When his glass runs empty of sands.*
>
> *White roses under the Moon,*
> *For the King without lands to give;*
> *But he reigns with the reign of June*
> *With his rose and his blackbird's tune,*
> *And he lives while Faith may live!*

The rose has been an emblem of Jacobean societies since this time.

Bonnie Prince Charlie did not reach his father before his death. His younger brother Henry, Duke of York, tried to persuade the Pope to recognize Charles as James's successor, but, after much deliberation, the Pope refused – one of the reasons being the strength of England after the success of the Seven Year's War. Although Charles had one illegitimate daughter, Charlotte, as the result of an affair with a Scottish girl, Clementina Walkinshaw, when he was a young man, he did not marry until fairly late in life. His cause seemed to have failed and he became an alcoholic. For company, it seems, he married Louise, Princess of Stolberg, a young girl of eighteen. After five sickening years, she finally left him for the favours of an artist and was later received in London by George III.

Charlotte, in the meantime, became legitimized and bore the title of the Duchess of Albany. She nursed her father tirelessly throughout his last illness until he died in 1788, at the age of sixty-eight. Robert Burns, the last laureate of the House of Stuart, immortalized Charles' daughter, the Duchess of Albany, in these words:

> *My heart is wae, and unco wae,*
> *To think upon the raging sea,*
> *That roars between her gardens green,*
> *And bonnie Lass of Albany.*
> *This lovely maid's of royal blood,*
> *That ruled Albion's kingdoms three,*
> *But oh, alas, for her bonnie face,*
> *They've wronged the Lass of Albany.*

Charlotte was killed in a riding accident a few months after her father's death.

When it became plain that the House of Stuart would never again threaten the English throne, the attitude of the English monarchy changed towards those who lived 'north of the border'. King George III was a great admirer of the Jacobite cause and ordered the restoration of lands to the remaining Scottish noblemen, and also gave monetary support to the exiled Stuarts. He was heard to say in the company of gentlemen from both nations, 'I have always regarded the attachment of the Scots to the Pretender – I beg your pardon gentlemen, to Prince Charles, I mean – as a lesson to me whom to trust in the hour of need'. An ancient verse says:

> *Treason does never prosper,*
> *What's the reason?*
> *For if it prosper,*
> *None dare call it treason.*

Sir Walter Scott was one of the people that collected and recorded the Jacobite songs remembered today. He travelled to the remote parts of Scotland to collect material for this purpose, but many airs were overlooked and have now sunk into oblivion, for their use and purpose became obsolete.

AULD LANG SYNE

It seems possible that it was Robert Burns himself who wrote the song *Auld Lang Syne*, which is now universally famous. It was originally included in a book of Scottish airs and songs entitled *The Interleaved Museum*, edited by the poet and published in 1796. Before publication, Burns wrote to a friend expressing admiration for the sentiment in the song which he said he had never seen in print, but had copied by ear from an old man singing in the streets. The historians have searched diligently for a record of this old ballad, but have discovered none using the content and feeling projected by Burns. This was a street song recorded about a hundred years before Burns's publication:

> *On old long syne,*
> *On old long syne, my jo,*
> *On old long syne;*
> *That thou canst never once reflect*
> *On old long syne.*

'Syne' is an ancient Scottish word meaning old kindness. This verse may have been based on an earlier ballad published in Watson's *Scot's Poems* in 1711 and attributed to an author living in the previous century:

> *Should old acquaintance be forgot,*
> *And never thought upon,*
> *The flames of love extinguished,*
> *And freely past and gone?*
>
> *Is thy kind heart now grown so cold*
> *In that loving breast of thine,*
> *That thou canst never once reflect*
> *On old, long syne?*

Other political or patriotic ballads were modelled on the form. This verse is aimed against the unification of England and Scotand:

> *Is Scotsmen's blood now grown so cold,*
> *The valour of their mind*
> *That they can never once reflect*
> *On old long syne?*

Another version is credited to a Scottish Loyalist after the Battle of Culloden, entitled *Langsyne*:

> Should old gay mirth and cheerfulness
> Be dashed for ever-more,
> Since late success in wickedness
> Made Whigs insult and roar.

It is possible that Burns took the title phrase and some of the words known to him, and created an entirely new ballad perhaps deliberately confusing the public by stating that the song was a copy of an earlier air, when in reality it was of his own creation. Burns had always suffered from ill health and, when he wrote this masterpiece, he must have been a very sick man. He was only thirty-seven when he died, six months before the publication of *Auld Lang Syne*. Perhaps he had a premonition of his own death, which increased his power of artistry and heightened his feelings towards old friends at this time. This may well explain the strong emotion which is felt whenever the song is sung. Here is *Auld Lang Syne* as we know it today:

> Should auld acquaintance be forget,
> And never brought to mind?
> Should auld acquaintance be forgot,
> And days o' lang syne?
>
> And for auld lang syne, my jo,
> For auld lang syne,
> We'll tak a cup o' kindness yet,
> For auld lang syne.
>
> And surely ye'll be your pint-stowp!
> And surely I'll be mine!
> And we'll tak a cup of kindness yet,
> For auld lang syne.
>
> And for auld lang syne, etc.
>
> We two hae run about the braes,
> And pou'd the gowans fine;
> But we've wander'd mony a weary foot
> Sin auld lang syne.
>
> And for auld lang syne, etc.

We two hae paidl'd i' the burn,
  Frae mornin sun till dine;
But seas between us braid hae roar'd
  Sin auld lang syne.

And for auld lang syne, etc.

And there's a hand my trusty fiere!
  And gie's a hand o' thine!
And we'll tak a right gude-willy waught,
  For auld lang syne.

And for auld lang syne, etc.

It is not known when the practice of singing this song at the end of convivial meetings first started. It is also difficult to establish when the company formed a circle and joined hands, although this probably arose from the last verse which promotes hand-clasping. The origin of the air is also obscure, but it was probably an adaptation of an old Scottish country dance tune or reel. Perhaps the circle and the linking of crossed hands are action remnants taken from old dances associated with the tune. One thing is certain, however the song is sung in a great many countries, and it must surely be a great symbol of unity in the world today.

SCOTTISH SHANTIES

Another old Scottish song well-known as a sea shanty is *Down Among The Dead Men*:

No hard fate can daunt a loyal spirit,
Till death shall remove all our cares below:
Then the delights that martyrs inherit,
Unsurping tyrants never shall know,
We'll own no power by rebels in convention,
Nor a king by such a rabble set on high;
Sooner than sell our country for a pension,
Down among the dead men,
Down among the dead men,
Down, down, down, down,
Down among the dead men let us lie.

The Keel Row is a Scottish traditional song that has become part of the English collection:

> *O' rosies, o' rosies,*
> *Wi' arms o' lily posies,*
> *To fauld a lassie in.*
> > *O merry day the keel row,*
> > *The keel row, the keel row,*
> > *Merry may the keel row,*
> > *The ship that my love's in.*
> *My love he wears a bonnet,*
> *A bonnet, a bonnet,*
> *A snawy rose upon it,*
> *A dimple on his chin.*
> > *O merry day the keel row, etc.*

This song with its unforgettable tune takes us back onto English soil once again, where we find that *Bobby Shafto* possesses similar words.

BOBBY SHAFTO

> *Bobby Shafto's gone to sea,*
> *Silver buckles at his knee;*
> *He'll come back and marry me,*
> *Bonnie Bobby Shafto!*
>
> *Bobby Shafto's bright and fair,*
> *Combing down his yellow hair;*
> *He's my ain for evermair,*
> *Bonnie Bobby Shafto!*
>
> *Bobby Shafto's looking out,*
> *All his ribbons flew about,*
> *All the ladies gave a shout,*
> *Hey for Bobby Shafto!*

The Shafto family has long been associated with the north of England and the family residence, which was purchased in 1652, Whitworth Hall, is still owned by a descendant of the popular nursery character. In a letter, Miss Shafto said that it has always been common family knowledge that Bobby Shafto owned ships and sometimes sailed in them. She also said that there were offices on the quayside at Newcastle belonging to the Shafto family. Shipping authorities cannot trace any mention of this, but as the earliest records only date back to 1834, it is probable that the song gives us more information on the subject than the recorded word, as is so often the case.

Miss Shafto said that Bonnie Bobby, as she calls him, was first engaged to Miss Bellasis of Brancepeth Castle, who died at the age of 21, either from a broken heart or tuberculosis. Bobby Shafto was fickle and married another heiress, Anne Duncombe of the Taversham family of Duncombe Park in Yorkshire. She possessed a large fortune, which Bonnie Bobby squandered at court. He was a celebrated man of fashion, as two more local verses bear witness:

> Bobby Shafto went to court,
> All in gold and silver wrought,
> Like the grandee as he ought,
> Bonnie Bobby Shafto!
>
> Bobby Shafto throws his gold,
> Right and left like knights of old,
> Now we're left out in the cold,
> Bonnie Bobby Shafto!

Robert Shafto lived from 1732 until 1797. He represented Durham in Parliament from 1760 to 1768, and afterwards represented the Borough of Downtown in Wiltshire during the reign of George III. It is not known if he was a Whig or a Tory, but he probably changed his loyalties to suit the party in power, like so many others. The second and third verses of the original ditty were written to bolster his election campaign. He was said to have been an uncommonly handsome and charming man, and although the ladies were not allowed a vote, they must surely have put pressure on their men folk to vote for him!

Shafto was 65 when he died, and was buried at Whitworth in the family Chapel. He had three sons: John, Robert and Thomas. John died without children, so Robert succeeded him and is Miss Shafto's great grandfather.

Miss Shafto also said that she possesses a painting of Robert Shafto and one of his sister, who became Lady Lisburne, both of which are reputed to have been painted by Joshua Reynolds.

ELSIE MARLEY

Elsie Marley is a character who has achieved eternal fame by way
of a nursery song. She lived in the same period as Bobby Shafto
and her home, too, was near Durham:

Do you ken Elsie Marley, honey?
The wife that sells the barley, honey?
She lost her pocket and all her money,
Aback o' the bush i' the garden, honey.

Elsie Marley is grown so fine,
She won't get up to feed the swine,
But lies in bed till eight or nine,
   Lazy Elsie Marley.

Elsie Marley is so neat,
It is hard for one to walk the street,
But every lad and lass they meet,
Cries, 'Do you ken Elsie Marley, honey?'

Elsie Marley wore a straw hat,
But now she's gotten a velvet cap,
She may thank the Lambton lads for that,
Do you ken Elsie Marley, honey?

Elsie keeps wine, gin and ale,
In her house below the dale,
Where every tradesman up and down,
Does call to spend his half-a-crown.

The farmers as they come that way,
They drink with Elsie every day,
And call the fiddler for to play
The tune of Elsie Marley, honey.

Those gentlemen that go so fine,
They'll treat her with a bottle of wine,
And freely will sit down and dine,
Along with Elsie Marley, honey.

So to conclude these lines I've penned,
Hoping there's none I do offend,
And thus my merry joke doth end
Concerning Elsie Marley, honey.

The lady in question was the attractive wife of the proprietor of The Barley Mow, nicknamed The Swan, at Picktree near Durham. The building has long since disappeared and no portrait of this fascinating female can be found. She was reported by a writer in the *Newcastle Magazine*, who saw her in her later years, to be 'a tall, slender, genteel-looking woman'. She had a gay personality and was also a very good business manager. As the song says, she was very popular with the men. The 'Lambton lads' mentioned in the song were five bachelor brothers who were all fond of her at one time.

When Elsie 'lost her pocket and all her money', she was going to Newcastle to pay the brewer's bill. She had twenty guineas in her purse, but her pocket was picked amongst a crowd on the journey and so she returned home. When she greeted her family, she cried out in great distress, 'Oh hinnies, hinnies, I've lost my pocket and all my money!' Her husband, Ralph Marley, immediately composed the first stanza of the song, though the rest were composed by an unknown hand. It would appear, though that the subsequent verses were written by a gossip-monger, who was not malicious perhaps but decidedly envious! At all events, the verses became so popular all over the district that Joseph Ritson included them in his famous Bishoprick Garland, published in 1784.

No one however would envy Elsie Marley's sad end. At the age of fifty-three she suffered a long and severe illness, and one night, having a high temperature, she got out of bed and, not knowing what she was doing, she wandered into a field near the house, where she fell into an old water-logged coal pit and was drowned. An account of her death was given in Sykes' *Local Records* in August 1768. A popular dance named after Elsie Marley is still performed in Scotland and the north of England today.

THE BRITISH GRENADIERS

Some talk of Alexander, and some of Hercules,
Of Hector and Lysander, and such great names as these,
But of all the world's brave heroes, there's none that can compare
With a tow row row row row row for the British Grenadier.

Those heroes of antiquity ne'er saw a cannon ball,
Or knew the force of powder, to slay their foes withal;
But our brave boys do know it, and banish all their fears,
Sing tow row row, etc.

When e'er we are commanded to storm the palisades,
Our leaders march with fusees, and we with hand grenades,
We throw them from the glacis* about the enemies' ears,
Sing tow row row, etc.

And when the siege is over, we to the town repair,
The townsmen cry 'Hurrah boys', here comes a Grenadier,
Here comes the Grenadiers my boys, who know no doubts or fears,
Sing a tow row row, etc.

Then let us fill a bumper, and drink a health to those,
Who carry caps and pouches, and wear the louped clothes;
May they and their commanders live happy all their years,
With a tow row row, etc.

'Glacis' were protective trenches or ditches. The Grenadier Guards were first introduced into the British Army in 1680. They were distinguished by their uniform caps and louped clothes, and they carried grenades in pouches and bayonets. The officers held the fusees (matches) to ignite the grenade fuses. Unlike other battalions, the Grenadier regiments were composed of hand-picked men, and developed a tradition of bravery and military strategy that has never been disputed throughout their long history. In battle these regiments took up posts on the right-hand side of the battalion and led it in every movement.

The Grenadier March has been known and played since 1690, and it is also believed to have had words attached to it, but it was not until the American War of Independence that the song *The British Grenadiers* gained universal esteem.

The war had not been going too well for the British forces on American soil until the Battle of Savannah in Georgia, in October 1779. A welcome dispatch arrived in England recounting how the British had gained a decisive victory over the French in this incident, due almost entirely to the courage of the 60th Regiment of the British Grenadiers under the leadership of Major Glasier. Every man distinguished himself in this campaign and special mention was made of Captain Wickham. The newspapers made much of the victory and bravery of the English soldiers, and it is probably due to this publicity that the idea for the song was engendered.

A popular comic opera/pantomime was currently in production at Covent Garden, and, when the news of the Grenadiers was published, the management decided to add an extra scene to the opera – and the theatre was closed over the Christmas period for rehearsals. The updated show entitled *Harlequin Everywhere* opened in 1780, and the new material included the stirring song *The British Grenadiers*. It was an instant success and the singer Charles Reinhold became the most popular performer of the day. The song was immediately published on separate song sheets, and was regarded as second only to the National Anthem in popularity at that time.

Hand grenades soon ceased to be used as offensive weapons, and the unique looped uniforms of the Grenadiers were adopted by other regiments. The Grenadiers were then only distinguished by their metre caps, matchboxes and grenade pouches. Today the Grenadier Guards form part of the cavalry attached to the Court.

YANKEE DOODLE

> *Yankee Doodle came to town,*
> *Riding on a pony;*
> *He stuck a feather in his cap*
> *And called it macaroni.*

It is difficult to pin-point exactly when this famous air was composed, but most historians agree that it is of American origin and was in the first place a song without words, probably 'tootled' on the flute or penny whistle. Not long afterwards it was used as a dance, these words being added:

> *Yankee Doodle keep it up,*
> *Yankee Doodle Dandy;*
> *Mind the music and the step,*
> *And with the girls be handy.*

The tune, it seems, was adopted in the first place by British troops fighting on American soil during the American War of Independance. The words composed to accompany the tune were derisive and insulting to the enemy – Yankee was used to describe the opposition in the same way as Gerry was used to describe the Germans during the last war. Here are two verses of the many sung by English troops at that time:

> *Yankee Doodle came to town,*
> *For to buy a firelock;*
> *We will tar and feather him,*
> *And so we will John Hancock.*

> *Madam Hancock dreamt a dream;*
> *She dreamt she wanted something;*
> *She dreamt she wanted a Yankee King,*
> *To crown him with a pumpkin.*

John Hancock was the first revolutionary leader to sign the Declaration of Independence in 1776 and was known to have ambitions to lead the combined states of America. However, after the defeat of the British at Bunker's Hill, the Americans were so delighted that they took over the tune, and made it their own. An excerpt from a letter written by a British officer, who took an active part in that engagement, says: 'But after the affair at Bunker's Hill, the Americans gloried in it. *Yankee Doodle* is now their paean, a favourite of favourites, played in their army, esteemed as warlike as *The Grenadier March* – it is the lover's spell, the nurse's lullaby. After our rapid successes, we held the Yankees in contempt, but it was not a little mortifying to hear them play this tune, when their army marched down to our surrender.'

The verses that follow are those sung by the Americans when victory over the English was in sight. The lot of the soldier was not to be envied, and the lines tell of the thoughts of a young boy who was frightened by what he saw of army life:

> *Father and I went down to camp,*
> *Along with Capt'n Gooding;*
> *And there we saw the men and boys,*
> *As thick as hasty pudding.*
> > *Yankee Doodle keep it up,*
> > *Yankee Doodle Dandy,*
> > *Mind the music and the step,*
> > *And with the girls be handy.*

And there we see a thousand men,
As rich as Squire David;
And what they wasted every day,
I wish it could be saved.
    Yankee Doodle, etc.

The leaders of each state naturally visualized that the first city of the new country should be based on their territory. To avoid unnecessary argument George Washington chose a piece of land on the Potomac river and declared it neutral. He named this land the District of Columbia and that is why to this day the capital of the U.S.A. is called Washington D.C.

Washington appointed a Frenchman, Major Pierre Charles L'Enfant, who had served with him during the war, to plan the new capital of the United States. L'Enfant was convinced that his country would one day be one of the great powers in the world and designed an imposing city, which would be in keeping with this. The President's house – the White House – was begun in 1792 and the Parliament building the year after.

In 1797, George Washington retired from public affairs and spent the last two years of his life at his home at Mount Vernon. He never lived in the White House. George Washington who it was said 'never told a lie', died at the age of sixty-seven in 1799, since which time he has been honoured by Americans as the 'father of his people' and the founder of the United States.

LUCY LOCKET

Lucy Locket lost her pocket,
Kitty Fisher found it;
Not a penny was there in it,
Only the ribbon round it.

While the song *Yankee Doodle* was achieving widespread fame in America, the above ditty, using the same air, became a popular dance tune in Britain at about the same time. It was called *Lydia Fisher's Jig*. Lucy Locket seems to be a traditional name, but Kitty Fisher actually existed. Kitty Fisher is said to have been a great beauty who served at Court during the reign of George III, and had a doubtful reputation, as the rhyme suggests.

THE GRAND OLD DUKE OF YORK

The Grand old Duke of York,
He had ten thousand men,
He marched them up to the top of the hill,
And he marched them down again.
And when they were up, they were up,
And when they were down, they were down,
And when they were only half way up,
They were neither up nor down.

This jingle, which is chanted so joyfully by our youngsters today, has immortalized the Duke of York in a very cruel way. He was the second son of George III and, in 1794, was the Commander-in-Chief of the English army in the Netherlands. In the summer of that year Colonel Wellesley, who later became the Duke of Wellington, set sail with 10,000 men to reinforce English troops in Flanders. During the early winter months the weather became severe, but the army was not provided with proper winter clothing and neither was there an organized food supply. In winter conditions like these it was usual to set up barracks and postpone fighting until warmer weather. The English leaders prepared to do just this, but the French had other ideas. They approached swiftly along the frozen canals, routed the English army, and sent it staggering towards Hanover, with the result that in a short time all the Dutch ports were captured by the French.

The Prime Minister, William Pitt, and his Parliament pressed for a withdrawal of command from the Duke of York, if only to satisfy public opinion. The Duke said about the whole affair to his father King George III, 'To say that I shall not feel this as a severe blow would be contrary to my own character'. The public, however, used the Duke of York as a scapegoat and the rhyme was widely publicized, and soon entered the oral collection.

In spite of this setback to his career, the Duke of York was made Commander-in-Chief of the English army in 1798 and held this post until 1807.

The English army at this time comprised a notorious collection of criminals, lunatics, old men and young boys. Commissions were bought by anyone who could pay regardless of character or training. The army wagon train was named after London's worst prison, the Newgate Blues.

After the bitter experience in the Netherlands, the Duke of York set out to improve the lot of the English soldier. He had also seen much active service in other parts of the world, and knew what was needed. Training was essential and the Duke of York founded the Royal Military College at Sandhurst. He also set up a Staff Headquarters and College, and a school for the children of soldiers billeted in England. He started a movement to introduce doctors, chaplains and veterinary surgeons to the battlefields.

However, the unfortunate Duke of York was ridiculed again by the public in 1807. His mistress, a devious lady by the name of Mary Ann Clark, was discovered to be supplementing her allowance by selling 'under the counter, and at cut prices, commissions, promotions and exchanges'. A couplet composed at the time said:

> *You'll be treated with Honours if you secrecy mark, Sir,*
> *For my Master is Noble and I am his Clark, Sir.*

The lady was dismissed by her royal lover in 1806 and was questioned by Members of Parliament about her misdemeanours, upon which she proceeded to ridicule the Duke of York in every way she could, saying that she even had to pin notes to their bedcurtains to remind her lover of his promises.

The Duke of York's effigy was burnt in Suffolk and Yorkshire, and Arthur Wellesley, later the Duke of Wellington, reluctantly came to the conclusion that York 'must have suspected Mrs Clark's practices'. The Duke of York resigned from the Horse Guards and the next day was replaced as Commander-in-Chief by old Sir David Dundas. In *An Epistle to Mrs Clark* Peter Pindar records the incident:

> *No longer now the Duke excites our wonder,*
> *'Midst gun, drum, trumpet, blunder bus and thunder;*
> *Amidst his hosts, no more with rapture dwells*
> *On Congreve's rockets, and on Shrapnell's shells,*
> *But quits with scornful mien, the field of Mars,*
> *And to Sir David's genius leaves the wars.*

Arthur Wellesley was doubtful of 'Sir David's genius', for he was old, set in his ways, and was averse to modern military strategy. In answering a complaint or a request for promotion in the Horse

Guards, Dundas always made the same remark, 'Wear flannel, man, wear flannel'. However, the Duke of York was a great favourite with his elder brother, the Prince Regent, and in 1811 he was reinstated as Commander-in-Chief of the army. He held this post for a number of years and died of dropsy in 1827.

THE MARSEILLAISE

The unrest in Paris exploded into the Revolution of 1789. A petition to ease the plight of the poor had been rejected by King Louis XVI and his wife, Marie-Antoinette, who when told that the poor lacked bread, simply said, 'Then let them eat cake'. The starving peasants unable to bear any longer the taxation and extravagance of the royal court, stormed the Bastille and set the prisoners free.

In 1792 France declared war on Austria, and the need for a French marching song was expressed by the Mayor of Strasbourg. A young captain of the Engineers billeted in that town, Claude Joseph de Lisle, heard of the mayor's suggestion, so, as he was a part-time musician, sat down to write the words and music for a marching hymn entitled *Chant de Guerre pour l'armee du Rhin*. It has been said that the whole composition was completed in one evening.

In a few months the popular air had caught the imagination of all France, and was renamed *Le Marseillaise* to mark the occasion when five hundred of the National Guard from Marseilles marched to Paris to celebrate the storming of the Bastille. They were singing their new marching song and it excited the mob to such a degree that they attacked the Tuileries, and took the royal family prisoner.

The Marseillaise became the unofficial national anthem of France in 1795, and it may be said that in some ways the song was responsible for the appalling bloodshed on the guillotine. Napoleon banned the song after the Restoration because of its revolutionary associations. It was not until 1873, when Ambroise Thomas was commissioned to prepare a definitive edition of the music that the *Marseillaise* was recognised as the national anthem.

Rouget de Lisle composed six stanzas, but the first and sixth are the most well-known:

Allons, enfants de la patrie!
Le jour de gloire est arrive!
Contre nous de la tyrannie,
L'étendard sanglant est levé,
L'étendard sanglant est levé!
Entendez-vous dans les campagnes,
Mugir ces feroces soldats?
Ils viennent jusque dans nos bras
Egorger nos fils, nos compagnes!

> *Aux armes, citoyens!*
> *Formez vos bataillons!*
> *Marchons! Marchons!*
> *Qu'un sang inpur abreuve nos sillons!*

Amour sacré de la Patrie,
Conduis, soutiens nos bras vengeurs!
Liberté, Liberté cherie,
Combats avec tes defenseure!
Combats avec tes defenseurs!
Sous nos drapeaux, que la victoire
Accoure a tes males accents!
Que tes ennemis expirants
Voient ton triomphe et notre gloire!

> *Aux armes, etc.*

The first verse of *The Marseillaise* was translated by Shelley in 1795:

Ye sons of France awake to glory,
Hark, hark what myriads bid you rise:
Your children, wives and grand-sires hoary,
Behold their tears and hear their cries,
Behold their tears and hear their cries!
Shall hateful tyrants mischief breeding
With hireling hosts, a ruffian band
Affright and desolate the land,
While peace and liberty lie bleeding?

> *To arms, to arms, ye brave!*
> *The avenging sword unsheathe!*
> *March on! March on!*
> *All hearts resolved on victory or death.*

The second verse was translated in 1943 by Mary Elizabeth Shaw, as a tribute to the French underground movement, during the Second World War:

> *O sacred love of France, undying,*
> *Th' avenging arm uphold and guide.*
> *Thy defenders, death defying,*
> *Fight with Freedom at their side.*
> *Soon their sons shall be victorious*
> *When the banner high is raised*
> *And their dying enemies, amazed,*
> *Shall behold thy triumph, great and glorious.*

NAPOLEON AND NELSON

A young soldier, who had proved himself to be a successful strategist, was making himself known in Paris. His name was, of course, Napoleon Bonaparte, and, because of his military successes and his diplomacy, he was soon elected First Consul of France. He and his wife, Josephine, were crowned Emperor and Empress of France in 1804 at a great ceremony held in the Cathedral of Notre Dame in Paris.

The leader of France, flushed with his military successes, decided, like so many before him, that he must conquer Britain, if he was to become the true dictator of Europe. Napoleon assembled a fleet of flat-bottomed boats at Boulogne and evolved complicated tactics to lure the British navy away from the all-important task of protecting the coastline of Great Britain. The British knew only too well of Napoleon's intentions, as James Hogg wrote:

> *Red glared the beacon on Pownell,*
> *On Skiddaw there were three;*
> *The bugle-horn on moor and fell*
> *Was heard continually.*

Mothers and nurses sang this lullaby to their children:

> *Baby, baby, naughty baby,*
> *Hush, you squalling thing, I say,*
> *Hush your squalling, or it may be*
> *Bonaparte may pass this way.*

> *Baby, baby, he's a giant,*
> *Tall and black as Rouen steeple;*
> *And he dines and sups, rely on't,*
> *Every day on naughty people.*

The majority of people, however, true to British tradition, put a brave face on things and satirists of the time made much of Napoleon's repeated threats to Britain:

> *The French are all coming, so they declare,*
> *Of their floats and balloons all the papers advise us,*
> *They're to swim through the ocean and ride on the air,*
> *In some foggy evening to land and surprise us!*

Old General Cornwallis was in charge of home defences and he wrote, 'When I consider the number of men that we have in arms and that they are all Britons, I cannot be afraid.' Wordsworth described Britain at that time as 'a bulwark to the cause of man', and continued:

> *No parleying now! In Britain is one breath;*
> *We are all with you now from shore to shore:*
> *Ye men of Kent, 'tis victory or death!*

As the autumn gave way to winter, the news that the French had mutinied in December when given orders to embark at Boulogne was received joyfully by the British. Confidence grew and London ballad sellers did a roaring trade with a broadsheet entitled *The Bellman and Little Boney:*

> *This little Boney says he'll come*
> *At merry Christmas time,*
> *But that I say is all a hum*
> *Or I no more will rhyme.*
>
> *Some say in wooden house he'll glide*
> *Some say in air balloon,*
> *E'en those who airy schemes deride*
> *Agree his coming soon.*
>
> *Now honest people list to me,*
> *Though income is but small,*
> *I'll bet my wig to one Penney,*
> *He does not come at all.*

The English nation was lulled into a sense of security, and a verse in a soldier's marching song went:

When rich men find their wealth a curse,
And freely fill the poor man's purse;
Then little Boney, he'll come down,
And march his men on London town.

In spite of the confidence of the Englishman that his country was
safe from invasion, the outcome might have been very different
had it not been for the courage and naval strategy of one man,
namely Horatio Nelson:

Old Lord Nelson lost one eye,
Old Lord Nelson lost the other eye;
Old Lord Nelson lost one arm,
Old Lord Nelson lost the other arm,
Old Lord Nelson lost one leg,
Old Lord Nelson lost the other leg;
Old Lord Nelson fell down dead.

This popular skipping chant has immortalized one of Britain's
most noble heroes in a rather derisive fashion – similar perhaps to
the unfortunate *Grand Old Duke of York*.

Horatio Nelson was born in 1758 in Burnham Thorpe in Norfolk, where his father was the vicar. He joined the navy when he
was twelve and for most of his adult life was engaged in active
service, as at that time Britain was involved in many wars. He lost
the sight of his right eye in a bid to seize the island of Corsica in
the Mediterranean. Later, while attempting to capture a town in
the Canary Islands, he was shot in the elbow of his right arm, and
it had to be amputated hurriedly by lantern light. He was given
leave to recover, and spent many months in England in great
pain.

Some time later Nelson was put in command of the British
forces in the Mediterranean with the sole purpose of defeating
the French fleet. Eventually the enemy were beaten in a decisive
battle off Egypt called the Battle of the Nile, during which Nelson
was wounded in the forehead.

While spending some leave in Naples, he met and fell in love
with the famous Lady Hamilton, who was the wife of the British
Envoy to Naples and Sicily. Because of this, Nelson never married, but kept true to his one and only love until his death.

Later, in a battle with the Danish fleet, when Nelson was
second in command, the bombardment was so fierce that the

commander, Admiral Parker, signalled an order to stop fighting. Nelson, so the story goes, put his telescope to his blind eye and declared that he saw no such signal; he continued the attack and won the battle against stern odds. In Britain, after his campaign, Nelson was acclaimed a national hero and given the title of Viscount Nelson.

In 1803, when Britain awaited the invasion of the French, Napoleon made a statement which can only be taken as a compliment by his enemy, 'England is not asleep, she is always on the watch.' To which Nelson replied, 'If we are true to ourselves, we need not mind Bonaparte.' Nelson, indeed, was true to himself and to his country, for he renewed his efforts to protect Britain's shores and combat the French fleet wherever possible.

A large contingent of French ships sailed for the West Indies, intending to return with reinforcements for the invasion. Nelson pursued them, but failed to catch up with the enemy. However, both fleets met later in the Mediterranean, where Nelson and Admiral Collingwood achieved a decisive victory at the Battle of Trafalgar. Cape Trafalgar is situated on the coast of southern Spain, not far from the Straits of Gibralter. The famous battle was fought approximately fifteen miles off the Cape. Before the engagement, Nelson summoned his sea captains onto the Victory, his own flag-ship, and explained his plan of campaign. Then he hoisted his well-known signal: 'England expects that every man will do his duty.' He then retired to his cabin and made a codicil to his will, entrusting the fate of Lady Hamilton and their child to the British Government.

During the battle Nelson was fatally wounded. He was carried below with face and medals covered, so that the rest of the crew would not learn that he had been hit and thus become disheartened. He lived a few hours longer, and learned that victory had been gained for the British. He asked his friend Hardy to kiss him and, with his last remaining breath, said that he left Lady Hamilton and his daughter Horatia as a legacy to his country. His last words were, 'Thank God I have done my duty to God and my Country'.

His death was mourned by the whole nation and he was buried in St Paul's Cathedral. Later, Nelson's Column was erected in Trafalgar Square in his honour and his ship, the Victory, can be viewed at Portsmouth.

WATERLOO

In spite of his defeat at Trafalgar, Napoleon made many successful military campaigns in Europe during the early nineteenth century. However, the British also possessed a military leader whose achievements on the battlefields were unsurpassed. Arthur Wellesley, the Duke of Wellington, defeated Napoleon once and for all in one of the bloodiest battles of all time. Not without good reason was the Duke of Wellington known as the Iron Duke.

The saying 'he has met his Waterloo', which is still in use today, is a direct reference to the fate of the French who suffered absolute defeat at the Battle of Waterloo in 1815.

On the eve of the campaign, a grand ball was given by the Duchess of Richmond in Brussels in honour of the military personnel involved. The Duke of Wellington was there, together with his senior officers and their wives, when a dispatch carrying the news that the French were making a quick advance threw the ball into confusion. Many soldiers left for the front still wearing their evening dress. Lord Byron recreated the scene:

> *Did ye not hear it? No, 'twas but the wind,*
> *Or the car rattling o'er the stony street;*
> *On with the dance! Let joy be unconfined,*
> *No sleep till morn, when Youth and Pleasure meet,*
> *To chase the glowing Hours with flying feet,*
> *But hark – that heavy sound breaks in once more,*
> *As if the clouds its echo would repeat;*
> *And nearer, clearer, deadlier than before!*
> *Arm! Arm! it is – it is – the cannon's opening roar.*

Thirty years later Thackeray based his novel *Vanity Fair* on this event.

The Prussian army came to the aid of the British and the Duke of Wellington formed his famous 'squares' of foot soldiers. After four days of bitter fighting, the French were routed and Napoleon made his way to Paris to try to escape to America. He was prevented from doing this, however, and was taken prisoner by the British, whom he described as 'the most powerful, the most determined, and the most generous of my enemies'. He was eventually exiled to the island of St Helena, where he died six years later.

There were approximately 45,000 dead and wounded left on the battlefield of Waterloo, a small village in Belgium. Today a memorial building stands on the spot and houses a large scale painting of the battle scene. Nearby, on a steep hillock, there stands the figure of a lion facing towards France.

After this decisive victory, sickened by the slaughter of war, Wellington gave up his military career in favour of politics. Although he was Prime Minister for two years, 1828-1830, he was not a great success with the commoners, partly because of his opposition to reform. Wellington died in 1852 and was given a state funeral, and buried in St Paul's Cathedral.

Although Wellington won many military campaigns, British soldiers did not rever him, as the French army did Napoleon, perhaps this was because Wellington had described his army as 'the mere scum of the earth'.

As Poet Laureate at this time it was Alfred Lord Tennyson's task to immortalize the death of Wellington; the opening lines read:

> *Bury the Great Duke*
> *With an empire's lamentation,*
> *Let us bury the Great Duke*
> *To the noise of the mourning of a mighty nation . . .*

Another verse goes:

> *Until we doubt not that for one so true*
> *There must be other nobler work to do*
> *Than when he fought at Waterloo,*
> *And Victor He must ever be.*

MADAME TUSSAUD

> *Tussaud's Beef-eater pay,*
> *To see her famed wax-work;*
> *Kings, queens, and ladies gay,*
> *Or English, French or Turk!*

This verse was probably published as an advertisement for Madame Tussaud's waxworks early in the nineteenth century.

The making of wax effigies was practised by pre-Christian Romans and has been a popular pastime ever since. Madame Tussaud, born Marie Grosholtz, at the age of six, went to Paris to live with her uncle, Dr Curtius, on the death of her father. Three years later, Curtius opened an exhibition of life-sized wax models and taught his niece the secrets of wax modelling. She soon became proficient at the art and at the age of seventeen, she made a portrait of Voltaire, which still exists today.

As a young woman, Marie spent much time at the French Court of Versailles teaching the King's younger sister to model in wax. In spite of this, Dr Curtius and his niece took part in the French uprising of 1789 and in the years of black terror which followed, Madame Tussaud and her uncle were forced to mould death masks of all those who were guillotined.

When her uncle died, Marie Grosholtz inherited the exhibition and married Monsieur Tussaud, an engineer, in 1795. They lived together for seven years and had three children. Madame Tussaud moved to England with her eldest son to promote her waxworks in 1802. She left her husband to manage the Paris shop, which he soon lost through gambling debts, and after her other two children had joined her, Madame Tussaud never saw or wrote to her husband again.

The exhibition twice toured the whole of Britain and a few jingles which were of course advertisements, survive to tell the tale, as the one published in the *Manchester Herald* in 1820 reveals:

> *Her Exhibition still attracts,*
> *Crowded still her Promenade*
> *All resort, or weak or active*
> *Old or young, or wives or maids.*
>
> *Swedenburgh all wish to see*
> *(See advertisement today)*
> *He, Kings, Queens and Bergami*
> *Are all soon going away.*

In 1835, after thirty-three years on tour, the exhibition was housed on a permanent site in Baker Street, London, and in 1884 it moved to Marylebone Road, where it has remained ever since. Madame Tussaud continued to make portraits until she died in 1850, at the age of eighty-one.

In 1845 Cruikshank satirized the exhibition as follows:

I dreamt that I slept at Madame Tussaud's,
With cut-throats and Kings by my side;
And that all the wax figures in those abodes,
At midnight became vivified.
I dreamt that Napoleon Bonaparte
Was waltzing with Madame Tee . . .

In 1919 a limerick verse appeared in *Punch:*

There was an old woman called Tussaud,
Who loved the grand folk in Who's Who so,
That she made them in wax,
Both their front and their backs
And asked no permission to do so.

TWINKLE, TWINKLE LITTLE STAR

Twinkle, twinkle little star,
How I wonder what you are!
Up above the world so high,
Like a diamond in the sky.

When the blazing sun is gone,
When he nothing shines upon,
Then you show your little light,
Twinkle, twinkle, all the night.

Then the traveller in the dark,
Thanks you for your tiny spark,
He could not see which way to go,
If you did not twinkle so.

In the dark blue sky you keep,
And often through my curtains peep,
For you never shut your eye,
Till the sun is in the sky.

As your bright and tiny spark
Lights the traveller in the dark,
Though I know not what you are,
Twinkle, twinkle, little star.

This poem has now become one of our best-known nursery rhymes. It was written by Ann and Jane Taylor, two sisters who wrote poems and hymns for young children at the beginning of the nineteenth century.

The Taylor sisters were born in a house opposite Islington church. Their father was an engraver and his two daughters were employed for long hours helping their father with his work. Due to reduced circumstances, the family moved to Lavenham in Suffolk in 1786 and Mr Taylor had the good fortune to be offered the post as minister at the non-conformist church in Colchester.

Mr Taylor educated his family himself and they all became interested in writing. Ann won a prize in a literary competition run by the publishing firm of Darton & Harvey and from then onwards she established a connection with the editor who was interested in using her work. *The Star* was first published in a book entitled *Rhymes For The Nursery* in 1806. The volume met with considerable success and by 1835 it was in its twenty-seventh edition.

While on holiday in 1813, Ann received a proposal of marriage from a Reverend Gilbert, whom she had never seen. Nevertheless, the couple were married in December of that year. Ann had many children and for a while her literary career was curtailed. She moved about the country with her family as her husband was offered various church posts. Jane died in 1824 at the age of 41, but Ann was determined to carry on the writing which had given her sister and herself so much pleasure. Mr Gilbert died in 1853 but Ann consoled herself in her written work as before. She lived in Nottingham and loved to travel around the country, revisiting childhood haunts. She died at Nottingham in 1866 at the age of eighty-four.

In 1860 J. Green set the poem to music, since when *Twinkle, twinkle, little star* has been in constant use throughout the English-speaking world as an infant hymn and secular song. The simple theme reflects the wonder of the universe as felt by child and adult alike from early times, and it is this mystery and charm which has helped the song to retain its popularity to the present day.

THE STAR-SPANGLED BANNER

The Star-Spangled Banner, the National Anthem of the United States of America, was written by Francis Scott Key and is sung to music composed by John Stafford Smith. It was officially adopted as the national anthem in March 1931 by Congress, but it had been regarded as the unofficial national song by the American army and navy long before this date.

As in most famous traditional songs there lies an interesting story behind its origin. During the War of 1812, the British forces captured William Beanes of Upper 'Marlborough and held him prisoner in a warship in Chesapeake Bay. President James Madison asked two Americans, a lawyer Francis Scott Key and John S. Skinner, to communicate with the British to obtain the release of Beanes. The two men boarded the warship just as it was about to launch an attack on Fort McHenry, which protected the important port of Baltimore. The British agreed to release Beanes after the battle, but held all three Americans prisoner throughout the attack in a prisoner exchange boat well away from danger, so that they could not communicate the British plans to the Americans.

The bombardment started one day in September 1814 and continued all through the night. The prisoners paced the deck until dawn, and could not tell who was winning the battle. When the smoke cleared, they saw that the American flag was still flying over Fort McHenry at Baltimore. The flag, patterned with stars and stripes, was fifty feet long – it can now be seen in the Washington History Museum, where it covers an entire wall. Key was so relieved to see the flag that he pulled a half-written letter from his pocket and on the back started to write the words of this famous song. He wrote most of the words during that memorable morning and the rest when he was released by the British later that day.

Within twenty-four hours the poem had been printed on handbills and distributed throughout the city of Baltimore. A few days later an actor, Ferdinand Durang, sang *The Star-Spangled Banner* to the tune of an old English drinking song called *To Anacreon in Heaven*, which was known to Americans as a political song called *Adams and Liberty*. Durang's performance brought immediate popularity to the song and it was later sung during the Battle of New Orleans.

By government permission the United States flag flies permanently over Key's grave at Frederick in Maryland and over Fort McHenry.

Oh! say, can you see, by the dawn's early light,
What so proudly we hailed at the twilight's last gleaming?
Whose broad stripes and bright stars, thro' the perilous fight,
O'er the ramparts we watched were so gallantly streaming?
And the rockets' red glare, the bombs bursting in air,
Gave proof thro' the night that our flag was still there.
Oh, say, does that star-spangled banner yet wave
O'er the land of the free and the home of the brave?

On the shore, dimly seen thro' the mist of the deep,
Where the foe's haughty host in dread silence reposes,
What is that which the breeze, o'er the towering steep,
As it fitfully blows, half conceals, half discloses?
Now it catches the gleam of the morning's first beam,
In full glory reflected, now shines on the stream.
'Tis the star-spangled banner. Oh! long may it wave
O'er the land of the free and the home of the brave!

And where is that land who so vauntingly swore
And the havoc of war and the battle's confusion
A home and a country should leave us no more?
Their blood has washed out their foul footstep's pollution.
No refuge could save the hireling or slave
From the terror of flight or the gloom of the grave,
And the star-spangled banner in triumph doth wave
O'er the land of the free and the home of the brave.

Oh! thus be it ever when freemen shall stand
Between their loved home and the war's desolation,
Blest with vict'ry and peace, may the Heav'n rescued land
Praise the Pow'r that hath made and preserved us a nation.
Then conquer we must, when our cause it is just,
And this be our motto, 'In God is our trust',
And the star-spangled banner in triumph shall wave
O'er the land of the free and the home of the brave.

IF I HAD A DONKEY

If I had a donkey that wouldn't go,
Would I beat him? Oh no, no,
I'd put·him in the barn and give him some corn,
The best little donkey that ever was born.

This comic song was inspired by the first Act of Cruelty to Animals passed in the British Parliament in 1822. Richard Martin, an Irish Member of Parliament for Galway, had devoted most of his life to championing the cause of dumb animals, for bear-baiting, cock fighting, monkey and dog fighting were very common, and horses and donkeys died in the streets from malnutrition and beatings. People accepted the cruel treatment of animals as a matter of course because they were not educated to think differently. When at last Parliament was made to see the debasement of civilization in allowing these harsh practices to go unpunished, Martin was sixty-seven years old and he felt that at last his life's work was bearing fruit. He was a very unorthodox man, with a lively personality, and conducted many of his cases in court himself. The story goes that he actually brought a costermonger's donkey into court to show the judge how it had been maltreated, but there has never been verification of this and the idea may have come from Jacob Beuler's song:

If I had a donkey wot wouldn't go,
D'ye think I'd wollop him? No, no, no!
But gentle means I'd try, d'ye see,
Because I hate all cruelty.
If all had been like me, in fact,
There ha' been no occasion for Martin's Act,
Dumb animals to prevent getting crackt, on the head.

For if I had a donkey wot wouldn't go
I never would wollop him. No, no, no!
I'd give him some hay and cry 'Geeo-Ho!' and 'Come up, - Ned'.

Wot makes me mention this, this morn,
I seed that cruel chap, Bill Burn,
Whilst he was out a-crying his greens,

His donkey wollop with all his means.
He hit him over the head and thighs,
He brought the tears up in my eyes,
At last my blood began to rise And I said,

If I had a donkey, etc.

Bill turned and said to me, 'Then perhaps,
You're one of these Mr Martin's chaps,
Wot is seeking for occasion
All for to lie an information'.
Though this I stoutly did deny,
Bill up and give me a blow in the eye,
And I replied, as I let fly, At his head,

If I had a donkey, etc.

As Bill and I did break the peace,
To us came the new Police,
And hiked us off, as sure as fate,
Afore the sitting magistrate.
I told his worship all the spree,
And for to prove veracity,
I wished he would the animal see For I said,

If I had a donkey, etc.

Bill's donkey was ordered into court,
In which he caused a deal of sport;
He cocked his ears, and ope'd his jaws,
As if he wished to plead his cause.
I proved I'd been uncommonly kind,
The ass got the verdict – Bill got fined;
For his worship and me were of one mind, And he said,

If I had a donkey, etc.

Bill said, 'Your worship, it's very hard,
But 'tisn't the fine that I regard;
But times are come to a pretty pass
When you mustn't beat a stubborn ass'.
His worship said nothing, but shut his book;
So Billy off his donkey took,
The same time giving me such a look; For I said,

Bill, if I had a donkey, etc.

This ditty became a bestseller in printed form and later joined the nursery collection.

People laughed at Richard Martin when he deplored the blood sports and inhuman treatment of animals, but in time the public realized that his attitude was right and humane. Richard Martin was too modest to allow himself to be credited as the founder of the R.S.P.C.A. but instead let his colleague, the Rev. Arthur Broome, take the honour.

Martin possessed the title of the Lord of Clare, in Ireland, and was an extensive property owner. He was a personal friend of George IV who first bestowed on him the nickname of Humanity Martin. He died when he was nearly eighty, and must remain one of the great humane characters in British history.

SEA SHANTIES

Until the mid-nineteenth century the pattern of British naval history has been reflected to some extent in traditional sea songs, though many have been lost and forgotten over the years, and at some time during the history of sailing, songs were forbidden by the humourless masters of ships long ago. It is known that the luxury of singing to help the hard toil of the labour force was forbidden in Scandinavian ships for many centuries, and this may also explain why there is a dearth of sea songs prior to the eighteenth century in this country.

During the reign of Queen Anne, Samuel Pepys preserved many naval traditions by recording sea songs, but after his death the recording of sea shanties was rare and many were allowed to perish in Georgian times. Later, steamships took over the work of the sailing vessels, and necessarily a decline in working sea songs followed. Nevertheless, sea shanties were sung and many of them are included in the community song books of today. The shanty was essentially a working song – a command and reply duet between the mate and the labourers – used when loading or unloading cargoes, when preparing the ship to cast off by turning the capstan or weighing the anchor, or when manipulating the sails out at sea.

The Rio Grande was and still is a firm favourite, although why Rio Grande was chosen nobody really knows, for it was not a port of any merit, being choked up with sand dunes, and did not possess any outstanding scenic features. Some say that the gold rush in the eighteenth century gave the place an aura. Stan Hugill, in his book *Shanties and Sailors' Songs*, presents some of the lines of the song like this:

> *Oh, a ship went a-sailing out over the bar,*
> *'Way for Rio –*
> *They've pointed her bow to the Southern Star*
> *And we're bound for the Rio Grand –*
> *Then away, bullies away –*
> *'Way for Rio –*
> *Sing fare ye well me Liverpool gals,*
> *And we're bound for the Rio Grande.*

Verse seven contains these words:

> *Cheer up, Mary Ellen, now don't look so glum,*
> *On white stockin' day you'll be drinking hot rum.*

Whitestocking Day was the day when sailors' wives and mothers went to the shipping offices to draw the half pay that their men folk had left them. They put on their best clothes, which included long white cotton stockings, for this special event and the town knew when it was pay day for sailors' dependents by the gathering of ladies wearing white stockings outside the shipping offices. This practice was carried out up to the last world war. Other 'hauling' songs recall the Napoleonic wars:-

> *Boney was a warrior*
> *Way, high, Ya!*
> *A warrior, a terrier,*
> *John Franswar!*

Jean Francois was the title of a French seaman's song. Another popular shanty was:

> *Boney beat the Prussians,*
> *The Osstrye-ans an' the Rooshye-ans,*
> *Boney went to school in France,*
> *He learnt to make the Rooshians dance.*
> *Oh, Boney marched to Moscow,*
> *Lost his army in the snow.*

Boney wuz a Frenchman,
But Boney had to turn again.
He wuz sent to Elba,
Wish'd he'd never bin there.
He whacked the Proosians squarely,
He beat the English nearly.
We licked him in Trafalgar's Bay,
Carried his main topm'st away.
'Twas on the plains of Waterloo,
He met the boy who put him through.
He met the Duke of Wellington,
And then his downfall wuz begun.
The long-nosed Dook he put him through,
He put him through at Waterloo.
Boney went a-cru-sye-in,
Aboard the Billy-Ruffye-an.
They sent him into exile,
He died on St Helena's Isle.
Boney was a war-rye-or,
A rorty-snorty war-rye-or.

The ordinary seaman led a miserable existence centuries ago: not only did he have to do extremely hard manual work, but he was never given enough good food and hardly any medical attention. Many died at sea or suffered scurvy at the least. The payment was low and treatment was harsh and cruel. The punishment for disobeying an order was many lashes with the 'cat'. Here are a few lines from *Aboard The Man-o'-War*:

They hung me up by my two thumbs,
And they lashed me till the blood did run;
They cut a net crosst me back and bum.
O! aboard the man-o'-war.

The treatment of slaves and the slave trade as a whole was abhorred by all. A verse taken from the *Roxburghe Ballads* entitled *The Algier Slave's Release* says:

Sometimes to the galleys I'm forced to go,
Though amongst all my fellows like a slave I do row;
And when I am spent with this labour and pain.
The thoughts of my love revive me again.

Because of the poor conditions offered to sailors, crews were hard to come by and press gangs were rife in the eighteenth century. Law-abiding citizens kept behind locked doors when these gangs roamed the streets. They were not particular who they took providing their age and health were suitable. Many sailors just home from long voyages were often pressed back to sea before they had had time to spend any leave or even get married in the orthodox way:

> *William Taylor was a brisk young sailor,*
> *He who courted a lady fair,*
> *Bells were ringing, sailors singing,*
> *As to church they did repair.*
>
> *Thirty couples at the wedding,*
> *All were dressed in rich array,*
> *Instead of William being married,*
> *He was press'd and sent away.*

Duke William, one of the sons of George III who later became William IV, spent many years in the navy. He sympathized with the harsh treatment suffered by ordinary seamen and made many alterations to improve living conditions. He also strove to abolish impressment and, in order to find out what really happened, he arranged for himself to be press-ganged. The story goes that, once aboard the ship, he was ordered to strip so that the mate could flog him. In the ballad called *Duke William's Frolic* he is reported to have said:

> *'No wonder my royal father cannot man his shipping,*
> *'Tis by using them so barbarously, and always them a-whipping,*
> *But for the future sailors all shall have good usage;*
> *To hear the news, together all cried, 'May God bless Duke*
> *William'.*

Impressment was abolished in 1815.

As mentioned in the section on street cries, many wounded sailors turned to begging for a living after the Napoleonic Wars:

> *I'm blind and I'm crippled,*
> *Yet cheerful would I sing,*
> *Were my disasters triple,*
> *'Cause why? 'Twas for my king.*

In the days before radio was invented, skippers recited rhymes to help them remember coastlines and to guide them into port. These pilot rhymes were especially useful when teaching younger seamen. Here is one dealing with the east coast of England:

> *First the Dudgeon, then the Sperm,*
> *Flamboro' Light comes next in turn;*
> *Scarboro' Light stands out to sea,*
> *And Whitby Light bears northerly.*
> *Huntley Foot that damned high land,*
> *Is five and twenty from Sutherland.*

Many naval terms have now been assimilated into everyday speech. The word 'skylarking', for instance, originated from the time when it was thought that to reduce scurvy sailors should exercise themselves, so, in the evenings, they were ordered to dance the hornpipe to the tune of the *Song and Skylark*. This, of course, produced merriment and relaxation, and continued, subject to the captain's orders, long after the ration of lime juice had been introduced.

Young boys are still called nippers and this word can be traced back to the times when the capstans aboard ship were turned to haul in the anchor cable and the larger capstan was linked to a smaller one by short ropes called nippers. While the adult men heaved at the large capstan, the young boys were put in charge of the nipper ropes and, in time, the boys themselves were called nippers.

The term 'son of a gun' originally meant 'bastard' from the time when the shore women boarded ships in port. Ordinary seamen slept in hammocks between the gun bulwarks and had no special quarters. Many a child was conceived under the gun and this explains the saying, which has a somewhat milder interpretation these days.

To conclude this section on sea songs here is *Blow The Man Down*, which probably dates from the mid-nineteenth century and has an interesting background:

> *Oh, as I was a-rolling down Paradise Street,*
> *Timme, way, hay, blow the man down!*
> *A fat Irish bobby I chance for to meet,*
> *Ooh! gimme some time to blow the man down!*

Sez he, 'Yer a Blackballer by the cut of yer hair,
An the long red-topped seaboots that I see you wear.
Ye've sailed in some packet that flies the Black Ball,
Ye've robbed some poor Dutchman of boots clothes and all.'

'Oh mister, O mister, ye do me great wrong,
I'm a flying fish sailor, just home from Hongkong.'
So I spat in his face, an' I stove in his jaw;
Sez he, 'Young fellar, yer breakin' the law.'

They gave me six months, boys in Liverpool town,
For bootin' an' kickin' and blowin' him down.
Now all ye young fellars what follow the sea,
Put yer vents on the wind and just listen to me.

I'll give ye a warnin' afore we belay,
Steer clear o' fat policemen, ye'll find it'll pay.
Wid a blow the man up, bullies, blow the man down,
An' a crew o' hard cases from Liverpool town.

This song dates back to the time when Dutch sailors were entering the British and American fleets. The natives disliked the 'square heads' or 'yaw-yaw' men for taking their jobs and took the opportunity to rob them whenever they could. This was called 'blackballing' and policemen were told to act severely in cases like this. The song became instantly popular and has remained in the traditional collection ever since.

VICTORIAN AND WINDSOR

QUEEN VICTORIA

In 1837 Victoria succeeded her uncle, William IV, and became Queen of Britain and the Commonwealth. On being appointed Poet Laureate, the first poem Tennyson published was a tribute to the new monarch. It was placed at the beginning of his work entitled *Poems* and thereafter appeared in every edition. Here are five stanzas from the complete version which consists of nine verses:

> *Revered, beloved – O you that hold*
> *A nobler office upon earth*
> *Than arms, or power of brain, or birth*
> *Could give the warrior kings of old,*
>
> *Victoria, since your Royal Grace*
> *To one of less desert allows*
> *This laurel greener from the brows*
> *Of him that utter'd nothing base;*
>
> *Take, Madam, this poor book of songs;*
> *For tho' the faults were thick as dust*
> *In vacant chambers, I could trust*
> *Your kindness. May you rule us long,*
>
> *And leave us rulers of your blood*
> *As noble till the latest day!*
> *May children of our children say,*
> *'She wrought her people lasting good;*
>
> *Her court was pure; her life serene;*
> *God gave her peace; her land reposed;*
> *A thousand claims to reverence closed*
> *In her as Mother, Wife, and Queen';*

When Victoria was eight months old, her father, the Duke of Kent, died, leaving her fifth in line to the throne. Before her in the line of succession were her grandfather, George III, and her three uncles, the Prince Regent, who was later George IV, the ill-fated Duke of York, and the Duke of Clarence, who later became William IV.

Victoria was only eighteen when she became Queen and for a while she enjoyed a life of gaiety and freedom unknown to her before, until she married Prince Albert and adopted his rather sombre, dedicated outlook on life. They had nine children and were very happy, enjoying holidays in Scotland at Balmoral, when affairs of State would allow. Albert died when he was only forty-two and the Queen never really recovered from the tragedy. She retired from public life and attended to affairs of the realm from behind closed doors. She became a morose and ill-tempered woman, and the saying accredited to her that 'We are not amused' reflected her general attitude to events and people around her.

THE CRIMEA

In her later years Queen Victoria became increasingly interested in the expansion of the British Empire, and was particularly impressed by the work that Florence Nightingale had accomplished in the field of nursing and hospital management, both at home and abroad. The Queen once again allowed herself to be seen publicly, and enjoyed the celebrations prepared for her on the occasion of her fiftieth anniversary and again on the sixtieth anniversary of her accession to the throne. She died in 1901 having reigned for sixty-five years, the longest reign of any British sovereign.

In 1854 a passage in *The Times* about 'some hideous blunder' spurred Tennyson to write his immortal poem *The Charge of the Light Brigade*. It has been said that Tennyson's impulse to take his own life in younger days found an outlet in this poem, in which to commit suicide was considered the honourable thing to do:

Half a league, half a league,
Half a league onward,
All in the valley of Death
  Rode the six hundred.
'Forward, the Light Brigade!
Charge for the guns!' he said;
  Into the valley of Death
  Rode the six hundred.

'Forward, the Light Brigade!'
Was there a man dismay'd?
No, tho' the soldier knew
Someone had blundered;
  Theirs not to make reply,
  Theirs not to reason why,
  Theirs but to do and die;
    Into the valley of Death
    Rode the six hundred.

Cannon to right of them,
Cannon to left of them,
Cannon in front of them
  Volley'd and thunder'd;
Storm'd at with shot and shell,
Boldly they rode and well,
  Into the jaws of Death
  Into the mouth of Hell
  Rode the six hundred.

Flash'd all their sabres bare,
Flash'd as they turn'd in air
Sabring the gunners there,
Charging an army, while,
All the world wonder'd;
  Plunged in the battery-smoke
  Right thro' the line they broke;
  Cossack and Russian
  Reel'd from the sabre-stroke
  Shatter'd and sunder'd.
    Then they rode back, but not,
    Not the six hundred.

Cannon to right of them,
Cannon to left of them,
Cannon behind them
   Volley'd and thunder'd;
Storm'd at with shot and shell,
While horse and hero fell,
They that had fought so well
Came thro' the jaws of Death,
Back from the mouth of Hell,
All that was left of them,
   Left of six hundred.

When can their glory fade?
O the wild charge they made!
   All the world wonder'd.
Honour the charge they made!
Honour the Light Brigade,
   Noble six hundred.

The Crimean War, fought against Russia by Turkey, France and Britain, was one of the worst-managed wars in history. Russia had decided that it was her right to protect Christians living on Turkish soil and therefore invaded Turkey, destroying Turkish ships in the Black Sea. Britain and France saw their chance to weaken Russia, who was becoming too powerful, and so they allied themselves with Turkey. Approximately 57,000 British troops invaded the Crimea, a peninsula on the Black Sea coast, and marched towards Sebastopol on Russian territory.

It was at the siege of Sebastopol that the now-famous incident took place. Several times the Russian forces tried to break through to relieve the city and they succeeded at one point in capturing some Turkish guns. The British commander, Lord Raglan, sent orders to the Light Cavalry to recapture them. The officer in charge, Nolan, made a terrible error and sent the Light Brigade in the wrong direction – straight into the Russian guns. Six hundred men obeyed an order which they knew to be a mistake and charged heroically to their deaths. Tennyson expressed the horror and the pride of the nation at the soldiers' heroism when he wrote *The Charge of the Light Brigade*. He was quick to point out that it was the loyal soldiers who suffered and died, while incompetent commanders went unpunished.

The poem was published in a newspaper in December 1854 and was an immediate success. The British troops fighting in the Crimea expressed great interest in the work and, in a response to demand, Tennyson had a thousand copies printed and sent out to the battle front.

If soldiers did not die of their wounds, they probably died of cholera, starvation or frostbite in this mismanaged campaign. Florence Nightingale was sent out to the Crimea, together with thirty-eight nurses, to establish a military hospital. When she arrived at Scutari, she found no bandages, no sanitation, no drugs and not even a cake of soap. She reorganized the hospital completely and consequently saved many soldiers' lives. Each evening she toured the wards carrying a lantern and the men came to call her 'the lady with the lamp'.

ANNIE LAURIE

Although Annie Laurie was born in 1685, it was not until the Crimean War that the original poem of the same name, written in 1703, was revised and set to music by Lady John Scott. It was published, together with other songs, to raise money to help the widows and orphans of the soldiers who had fought in this campaign.

The story goes that, when Annie was eighteen, she fell in love with a young man with strong Jacobite connections called William Douglas of Fingland. They met at a ball in Edinburgh and, as Annie's father, who was first Baronet of Maxwelton, did not condone the match for political reasons, the lovers met secretly for many months in the extensive grounds of Maxwelton, where Annie lived. The pressure on the Stuart invasion was such that Douglas was recalled to Edinburgh and was forced to flee to the Lowlands to avoid capture. On the eve of his departure, he was said to have written this poem to Annie:

> *Maxwelton Banks are bonnie,*
> *Whare early fa's the dew,*
> *Whare me and Annie Laurie*
> *Made up the promise true,*

Made up the promise true;
And ne'er forget will I;
And for bonnie Annie Laurie
I'd lay down my head and die.

She's backit like a peacock
She's breistit like a swan,
She's jimp about the middle,
Her waist ye weel may span,
Her waist ye weel may span;
And she has a rolling eye;
And for bonnie Annie Laurie
I'd lay down my head and die.

Annie Laurie, who was the youngest of a large family, was said to be very beautiful, with rich brown hair that was unpowdered, contrary to current fashion, a lovely Grecian face, blue eyes and a slim figure to match. As in the song, she did have a 'rolling eye' and was not broken-hearted when her lover had to leave the country. In fact, she never saw him again. She had many affairs and finally married Alexander Ferguson, the rich laird of Craigdarroch, when she was about twenty-eight. It was reported that she enjoyed a very happy married life and had every luxury. In later years she achieved the reputation of being a matchmaker, probably drawing on her own experiences, and she also took snuff!

Annie designed the new building at Craigdarroch and also the Georgian gardens behind. In all her letters throughout the years she only mentioned Douglas once, saying she hoped that he had renounced his treasonable opinions and that he was content. William Douglas also did not seem unduly worried at the end of the romance and he had many more affairs, before making a runaway marriage with a lady named Elizabeth Clerk, by whom he had four sons and two daughters. He was a notable swordsman and was reported to have fierce, squinting eyes – perhaps that was the reason why Annie Laurie changed her mind about him! He wrote other poems, but *Annie Laurie* is the only one to have survived.

Lady John Scott omitted the original second verse and substituted two more of her own, which she thought in better taste. Here are the second and third verses of the song as published in 1853;

Her brow is like the snaw-drift,
Her neck is like the swan,
Her face it is the fairest
That e'er the sun shone on;
And dark blue is her e'e;
And for bonnie Annie Laurie
I'd lay me doun and dee.

Like dew on the gowan lying
Is the fa' o' her fairy feet;
And like the winds in summer sighing,
Her voice is low and sweet;
And she's a' the world to me;
And for bonnie Annie Laurie
I'd lay me doun and dee.

HOME SWEET HOME

The song *Home Sweet Home* has strong Victorian connotations for many people. It was written by an American, John Howard Payne, who came to England from his home in Long Island as a teenager. He was very interested in the theatre and, although he was not an outstanding actor, he took any job connected with the stage that was offered to him: he scrubbed floors, moved scenery and did anything that helped him to survive. However, times were very hard and, even when he took to writing plays and musical scripts, luck was not with him. He was imprisoned for debt in London and was released when he finally sold a successful translation.

One evening, when he was near starvation and was wandering in bitter weather about the streets of London, he strayed into the West End. He looked through the lighted window of a large house and saw a young lady playing the piano. The air was unfamiliar to him, but he was much taken with it. Then the family retired to the dining room at the back of the house to consume a wonderful meal in sumptuous surroundings. Payne crept round the back and peeped in. The sight of so much rich food made his own plight seem all the more horrible, and he swore and dashed down the street back to his own hovel. He worked all night on the song *Home Sweet Home*, inspired by what he had seen and thoughts of his own home that he had left in America. He based the melody on the air that he had heard earlier.

Eventually Payne wrote a musical play called *Clari, The Maid of Milan*, which included *Home Sweet Home* and it was bought by a musical director named Bishop for £50. The song was so successful that it was soon sold as sheet music, and Payne never looked back from that time. He continued to write songs and plays, and returned to America in 1832. It is strange that the man who wrote *Home Sweet Home* never married and never knew the comforts of a real home. This fact alone perhaps makes the song even more nostalgic.

In 1843 Payne was appointed American Consul in Tunis, a post which he held until his death nine years later. It was not until thirty years after his death that a certain Mr Corocoran of Washington, who had known Payne, obtained permission to bring back his remains to America. At an emotional reinterment service held at Oak Hill Cemetery, Washington, a thousand voices sang *Home Sweet Home:*

'Mid pleasures and palaces, though we may roam,
Be it ever so humble there's no place like home;
A charm from the skies seems to hallow us there,
Which, seek through the world, is ne'er met with elsewhere.
Home, home, sweet, sweet home,
There's no place like home, there's no place like home!

An exile from home, splendour dazzles in vain,
Oh, give me my lowly thatched cottage again;
The birds singing gaily that came at my call,
But give me the peace of mind dearer than all!
Home, home, sweet, sweet home,
There's no place like home, there's no place like home!

I gaze on the moon as I trace the deer wild,
And feel that my parent now thinks of her child;
She looks on that moon from her own cottage door,
Through woodbines whose fragrance shall cheer me no more,
Home, home, sweet, sweet home,
There's no place like home, there's no place like home!

To thee I'll return overburdened with care,
The heart's dearest face will smile on me there;
Let others delight 'mid new pleasures to roam,
But give me, oh give me, the pleasures of home.
  Home, home, sweet, sweet home,
  There's no place like home, there's no place like home!

JOHN BROWN'S BODY

Another song with strong American roots found in Community songbooks is *John Brown's Body* which dates from before the American Civil War. John Brown was a man who was violently opposed to slavery and did his best to abolish it in every way he could. Moves were afoot to solve the question peacefully, but John Brown, who was then fifty-nine, believed that the only way to end the problem was to arm the negroes and give them a chance to fight for their independence. One night he and eighteen followers seized an arsenal at Harper's Ferry, Virginia. Brown expected the slaves to support him by revolting and joining him and his men, this did not happen, and the next day a force of United States marines, led by Robert E. Lee, captured the rebels. Fifteen men were killed and John Brown was taken prisoner. He was later tried on charges of treason and murder, and was hanged in 1859.

The Civil War broke out in 1861, in which the Northern States fought the Southern States, where negroes were employed as slaves. The song was adopted by the Northern troops as a marching song. The chorus 'and his soul goes marching on' was enjoyed by all foot soldiers. Some reports say that this song had nothing to do with the erudite John Brown, but came from a poem written about a sergeant in the Massachussetts Infantry Regiment and only achieved popularity because people thought it referred to the infamous John Brown. Here are the original words of the song we know so well, as sung by the Union soldiers and written down by W. J. Wetmore:

John Brown's body lies a-mouldering in the grave,
John Brown's body lies a-mouldering in the grave,
John Brown's body lies a-mouldering in the grave,
His soul goes marching on!

Glory, glory, hallelujah!
Glory, glory, hallelujah!
Glory, glory, hallelujah!
His soul goes marching on!

We mourn for the fallen one, we weep for the brave,
Who to a holy cause his noble life he gave,
Sadly, yet proudly, we shout forth his name,
As we go marching on!

Glory, glory, hallelujah, etc.

John Brown's knapsack is strapped upon his back,
John Brown's knapsack is strapped upon his back,
John Brown's knapsack is strapped upon his back,
His soul goes marching on!

Glory, glory, hallelujah, etc.

He's gone to be a soldier in the army of the Lord,
He's gone to be a soldier in the army of the Lord,
He's gone to be a soldier in the army of the Lord,
His soul goes marching on!

Glory, glory, hallelujah, etc.

The tune to which this is sung had been used as early as 1855 as a camp meeting hymn entitled *Say Brothers Will You Meet Us On Canaan's Happy Shore.* Julia Ward Howe wrote her immortal words for *The Battle Hymn of the Republic,* set to the well-known marching melody, in 1861. She is reported to have been inspired by the Union camp fires while looking through the window of her hotel, Willard's in Washington. Her version was published in February 1862 in *Atlantic Monthly* and it was an immediate success:

Mine eyes have seen the glory of the coming of the Lord;
He is trampling out the vintage where the grapes of wrath are
stored;
He hath loos'd the fateful lightning of his terrible swift sword,
His truth is marching on.

Glory, glory, hallelujah!
Glory, glory, hallelujah!
Glory, glory, hallelujah!
His truth is marching on.

I have seen him in the watch fires of a hundred circling camps;
They have builded Him an altar in the ev'ning dews and damps;
I can read his righteous sentence by the dim and flaring lamps.
His day is marching on.

Glory, glory, hallelujah, etc.

I have read the fiery gospel writ in burnish'd rows of steel;
'As ye deal with My contemners, so with you My grace shall deal'.
Let the hero born of woman crush the serpent with his heel,
Since God is marching on.

Glory, glory, hallelujah, etc.

He has sounded forth the trumpet that never call retreat;
He is sifting out the hearts of men before his judgement seat.
Oh be swift my soul to answer Him, be jubilant my feet!
Our God is marching on.

Glory, glory, hallelujah, etc.

In the beauty of the lilies Christ was born across the sea,
With a glory in his bosom that transfigures you and me;
As he died to make men holy, let us die to make men free,
While God is marching on.

Glory, glory, hallelujah, etc.

ETON BOATING SONG

Although Eton and Westminster schools have a long history of
boat racing, preferred by most boys to cricket as the river flows so
near the school, it was not until the 1860s that the famous Eton
school song was composed:

> *Jolly boating weather,*
> *And a hay-harvest breeze;*
> *Blade on a feather,*
> *Shade off the trees.*
> > *Swing, swing together,*
> > *With your bodies between your knees.*
> > *Swing, swing together,*
> > *With your bodies between your knees.*

Twenty years hence this weather
May tempt us from office stools;
We may slow on the feather,
And seem to the boys old fools,
    But we'll still swing together,
    And swear by the best of schools,
    And we'll still swing together,
    And swear by the best of schools.

The lyrics were written by William Johnson, a master at Eton, who sent them to an old pupil of his, Algernon Drummond, serving in the Punjab in the Rifle Brigade. Although he was no musician, Drummond was so impressed by the words that he and another officer composed the tune as we know it today. The melody was partly based on Tennyson's *Break, Break, Break*. In the officer's mess there was a 'tinny old piano' and this is where the song was born. There were other old Etonians in the battalion and they sung the new composition in the evenings with great pleasure. The song became so popular that it was adopted as a second school anthem – the original being in Latin and not so well known. The tune had a good waltz rhythm and was played constantly at balls and parties in Victorian times. The song is still sung sometimes when old Etonians meet. The royalties are paid to the Bursar of Eton and are put towards a prize for music, named after the young officer stationed in India who composed the song.

BOAT RACE DAY

In 1829 the first boat race between the universities of Oxford and Cambridge was rowed at Henley. In the first race Cambridge wore leander pink, while Oxford wore the traditional royal blue. After much discussion, it was decided that pink was not an appropriate colour for a boat race crew, so the 'light blues' of Eton were adopted by Cambridge and have been worn by them ever since.

In 1836 the race was rowed on a tideway and soon became an annual event on the Putney to Mortlake course. The boat race of

1866 was recorded in a popular song of the day, written and sung by Harry Sydney, a topical songster and entertainer. The year marked the first attempt by the Thames Conservancy to curtail barges and other river traffic while the race was in progress. Up to this time sailing boats, paddle steamers and the like were allowed to churn up the water and prevented the boat race from progressing in a fair manner:

> *In some person's estimation*
> *Not a contest that takes place*
> *Causes half as much sensation*
> *As the 'Varsity Boat Race.*
> *Dark Blue urging on the Dark Blue,*
> *Cambridge calling on the Light;*
> *Whether Dark Blue or the Light Blue,*
> *Each believes his Blue the right.*
>   *Now give way!*
>
> *Great is the excitement on the Boat Race Day,*
> *Ev'ry one desiring that they should have fair play;*
> *With confidence and courage both the race begun.*
> *And freely we acknowledge that the best men won.*

Sydney continues his song to tell how a sailing barge off Chiswick meadows made Cambridge divert their course and lose the race:

> *Always an excuse for losing,*
> *Oft trifles we enlarge,*
> *Be the course of doubtful choosing,*
> *Thousands shout, 'Confound that barge!'*
> *Cambridge men once more defeated*
> *Striving for pride of place,*
> *Should such ill-luck be repeated,*
> *They meet defeat, but not disgrace.*
>   *Now give way!*
>
> *Fair was the weather on the Boat Race Day,*
> *Starting both together they have had fair play.*
> *With confidence and courage both the race begun,*
> *And freely we acknowledge that the best men won.*

Although this song is not familiar today, it does recall conditions and incidents which are a part of history, now long forgotten. Harry Sydney sang the refrain in the music halls, where it was received with enthusiasm. Many other songs written in the Victorian era and later were first sung in these places of entertainment, and have remained in the hearts and minds of the British public from that time.

POP GOES THE WEASEL

Like many old rhymes and songs that have been examined, the music hall ditties contain sound observation and psychology, as Harold Scott said, 'A revealing cynicism which, by bringing into comic relief the unpleasant facts of daily life, removed the sting from them!' Never has the British public's sense of humour been so bright, as it was during the music hall era. The poor and oppressed, namely the working classes, found that they could laugh at their fate when it was mirrored in comic songs, presented by talented artistes. When an audience came out of a music hall, it came out bubbling, whistling, laughing and humming choruses. This alone endorsed the fact that the show had provided exactly the type cheering effect that was needed. Music halls began in rough taverns and inns which provided food, drink and some form of show, in which the patrons were usually invited to join to swell the choruses and provide a sing song for all concerned. The ever-popular nursery rhyme 'Pop goes the weasel' commemorates one of the first halls in existence:

> *Up and down the City Road,*
> *In and out the Eagle;*
> *That's the way the money goes,*
> *Pop goes the weasel.*

> *Half a pound of tuppenny rice,*
> *Half a pound of treacle,*
> *That's the way the money goes,*
> *Pop goes the weasel.*

The Eagle tavern replaced the gardens of the Shepherd and Shepherdess when the City Road was built in the East End of

London in 1825. The new proprietor was a man called Rouse, commonly known as 'Bravo Rouse'. He was an adventurous man, who provided new entertainment to attract his customers. He arranged balloon ascents, built the Russian Mountain made of scenic model railways, and in 1831 converted the ornaments used at the coronation of William IV into a large ornamental entrance to his pleasure gardens. He extended the Eagle tavern and the site was then called Royal Eagle Coronation Pleasure Grounds. In 1832 he built the Grecian saloon and provided dancing and entertainment within its walls, thus extending the Eagle even more. Later the saloon became the Grecian Theatre, but did not thrive as such and, in 1882, it was taken over by the Salvation Army. Until its demolition at the turn of the century, the Grecian Theatre could easily be distinguished by the two stone eagles set on pillars on each side of the entrance.

The song 'Pop goes the weasel' was written in the 1830s by Charles Sloman and sung by him in such places of ill-repute as the Cyder Cellars and the Coal Hole. His version does not contain the words that are so familiar to us today. There were six verses in the original song, all in the same vein as the first:

> *Something new starts every day,*
> *Pop goes the Weasel,*
> *Fashion ever changes sway,*
> *Pop goes the Weasel.*
> *As one comes in another goes out,*
> *Pop goes the Weasel.*
> *The newest one, there is no doubt, is*
> *Pop goes the Weasel.*

The lyrics comment on the changing fashion of catch phrases and 'pop goes the weasel' was a saying at the time. The 'weasel' was a tailor's 'goose' or heavy iron, a commodity which could easily be pawned. Another explanation of this rhyme was suggested by Arthur Moore, who says he had always understood that the Eagle tavern had been a betting shop, where money was lost and poachers pawned their weasels to pay their debts.

James Robinson Planché used the verse that we know today in his revue *The Haymarket Spring Meeting* and adapted it to the Eagle tavern, where it was first produced.

NURSERY RHYMES

Surprisingly, many nursery rhymes have their roots in music hall songs. 'A frog he would a-wooing go', originally derived from an obscure sixteenth century ballad, was composed and sung by John Liston at Covent Garden and was later sung by Grimaldi and Sam Cowell at Evan's Supper Rooms in 1850.

'Diddle diddle dumpling' is a ditty taken from the cry of the hot dumpling sellers in the streets of London:

> *Diddle diddle dumpling, my son John*
> *Went to bed with his trousers on,*
> *One stocking off, and one stocking on,*
> *Diddle diddle dumpling, my son John.*

It was brought to fame by Arthur Lloyd, a versatile performer, who claimed to be the author, and it quickly found its way into the nursery collection.

'Oh where, Oh where has my little dog gone' is a firm favourite with children today, but, like so many others, it was not written with children's amusement in mind. The composer was an American music publisher, Septimus Winner, who was also a critic and had as many as two thousand pieces to his credit. He died in 1902 in Philadelphia at the age of seventy-six, since when this rhyme has achieved immortality:

> *Oh where, oh where has my little dog gone?*
> *Oh where, oh where can he be?*
> *With his ears cut short and his tail cut long,*
> *Oh where, oh where can he be?*

Originally called *Der Deitcher's Dog*, the song was registered in 1864 and described as a 'comic ballad'. As the title suggests, it relates the fears of a German dog owner when he loses his pet. Here are three other original stanzas:

> *I loves mine lager, 'tish very goot beer,*
> *Oh where, oh where can he be?*
> *But mit no money I cannot drink here,*
> *Oh where, oh where ish he?*

Across the ocean in Garmanie
Oh where, oh where can he be?
Der deitscher's dog ish best companie
Oh where, oh where ish he?

Un sasage ish goot, bolonie of course,
Oh where, oh where can he be?
Dey makes un mit dog und dey makes em mit horse,
I guess dey makes em mit he!

The song was often sung at college gatherings at the turn of the century, and through misuse is now often referred to as *The Dutchman's Dog*.

The famous chant of *Jingle Bells*, now part of the modern Christmas scene, was brought over from America by the Christy Minstrels and sung on the music hall stage. Many songs now part of the oral tradition were introduced to this country in this way and song writers depended on travelling minstrel shows to advertise their latest 'hits'. George Leybourne was one of the early stars of the music hall, who was responsible for the popularity of yet another nursery rhyme:

Polly put the kettle on,
Polly put the kettle on,
Polly put the kettle on,
We'll all have tea.

Sukey take it off again,
Sukey take it off again,
Sukey take it off again,
They've all gone away.

This rhyme was set to a well-known country dance tune of the eighteenth century called *Jenny's Bawbee*. Leybourne wrote the words and sung them constantly in 1870 on the stage, until the title became a household catch-phrase.

Leybourne was originally an engine fitter, who came up to London from his home town, Wolverhampton, for a holiday. While in the capital, he tried out his act in the 'free and easies', which were pubs that provided a crude sort of entertainment. He was soon asked by Charles Morton, 'the Father of the Halls', to make his debut at the Canterbury and his future was assured. At the peak of his career, he was earning £120 per week which was a substantial amount in those days. The manager of the Canterbury built up Leybourne's reputation as a man-about-town by buying him a carriage and four white horses in which he drove from one hall to another. His hit song *Champagne Charlie* has never been forgotten and was the craze of the time. The champagne merchants provided free champagne for George Leybourne, to the tune of twenty pounds a week, because they thought the advertisement for their commodity was well worth it:

> *Champagne Charlie is my name,*
> *Champagne drinking is my game,*
> *There's no drink as good as fizz! fizz! fizz!*
> *I'll drink every drop there is, is, is!*
> *All round town it's the same,*
> *By pop! pop! pop! I rose to fame,*
> *I'm the idol of the barmaids,*
> *And Champagne Charlie is my name.*

George Leybourne was a 'swell' on the stage and off – drinking champagne at all times. He lived beyond his means and kept very irregular hours. This way of life brought on ill health and an early death at the age of forty-two in 1884. Leybourne also wrote and sang *The Man On The Flying Trapeze*, another very popular song, with music by Alfred Lee, who also composed the music for *Champagne Charlie*:

> *He'd fly through the air with the greatest of ease,*
> *A daring young man on the flying trapeze,*
> > *His movements were graceful,*
> > *All the girls he could please*
> *And my love he purloined away!*
>
> *He taught her gymnastics and dressed her in tights*
> *To help him live at his ease,*
> *And made her assume a masculine name,*
> *And now she goes on the trapeze.*

The song was based on the act of Leotard, the Frenchman who first introduced the trapeze to British audiences in 1860. He performed nightly at the Alhambra Theatre to a silent and amazed audience. The song was revived in the 1930s.

In the early days, composers and lyric writers were very poor and never received the reward they were entitled to if they wrote a bestseller. Songs were usually written for one artiste, who paid the composer a nominal sum, for instance, when Alfred Lee came to London with the score of *Champagne Charlie* in his pocket, he had so little money that he could not pay the toll at Waterloo Bridge. He waited in near despair, while the publisher decided whether or not to accept the song, for which he was eventually paid an advance of £20.

CHARLES COBURN

Fred Gilbert wrote many songs for Charles Coburn, of which his most successful was *The Man Who Broke The Bank At Monte Carlo*, based on a true incident in which a man named Charles Wells won £60,000 at the gaming tables and thus broke the Monte Carlo Casino Bank. Gilbert had a hard job to sell this song, but eventually Coburn himself bought it for a guinea. Later Coburn advanced the composer £10 for his share in the publication, while he himself drew £600 in royalties, but that was all. The song was first sung in public in 1890:

> I've just got here, thro' Paris, from the sunny southern shore;
> I to Monte Carlo went, just to raise my winter's rent.
> Dame Fortune smil'd upon me as she'd never done before,
> And I've now such lots of money, I'm a gent.
>
> As I walk along the 'Bois Bou-long'
> With an independent air,
> You can hear the girls declare,
> 'He must be a millionaire';
> You can hear them sigh
> And wish to die,
> You can see them wink the other eye
> At the man who broke the bank at Monte Carlo.
>
> I stay indoors till after lunch and then my daily walk
> To the great Triumphal Arch is one triumphal march,
> Observed by each observer with the keenness of a hawk,
> I'm a mass of money, linen, silk and starch,
> I'm a mass of money, linen, silk and starch.
>
> As I walk along the 'Bois Bou-long', etc.

I patronized the tables at the Monte Carlo hell
Till they hadn't got a sou for a Christian or a Jew;
So I quickly went to Paris for the charms of Madamoiselle,
Who's the loadstone of my heart, what can I do,
When with twenty tongues she swears that she'll be true?

As I walk along the 'Bois Bou-long', etc.

Charles Coburn, whose real name was Colin MacCallum, started working in music halls in 1879, and the song which brought him sudden fame was one that he wrote himself entitled *Two Lovely Black Eyes* or *No More Politics For Me*, adapted from a forgotten ballad called *My Nellie's Blue Eyes*. His first rendition of the song was at the Paragon in Mile End Road, where he was booked for a fortnight, but stayed fourteen months:

Strolling so happy down Bethnal Green,
This gay youth you might have seen,
Tompkins and I, with his girl between,
Oh! What a surprise!
I praised the Conservatives frank and free,
Tompkins got angry so speedilee,
All in a moment he handed to me,
Two lovely black eyes!

Two lovely black eyes,
Oh! what a surprise!
Only for telling a man he was wrong,
Two lovely black eyes!

Next time I argued I thought it best,
To give the Conservative side a rest,
The merits of Gladstone I freely press'd,
When oh! What a surprise!
The chap I had met was a Tory true,
Nothing the Liberals right could do,
This was my share of that argument too,
Two lovely black eyes!

Two lovely black eyes, etc.

The moral you've caught I can hardly doubt:
Never on politics rave and shout,
Leave it to others to fight it out,
If you would be wise.

Better, far better it is to let
Liberals and Tories alone, you bet,
Unless you're willing and anxious to get
Two lovely black eyes!

Two lovely black eyes, etc.

The song became an instant success in the West End of London and was even translated into other languages, though the French version is poor:

Deux beaux yeux noire
Ah! ciel . . . quel horreur!

The Duke of Clarence, while listening to Coburn one evening at a smoking concert at the Beaufort Club, jotted down a better version:

Deux beaux yeux poches!
Me v'là épaté.
Je n'ai que dit;
'T' as tort, mon petit',
Deux beaux yeux poches!

The song was so popular that, like *Champagne Charlie*, it was adopted by the Salvation Army and the tune used for a hymn.

Charles Coburn remained at the top of the bill for the rest of his life, doing much good work to improve the conditions and pay of entertainers, and he helped to form the union which is now called Equity. He died in 1945 aged ninety-three.

FOR HE'S A JOLLY GOOD FELLOW

For He's A Jolly Good Fellow has very mysterious origins, in fact, it seems to be impossible to trace its origin with any certainty. Apparently the tune has been known in Europe for many centuries and may have been heard first in Jerusalem when the Crusaders fought the Arabs during the Middle Ages. The air became very popular in France when it was used as a nursery song by a nursemaid at the birth of one of Marie Antoinette's children in 1781. It was sung as a lullaby and the Queen of France was so taken with it that soon the whole French Court was singing it:

Malbrook s'en va-t-en guerre,
Mironton, mironton mirontaine.
Malbrook s'en va-t-en guerre
Ne sait quand reviendra.

The lyrics refer to the first Duke of Marlborough, who was a brilliant general and much admired even in France. The song took Europe by storm, and many countries adopted it and supplied their own variations on the words. The British soon followed suit and wrote a version about a military campaign. There are many verses, of which this is the first:

D'Artois returns from Spain
Oh what a rare campaign!
Oh what a rare campaign!
We thought that with a look
He would the place have took,
But the thunders of his wrath
Was not a cracker worth.

The air was used for other British songs including *The Maid of Primrose Hill*, but it was not until the mid-nineteenth century that a song was published that had any significance:

We won't go home till morning,
We won't go home till morning,
We won't go home till morning,
And so say all of us.

For he's a jolly good fellow,
For he's a jolly good fellow,
For he's a jolly good fellow,
And so say all of us.

This song has been described as 'convivial', being most frequently sung in pubs and meeting houses. How the second verse became national property is a mystery that none can solve. It seems to have escalated to fame in the same way as *Auld Lang Syne*, and it is now sung in praise of a fellow man or woman on many occasions. It is rather sad to relate that the original 'jolly good fellow' remains anonymous, though there is no doubt that the author must have had someone in mind when he wrote the words, even if it were only the popular landlord of a local pub. In America the tune is sung with alternative lyrics, *The Bear Went*

Over The Mountain, and this rendering is thought to be of fairly modern origin. The idea that *For He's A Jolly Good Fellow* is an American college song is quite unfounded – the words are unmistakably British.

HAPPY BIRTHDAY TO YOU

Happy Birthday To You ranks as one of songs most frequently sung in the world today. It has a surprising history which started when a twenty-one year old young lady, Patty Hill, graduated from the Free Kindergarten teacher's training school in Louisville, Kentucky, in 1889. Patty Hill possessed some revolutionary ideas on teaching young children and the principal of the college was so impressed with her work that she offered her the post as head of the school attached to the college, which was used for demonstration purposes. So, together with her sister Mildred, who was a music teacher, Patty took charge of the infant school and put her ideas into practice. Her aim was to make school a joyful place in which to be and at the same time a place where good work was done. She and her sister found that one of the best ways to create a happy and relaxed atmosphere was to use songs as communication. To start the day they created a song called *Good Morning To All*. On the sheet music the instructions were that it had to be sung standing and sung 'brightly':

> *Good morning to you,*
> *Good morning to you,*
> *Good morning dear children,*
> *Good morning to all.*

The song was designed to be sung at the commencement of the morning session and the sisters thought it especially suitable for children's voices. As a matter of interest, they also composed a *Goodbye Song* to be sung at the close of school. These two songs and others were published in a music book called *Song Stories for the Kindergarten* in 1896.

Later, the sisters rewrote the morning song with entirely new lyrics and it was called *Happy Birthday To You*, sung supposedly on the event of birthdays within the school. Teachers and students were impressed by what they saw while attending Miss

Hill's classes, and returned to their own domains to practise the new methods. The song *Happy Birthday To You* was easy to remember and spread quickly – teachers singing it to children, children singing it to families and so on. The song could be sung at any age to anybody and was unique. It was not until 1936 that Patty Hill was persuaded by the publishers to subject the song to copyright!

> *Happy Birthday to you, Happy Birthday to you,*
> *Happy Birthday dear ...., Happy Birthday to you.*
> > *From good friends and true,*
> > *From old friends and new,*
> > *May good luck go with you,*
> > *And happiness too,*
> > *And happiness too.*

To a dedicated educationist such as Miss Hill, the success of this song was something of an embarrassment. Nevertheless, she was persuaded by her lawyers to allow herself and her family a fair share of the royalties. Miss Hill died in 1946, and the remaining heir had indicated that he will leave his share of the estate to a charitable trust for small children in honour of Patty S. Hill.

LILY OF LAGUNA

Eugene Stratton was a black artist who was born in Buffalo, U.S.A., and came to Britain with a minstrel troupe called The Haverley Minstrels in 1880. Leslie Stuart wrote most of Stratton's songs, particularly when the latter started. He branched out as a solo act in the halls in 1892. Stratton was a great success and topped the bill wherever he went. His soft shoe shuffle to *Lily of Laguna* became a famous act. Seymour Hicks described him as, 'A dancer beautiful beyond words, who seemed to be a feather blown hither and thither by Leslie Stuart melodies which he taught the town to sing'. Like many other classic songs it is only the chorus that is clearly remembered. Lily of Laguna was in fact a shepherdess. Here is the first verse plus the chorus

It's de same old tale of a pal-pa-ta-ting niggar ev'ry time, ev'ry time;
It's de same old trouble of a coon dat wants to be married very soon;
It's de same old heart dat is longing for it's lady ev'ry time, yes, ev'ry time,
But not de same gal, not de same gal, she is ma Lily, ma Lily, ma Lily gal!
She goes ev'ry sundown, yes, ev'ry sundown callin' cattle up de mountain;
I go cos she wants me, cos she wants me help her do de countin'.
She plays her music to call de lone lambs dat roam above,
But I'm the black sheep and I'm waitin' for de signal of ma little lady love.

> *She's ma lady love, she is ma dove, ma baby love,*
> *She's no gal for sittin' down to dream,*
> *She's the only queen Laguna knows;*
> *I know she likes me, I know she likes me*
> *Bekase she says so,*
> *She is de Lily of Laguna,*
> *She is ma Lily and ma Rose.*

Stratton then sung a yodelling chorus called *Shepherd's Mountain Call*, before launching into the second verse. Laguna is a beautiful resort situated on the east coast of Brazil.

Leslie Stuart has been described by some as the best song writer that the music hall ever had. He was born in Southport in 1864 and was christened Thomas Augustine Barrett. At the tender age of fifteen he was both organist and choirmaster at a local church. Eventually he became organist at St John's Cathedral in Manchester, but his interest in less classical music grew so that, when he wrote popular songs, he had of necessity to use a pseudonym.

Eugene Stratton remained at the top of the bill until he retired in 1914.

BLAYDON RACES

George Ridley was a collier, who, after sustaining injuries in a pit accident which left him a cripple, decided to entertain the public for a livelihood. He composed and sang many songs, mostly about horse racing, with a lively and humorous air. *Blaydon Races* is a song that portrays a true event on an outing to those famous races and is set to a tune called *Brighton*. The proprietor of the Wheatsheaf Inn, where the song was first sung, was a man called Balmbra and his name is immortalized in the song:

1. *Aa went to Blaydon Races, twas on the ninth of June*
    Eighteen hundred and sixty-two on a summer's afternoon;
    Aa tyuk the bus fra Balmbra's and she was heavy laden
    Away we went along Collingwood Street thats on the road to
        Blaydon.

    Oh lads, ye shud a seen us gannin
    Passin' the folks upon the road
    Just as they were stannin,
    Thor wis lots of lads and lasses there
    Sull wi' smilin' faces
    Gannin alang the Scotswood Road
    To see the Blaydon Races.

2. *We flew past Armstrong's factory an' up te the Robin Adair*
    Just gannin doon te the railway bridge the bus wheel flew off there,
    The lassies lost thor crinolines an' the veils that hide thor faces,
    Aa got two black eyes and a broken nose i' gan te Blaydon Races.

    Oh lads, ye shud a seen us gannin, etc.

3. *When we gat the wheel put on, away we went ageyn,*
    But them that had thor noses broke, the' cam back ower hymen,
    Sum went to the dispensary an' sum to Dr Gibbs,
    And sum to the informary to mend thor broken ribs.

    Oh lads, ye shud a seen us gannin, etc.

6. *The rain it poured aall the day an' mayed the grounds quite muddy,*
    Coffy Johnny had a white hat on – they yelled, 'Who sold the
        cuddy?'
    Thor was spice staalls an' munkey shows, an' aad wives selling
        ciders,
    An a chep wi' a hapenny roondeboot shootin', 'Noo me lads for
        riders!

    Oh lads, ye shud a seen us gannin, etc.

The fourth and fifth verses describe how they eventually arrived at the races with George Ridley singing to amuse the passengers and the crowds.

Ridley sang his songs in pubs in the Newcastle area, especially in the old Wheatsheaf in the Cloth Market, where a singing room was built on. It might be classed as one of the early music halls. George Ridley was invited to make his first professional appearance at the Grainger Music Hall in 1862, but his career was short and he died when he was only thirty years old through injuries gained at the pithead. The Grainger Music Hall changed hands and names many times during the ensuing century, but in June 1962 it was used under the name of Balmbra's Music Hall and presented a show celebrating the centenary Of the immortal *Blaydon Races*. The song is used nowadays by supporters of the Newcastle Football Team and was sung repeatedly at the 1974 Cup Final.

GOODBYE DOLLY GRAY

The only ditty to be remembered from the Boer War is *Goodbye Dolly Gray*, which was first sung by Hamilton Hill, a strong Australian baritone, who was distinctive because he would not dress up to perform, but would do his act in everyday attire. Here are some of the words written by William Cobb, which were put to music by Paul Barnes:

> *I have come to say goodbye Dolly Gray;*
> *It's no use to ask me why Dolly Gray.*
> *Goodbye Dolly I must leave you,*
> *Though it breaks my heart to go.*
> *Something tells me I am needed*
> *At the front to fight the foe.*
> *Look the soldier boys are marching,*
> *And I can no longer stay,*
> *Hark! I hear the bugle calling;*
> *Goodbye Dolly Gray.*

The Boer War broke out when Cecil Rhodes, who was Prime Minister of the Cape in 1890, tried to unite several of the independent states of South Africa. He controlled the diamond mines at Kimberley and, when gold was discovered in the Rand, it produced a gold rush. Most of the prospectors were from Britain

and they invaded the Transvaal in their thousands – outnum-
bering the original Boer settlers. Farming settlers from Holland
called themselves *boeren*, which is Dutch for farmer. The *boeren*
did not take kindly to the idea that their territory should be
governed by Britain and in 1899 they declared war.

In the beginning the Dutch were very successful – they seized
the Kimberley diamond mines and besieged the strategic towns of
Ladysmith and Mafeking, which were British strongholds. In
Britain it was soon realized that recruits were necessary and a
large army was sent out to South Africa. Lord Roberts was
Commander-in-Chief and Lord Kitchener was Chief of Staff. The
marching song *Goodbye Dolly Gray* became a favourite with the
infantry soldiers.

Gradually the tide turned in favour of the British, so that the
Transvaal and Orange Free State were under British command.
Mafeking was relieved, and the British commander within its
walls was Colonel Robert Baden-Powell, who later became the
founder of the Boy Scout movement. Many of the Boers had
taken to the hills and continued to make lightning 'commando'
raids on British encampments. Finally, hostilities came to an end
and the peace treaty was signed in 1902. The Boers had suffered
many hardships inflicted by the British during this campaign and
later the British government paid over £3,000,000 to the Boers in
compensation.

The Transvaal was given rights of self-government in 1906 and
the Orange Free State a year later. In 1910 the Union of South
Africa was formed and became part of the Commonwealth. Cecil
Rhodes' dream had come true at last.

EDWARD VII

Queen Victoria died in 1901 and her son succeeded her as Edward
VII. Harry Pleon, actor, comedian and writer often indulged in
taunting royalty and made a hit with this song called *On The Day
King Edward Gets His Crown On*:

> *Father's going to give a dinner to prove he's lots of pelf,*
> *On the day King Edward gets his crown on.*
> *To make the neighbours jealous he'll eat it all himself,*
> *On the day King Edward gets his crown on.*

Auntie'll be dressed in khaki, ribbons down her back,
We can't afford to buy new clothes, but loyalty will not lack,
Ma's going to patch up father's pants with a piece of Union Jack,
On the day King Edward gets his crown on.

Up and down the Strand, up and down the Strand,
Wait until you hear the trumpets sound,
Shouting, 'Hip Hurray' all the blooming day,
When our good King Edward gets his crown on.

After sixty-five years of Queen Victoria's rule, the British public on the whole was pleased to have a change of monarch and Harry Pleon cleverly states the views of the commoners on this subject. In sharp contrast here is an 'official' song commemorating the event, *Land of Hope and Glory:*

Dear Land of Hope, thy hope is crowned,
God make thee mightier yet!
On Sov'ran brows, beloved, renowned,
Once more thy crown is set.
Thine equal laws by Freedom gained – by Truth maintained,
Thine Empire shall be strong.

The Land of Hope and Glory,
Mother of the Free,
How shall we extol thee, who are born of thee?
Wider still and wider shall thy bounds be set;
God, who made thee mighty, make thee mightier yet,
God, who made thee mighty, make thee mightier yet.

Thy fame is ancient as the days,
As oceans large and wide;
A pride that dares and heeds not praise,
A stern and silent pride;
Not that false joy that dreams content
With what our sires have won;
The blood a hero sire hath spent
Still nerves a hero son.

Land of Hope and Glory, etc.

This was one of the marches in *Pomp and Circumstance* written for the coronation of Edward VII by Edward Elgar, who lived from 1857 until 1934 and devoted his life to composing. He was born at Broadheath near Worcester, where he obtained his musical education principally at his father's music shop and local academies. Elgar was heralded as one of the greatest of all British composers. The above song has remained firmly in the traditional British repertoire and is often sung at community meetings and always at the closing of the Promenade Concerts at the Albert Hall. The words were written by Arthur C. Benson. This song is also chosen to represent England at the Commonwealth Games.

'He'd have to get under, get out and get under' is a veteran car song that has survived the years and tells of the perils and frustrations felt by the owners of the new machines. The lyrics remind us that whenever the driver wanted 'to cuddle his queen', the car would break down and he would have to 'get out and get under'!

In 1896 the motor car was seen for the first time on the roads of Britain, and that same year saw the first run to Brighton on 'emancipation day' and the old crocks' race has been an annual event ever since. Horses were, of course, terrified of these noisy, unpredictable monsters and bolted at once. A man with a red flag was ordered to walk in front of the car to warn others of its approach and speed was limited to four miles per hour. In the early days cars were understandably very unreliable and were taken to blacksmiths for repairs!

There is a charming story about a wonderful invention called the King's Car, a splendidly furnished 'room', which was intended to carry Edward VII and his party from the foyer of the Coliseum Theatre to the Royal Box entrance. The contraption was supposed to move on a track on the floor at a given signal. When the King arrived one evening, he and his party were ushered into this 'lounge' for drinks and, when ready, they were to give a signal to be moved forward to the entrance of the Royal Box in private. Alas, a fuse blew at the crucial moment and the car remained stationary. The King thought the whole matter a huge joke and proceeded to walk to the box as usual, much to the chagrin of the organizers. The 'car' was never set in motion again, but was kept in storage for many years. During the 1930s it was used as a booking office at the Stoll Theatre in Kingsway.

DAISY BELL

The song *Daisy Bell* recalls the invention of another form of transport, namely, the bicycle. It was written and composed by Harry Dacre, and sung by a little-known lady called Katie Lawrence in 1892. She sang the song on the stage wearing man's attire – knicker-bockers and stockings. Like many other songs it is only the chorus that is commonly remembered today, but all three verses are given here as the lyrics are so charmingly naive, using all sorts of unbelievable puns!

There is a flower within my heart, Daisy, Daisy,
Planted one day by a glancing dart,
Planted by Daisy Bell!
Whether she loves me or loves me not,
Sometimes it's hard to tell,
Yet I am longing to share the lot
Of beautiful Daisy Bell!

Daisy, Daisy, give me your answer do!
I'm half crazy, all for the love of you;
It won't be a stylish marriage,
I can't afford a carriage
But you'll look sweet upon the seat,
Of a bicycle made for two!

We will go tandem as man and wife, Daisy, Daisy!
Peddling away down the road of life,
I and my Daisy Bell!
When the road's dark we can both despise
P'licemen and lamps as well;
There are bright lights in the dazzling eyes
Of beautiful Daisy Bell!

Daisy, Daisy, give me your answer do, etc.

I will stand by you in wheel or woe, Daisy, Daisy,
You'll be the bell which I'll ring you know!
Sweet little Daisy Bell!

You'll take the lead in each trip we take,
Then if I don't do well,
I will permit you to use the brake,
My beautiful Daisy Bell!

Daisy, Daisy, give me your answer do, etc.

By the late nineteenth century the bicycle had become a useful and manageable form of transport. It developed out of the hobby horse, which was invented by a Reading schoolmaster in 1760, and later it was known as the dandy-horse, because of the dandies or fashionable men who rode it. A crankshaft was introduced by a Scotsman named Kirkpatrick Macmillan, who rode his machine in 1842 from Keir in Dumfrieshire to Glasgow and was fined for knocking down a child. Later pennyfarthings were introduced and they in turn gave way to models similar in design to modern ones thanks to J. K. Starling, who made a machine called a Rover. J. B. Dunlop invented pneumatic tyres in 1888. The bicycle industry in Britain was mainly established in Coventry.

Before the tandem there existed a model called the companionable, designed to take two people side by side. However this idea was soon discarded in favour of the tandem, which is still in use today and is often referred to as a 'daisy'. Therefore, by the turn of the century the bicycle had gained surprising popularity especially with the women, for whom it provided freedom of transport and an independence hardly known before. Special mannish clothes suitable for the saddle were designed and the attire of Katie Lawrence on stage reflected the daring fashions of the day.

DON'T DILLY DALLY ON THE WAY

Marie Lloyd is the accepted queen of music hall stars and she sang many songs which are still very popular today. Perhaps her most famous song was *Don't Dilly Dally On The Way*, written and composed by Charlie Collins and Fred Leigh. The chorus in particular is often sung and has become part of the oral collection. The song endorsed the gaining popularity of the motor car in those early days:

We had to move away,
'Cos the rent we couldn't pay,
The moving van came round just after dark,
There was me and my old man,
Shoving things inside the van,
Which we'd often done before, let me remark.
We packed all that could be packed
In the van and that's a fact;
And we got inside all we could get inside,
Then we packed all we could pack
On the tailboard at the back,
Till there wasn't any room for me to ride.

My old man, said, 'Follow the van, and don't dilly dally
    on the way'!
Off went the cart with the home packed in it,
I walked behind with my old cock linnet,
But I dillied and dallied, dallied and dillied,
Lost the van and don't know where to roam,
I stopp'd on the way to have the old half quarter,
And I can't find my way home.

I gave a helping hand
With the marble wash-stand,
And straight, we wasn't getting on so bad;
All at once the carman bloke
Had an accident and broke,
Well the nicest bit of china that we had.
You'll understand of course,
I was cross about the loss,
Same as any other human woman would;
But I soon got over that,
What with two out and a chat,
'Cos it's little things like that what does you good –

My old man said ...
Lost the van and don't know where to roam,
Now who's going to put up the old bedstead,
If I can't find my way home?

Oh' I'm in such a mess
I don't know the new address,

Don't even know the blessed neighbourhood,
And I feel as if I might
Have to stay out all the night,
And that ain't a-going to do me any good.
I don't make no complaint,
But I'm coming over faint,
What I want now is a good substantial feed
And I sort o' kind o' feel,
If I don't soon have a meal,
I shall have to rob the linnet of his seed.

My old man said . . .
Lost the van and don't know where to roam.
You can't trust the specials like the old time coppers
When you can't find your way home.

The lyrics give a fairly good picture of life in the disreputable parts of London and the uncertain movements of a cockney couple who did 'moonlight flits' from one lodging house to another to avoid paying the rent.

Marie Lloyd's real name was Matilda Wood and she was born in 1870. She first performed as Bella Delmere at the Eagle music hall for fifteen shillings per week. She then decided to change her luck by changing her name again and, as Marie Lloyd, she became world-famous. She was heralded as the foremost comedienne of her day, although she had a fair amount of talented competition, but her personality and sex appeal made every song she sang a winner and she became 'the darling of them all'. *Oh Mr Porter* and *One Of The Ruins Cromwell Knocked About A Bit* are two other well-known songs that were written for her, and she also revived Nellie Power's song *The Boy I Love Is Up In The Gallery*.

Marie Lloyd married three times, but never very happily. One of her husbands was Alec Hurley, the coster comedian. Owing to her coarse humour, she was never asked to perform at the Coliseum, which ran family entertainment, and in 1912, at the height of her fame, she was pointedly left out of the cast of the first Royal Command Performance. She was a big-hearted woman who did not give up easily and she often performed in great physical pain during the last years of her life. She was taken ill while playing at Crouch End Hippodrome and died in 1922 when she was only fifty-two years old.

POLICEMEN SONGS

In 1822, when the police force was first started, the pay was one guinea per week for a single man and, indeed until the turn of the century, the pay was less than £1.50. Rattles were used instead of whistles in the early days and the only qualifications needed to join the force was a smattering of the three Rs. Policemen were called 'peelers' after Sir Robert Peel, who organized the London Metropolitan Police Force – a name that has survived. They were also called 'bobbies', after the same man, and 'coppers' after the slang 'to cop', which means to catch. At first the uniform consisted of top hats and tail coats, but a jacket soon replaced the tail coat, and in 1864 a helmet replaced the top hat. The force was not armed but carried wooden batons and a watch!

Special constables were appointed to help the regulars in emergencies, when riots occurred and so on. The 'specials' were dismissed when the danger was over and could only be classed as casual labour. As we have seen, Marie Lloyd sang about them in her song *Don't Dilly Dally*, 'You can't trust the specials like the old time coppers, when you can't find your way home'. This was probably very true.

The *Gendarmes Duet* in 1871 was a great hit and was first sung in Offenbach's *Genevieve de Brabant*. The original gendarmes took seventeen encores on the first night. This song has been revised and translated, and used often in a paradoxical sense ever since it was introduced to the public. The English version of *We Run Them In* gave ample opportunity for poking fun at British policemen and started a whole spate of 'policemen songs'.

The policemen in Gilbert and Sullivan's opera *The Pirates of Penzance* were a huge success, especially when they sang:

> When Constabulary duty's to be done,
> A Policeman's lot is not a happy one.

The duties of the police varied between town and country, but it was the London 'coppers' that were most sung about. James Fawn, a talented artiste who performed towards the end of the nineteenth century, contributed to the traditional flow when he sang *Ask A Policeman*, written by E. W. Rogers and composed by A. E. Durandeau. Here are the first, second and fifth verses with the choruses:

1. The P'lice force is a noble band
    That safely guard our streets,
    Their valour is unquestioned and
    They're noted for their feats!
    If anything you wish to know,
    They'll tell you with a grin,
    In fact each one of them
    Is a complete 'Enquire within'.

    If you want to know the time,
    Ask a P'liceman!
    The proper Greenwich time
    Ask a P'licemen!
    Ev'ry member of the force
    Has a watch and chain, of course;
    If you want to know the time
    Ask a P'liceman.

2. And if you stay out late at night
    And pass through regions queer,
    Thanks to those noble guardians,
    Of foes you'll have no fear.
    If a drink you want and 'pubs' are shut,
    Go to the man in blue,
    Say you're thirsty, and good natured,
    He'll show you what to do.

    If you want to get a drink,
    Ask a P'liceman!
    He'll manage it, I think,
    Will a P'liceman!
    He'll produce the flowing pot,
    If the 'pubs' are shut or not,
    He could open all the lot,
    Ask a P'liceman!

5. Or if you're called away from home,
    And leave you're wife behind;
    You say, 'Oh! would that I a friend
    To guard the house could find,
    And keep my love in safety',
    But let all troubles cease;
    You'll find the longed for keeper
    In a member of the P'lice.

If your wife should want a friend,
Ask a P'liceman!
Who a watchful eye will lend,
Ask a P'liceman!
Truth and honour you can trace,
Written on his manly face;
When you're gone he'll mind your place,
Ask a P'liceman!

James Fawn was well-known to every policeman in London, especially in the West End. He distributed money to the force every time he was recognized and saluted!

The name P.C. 49 is one that we all have heard and is still used by the callers at bingo halls. The origin may be found in another song about the police force written by William Hargreaves in 1910 and sung by J. W. Rickaby:

When I was out of work the missus nagged me so much you see,
I went down to the station to see if I'd make a 'D'.
They dressed me in this uniform, and then they said to me,
'You're P.C. 49'.

The first day I came out the kids threw mud and spoiled my clothes,
A dozen navvies looked at me, then punched me on the nose;
I don't suppose Jack Johnson ever stopped so many blows
As P.C. 49.

P.C. 49! Anyone can have this little job of mine.
They threw me in some melted tar till I was nearly dead,
Then got a big steam-roller, which they ran across my head;
When I got back the sergeant cried 'Who are you?' so I said,
'I'm P.C. 49'.

One night they held a meeting to advance the suffragette,
The sergeant said, 'We need a lot of men they can't upset',
He looked around the station, then he shouted you can bet,
For P.C. 49.

But how those women mauled me when they caught me by the throat,
They tore the clothes right off my back, to try and get the vote.
For all they left me wearing was the collar of my coat,
With P.C. 49.

P.C. 49! Anyone can have this little job of mine,
They ripped my clothes to ribbons so for help I had to call;
The sergeant looked at me and said, as I stood by the wall,
'I thought it was Maud Allen, but it isn't her at all –
It's P.C. 49'!

The reference to the suffragette movement trying to procure votes for women was very topical before and during the First World War. The suffragettes were a constant source of embarrassment to the authorities and severe measures were taken. Women offenders were subjected to harsh treatment in prison, including forced feeding when they went on hunger strike. Emily Pankhurst was one of many who suffered severely for the movement – her health broke down and she died prematurely. Another supporter committed suicide when she threw herself in front of the King's horse at the Derby in 1913. It was not until 1918 that women finally gained the right to vote.

Another song with close associations with the police force is *Put Me Amongst The Girls*, sung by a north country comedian called Charlie Whittle. The gist of the song is that the 'bobby' in question, like P.C. 49, is not the tough customer that he is supposed to be. In spite of the sergeant's orders to 'get amongst the rough', the timid policeman sighs, 'Put me amongst the girls – those with the curly curls'.

SEASIDE SONGS

Mark Sheridan sang '*I Do Like To Be Beside The Seaside*, written by Glover and Kind, in 1909 and it reflected the fashion for holidays by the sea. The new venue took the place to a certain extent of the health resorts and water spas, such as Bath and Leamington. The sea, it was discovered, contained health-giving properties and the air was very good too. Those who could afford it flocked to inhale the ozone, holiday resorts sprang up, piers were built and pavilions mushroomed. Brighton was perhaps the most popular of all resorts at that time. Royalty blessed this new attraction and of course set the fashion. Seaside songs began to be sung on the stage and this is one that has survived – here is the first verse and chorus:

Everyone delights to spend their summer holiday
Down beside the silvery sea.
I'm no exception to the rule – in fact if I'd my way,
I'd reside at the silvery sea.
But when you're just the common-a-garden Smith, Jones or
  Brown
At business up in town, you've got to settle down;
You save up all the money you can till summer comes around.
Then away you go to a spot you know
Where the cockle shells are found.

Oh, I do like to be beside the seaside,
I do like to be beside the sea,
I do like to be beside the prom, prom, prom,
Where the brass bands play 'Tiddley-om-pom-pom!'
So let me be beside the seaside,
I'll be beside myself with glee;
And there's lots of girls besides
I would like to be beside
Beside the seaside, beside the sea!

Mark Sheridan was born in Hendon, County Durham, and his real name was Fred Shaw. He usually performed his act dressed in bell-bottomed trousers and an old-fashioned frock coat, and whacked the back-cloth lustily with his cane while rendering a number. He was a good entertainer, who also sang songs such as *Who Were You With Last Night?*, which he wrote in collaboration with Fred Godfrey, and *Here We Are Again,* but it is his seaside song that has put him in the ranks of the immortals. He became depressed during the First World War and believed that his popularity was waning; while in a pantomime at the Glasgow Coliseum, he went into a park one day and blew his brains out. Everyone who knew him was shocked at the tragedy and Noel Coward used the seaside song in his film *Cavalcade,* which revived its popularity.

Mr. Reginald Dixon, M.B.E., for many years resident organist at the Tower Ballroom, Blackpool, used this song as his signature tune. He has an original copy as sung by Sheridan and, although he does not know who the composer was, it is recorded as Glover-Kind and he supposes this to be correct.

With bathing very much the vogue in the mid-nineteenth century, a song was popularized by the Great Vance in 1868. He sung about Martha Gunn, the bathing woman on duty at Brighton for over seventy years. She enticed would-be bathers out of the bathing machines to feel the sea, and perhaps even swim in it! The character of Martha Gunn is clearly portrayed in this song composed and sung by Alfred Vance, which reflects the attitude to sea bathing at the time:

> *I am a female Neptune, a sort of mermaid race,*
> *My nature is amphibious, and smiling is my face.*
> *I bathe the ladies young and old, and bless the pretty birds,*
> *My cry's familiar in their ears as any 'ousehold words:*
>
> *Come to your Martha, come, come, come.*
> *The water is warm in the sun, sun, sun.*
> *Don't shiver dear, there's nought to fear,*
> *But come to your Martha, come.*
>
> *I has to study customers and, if the sea is rough,*
> *My manner is so smooth I make 'em think it's calm enough;*
> *Though timid ones, when they behold the ocean cold and grey,*
> *If I was not to collar 'em, would quickly run away.*
>
> *Come to your Martha, etc.*
>
> *I ain't alone the favourite of ma's and pretty girls,*
> *I've bathed a many a markisses, and dipped a many a earls;*
> *They were but young, but if they could remember it they'd say,*
> *With you, that Martha Gunn is quite a 'great gun' in her way.*
>
> *Come to your Martha, etc.*

Alfred Vance was born in 1840 in the north of England (see 'The Northern Music Hall by G. J. Mellor) and his real name was Alfred Peck Stevens. Vance was a rival to Leybourne and led the same kind of life. He appeared many times at the Leeds City Varieties, now used for the B.B.C. production 'The Good Old Days'.

Vance, Leybourne, Macdermott and Mackney were four performers brought to fame by Charles Morton. Morton dubbed these four stars 'great' and they were billed as such to the end of their working days. The Great Mackney was the first black-faced minstrel and made famous the song *I Wish I Was In Dixie*. Later, his recitation *The Whole Hog Or None At All* was such a success that the term 'whole hog' is still used.

TWENTY-ONE TODAY

Jack Pleasants, a shy Yorkshire comedian, was responsible for the special coming of age song sung by all British people, even though the age has now been lowered to eighteen. It was written and composed by Alec Kendall, and quickly found its place in the traditional repertoire. Here are the first and fifth verses, and the chorus:

Excuse me shouting out like this
And making all this noise!
  I've finished up with college life,
  Now I'm one of the boys.
I mean to paint the town tonight,
And give each girl a wink;
  Britons never shall be slaves,
  So let your glasses chink!

I'm twenty-one today!
Twenty-one today!
I've got the key of the door,
Never been twenty-one before,
And Pa says I can do as I like,
So shout, 'Hip, hip hurray!
He's a jolly good fellow!'
I'm twenty-one today.

A girl stopp'd me in Leicester Square,
And cried, 'I'm full of glee,
  I'd love to marry you young man,
  But one thing's stopping me'.
She said, 'Why don't you grow a beard?'
I said, 'May I be hung,
  I wouldn't mind a fair moustache,
  But for whiskers I'm too young.

I'm twenty-one today! etc.

Jack Pleasants was born in Bradford in 1874 and spent his youth singing comic songs to his friends. His ambition was to go on the stage, but when he left school he was put to work in a warehouse. Soon, however, his talent was acknowledged and he obtained work first at the Bradford singing rooms, and later at the Bradford

Palace. He was a great success and toured the provinces appearing at the top of the bill wherever he went. He also played in many pantomimes in the North and his songs became well known. *I'm Twenty-one Today* was written in about 1910 and Bert Feldman, the music publisher, bought the copyright in 1911. Jack Pleasants continued to perform on the stage until one day in January 1924, while appearing as Simple Simon in the pantomime of that name at the Princess Theatre in Bradford, he was suddenly taken ill and rushed to hospital. The operation to remove his appendix was successful by all accounts but he had a relapse the following night and died early the next morning. All Bradford and indeed all music hall fans in Britain mourned this well-loved entertainer. Pleasants was also well-known for his rendering of *I'm Shy Mary Ellen, I'm Shy*.

HELLO! HELLO! WHO'S YOUR LADY FRIEND?

Harry Fragson was an Anglo-French comic and composer. He had an English mother and was born in London, but his father was Belgian and spoke nothing but French. Harry lived with his father in Paris and at an early age received engagements to sing in small night clubs and cafés. In 1905 Arthur Collins saw his act and took him to London with his father. Harry taught himself to speak pure Cockney, which greatly helped his progress on the London stage. He starred at Drury Lane and many other well-known music halls both in England and France. Fragson was a great favourite with the ladies and his greatest hit song was *Hello! Hello! Who's Your Lady Friend?*. He wrote the tune and the lyrics were written by Worton David and Bert Lee. Here is the first verse and chorus:

> *Jeremiah Jones a lady's man was he,*
> *Ev'ry pretty girl he'd love to spoon,*
> *Till he found a wife and down by the silvery sea*
> *Went to Margate for the honeymoon;*
> *But when he strolled along the promenade*
> *With his little wife just newly wed*
> *He got an awful scare when someone strolling there*
> *Came up to him and winked and said,*

> *Hello! Hello! who's your lady friend?*
> *Who's the little girlie by your side?*
> *I've seen you with a girl or two,*
> *Oh' Oh' Oh' I am surprised at you,*
> *Hello! Hello! stop your little games,*
> *Don't you think your ways you ought to mend?*
> *It isn't the girl I saw you with at Brighton,*
> *Who, who, who's your lady friend?*

Fragson's father became so insanely jealous of his son's success on the stage and off, and his popularity with the fair sex in general, that in 1913 he shot Harry with a revolver!

TEDDY BEARS

> *Round and round the garden*
> *Like a teddy bear,*
> *One step, two step,*
> *Tickle you under there!*

This is a frequently used child's tickling rhyme, which is chanted and performed with great glee by both adults and children. Strangely enough there are very few rhymes about teddy bears which may be due to the fact that prior to 1907 the toy as such was unknown. The story goes that Theodore Roosevelt, President of the U.S.A., was persuaded, rather against his will, one day to go on a shooting expedition. He was a soft-hearted man where animals were concerned and when he was confronted with a bear cub, whose mother had just been killed, he refused to shoot it and returned home empty-handed. The newspapers made much of this event and one edition produced a cartoon based on the incident. The bear cub was portrayed so convincingly by the cartoonist that it took the fancy of a penniless toy manufacturer. He created a cuddly bear cub fashioned on the lines of the cartoon image and sent it to the President. In an accompanying letter the man asked if permission could be given for the animal to be manufactured and sold as a cuddly toy under the name of 'teddy bear', after the nickname of the president, 'Teddy' Roosevelt. Permission was granted and so the world famous teddy bear was born.

The old favourite, *The Teddy Bear's Picnic* was in fact written after the bear cub story was published by Jimmy Kennedy and the music was composed by John W. Bratton. It was not initially a huge success, however, until Henry Hall, the band leader, revived it with slightly different lyrics in 1932, since when it has found a niche in children's traditional material and has never been forgotten.

IT'S A LONG WAY TO TIPPERARY

There seems to have been some mystery at one time as to who was the author and composer of the very well-known song *It's A Long Way To Tipperary*. After research done in 1934 in connection with the film *Royal Cavalcade*, a letter came to light which a man called Jack Judge wrote to a certain Mr Whittaker, a shopkeeper in Stalybridge, Cheshire. In the letter Judge explained in detail how he came to write the song and the document was displayed in Mr Whittaker's shop window for some time afterwards. The gist of the contents was as follows. Just after midnight on 31 January 1912, Judge emerged from a club in Stalybridge with his friends, having bet one Frank Newberry five shillings, that he could write, compose and sing a new song that very day. He bid a jocular goodbye to his friends and, on the way to his lodgings in Portland Place, he overheard one man say to another, 'It's a long way to . . .' somewhere or other. This phrase immediately stuck in Judge's mind and he added the name 'Tipperary'. He then slept on the idea and the next morning, after a good breakfast, he walked to the Newmarket Inn, sat down and wrote the lyrics as if he already knew them off by heart. Some time later, he hummed the tune to the musical director of the Grand Music Hall, opposite the pub, where he was currently appearing. Horace Vernon, the conductor, hastily wrote a score and Jack Judge sang his song that very night, and won his bet. It is interesting to note that Judge's mother came from Tipperary, which is probably why he chose this particular town:

> *Up to mighty London came an Irishman one day,*
> *As the streets were paved with gold, sure ev'ry one was gay;*
> *Singing songs of Piccadilly, Strand and Leicester Square,*
> *Till Paddy got excited then he shouted to them there,*

It's a long way to Tipperary,
It's a long way to go.
It's a long way to Tipperary,
To the sweetest girl I know!
Goodbye Piccadilly,
Farewell Leicester Square.
It's a long way to Tipperary,
But my heart's right there! It's there!

Paddy wrote a letter to his Irish Molly O,
Saying, 'Should you not receive it, write and let me know!
If I make mistakes in spelling, Molly dear', said he,
'Remember it's the pen that's bad, don't lay the blame on me.'

It's a long way to Tipperary, etc..

Molly wrote a neat reply to Irish Paddy O,
Saying, 'Mike Maloney wants to marry me, and so
Leave the Strand and Piccadilly, or you'll be to blame,
For love has fairly drove me silly − hoping you're the same'.

It's a long way to Tipperary, etc.

So great was the confidence of Judge that he had written a winner
that a few weeks later he put the following advertisement for the
song in a theatrical magazine:

It's a long way to Tipperary
A song that's full of go.
The wildest men will sing it
In the wilds of Borneo.
The wild, wild waves will roar it
You'll find these words prove true,
Wild elephants will dance it,
So will monkeys at the zoo.

Judge repeatedly sang the song at his various engagements
round the country, as did Florrie Forde, and it was sung to the
troops on manoeuvres in Ireland and in the Isle of Man. Judge
also had a regular date to entertain the 7th Battalion of the
Worcestershire Regiment each summer and he sung his favourite
song to them many times before World War I broke out. Thus,
most regular soldiers in Judge's territory were well acquainted
with the song and took it to the Continent with them.

When a struggling music publisher named Bert Feldman

bought the score from Judge and arranged for the sale of sheet music, the song really reached the height of its fame. It is true to say that as Feldman made *Tipperary*, so *Tipperary* made Feldman. He became one of the leading music publishers of the day and his name is still well-known in the music world. He replaced the image of Florrie Ford on the frontispiece with an illustration of British troops marching into battle, with the title 'Soldiers of the King'. Although the song was not originally written with war in mind, it was in this context that it made its mark.

Jack Judge was a fishmonger and, when not engaged in music hall work, he would be at this fish stall in Oldbury market near Birmingham, where he and his family lived. He was known as the 'cheerful singing fishmonger' and would entertain his customers with songs and patter while serving them. Although of Irish extraction, Judge and his family of nine were brought up in Oldbury. People who knew him say he was a very cheerful and happy man, who was always ready to help those not so fortunate as himself. At one function, a regimental dinner for the Buffs, he was called on to make an impromptu speech and he began by saying: 'May the good ceiling never fall in and the good fellows below never fall out!'

The story of *Tipperary* does not finish there however, for many people claimed to have heard the song before 1912 and that a cripple named Harry Williams composed it with Jack Judge – long before the official date of publication. Judge was a great friend of Harry's, who was a musician and lived with his brother at the Plough Inn (later renamed the Tipperary Inn) at Meer End in Warwickshire. The pair often composed and sang tunes together to entertain the customers around the piano. Williams died in 1925, but among his papers was a song written in Judge's handwriting, with the score composed by Williams. The song was called *Connemara* and this was undoubtedly the song that had been sung before 1912. What happened, it seems, is that Judge changed the title and some of the words, and produced it as a new song called *It's A Long Way To Tipperary*. In any case, both Judge and Williams received royalties from the song from Feldman, which perhaps settles the matter.

'Tipperary' was popular with the troops in the Second World War also, possibly for the nostalgic quality of the lines 'Goodbye Piccadilly, Farewell Leicester Square'.

FLORRIE FORDE

As previously mentioned, Florrie Forde, the well-known chorus singer, sang *Tipperary* in the early days for Jack Judge, but without much success. In fact, it was her only failure. She was a great friend of Bert Feldman's and he in turn worshipped Florrie, and spent much time with her when she performed in Douglas on the Isle of Man and in Blackpool. Florrie was born in Australia, but emigrated to England as a young girl and immediately went on the stage. She was renowned for her expensive dresses and fabulous hats. In a pantomime at the York Empire in 1902 Florrie wore a huge hat costing £7 sterling. Her songs were all supplied by Feldman and included *Down At The Old Bull And Bush*, *Antonio*, *When Irish Eyes Are Smiling*, *I'm A Lassie From Lancashire*, *Has Anybody Here Seen Kelly?* and *Flanagan*.

Feldman introduced a copyright system in 1904. Up to that time songs were bought outright for a small fee by individual artistes. Feldman's idea that a system of copyright would give the publishers and composers a fair deal got an immediate response, and sheet music was introduced. According to Arthur Moore, Feldman was a Jew who in his early days was too poor to pay his rent. A story goes that one week he did not have enough money to pay his cleaning woman and, when he told her so, she replied that she did not want payment. Feldman promised that when he made his fortune she would be his housekeeper. This all came true and Mrs Wright, the lady in question, was Feldman's housekeeper for many years.

It was expected that Florrie Forde and Bert Feldman would wed, but this never happened, and later she married a variety agent and Feldman died a bachelor. For many years Florrie Forde owned a small cottage on the west coast of the Isle of Man and performed at the Derby Castle Music Hall for about 30 consecutive summers. She died in 1940.

Just after the First World War Florrie brought together two men that were to become one of the most famous of all double acts. A man called Chesney Allen wanted a stooge and Florrie recommended a man called Bud Winthrop. When the two men were introduced, they found that they had met before in very different circumstances – in France during the war, in fact. Their act was a great success and made the names of Flanagan and Allen world-famous.

NELLIE DEAN

The song most frequently sung in pubs during the present century must surely be *Nellie Dean*. The reason for this seems obscure, but perhaps the tune lends itself to 'letting one's hair down' after a few drinks have been consumed. The song has two verses of which the first verse and chorus, written and composed by Henry W. Armstrong, are given here:

> *By the old mill stream I'm dreaming, Nellie Dean,*
> *Dreaming of your bright eyes gleaming, Nellie Dean,*
> *As they used to fondly glow,*
> *When we sat there long ago,*
> *List'ning to the waters flow, Nellie Dean.*
> *I can hear the robins singing Nellie Dean;*
> *Sweetest recollections bringing Nellie Dean.*
> *And they seem to sing of you*
> *With your tender eyes of blue,*
> *For I know they miss you too, Nellie Dean.*

> > *There's an old mill by the stream, Nellie Dean,*
> > *Where we used to sit and dream, Nellie Dean,*
> > *And the waters as they flow*
> > *Seem to murmur sweet and low,*
> > *You're my heart's desire, I love you, Nellie Dean.*

The person responsible for the fame of this well-loved song was Girtie Gitana, an esteemed 'top of the bill' artiste who worked in the music halls during and after the First World War. She was the daughter of a pottery manager from Hanley in Staffordshire and when she was only four she took the stage name of Little Gitana and toured the potteries with a concert party act called Thompson's Gipsy Choir. Her real name was Gertrude Astbury and her mother had a small shop in Frederick Street, which conveniently led into the stage door of the theatre.

At the age of ten, she performed in her first professional engagement at the Holborn Theatre in London, doing a little girl act with dolls. In her early teens she changed her name to Girtie Gitana and, when she received the score of *Nellie Dean* from a friend in America, she was thought by her manager to be too young to sing about love, and was advised to keep the score for two years. When she eventually did sing it, everyone was surprised and pleased at its success. *Nellie Dean* remained Girtie Gitana's favourite song for the rest of her life. During the Great War she raised many thousands of pounds to rehabilitate the wounded from the front by the sale of her picture postcards and numerous charity performances. Miss Gitana married a Mr Ross who was her juvenile lead in 1928, and he later became a theatrical agent and producer. He presented the radio show 'Thanks for the memory', a revival of the old time music halls in which his wife performed. She died at the age of sixty-eight in her home which was named Neldean after the song. Three years before her death the town of Hanley renamed Frederick Street, Gitana Street, as a mark of honour and respect.

PACK UP YOUR TROUBLES

Francis & Day, a firm of music publishers, held a competition for the best marching song submitted to them in 1914. There were hundreds of entries for the prize of one hundred guineas. The song that won was *Pack Up Your Troubles In Your Old Kit-bag*, which has become almost as famous as *Tipperary*:

Private Perks is a funny little codger,
With a smile, a funny smile,
Five feet none, he's an artful little dodger,
With a smile, a sunny smile,
Flush or broke, he'll have his little joke.
He can't be suppress'd.
All the other fellows grin
When he gets this off his chest, Hi!

Pack up your troubles in your old kit-bag and smile, smile, smile.
While you've a Lucifer to light your fag,
Smile boys that's the style,
What's the use of worrying?
It never was worthwhile, so
Pack up your troubles in your old kit-bag, and smile, smile, smile.

Private Perks went a-marching into Flanders,
With his smile, his funny smile.
He was loved by the privates and commanders
For his smile, his sunny smile.
When a throng of Germans came along
With a mighty swing
Perks yell'd out, 'This little bunch is mine!
Keep your heads down boys and sing, Hi!'

'Pack up your troubles', etc.

Private Perks came back from Bosch shooting,
With his smile, his funny smile.
Round his home he then set about recruiting
With his smile, his sunny smile.
He told all his pals, the short, the tall,
What a time he'd had
And as each enlisted like a man
Private Perks said, 'Now my lad, Hi!'
'Pack up your troubles', etc.

There was certainly nothing to smile about for the troops that fought on the Continent in the First World War. Of course, Felix Powell, who composed the tune, and George Powell, who wrote the lyrics, could not have envisaged what was to happen but nevertheless the message in the lyrics bears little relation to the real horror of war. Prior to 1914 the Powell brothers, who were of Welsh origin, were in the entertainment business as pierrots: Felix played the piano and George was the vocalist. The troupe in which they played appeared at the old wooden Bridge Pavilion at Ilkley in Yorkshire, and later the cast moved to Bradford. The song *Pack Up Your Troubles* was not composed specifically for the Francis and Day competition, but months before, owing to lack of success, it was put in a drawer and more or less forgotten, until the competition for a marching song was publicized.

Felix Powell later served on the Continent and was stationed with the army of occupation in Cologne after the armistice. Here, his popular song was sung with gusto by the troops and general public alike. In 1922 Felix went to live in Peacehaven, Sussex, and later became an estate agent. He was well-known in the district for his musical compositions, which included *Come to Peacehaven*, and was a leading light in the local philharmonic and operatic societies.

When the Second World War broke out, the Powell brothers must have felt very gratified to learn that their song had become a firm favourite with a fresh generation of troops. Felix Powell joined the Home Guard and enjoyed the comradeship it offered, but in February 1942 a colleague found Powell lying wounded in the headquarters of the Peacehaven Home Guard. When asked what was the matter, he replied, 'I have shot myself'. He died in a Brighton hospital from a stomach wound. Though he had not long before written a marching song for the Home Guard, after his death a note was found saying farewell to his friends and explaining that he had been unable to work for some time, and could see only one way out. The coroner recorded a verdict that Felix Powell took his life while the balance of his mind was disturbed. George Powell also wrote under the name George Asaaf, a pseudonym probably inspired by the fact that in his youth Felix was a chorister at St Asaaf's Cathedral in Wales. George died in 1951 at the age of seventy-one

WORLD WAR I

During the First World War a surprising number of young men found time and inspiration to write verses of high quality about their personal experiences. For the first time we are given a sense of realism, a true picture of the horror and futility of trench warfare, in which hundreds of thousands of young men were killed and a huge number were maimed, blinded or shell-shocked for the rest of their lives. One of these trench poets was Charles Hamilton Sorley, a brilliant undergraduate at Oxford, who enlisted in the Suffolk Regiment in 1914 and, when only twenty, held the rank of captain. While at Oxford he had had some of his poetry published and was considered by John Masefield to be one of the most promising poets of his generation. He endured six months on the Western Front, and sent home poems with apologies for their crumpled and dirty condition! He was killed at Loos in 1915 and among the contents of his kit-bag, which was brought back to England, was a sonnet which began:

> *When you see millions of the mouthless dead*
> *Across your dreams in pale battalions go,*
> *Say not soft things as other men had said . . .*

Rupert Brooke, the most well-remembered of the younger war poets, made a name for himself as a writer and journalist before the war. Having been at school at Rugby, where his father was a master, he entered Cambridge University and was apparently an outstanding scholar. He then travelled round the world and represented the *Westminster Gazette* in the United States and Canada. He was a close friend of the sons of Asquith, who was Prime Minister of Great Britain at the time, and consequently he was often invited to stay at 10 Downing Street. In 1914 he went to war as a sub-lieutenant in the Royal Navy. Brooke was very patriotic and belonged to the school of poets that wrote majestically about war and the idealism that lay behind it – he was not afraid to die for his country. In fact, however he was not killed in action; he became very ill on the way to the Gallipoli front and died of acute blood poisoning. His most famous war poem is entitled *The Soldier* and was published with four other sonnets in a volume called *1914*. They were written soon after Brooke had joined the army; the first eight lines of *The Soldier* are:

> *If I should die, think only this of me:*
> *That there's one corner of a foreign field*
> *That is forever England. There shall be*
> *In that rich earth a richer dust concealed;*
> *A dust whom England bore, shaped, made aware,*
> *Gave once her flowers to love, her ways to roam,*
> *A body of England's, breathing English air,*
> *Washed by rivers, blest by suns of home.*

Friends buried him on the Greek island of Syros high on a hill. The burial procession, led by a sailor carrying a white cross with Brooke's name written on it in black, took nearly two hours to reach the summit. Then the ceremony was performed, the Last Post was sounded and the grave was marked with slabs of marble, which were lying around. Brooke left the royalties of his works to his three friends: Lascelles Abercrombie, Wilfred Gibson and Walter de la Mare. In 1960 a contingent from the Royal Navy landed on the island and found the grave overgrown and forgotten.

Meanwhile in Great Britain, although conscription did not start until 1916, young men were continually being persuaded to volunteer for service on the battlefields of Europe, Winston Churchill was the minister responsible for equipment at the time and he had ordered the development of an armoured vehicle, which was later called 'the tank'. Because it was intended to be the British secret weapon, at first only a limited number were produced. The Government were very impressed by the new vehicles and immediately made plans to put the tanks into action. Churchill argued that an offensive using a limited number of tanks would be useless, but because he was not a member of the Cabinet, his warnings were not heeded. The tanks were used in the battle of the Somme in 1915 and, as Churchill had predicted, the whole campaign was a disaster. On the first day alone 60,000 men were lost by the British and altogether the Allies lost 615,000 men in this battle.

Churchill appealed to the miners, factory hands and steel workers to toil unceasingly to produce arms for the war. The miners reaction is recorded in a verse by D. S. MacColl entitled *The Miner's Response:*

> We do; the present desperate stage
> Of fighting brings us luck';
> And in the higher war we wage
> (For higher wage) we struck.

The conditions under which the miners worked in those days were appalling and the wages were very low.

At the Front young men were being mowed down in their thousands and one of them was the only son of Rudyard Kipling, who was killed in action at Loos in 1915. Rudyard Kipling was a highly respected writer and journalist before the outbreak of war, and was awarded the Nobel Prize for Literature in 1907. His son was a lieutenant in the Irish Guards and after the news of his death Kipling was never quite the same again; his war verses became very bitter, as can be seen from the last eight lines of the poem *A Death Bed:*

The war was forced on me by my foes.
All that I sought was the right to live.
(Don't be afraid of the triple dose;
The pain will neutralize half we give.

Here are the needles. See that he dies
While the effects of the drugs endure.
What is the question he asks with his eyes?
Yes, All-Highest, to God, be sure.)

After the armistice, Kipling devoted much of his time to writing the history of the Irish Guards, and it became one of the finest of all regimental histories. For many years after the war he arranged for the Last Post to be played every night at the Menin Gate at Ypres, in memory of his son and others who died. He refused the honour of Poet Laureate three times. Kipling died in 1936 aged 71.

Above all I am not concerned with Poetry.
My subject is War, and the pity of War.
The Poetry is in the pity.

These lines were written by Wilfred Owen, who at the age of twenty worked as a private tutor in Bordeaux, after graduating from London University. In 1915, although not in good health, he joined the British army as an officer in the Manchester Regiment. He survived the trenches for six months in 1917 and was then sent home to England with his nerves shattered. While convalescing, he met another poet, Sassoon, who, recognising that he possessed great potential, encouraged him with his poetry.

Owen was sent back to France as a company commander to try, as an obvious leader of men, to help them out in every way he could. Towards the end of the campaign he wrote to his mother, 'My senses are charred; I don't take the cigarette out of my mouth when I write Deceased over their letters.' He also wrote about this time a poem called *Dulce et Decorum* of which this is the first verse:

Bent double, like old beggars under sacks,
Knocked-kneed, coughing like bags, we cursed through sludge,
Till on the haunting flares we turned our backs,
And towards our distant rest began to trudge.
Men marched asleep. Many had lost their boots;
Drunk with fatigue; deaf to the hoots
Of gas-shells dropping softly behind.

Shortly after this poem was published, Owen was awarded the Military Cross for exceptional bravery in the field. He was killed at the age of twenty-five by machine-gun fire, whilst trying to get his company over the Sambre canal, a week before the armistice was signed.

As we have seen, the poets of the Great War were their own war correspondents. John Macrea was born in 1872 and graduated as a Doctor of Medicine in Canada. He was a serious scholar who wrote an important book on pathology, as well as many poems, and became a well-known, respected member of society. He went to Europe to fight with Canadian troops as a gunner, but was transferred to the medical corps. Macrea wrote a poem called *In Flanders Fields*, which became one of the most famous poems of the war, because it gave a message from the soldiers who died to those who lived to fight on:

> *In Flanders' fields the poppies blow*
> *Between the crosses, row on row*
> *That mark our place; and in the sky*
> *The larks, still bravely singing, fly*
> *Scarce heard amid the guns below.*
>
> *We are the Dead. Short days ago*
> *We lived, felt dawn, saw sunset glow,*
> *Loved and were loved, and now we lie*
> *In Flanders' fields.*
>
> *Take up our quarrel with the foe;*
> *To you from failing hands we throw*
> *The torch; be yours to hold it high*
> *If ye break faith with us who die*
> *We shall not sleep, though poppies grow*
> *In Flanders' fields.*

This poem was written during the second battle of Ypres, when Macrea had for his dressing station a hole in a bank of the Ypres canal, where casualties literally rolled in when shot. The poem was first published in *Punch* in December 1915. Macrea was put in charge of no. 3 General Hospital at Boulogne and in January 1918 was appointed consultant to all British armies in France, but he died of pneumonia before he could accept.

WORLD WAR I

Robert Service was born in Preston, Lancashire, but went to Canada at an early age. He was already in his forties when war broke out and, being too old to enlist, he became a stretcher bearer. He wrote a good deal of poetry, especially for 'the poor bloody infantry'. Perhaps Service's most poignant war poem was *Tipperary Days*, of which these are the second and third verses with the choruses:

> *Come Yvonne and Juliette! Come Mimi and cheer for them!*
> *Throw them flowers and kisses as they pass you by.*
> *Aren't they lovely lads! Haven't you a tear for them*
> *Going out so gallantly to dare and die?*
> *What is it they're singing so? Some hymn of Motherland?*
> *Some immortal chanson of their Faith and King?*
> *Marseillaise or Brabançon, anthem of that other land?*
> *Dear, let us remember it, that song they sing:*
>
> *C'est un chemin long 'to Tepararee'*
>   *C'est un chemin long, c'est vrai;*
> *C'est un chemin long 'to Tepararee'*
>   *Et la belle fille qu'je connais;*
>   *Bonjour, Peekadeely!*
>   *Au revoir, Leistaire Square!*
>   *C'est un chemin long 'to Teparee'*
>   *Mais mon coeur 'ees saire'.*
>
> *The gallant old 'Contemtibles!' there isn't much remains of them,*
> *So full of fun and fitness, and a-singing in their pride;*
> *For some are cold as clabber and the corby picks the brains of them,*
> *And some are back in Blighty, and a-wishing they had died.*
> *Ah me! It seems but yesterday, that great glad sight of them,*
> *Swinging into battle as the sky grew black and black;*
> *Yet oh, their glee and glory, and the great grim fight of them!*
> *Just whistle Tipperary and it all comes back!*
>
> *It's a long way to Tipperary*
> *(which means 'ome anywhere);*
>   *It's a long way to Tipperary*
> *(And the things wot make you care).*

Goodbye, Piccadilly.
(Ow I 'opes my folks is well ;)
It's a long way to Tipperary,
('R ain't war just 'ell?) –

Service risked his life many times to bring in the wounded, but he survived the war and continued to write poetry and prose, championing the cause he held so dear.

RHYMING SLANG

After perhaps one of the saddest periods in our more recent history, we come to what may be the brightest – at least as far as oral rhymes are concerned. I refer to the Cockney rhyming slang, so much a part of our language today that it is difficult to trace its source. No one knows for sure when it originated and, indeed, it may be a good deal older than we first thought, for instance, a boy was known as a 'hobbledehoy' as long ago as 1540 and Defoe talks of a 'baa-cheat' when referring to a sheep rustler in his book. *Street Robberies Considered*, published in 1728. As we have seen before, oral rhymes were not thought of sufficient importance to warrant record and so for centuries have only existed on the tongue and in the memory.

When the police force came into being in 1822, the first 'coppers' were mystified by the language of the miscreants, who spoke as if in a foreign tongue, in riddles, which seemed to evoke humour even in situations of apparent distress. The policemen in London, therefore, quickly made it their business to learn this strange jargon, principally so they could understand what the prisoners were saying to each other. This was the first record of rhyming slang made available to the general public and, because it was learned from thieves and other wrong-doers, a stigma was attached to it, which remained for nearly a century. The cult was regarded as evil and one that should not be repeated or copied by law-abiding citizens. What these good people did not realize was that not only was it the common language of the underworld, but also the general means of communication of all Cockneys – be they workmen, navvies, costermongers or dockers. Many historians date the origin of rhyming slang around the beginning of the nineteenth century, but I believe that it may be a good deal older than this. For instance, the substitute for 'haven't got a penny' is 'haven't got a coal-heaver', which in its turn was originally coupled with 'stiver'. A 'stiver' was a coin in general use when William and Mary were on the throne, nearly three hundred years ago. According to Adam Joseph, the Cockney historian, this kind of slang developed after the Great Fire of London in 1666 – and I am inclined to agree with him. Many of the sayings have an Irish flavour, for example 'Rory O'More' for 'door, and it is known that a great many Irish navvies were imported from Ireland at that time of rebuilding. It is easy to imagine how the garrulous wit of the Irish fused with the Cockneys' sense of fun to produce the most humorous rhyming of all.

Rhyming slang seems to have thrived on adversity. The working class of London used it and through the centuries, up to the present day, it has personified the underdog, the underprivileged and the uneducated. It must have gathered momentum after the Industrial Revolution, when the conditions of workers and employed alike deteriorated considerably, before improvements were made. Yet out of misery, squalor and oppression came this marvellous sense of fun, simple and effective, without malice, opening up a whole new word language to the uninitiated. To listen to a couple of 'masters' is as good a form of entertainment as any. When a cockney says to his 'china', "How's the trouble and gawdfers?" what he means is, "How's the trouble and strife?" (wife) and "gawdferbids" (kids)!

> I was sitting in front of the Ave Maria
> Warming me plates of meat,
> When I heard a knock at the Rory O'More,
> That made me raspberry beat.

This rhyme was printed in a small book entitled *Dictionary of Rhyming Slang*, published in 1941. For those who do not understand, 'Ave Maria' means fire, 'plates of meat' are feet, 'Rory O'More' is door, and 'raspberry' is short for raspberry tart – heart.

Many of the expressions that we use today originated in slang rhymes, for instance, when you are on your 'Tod' or 'Jack Jones', you are really on your own, alone; 'Tod' is short for Tod Malone. Having a 'butcher's' (look) is short for butcher's hook. The meat inspectors at meat markets were very careful to inspect meat where the hanging hook had been thrust. 'Using your loaf' means loaf of bread (head). Having a harmless Jimmy Riddle' is used instead of piddle. The term 'I should cocoa' comes from coffee and cocoa – I should say so. When you are 'tiddley', you are tiddley wink – worse for drink. When you 'scapa' (go), you are really saying Scapa Flo. When a friend says, 'I'll give you my Richard', he means Richard III (word) and the term 'won't say a dickie bird' comes from this too. When the phrase 'it's taters outside' is used, meaning cold, it springs from the old saying 'taters in the mould' – cold. Similarly 'peas' means hot, stemming from 'peas in the pot'.

I wonder how many Cabinet Ministers, when using the term 'getting down to brass tacks', realize that they are using rhyming slang for facts. When a Cockney calls his mate 'china', he is abreviating 'china plate', which stems from the time when the best china was produced to entertain respected friends. The term 'elephant's trunk' (drunk) was recorded as early as 1859 and is still widely used. It probably gave rise to the fallacy that pink elephants are seen when 'tiddley'! 'Rabbit and pork' for talk has been shortened to 'rabbit', when people 'tell on you'. 'Dutch treat' is the Cockney for eat and has connections with going 'Dutch', paying for one's own meal. 'Lollipop' originally meant 'drop' (tip or money), hence the name given to cash today – 'Lolly'!

The Cockney of London, although rough and ready, usually has a heart of gold, especially where children are concerned. Many nursery rhymes have proved simple and effective for the 'gawdferbids': Johnnie Horner – corner, Jack and Jill – hill, Hey diddle diddle – fiddle, Old King Cole – dole (introduced in 1925), Dickory dock – clock, Simple Simon – diamond, Tommy Tucker – supper, Bo-Peep – sleep, Rub-a-dub dub – pub, Jack Sprat – fat meat, Mother Hubbard – cupboard, and Hot Cross Bun – on the run. Perhaps the most widely used rhyme of all is 'up the apples and pears', meaning up the stairs. It has always puzzled me why this particular link was made. Now it is evident that the costermongers stack their fruit on the barrows in 'steps and stairs' – and of course the fruit most appropriate for this kind of display are apples and pears! The fruit is graded so that the best is in the front, going up in steps and stairs, with the smallest at the top.

It was a surprise too to learn that different professions have different sets of rhymes, which are still widely used. The betting community use the slang 'evens', which is short for 'evens Steven's' from Major Stevens and 'nose and chin', meaning a win. Theatrical people use certain language patterns not generally known to the public, for instance 'mickey mouse' for house, meaning theatre, and 'just as I feared' for beard. 'Harry Tagg' is also a phrase commonly used by actors meaning a bag – the suitcase plays a large part in the lives of travelling players. The armed forces have their own versions: 'battle and cruiser' for 'boozer' (pub) and 'jam jar' for armoured car. These are only two examples of the many slang terms still used today.

In America and Australia this kind of jargon is very popular, probably more so than in Britain: 'head and tail' means jail and 'frog a log' means dog in the U.S.A. Australia boasts many sayings also; 'fried eggs' for legs and 'Joan of Arcs' for sharks are just two of many. It was thought that the immigrants and wrong-doers who were shipped to these two countries infused the national vocabulary with rhyming slang at an early date.

Here is part of a sonnet in slang called *Meg's Diversion*, published in 1897. It describes the sad story of Meg, a young girl who had no money and tried to pawn the landlord's trousers:

> *Now, a tear-drop fell from the girl's mincepies*
> *And her raspberry tart was torn*
> *With anguish; for she had an empty sky,*
> *And she'd nothing to bullock's horn.*
>
> *But she cooled each mince with a little scent,*
> *And her Barnet arranged with grace;*
> *Then down the apples and pears she went*
> *With a sorrowful Chevy Chase.*
>
> *And she saw, as she passed her landlord's shed,*
> *That the Rory he'd failed to close;*
> *And the thought came into her loaf of bread,*
> *Just to pop in here, I suppose.*
>
> *And she did and a quick glance round she flung,*
> *The old pot and pan wasn't there;*
> *But a pair of his round the houses hung,*
> *At the Anna Maria to air.*

She said to herself, "They're decent stuff,
It's all harbour, I think they'll do;
I'll half inch 'em – they're sure to fetch enough
To purchase a Brian or two!"

mincepie – eye; sky – pocket; bullock's horn – pawn; Barnet –
Barnet Fair – hair; Chevy Chase – face; pot and pan – old man or
father; round the houses – trousers; harbour – all right; half inch
– 'pinch' or steal; Brian – Brian O'Flynn – gin, later called
'mother's ruin'.
(From 'A Dictionary of Rhyming Slang' by Julian Franklin)

CHARLIE CHAPLIN

Charlie Chaplin went to France
To teach little French girls how to dance;
First they did the wibble wobbles, then they did the kicks,
Then they did the can-can, then they did the splits.

This children's skipping chant, now firmly established in the oral
collection, has already immortalized the name of Charlie Chaplin, one of the greatest actor/comedians of this century.

Chaplin was born in a small back room in Kennington Road,
London, in 1889. His father, Charles Chaplin, was a comic singer
and an habitual drunkard, who died from the effects of drink
when he was thirty. His mother, Hannah Chaplin, was a singer
and dancer of Irish descent. The loss of her second husband
proved too much for her and she became mentally ill and incapa-
ble of looking after Charlie and his half brother, Sydney, who was
four years older. The two boys were sent to a poor boys' institu-
tion called Old Cuckoo School, where they spent a miserable
time. A teacher, who said she remembered Charlie at this school
described him as a 'dear little boy, sweet and shy, with big eyes
and a mass of dark curly hair'. He copied his famous walk, she
said, from an old man who used to feed and water the horses
outside the Elephant and Castle pub.

Sydney Chaplin, who was in due course released from school,
returned to live with his mother and later went to sea as a cadet.
Charlie was allowed to return to his mother's care later, when she

had given up the stage and earned a living sewing. They lived a very meagre existence, and Charlie sold newspapers and fetched free pea soup from the Old Church in Waterloo Road. Charlie grew fond of dancing apparently and often danced in the streets to amuse his friends and passers-by. One day he was spotted by a member of the Jackson Lads, a troupe specialising in clog dancing. When one of the members fell sick, Charlie was asked to step in. He was so good that he kept the job, usually performing as the 'dude', the smallest and funniest of the act. The Jackson Lads toured the Continent and were especially welcomed in Paris. (Perhaps this is where the skipping rhyme originated.) In 1913 Chaplin was signed up with an American film company by Stan Sennet, the film producer famous for the Keystone Cops, but Chaplin did not find real fame until he had developed the image of the little man with the bowler hat and cane. He did this, so the story goes, by 'fooling around' in the Keystone Cops' dressing room one day. He put on a coat that was much too small, some large baggy trousers, a pair of large 'cop' boots, a bowler hat, and added a moustache and cane for effect. The result was so comical that, when he strutted around with his 'flat-footed' walk, the producer was only too eager to make a film with Charlie as the principal lead. In 1975 Charlie Chaplin was knighted by Queen Elizabeth. Now, of course, he lives in Switzerland, enjoying a comfortable old age, with his wife, Oona, and several of his family.

WORLD WAR II

In September 1939 a Second World War broke out in which the Germans were so successful that by the middle of 1940 Hitler had decided to invade Britain. His air force began to bomb ports, air fields and other strategic positions in the British Isles. After the defeat of France, Winston Churchill knew better than most how precarious the position was. In one of his most powerful speeches he said these immortal words, which stirred and lifted morale, 'In the face of immediate invasion, we shall fight on the beaches, we shall fight on the landing grounds, we shall fight in the fields, and in the streets, we shall fight in the hills, we shall never surrender. . . ' During August and September of that year the air crews and ground staff of the R.A.F. were almost constantly engaged in enemy action. Heavy casualties were suffered on both sides, but in the end the Luftwaffe had to admit defeat in this campaign. A poem entitled *Dawn Patrol*, written by Warren Hastings and Herbert Jordan, reflects the scene:

> *I had a brother dressed in blue,*
> *An airman young and fine.*
> *At dawn beside his Hurricane*
> *I took his hand in mine.*
> *He said with a smile I knew so well,*
> *"Just off for a spot of fun".*
> *I placed his hand in the hand of God,*
> *And he flew towards the sun.*

The main brunt of the battle was born by the squadrons of No. II Group Fighter-Command under Air Vice-Marshal Keith Park (later Air Chief Marshal Sir Keith Park.) It may be said that in those few weeks the fate of Britain, and maybe the whole world, lay in the hands of a few pilots. One afternoon, at the height of the Battle of Britain, Churchill was in the central operations room, when news was received that a great force of German raiders was approaching London. The last available fighter squadron was sent up; the German attack was broken up and turned tail over the Channel. Churchill then reported to have said quite spontaneously, "Never in the field of human conflict was so much owed by so many to so few". This was later included in one of the Prime Minister's broadcasts to the British people, and the words have immortalised the bravery of those who fought in the Battle of Britain.

The Second World War brought the civilian into the front line for the first time. Many children were evacuated to the country, but adults stayed in the big cities to maintain essential services and to help with the war effort. Home Guard training and A.R.P. duties were carried out in the evenings, and, if they were not on fire-watching duty, most people slept in dug-outs or underground tube shelters at night. The important ports and cities were subjected to numerous attacks by German bombers. In addition the Germans used their secret weapons – flying bombs and, later, rockets – to wear down the morale of the British public. Huge areas were reduced to rubble and many lives were lost. Here is part of *The Rhyme of the Flying Bomb* written by Mervyn Peake, which tells the traumatic story of a tough sailor and a newborn child, who took refuge from the blitz in a Church:

> And the church leapt out of a lake of light
> And the pews were rows of fire,
> And the golden cock crowed thrice and flew
> From the peak of the falling spire.
>
> And the candle wax swam over the stones,
> And the tail of the flying bomb
> Stuck out of the floor to point the place
> That it had journeyed from.
>
> While plunged below in the shattered crypt
> Was the skull of the scalding head,
> And the short black wings that made the cross
> Were splashed with sailor's blood.
>
> And the dust rose up from the hills of brick
> And hung over London town,
> And a thousand roofs grew soft and thick
> With dust as it settled down.
>
> And the morning light shone clear and bright
> On a city as gold as grain,
> While the babe that was born in the reign of George
> Lay coiled in the womb again.

George VI, father of Queen Elizabeth, reigned until 1952.

A complete contrast is provided by a poem written during the blitz by Sir John Betjeman, the present Poet Laureate. Although he does not like to be described as a humorous poet, Betjeman's work sometimes shows a refreshing sense of humour. Here are three verses from *Slough*, taken from *Collected Poems*:

> Come, friendly bombs, fall on Slough,
> It isn't fit for humans now,
> There isn't grass to graze a cow.
> Swarm over, Death!
>
> Come, bombs and blow to smithereens
> Those air-conditioned, bright canteens,
> Tinned fruit, tinned meat, tinned milk, tinned beans,
> Tinned minds, tinned breath.

Come, friendly bombs, and fall on Slough
To get it ready for the plough.
The cabbages are coming now;
The earth exales.

Sir John Betjeman has a great interest in restoring old buildings, especially those of the Victorian period, and, as is evident in the poem, he abhors new buildings, concrete office blocks and other structures which offend the eye.

Alun Lewis was an esteemed poet and writer, who served as a second lieutenant during World War II. For a while he was stationed in England and his writings describe the life of a sensitive man in unsensitive surroundings. He had a horror of war but endeavoured to do what was expected of him. When he was sent to India, his works took on an ethereal quality, difficult to explain. In fact, he might be described as the Rupert Brooke of World War II, because, like his predecessor, he had a premonition of death. These lines written by Lewis in India come from a poem entitled *Mahratta Ghats* and reflect to some extent a soldier-poet's thoughts on the fight for survival, both in peace and in war:

Who is it climbs the summit of the road?
Only the beggar bumming his dark load.
Who was it cried to see a falling star?
Only the landless soldier lost in war.

And did a thousand years go by in vain?
And does another thousand start again?

At the beginning of 1944, Lewis's regiment was moved to the Burma Front. Lewis was Intelligence Officer at the time and, as such, it was not necessary for him to fight, but he repeatedly requested experience in open combat and in March, although not actively engaged in battle at the time, Lewis 'was accidentally wounded by a pistol shot'. He never recovered and died in the base hospital, and was buried in a cemetery near Bawhi Bridge. He was only twenty-nine years old. Lewis came from a Welsh mining family, each member of which possessed a good deal of natural talent, favouring education and the arts. He wrote many war poems, including *The Soldier*, *After Dunkirk* and *On Embarkation*.

After the failure to capture Britain during the Battle of Britain, Hitler decided to blockade the British Isles with U Boats. He tried to strangle the life blood of food and ammunition shipped across the Atlantic from the United States of America. Churchill had previously requested that President Roosevelt ensure a supply of basic needs. In his own undaunted way he said, 'Give us the tools, and we will finish the job'. This material help was described as 'lease lend'. The men of the Merchant Navy were heroes in their own right, for they ran the gauntlet untiringly to deliver the goods that Britain so badly needed – often with less than adequate protection from the war-scarred Royal Navy. The following short extract from *Merchant Navy*, written by V. F. Stevens and S. Brown, records briefly the part played by merchant seamen:

> *No braid adorns their reefers, no flash, no stripes, no pips,*
> *But a tiny 'M.N.' denotes they're the men who go down to the sea in ships,*
> *Out where the convoys muster on the wide eternal blue;*
> *'Midst mine, torpedo, bomb, and shell, they've got a job to do.*

Back on land the war effort was well under way, land was ploughed to grow crops, allotments were a necessity and food was rationed. Although housewives had to spend many hours queueing for 'extras', as a nation the British were much better fed than during the First World War. A song that has now joined the oral tradition and is reminiscent of the 'extras' which made life bearable in the dark days is *Run Rabbit, Run,* written by Ralph Butler and Noel Gay (Copyright 1939 Noel Gay Music Co. Ltd., London):

> *On the farm, ev'ry Friday,*
> *On the farm, it's rabbit pie day.*
> *So ev'ry Friday that ever comes along*
> *I get up early and sing this little song:*

> > *Run rabbit, run rabbit, run, run, run,*
> > *Run rabbit, run rabbit, run, run, run.*
> > *Bang, bang, bang, bang, goes the farmer's gun,*
> > *Run rabbit, run rabbit, run, run, run.*
> > *Run rabbit, run rabbit, run, run, run,*
> > *Don't give the farmer his fun, fun, fun.*
> > *He'll get by without his rabbit pie,*
> > *So, run rabbit, run rabbit, run, run, run.*

This song was not originally written with war in mind, but for Flanagan and Allen to sing in a Crazy Gang Show called The Little Dog Laughed, at the London Palladium in 1938. During the war it was revived for obvious reasons and became an instant success. In fact, with its simple tune and easily remembered words, it has never been forgotten. Although the sheet music has been out of print for a number of years, it has now joined the oral collection.

Other war-time songs which may be remembered in the years to come are *Lily Marlene*, the German marching song, which was adopted by British troops, *Roll Out The Barrel* and *Quartermaster's Stores*, which is flourishing with differing words in Scout and other summer camps where community singing is called for.

The great war-time comedian Tommy Handley and his show ITMA (It's That Man Again) did much to keep up morale. Such phrases from the show as 'Can I do you now, sir? 'I don't mind if I do' and 'After you, Claude' have become a colloquial part of the English language.

> *Whistle while you work,*
> *Hitler is a twerp.*
> *He's half barmy*
> *And his army.*
> *Whistle while you work.*

This jingle, a parody on the dwarfs' song from Walt Disney's cartoon film *Snow White and The Seven Dwarfs*, was chanted constantly and defiantly by children in Britain during the last war, and is now entering the oral collection as following generations take it up.

D Day, the day on which the land offensive on Europe was launched by British, Canadian and American troops, was originally planned for mid-May 1944, but owing to freak weather conditions the landings were not made until 6 June. The Germans had expected a Dover Crossing, but the attack came from much further down the Channel. The British troops took their own harbours with them, towing two Mulberry floating landing-stages across the Channel. The fact that one was lost in a severe storm did not halt the attack, which was accomplished on the remaining portable harbour on the Normandy beaches. The term 'D Day' is now a term used in every day speech, denoting the commencement of any important event.

After the attack on Pearl Harbour in 1941, the U.S.A. declared war on Japan, and American children began to chant this parody of a well-known counting-out rhyme:

> *Eena, meena, miny, mo,*
> *Catch old Tojo by his toe;*
> *If he hollers, make him say,*
> *'I surrender, U.S.A.'*

Tojo was one of the Japanese war leaders. It was not until an atom bomb was dropped in Hiroshima on August 6 1945 and another, even more powerful one was dropped on Nagasaki that Japan surrendered.

MOUNT EVEREST

In a very lonely and isolated part of Nepal the highest mountain in the world was discovered in 1850. British surveyors in northern India, mapping the area for the first time, noticed the white pyramid on the horizon and calculated its height to be over 29,000 feet. It was given the name Everest in honour of Sir George Everest, who was Surveyor General in India at the time of its discovery. It was not until the 1920s that permission was granted by the Tibetan Government for an expeditionary force to attempt to climb the mountain. There were eight attempts before the summit was reached in 1953 by Edmund Hillary and Sherpa Tenzing, members of the British Expedition led by John Hunt. Here are the last ten lines of a fascinating poem by Ian Serraillier, entitled *Everest Climbed*, in which he describes the ascent in a very realistic manner:

> *Was the summit theirs? – they puffed and panted.*
> *No, for the ridge still upwards pointed.*
> *On they plodded, Martian-weird*
> *With pouting mask and icicle beard*
> *That cracked and tinkled, broke and rattled,*
> *As on with pounding hearts they battled,*
> *On to the summit,*
> *Till at last the ridge began to drop.*
> *Two swings, two whacks of Hillary's axe,*
> *And they stood on the top.*

For posterity Hillary took a photograph of Tenzing standing on the summit with the flags of Nepal, the United Nations and India, and the Union Jack flying from his ice pick. Sir John Hunt wrote the foreword to this poem and seemingly approved the avid description of the exercise, 'Thus interpreted, it is but natural that the story of Everest should have been translated from cold prose and photography into poetry and painting.'

SPACE TRAVEL

Man's venture into space in the second half of the twentieth century might be regarded as his most outstanding achievement to date. Orbiting and walking in space, journeying round the dark side of the Moon, and the inevitable Moon walk-abouts have all been carried out very successfully, though the Moon landings only endorsed the scientists' opinion that the Moon is a dead planet. Three verses from *Rockets* by Peter Bird give food for thought;

> *A mother cannot feed her child,*
> *Another feeds hers with a silver spoon,*
> *The Welfare State is going wild*
> *And we send rockets to the moon.*
>
> *The desert bare – no crops grow there –*
> *We'll have to succour millions soon,*
> *Yet still few plans to fertilize,*
> *For we send rockets to the moon.*
>
> *The world is full of misery*
> *(And atom bombs and big fast cars)*
> *So let us suffer! let us die!*
> *We'll soon be flying up to Mars.*

The Chinese first used rockets as weapons during the thirteenth century, though they had used fireworks as a display for much longer. With the invention of guns, however, rockets were only used at firework displays in Europe, until the British successfully developed them as war weapons during the Napoleonic Wars. During the Second World War the Germans evolved the rocket known as the V2 (Vergeltungswaffe 2). For a while the space programme has been somewhat curtailed, but this inactive period will perhaps be only temporary.

TODAY

Some of the verses recorded in this book may be new to many people; most of the rhymes and songs selected however, are more than familiar to us – they are part of our heritage and to a certain extent record our history. For centuries they have been passed down by word of mouth and stored in the memory. Nowadays radio, television and records promote traditional folk songs, verses and sayings. Although it is not possible to say whether any one song or poem will eventually join the oral collection, it does seem probable that one or two at least of the ones well-known today will be remembered and passed on to the next generation. Perhaps songs such as *Yes, We Have No Bananas* or *Where Did You Get That Hat?* will form part of the oral collection of the twenty-first century. How shall we be seen in the future? The following lines from *Young Poets At The Big Match* by Wes Magee depict the football matches of today, as seen through the eyes of young supporters:

> We arrived late on the scene.
> All ready our team was out,
> slick under the high floodlights,
> flicking the ball with
> ease till one (bald and lanky)
> slipped and messed his pants. Behind
> the goal we fell about, howled
> for the ref and, once the game
> got going, sang lyric lines
> and randy rhymes that always
> earned a laugh. Then, bored by square
> movements with never a goal,
> mouth incident or punch-up
> in sight, we fired the programme,
> sent up in smoke the rules and
> pages of posed photographs.

Or perhaps the following gives a wider view of the world today?

Winter package holidays are quite within our means,
We fly abroad to happiness and savour sunny scenes;
But when it is all over, we are brought back with a thud,
To strikes and bombs and power cuts,
And M.P.s slinging mud.

Perhaps, after all, it is better to be optimistic:

Let's laugh at the comics,
Let's clown with the kids;
Let's make Auntie giggle
When she's round cousin Syd's.

Let's hope that the Sports
At the Commonwealth games
Can pass on their goodwill
To other Big Names.

Hurrah for the Queen!
Long may she reign,
It's the Royal Family
That keeps us all sane.

Hurrah for the Queen!
It's her jubilee –
The pomp and the pageant
Will reflect history.

We've had some 'lucky strikes'
And the oil's flowing free –
The national debt,
Will be paid off with glee!

Let's praise Jesus Freaks
And others who say
'Make love not war'
And then lead the way.

Let's cheer the streakers,
And those who dare
To reveal all the facts,
And lay themselves bare.

Let's forget bees and honey
Just for a while –
LET'S PACK UP OUR TROUBLES
AND SMILE.

ACKNOWLEDGMENTS

The author and publishers would like to thank the following for permission to reproduce copyright material in the text:

George Allen and Unwin Ltd, London, for an extract from 'The Mahratta Ghats' out of *Ha Ha Among The Trumpets* by Alun Lewis.

John Murray (Publishers) Ltd, London and Houghton Mifflin Co, U.S.A., for verses from the poem 'Slough' from *Collected Poems* by John Betjeman.

Colin Smythe Ltd, Publishers for five verses of *The Rhyme of the Flying Bomb* by Mervyn Peake.

The Hamlyn Publishing Group Limited for extracts from *Churchill – His Life And Times, 1874-1965* by Malcolm Thompson.

Ernest Benn Publishers, London, McGraw-Hill Ryerson Ltd of Canada, and Dodd, Mead & Co Inc, New York, for two verses and two courses of 'Tipperary Days' by Robert Service from *Collected Poems of Robert Service*. Copyright 1916 by Dodd, Mead and Company Inc. Copyright renewed by Robert Service 1944.

Constable Publishers for 'The Miners' Response by D. S. Maccoll from *Bull and Other War Verses*.

Mrs George Bambridge, Eyre Methuen Ltd, Macmillan Co of Canada and Doubleday & Company, Inc, New York, for eight lines from 'A Death Bed' from *The Years Between* by Rudyard Kipling. Copyright 1919 by Rudyard Kipling.

Derbyshire Countryside Ltd for an extract from *The Well Dressing Guide* by Crichton Porteous.

Wes Magee for an extract from 'Young Poets at the Big Match' from *New Poems 1970-71*, the fourteenth P.E.N. Anthology of contemporary poetry.

Peter Bird for an extract from 'Rockets' as published in *Top Poets of 1968* by Golden Eagle Press.

Ian Serraillier for the last ten lines of his poem *Everest Climbed* published by Oxford University Press. © Ian Serraillier 1955.

E.M.I. Music Publishing Ltd for *Dawn Patrol* by Warren Hastings and Herbert Jordan and four lines from *Merchant Navy* by V. F. Stevens and S. Brown, from *The Old Times Star's Book of Monologues* compiled by Reynolds and published by Wolfe Publishing Ltd, London for extracts from the lyrics of the following songs: 'Don't Dilly Dally' by Charles Collins and Fred Leigh; 'I'm Twenty-one Today' by Alec Kendall; 'Hello, Hello' Who's your lady friend?' by Harry Fragson, Worton David and Bert Lee; 'It's a Long Way to Tipperary' by Jack Judge and Harry Williams; 'P.C. 49' by William Hargreaves; 'Goodbye Dolly Gray' by William Cobb and Paul Barnes; 'Nellie Dean' by Henry W. Armstrong, all originally published in Britain by B. Feldman & Co. For extracts from the lyrics of the following songs: 'Daisy Bell' by Harry Dacre; 'If you want to know the time, ask a policeman' by E. W. Rogers and A. E. Durandeau; 'Lily of Laguna' by Leslie Stuart; 'Pack Up Your Troubles' by Felix Powell and George Asaaf; 'Two lovely black eyes' by Charles Coburn', all originally published in Britain by Francis Day and Hunter. For the lyrics of 'A happy birthday to you' by Patty S. Hill and Mildred J. Hill, formerly published by K. P. M. Music Group.

M. Witmark and Sons, New York, for extracts from 'Nellie Dean' by Henry W. Armstrong, originally published in Britain by B. Feldman & Co.

Clayton F. Summy Co, Chicago, for lyrics of 'Happy Birthday to you' by Patty S. Hill and Mildred J. Hill.

Summy-Birchard Company, Illinois for the lyrics of 'Good Morning to All' from *Song Stories for the Kindergarten* by P. S. Hill and M. J. Hill.

Noel Gay Music Company Ltd, for the lyrics of 'Run Rabbit Run' by Noel Gay and Ralph Butler. Copyright 1939.

Boosey & Hawkes Music Publishers Ltd for two verses and chorus of 'Land of Hope and Glory' by A. C. Benson and Edward Elgar.

Ascherberg, Hopwood & Crew Ltd, for eight lines and chorus taken from the 'The Day King Edward gets his crown on' by M. Lorne and Harry Pleon, 1902.

The author also gratefully acknowledges the help of:

Peter Stockham, J. Symons, A. Moore, Rev. Bland, Miss Shafto, F. Seale, Lord Hunt, Reginald Dixon, Mike Ayton, Ruth Pickard, Mrs Laing, Rev. Pallant, Brown Bros, L. S. Colchester, C. H. Gibbs-Smith, Sheila Harrowven, Cynthia Felgate, Mrs Annie Courtney, Rev. R. Tydeman, Rev. Joseph McCulloch, the R.S.P.C.A., Ronald Pearsall, McCulloch Properties Inc. and also the many librarians and archivists throughout Britain, in Dublin and New York, without whose help and diligence this book would never have been written.

Illustration acknowledgments.
1. By permission of the Public Record Office, Chancery Lane, London.
2. By permission of the authorities of Norwich Cathedral. Photograph by Colin Brown.
3. By permission of the authorities of Wells Cathedral. Photograph by L. S. Colchester.
4. By permission of The British Museum, Crown Copyright.
5. By courtesy of Chester Public Library.
6, 7, 8, 9. By permission of the British Museum, Crown Copyright.
10. By courtesy of Blinkhorns of Banbury.
11. By permission of the Ashmoleau Museum, Oxford.
12. By permission of the British Museum, Crown Copyright.

BIBLIOGRAPHY

Airne, C. W., *The Story of Tudor and Stuart Britain*, Sankey, Hudson & Co., Manchester, 1933.
Alford, Violet, *An Introduction to English Folklore*, Bell, 1952.
Allen, A. B., *The Middle Ages 1154-1485*, Rockliff Publishing Co., London, 1951.
Anson, Peter, *Fisher folk-lore*, Faith Press, London, 1965.
Armstrong, Edward, *The Folklore of Birds*, Collins, 1965.
Ashton, John, ed., *Real Sailor-Songs*, Leadenhall Press, 1891.
Baker, Margaret, *Discovering English Fairs*, Shire Publications, 1968.
Baring-Gould, S., *Curious Myths of The Middle Ages*, Rivingtons, 1888.
Benedictines, ed., *The Book of Saints*, 5th ed., Adam & Charles Black, 1960.
Bennett, Richard Rodney, *All The King's Men*, Universal Edition, 1968.
Black, E. L., ed., *1914-18 in Poetry*, University of London Press, 1970.
Blunden, E., ed., *War Poets 1914-1918*, Longmans & Green, 1958.
Brain, John A., *Berkshire Ballads*, Thomas Thorpe, Reading, 1904.
Brophy, J., and Partridge, E., *The Long Trail*, revised ed., Deutsch, 1965.
Brown, R. L., *A Book of Superstitions*, David & Charles, 1970.
Bryant, Sir Arthur, *The Medieval Foundation*, Collins, 1966.
Chambers, Robert, *Popular Rhymes of Scotland*, Chambers, 1842.
Chaundler, Christine, *Everyman's Book of Superstitions*, Mowbray, 1970.
Claire, Colin, *Unnatural History*, Abelard Schuman, 1967.
Crockett, W. S., *The Scott Country*, Adam & Charles Black, 1902.
Daiken, Leslie, *The Lullaby Book*, Edmund Ward, 1959.
Ditchfield, P. H., *Old English Customs*, Methuen, 1901.
Duckworth, Francis, *Chester*, 2nd ed., Adam & Charles Black, 1927.
Ekwall, Eilert, *Street-Names of The City of London*, Clarendon Press, 1954.
Fairholme, E. G., and Pain, W., *A Century of Work for Animals*, John Murray, 1925.
Firth, C. H., *Cromwell's Army*, Methuen, 1902.
Firth, C. H., *Naval Songs and Ballads*, Naval Records Society, 1907.
Ford, Robert, *Song Histories*, Hodge, Glasgow and Edinburgh, 1900.
Forrester, D. M., *Logiealmond*, Oliver & Boyd, Edinburgh and London, 1944.
Franklyn, Julian, *A Dictionary of Rhyming Slang*, Routledge & Kegan Paul, 1960.
Fraser, Antonia, *Cromwell: Our Chief of Men*, Weidenfield & Nicholson, 1973.
Fuld, James J., *World Famous Music*, revised ed., Crown, New York, 1971.
Fuller, Thomas, ed., *The History of the Worthies of England*, 4 parts, I.G.W.L. & W.G., London, 1662.
Woodward, Marcus, ed., *Leaves from Gerard's Herball*, Gerald Howe, London, 1931; Bodley Head, 1972.
Gerish, W. B., *Hertfordshire Folklore*, S. R. Publications, 1970.
Gibbs-Smith, C. H., *Bayeux Tapestry*, Phaidon Press, 1973.
Glyde, John, Jun., *The Norfolk Garland*, Jarrold, London, 1872.
Gomme, G. L., *Folklore as an Historical Science*, Methuen, 1908.
Gunston, David, 'Counting Sheep', *Country Quest*, vol. 7, 1966.
Halliday, W. J., and Umpleby, A. S., ed., *The White Rose Garland of Yorkshire*, Dent, 1949.
Halliwell, James O., *Nursery Rhymes of England*, 4th ed., London 1846; Bodley Head, 1970.
Hart, Rev. Richard, 'On Misereres', *Norfolk Archaeology*, vol. 2, Norfolk and

Norwich Archaelogical Society, 1849, pp. 234-252.

Hogg, James, *Jacobite Relics of Scotland*, 2 vols., W. Blackwood, Edinburgh, 1819-21.

Hugill, Stan, *Shanties and Sailors' Songs*, Herbert Jenkins, London, 1969.

Hussey, Christopher, 'Mells, Somerset: The Manor House', *Country Life*, vol. 93, 1943, p. 748.

Hyett, F. B., ed., *Fifty London Rhymes for Children*, Blackwell, Oxford, 1926.

Lang, Andrew, *The Nursery Rhyme Book*, Frederick Warne, London, 1897.

Lawrence, Berta, *Somerset Legends*, David & Charles, 1973.

Leach, Maria, and Fried, J., ed., *The Standard Dictionary of Folklore and Legend*, 2 vols., Funk & Wagnall, New York, 1949.

Leigh, Effie, *Ballads and Legends of Cheshire*, L. P., London, 1867.

Lucas, Hedley, *Homage to Cheshire*, 6th ed., Independent Press, 1960.

Mackinlay, James, *Folklore of Scottish lochs and springs*, Hodge, Glasgow, 1893.

Mander, R., and Mitchenson, J., *British Music Hall*, Studio Vista, 1965.

Marshall, H. E., *Our Island Story*, T. C. & A. C. Jack, London, 1905.

McCulloch, Rev. Joseph, *St. Mary Le Bow*, Pitkin Pictorials, 1964.

McNeill, Forence, *The Silver Bough*, William MacLellan, Glasgow, 1957.

McWhirter, Norris and Ross, ed., *Guiness Book of Records*, 21st ed., Guiness Superlatives, 1974.

Mellor, G. J., *The Northern Music Hall*, F. Graham, England, 1970.

Milliken, E. K., *Lancastrian and Tudor*, Harrap, 1949.

Montgomerie, Norah, ed., *The Hogarth Book of Scottish Nursery Rhymes*, Hogarth Press, 1964.

Neuberg, Victor E., *The Penny Histories*, Oxford University Press, 1968.

Northall, G. F., *English folk-rhymes*, Kegan, 1892.

Opie, Iona and Peter, ed., *The Oxford Dictionary of Nursery Rhymes*, 2nd impression, Oxford University Press, 1969.

Opie, Iona and Peter, ed., *The Nursery Rhyme Book*, Oxford University Press, 1955.

Pearsall, Ronald, *Victorian Popular Music*, David & Charles, 1973.

Porteous, Crichton, *The Well Dressing Guide*, Derbyshire Countryside Ltd., 1967.

Pulling, Christopher, *They were singing*, Harrap, 1952.

Radford, E. and M.A., ed., *Encyclopaedia of Superstitions*, Rider, London, 1948.

Rusher, J. G., *The Cries of Banbury and London*, Rusher, Banbury, (1820?)

Sackville West, V., *Nursery Rhymes*, Dropmore Press, 1947; Michael Joseph, 1950.

Sexby, J. J., *The Municipal Parks, Gardens and Open Spaces of London*, E. Stock, London, 1898.

Smith, W. G., ed., *The Oxford Dictionary of English Proverbs*, 2nd, ed., Oxford University Press, 1948.

Smythe, A. M., *A Book of Fabulous Beasts*, Oxford University Press, 1939.

Surtees, R., *The History and Antiquities of the County Palatine of Durham*, vol. III, L. P., London 1823.

Thomson, Malcolm, *Churchill: His Life and Times*, Odhams, 1965.

Todd, James Henthorn, *St. Patrick, Apostle of Ireland*, Dublin, 1864.

Tuer, Andrew W., ed., *London Cries: with six charming children*, Field & Tuer, London, 1883.

Tydeman, Richard, *Without a City Wall*, (pictorial guide to Church of the Holy Sepulchre), Foster Press, London, 1971.

Williamson, H. R., *The Flowering Hawthorn*, Peter Davies, 1962.

Wire, William, 'Old Street Names of Colchester', *Essex Review*, vol. 42, 1933, p. 9.

Wright, A. R., and Lones, T. E., ed., *British Calendar Customs*, 3 vols, published for The Folklore Society by William Glaisher, 1936, 1938, 1940.

Wright, Thomas, *The Romance of the Lace Pillow*, H. H. Armstrong, Bucks, 1919.

INDEX OF FIRST LINES

Aa went to Blaydon Races, twas on the ninth of June, 284
Above all I am not concerned with Poetry, 312
After dinner rest a while, 47
Ah'll tee on my bonnet, 13
All work and no play makes Jack a dull boy, 47
All you that in the condemned hole do lie, 152
Allons, enfants de la patrie!, 239
'Although I am ragged and not so well dressed, 71
Amidst the mists and coldest frosts, 52
And so great Arthur's seat ould Winchester prefers, 56
Apple pie without the cheese, 63
April noddy's past and gone, 70
Arthur O'Bower has broken his band, 57
As I was a-walking on Westminster Bridge, 50
As I was going by Charing Cross, 176
As I was going to Banbury, 136
As I was going to Jordan wood, 125
As round as an apple, 50
As you waste away, may she waste away, 20
Ash tree, Ashen tree, 128
Ashes in the river, 189
At Islington a fair they hold, 135
At Rusher's fam'd Warehouse, 168
Away in a manger, no crib for a bed, 4
Awd Grimey sits upon yon hill, 172

Baa, baa, black sheep, 113

Baby, baby, naughty baby, 3, 240
Baby Jesus, sweetly sleep, 4
Baldur rade, the foal slade, 21
Be it weal or be it woe, 64
Before St Chad, 85
Behold the wonder of this present age, 134
Bent, double, like old beggars under sacks, 312
Bessy Bell and Mary Gray, 191
Best never been born if Sunday shorn, 73
Better a child had ne'er been born, 72
Betty Botter bought some butter, 54
Between Calder and Aire, 15
Beware of that man, 73
Beware of the oak, it draws the stroke, 59
The big black bug bit a big black bear, 53
Birds of a feather flock together, 46
Black bat, bear away, fly over here away, 116
Bless you, bless you, burnie-bee, 27
Blest be the day that Christ was born, 66
Bloodthirsty Dee, 12
A bloom on the tree when the apples are ripe, 63
Bobby Shafto's gone to sea, 228
Boney beat the Prussians, 254
Boney was a warrior, 254
The boughs do shake, and the bells do ring, 65
Bounce buckram, velvet's dear, 69
Bread and cheese, work at your ease, 66
The bridegroom's health we all will sing, 77
Buck, buck, 45
Bury the Great Duke, 245
Buttons a farthing a pair, 203

Buy my fine Gooseberries, fine Gooseberries, 195
Buy my Oysters, live Oysters, O!, 196
Buy ripe Strawberries, fine Strawberries, 194
By the old mill stream I'm dreaming, Nellie Dean, 306

Can a boy jump higher than a lamp post?, 51
Champagne Charlie is my name, 276
Charlie Chaplin went to France, 319
The charm of God the Great, 125
'Cherries, ripe cherries', the old woman cried, 195
A cherry year, 67
Christmas is coming and the goose is getting fat, 69
Churn butter dash, 117
Clear moon, 9
A clover, a clover of two, put it in your right shoe, 62
Cobbler, cobbler, mend my shoe, 186
Cock a doodle doo!, 164
Come all you young ladies and make no delay, 200
Come boat me o'er, come row me o'er, 221
Come butter, churn, 117
Come buy my gudgeons fine and new, 193
Come, friendly bombs, fall on Slough, 322
Come my boys with hearty glee, 132
Come visit the fountain adorned with flowers, 17
The Country teems with Wealth, 212
Crow, crow, get out of my sight, 31
The cuckoo comes in April, 28
Cut them on Monday, cut them for health, 72
Cut thistles in May, 67

Dam the lad, 118
Dame get up and bake your pies, 69
D'Artois returns from Spain, 280
Dear Land of Hope, thy hope is crowned, 287
Deux beaux yeux noire, 279
Deux beaux yeux poches!, 279
Did ye not hear it? No, 'twas but the wind, 244
Diddle diddle dumpling, my son John, 274
A dimple on your cheek, 74
Divorced, beheaded, died, 154
Do you ken Elsie Marley, honey?, 230

Doctor Foster went to Gloucester, 103
Don't cast a clout, 124
Don't on a Friday buy your ring, 124
Down in yon lum we have a mill, 102
Down with the Rosemary and so, 62
Drag forth the legal monsters into light, 214
The drummer goes round, 206
A Duck and a Drake, 45

Early to bed and early to rise, 47
Een, teen, tuther, futher, fipps, 34
Eena, meena, miny, mo, 33, 326
Elizabeth, Elspeth, Betsy and Bess, 50
Even ash, even ash, I pluck thee, 61
Even ash I do thee pluck, 61
Everyone delights to spend their summer holiday, 297
Excuse me shouting out like this, 299

Fair lady mourn the memory of all our Scottish fame, 220
Fairies small, two feet tall, 121
Far o'er yon hills of the heather so green, 222
A far off brough, 9
Father and I went down to camp, 234
Father's going to give a dinner to prove he's lots of pelf, 286
Fire come, fire go, curlin' smoke keep out o'pan, 119
The first cock of hay, 29
First the Dudgeon, then the Sperm, 257
First William the Norman, 90
For every evil under the sun, 47
For every fog in March, 60
For ev'ry realm, the careful factors meet, 114
For the want of a nail the shoe was lost, 46
Four stiff standers, 49
The French are all coming, so they declare, 241
Friday flits, 124
Friend, foe, letter, lover, journey to go, 72
From Billingsgate industrious Will, 196
'From Colchester there rose a starre, 37

A garthful of geese and no turds, 124
A gift on the thumb is sure to come, 72
Gin ye ca' me imp or elf, 19
Girls and boys come out to play, 185
Go to bed first, a golden purse, 121
God bless our lord the King!, 218

God bless our meat, 159

God cannot love (says Blunt with tearless eyes), 213

God rest you merry, gentlemen, 69

God save our gracious King, 217

Good Friday comes this month, the old woman runs, 198

Good Master and good Mistress, 66

Good morning Mister Capstick, 68

Good morning to you, 281

Good morning to you Valentine, 84

Good tooth, bad tooth, 126

Goose Fair comes and Goose Fair goes, 138

The Grand old Duke of York, 236

Green and white, 76

Gunpowder Plot, 172

Gunpowder Plot will never be forgot, 172

Guy Fawkes and his companions did contrive, 171

Haley, Maley, tipsy tee, 32

Half a league, half a league, 261

Hallowe'en, Hallowe'en, 117

Haly on a cabbage stalk, 118

Happy Birthday to you, Happy Birthday to you, 282

Happy is the bride the sun shines on, 76

Happy they'll be that wed and wive, 76

Hark, Hark, the dogs do bark, 149

Have you seen the muffin man, 198

Hay is for horses, 67

He is a lord for a year and day, 112

He that lies at the stock, 121

He'd fly through the air with the greatest of ease, 276

Hempseed I sow, 119

Her Exhibition still attracts, 246

Here are fine golden pippins, 194

Here I am with my rabbits, 199

Here, ladies, are cotton, 204

Here lies Fred, 211

Here oranges sweet, 194

Here rabbits wild and tame, 199

Here strawberries, the best, 195

Here's a health unto his Majesty, 176

Here's a large one for the lady, 203

Here's fine rosemary, sage and thyme, 200

Here's Finiky Hawkes, 205

Here's that will challenge all the fair, 130

Hey diddle diddle, the cat and the fiddle, 157

Hey diddle dinkety, poppety pet, 112

Hey-how for Hallowe'en!, 117

Hiccup, hiccup, go away, 127

Hick-up snick-up look-up right-up, 127

Hickup, snickup, Rise up, right up, 53

High diddle ding, 179

His was the Word that spake it, 159

Hob-hole Hob!, 20

Holly berries shining red, 59

Home came the jovial Horkey load, 65

Hot cross buns, hot cross buns, 197

How many miles to Babylon?, 3

How shall I speak of that triumphant day, 179

Humpty Dumpty lay in the beck, 175

Humpty Dumpty sat on a wall, 174

Hush-a-ba, birdie, croon, croon, 2

Hush you, hush you, 107

I am a female Neptune, a sort of mermaid race, 298

I bind myself today, 79

I do not want to hurt thee frog, 127

I dreamt that I slept at Madame Tussaud's, 247

I had a brother dressed in blue, 321

I had a little nut tree, 142

I have an apple I can't cut, 49

I have come to say goodbye Dolly Gray, 285

I knock this rag upon this stane, 116

I see the moon, and the moon sees me, 8

I seiz'd the vermin, home I quickly sped, 25

I shall goe into an hare, 116

I tell of Christmas mummings, New Year's day, 68

I was sitting in front of the Ave Maria, 316

I washed my face in water, 49

I wish you a merry Christmas and a happy New Year, 69

Ic Dictation, 34

If a rainbow comes at night, 58

If all the world were paper, 43

If bees stay at home, 60

If he stays until September, 29

If I had a donkey that wouldn't go, 251

If I had a donkey wot wouldn't go, 251

If I should die, think only this of me, 310

If one day you would wed, 122

If she be a good goose, her dame well to pay, 84

If you have none of these pretty little elves, 197

If you love me, bounce and fly, 63

If you marry in Lent, 76

If you sing before breakfast, 73

If your whip stock's made of rowan, 118
If you're the lady as I take you to be, 73
I'll to thee a Simnel bring, 68
I'm blind and I'm crippled, 256
I'm the king of the castle, 44
In and out the dusky bluebells, 19
In comely sort their foreheads did adorne, 133
In Flanders' fields the poppies blow, 313
In fourteen hundred and ninety two, 141
In good King Charles' golden days, 209
In London thirty years ago, 177
In seventeen hundred and fifty three, 40
In sixteen hundred and sixty-six, 190
In some person's estimation, 271
In the blood of Adam death was taken, 125
In the month of Averil, 30
In the name of the Lord, 128
In Yorkshire ancient people say, 59
Ip, dip, 34
Is Scotsmen's blood now grown so cold, 225
It was on the eighteenth of October, 134
It's a long way to Tipperary, 303
It's de same old tale of a pal-pa-ta-ting niggar ev'ry time, ev'ry time, 283
It's Punkie Night tonight, 120
I've just got here, thro' Paris, from the sunny southern shore, 277
I've placed my cradle on yon holly top, 2
Ivy, Ivy, I love you, 62

Jack and Jill went up the hill, 10
Jack be nimble, 144
Jack Horner was a pretty lad, 147
Jack Spratt could eat no fat, 46
Jeremiah Jones a lady's man was he, 300
Jim and George were two great lords, 185
John Brown's body lies a-mouldering in the grave, 267
Jolly boating weather, 269
Just at the mirk and the midnight hour, 120

King Arthur lives in merry Carlisle, 57
King Charles the First walked and talked, 176
Kyng Edward, 104

Lady, Lady, Landers, 28
Ladybird, ladybird, fly away home, 27
The Leith police dismisseth us, 54
Let's joy in the Medal with James III's Face, 183
Let's laugh at the comics, 329

Lincoln was, London is, but Yorke shall be, 111
The lion and the unicorn, 21
Little bird of paradise, 50
Little Bo-Peep fell fast asleep, 160
Little Bo-Peep has lost her sheep, 160
Little Boy Blue, come blow up your horn, 143
Little General Monk sat upon a trunk, 178
Little Jack Horner, 146
Little Jack Horner sat in a corner, 145
Little Miss Muffet, 173
Little Nancy Etticoat, 51
London Bridge is broken down, 85, 87, 90
A long tail'd pig, 197
Lord grant that Marshall Wade, 217
The Lord rade. The foal slade, 21
Lucy Locket lost her pocket, 235

Mackerel sky, 59
Magpie, magpie, flutter and flee, 30
Malbrook s'en va-t-en guerre, 280
The man in the moon came down too soon, 10
The Man in the Moon was caught in a trap, 8
The man o' the moon, here's to him, 10
A man of words and not of deeds, 48
Mark well her grot, don't miss this place, 15
Mary, Mary, quite contrary, 162
Mary, Mary, where are you now Mary?, 131
Matthew, Mark, Luke and John, 42
Maxwelton Banks are bonnie, 263
Maydens of Englonde, sore maye ye morne, 104
'Mid pleasures and palaces, though we may roam, 266
The milk-woman's here, 199
Miller, miller, mooter poke, 102
Mine eyes have seen the glory of the coming of the Lord, 268
Monday for danger, Tuesday kiss a stranger, 74
Monday for wealth, 75
Monday's child is fair of face, 72
Moon, moon, 9
Moon.penny bright as silver, 9
The moon shines bright, 19
The more you feed it, 49
Moses supposes his toeses are roses, 54
A mother cannot feed her child, 327

Mouse! Here I give thee a tooth of bone, 126
My bell I keep ringing, 198
My dame hath a lame tame crane, 53
My first is in apple, and also in pear, 49
My grandmother sent me a new fashioned three-cornered cambric country-cut handkerchief, 54
My head is made of iron, 106
My heart is wae, and unco wae, 224
Mythologists might, in this cave lay odds, 15

Nail horseshoe over door, saying, 78
Nimble Heels henceforward shall be his name, 130
No braid adorns their reefers, no flash, no stripes, no pips, 324
No hard fate can daunt a loyal spirit, 227
No longer now the Duke excites our wonder, 237
No parleying now! In Britain is one breath, 241
'No wonder my royal father cannot man his shipping, 256
A north-west breeze as big as a sheet, 61
Now, a tear-drop fell from the girl's mincepies, 318
Now the dustman's arrived, 206

O may thy virtue guard thee thro' the roads, 214
O Mr Mayor, O Mr Mayor, 135
O, Pearlin Jean!, 118
O' rosies, o' rosies, 228
O sacred love of France, undying, 240
O, Suffolk is a noble county, full of lovely views, miss, 137
O what's the rhyme to porringer?, 182
Oak before ash, all wet and splash, 60
Of all the days that's in the year, 185
Oh, a ship went a-sailing out over the bar, 254
Oh, as I was a-rolling down Paradise Street, 257
Oh Bessie Bell an' Mary Gray, 192
Oh! here comes I St George, 105
Oh! say, can you see, by the dawn's early light, 250
Oh, we've been rambling all this night, 97
Oh where, oh where has my little dog gone?, 274
Old Chairs to mend, Old Chairs to mend, 205

Old King Cole was a merry old soul, 36
Old Lord Nelson lost one eye, 242
On Good Friday rest thy plough, 65
On old long syne, 225
On the farm, ev'ry Friday, 324
On the first of March, 60
On yonder hill there is a red deer, 49
One crow was bad luck, 30
One for a kiss, two for a wish, 74
One for sorrow, two for mirth, 30
One half the play they spend in noise and brawl, 181
Onery two-ery, six and seven, 32
Onion skin, 64
Oranges and lemons, 150
Out nettle, in dock, 127
Over the water and over the lea, 221
Over thy head I ring this bell, 130
Oyez! Oyez! Oyez!, 129

Pancake day, pancake day, 70
Pease pudding hot, pease pudding cold, 44
The people say, 75
Peter Piper picked a peck of pickled pepper, 53
Peter was sitting on a marble stone, 126
Pick 'en up 'e' 'orse shoe, and spatter en wi' spittle, 78
A pin to look in, 123
A pin to see a puppet show, 123
A pinnet a piece to look at a show, 123
Pity a poor old man, 207
The P'lice force is a noble band, 294
A plot's now on foot, look about, English boys, 184
Polly put the kettle on, 275
The postman hurries forth to bring your daily news, 205
Potatoes and apples, 195
Private Perks is a funny little codger, 307
Punch and Judy, 206

Rain before seven, 58
Rain, rain, go away, 44
The rat ran over the roof of the house, 53
Ratton and mouse, 188
Red glared the beacon on Pownell, 240
Red roses under the sun, 223
A red sky in the morning, 58
Reed reed sodger fly away, 28
Remember, remember the fifth of November, 169
Revered, beloved — O you that hold, 259

Ride a cock-horse to Banbury cross, 166, 167
Ride on a horse, 168
Right cheek, left cheek, why do you burn?, 75
Right for spite, 74
Ring-a-ring o' roses, 187
Rob a robin, 63
Robert Rutter dreamed a dream, 52
The robin and the redbreast, 63
Robin Hood, Robin Hood, 107
Robin takker, robin takker, 63
Rock-a-bye baby on the tree top, 2
Rock-a-bye baby, thy cradle is green, 3
Rock cradle empty, rock in plenty, 72
The rose is red, the violet blue, Gillies are sweet and so are you, 84
Roses are red and violets are blue, 84
Round and round the garden, 301
Rowley, Powley, puddin' and pie, 180
Royal Oak Day, 179

Said the Devil when flying o'er Harrogate Wells, 16
St Dunstan as the story goes, 82
St John to see the girls, 14
St Olav's Well, low by the sea, 16
Sair back an' sair banes, 14
Sally an' I, Sally an' I, 103
Sandy he belongs to the mill, 102
Saturday new and Sunday full, 9
A Saturday's Moon, 9
A Scarborough Warning, 157
Seagull, seagull, get thi on t' sand, 60
See a pin and pick it up, 122
See saw, sack-a-day, 180
See the rustic in the moon, 7
September blow soft, 67
Shall those who drudge from morn till night, 213
She seldom sells shellfish, 53
Should auld acquaintance be forgot, 226
Should old acquaintance be forgot, 225
Should old gay mirth and cheerfulness, 226
The side was steep, the bottom deep, 13
Silent night, Holy night, 5
Sing a song of sixpence, 147
Sir Christopher Wren, 191
Smiling girls, rosy boys, 198
Snail, snail, come out of your hole, 25
Snailie, snailie, shoot out your horn , 25
Snaw, snaw, come faster, 59
Sneel, sneel, put out yer hoan, 25

Sneeze on Sunday morning fasting, 74
Some talk of Alexander, and some of Hercules, 231
Something new starts every day, 273
Something old, something new, 76
A son's a son till he gets him a wife, 47
A soul cake, a soul cake, 120
Sow peas and beans on David and Chad, 64
The Spanish Armada met its fate, 162
Spider as you waste away, 127
A spraggy cod'll grow no fatter, 61
Sprats alive oh!, 196
Spring: Slippy, drippy, nippy!, 64
Stand fast root, 67
A stick and a stake, 172
Stir up the fire, and make it low, 124
Strolling so happy down Bethnal Green, 278
Summer is icumen in, 96
A swarm of bees in May, 26
Sweet Agnes work thy fast, 38
Sweet and low, sweet and low, 5
Swim son, swim, show me you're a swimmer, 54

Take two that's red and one that's black, 119
Tell-oie-tit, 31
That house doth everyday more wretched grow, 124
A thatcher of Thatchwood went to Thatchet a-thatching, 53
Thatcher, thatcher, thatch a span, 103
Then we'll set a man to watch, 87
There came three angels out of the east, 16
There children dwell who know no Parent's care, 213
There is a flower within my heart, Daisy, Daisy, 289
There was a jolly miller and he lived by himself, 101
There was a jolly miller once, 98, 100, 101
There was a man came from the moon, 10
There was a wind, it came to me, 212
There was an old owl lived in an oak, 24
There was an old woman called Tussaud, 247
There were three crows sat on a stone, 30
There, where on Sundays I go alone, 18
There's a little short gentleman, 27
There's meat hung down before the fire to roast, 102
They never can be half so merry as we, 97

They that wash on Monday, 123
They that wive between sickle and scythe, 76
Think on this sacred festival, 43
Thirty days hath September, 39
This is Hallowe'en, 118
This little Boney says he'll come, 241
This man cries Old Clothes!, 204
Three blind mice, three blind mice, 155
Three crooked cripples went through Cripplegate, 53
Three grey geese in the garden grass grazing, 52
Three wise men of Gotham, 96
Through storm and wind, 67
Tickle, tickle, on the knee, 73
Tid, Mid, Miserae, 43
Tid, Mid, Miseray, 43
Tinker, tailor, 113
Tip at the toe, live to see woe, 186
'Tis no these pins I wish to burn, 122
To change the name and not the letter, 76
To the Maypole haste away, 97
Today, my Julia, thee must make, 159
Tom he was a Piper's son, 211
Tom Pearce, Tom Pearce, lend me your grey mare, 138
Treason does never prosper, 224
The tumbler's expert, 206
Turn again, Whittington, 110
Tussaud's Beef-eater pay, 245
'Twas Goose Fair cracked the merriest wheeze, 137
'Twas on a Monday morning, 215
Tweed said To Till, 12
Twinkle, twinkle little star, 247
Two brothers we are, 187
Two legs sat upon three legs, 50

Up and down the City Road, 272
Up to mighty London came an Irishman one day, 302
Upon Paul's steeple stands a tree, 154

Wallflowers, wallflowers, growing up so high, 145
We arrived late on the scene, 328
We do; the present desperate stage, 311
We had to move away, 291
We have a pretty witty king, 180
We won't go home till morning, 280
A weddin', a woo, a clog an' a shoe, 76
Weel bun' an' better shorn, 66

We've cheated the Parson, we'll cheat him again, 65
Wharfe is clear, and Aire is lythe, 13
What are little boys made of?, 46
What can a blind man see?, 51
What God never sees, 51
What goes between London and Glasgow without moving?, 51
What is the most difficult riddle?, 51
What is the rhyme for porringer?, 181
The wheelwright makes his wheel, 205
When a picture leaves the wall, 125
When a Twister a-twisting will twist him a twist, 55
When Advent comes do thou refraine, 75
When Britain first at Heaven's command, 208
When Candlemas day is cloudy and black, 60
When clouds appear like rocks and towers, 59
When Constabulary duty's to be done, 293
When good King Arthur ruled this land, 55
When I was out of work the missus nagged me so much you see, 295
When lords and ladies stinking water soss, 16
When my master has thatched all his straw, 103
When rich men find their wealth a curse, 242
When the bell begins to toll, 77
When the mist comes from the hill, 60
When the pancake bell begins to ring, 70
When the wind goes opposite the sun, 61
When the wind is in the east, 61
When thou dost hear a toll or knell, 77
When you see millions of the mouthless dead, 310
Where's Troy, and where's the Maypole in the Strand?, 213
Which travels faster, heat or cold?, 51
Whistle while you work, 325
A whistling woman and a crowing hen, 124
White bird featherless, 51
White sand, grey sand, 205
Who comes riding thither as black as coal, 171
Who is it that climbs the summit of the road?, 323
Who kept a brace of painted creatures to be hand, 173
Who killed Cock Robin?, 93

Whoever eats Hammer nuts, 17
Who'll buy my lavender, fresh lavender, 199
Who'll buy my Mitcham lavender?, 199
Why did the beetroot blush?, 51
William and Mary, George and Anne, 183
William Taylor was a brisk young sailor, 256
William the Conqueror 1066, 91
Within the sound of the great bell, 78
Winter package holidays are quite within our means, 329
Wishing well, wishing well, 17

Wyndham, Horner, Popham and Thynne, 147

X shall stand for playmates Ten, 41

Yan, tan, tethera, pethera, pimp, 35
Yankee Doodle came to town, 233, 234
Ye sons of France awake to glory, 239
Yorke, Yorke, for my monie, 111
You must not wash blankets in May, 124
You'll be treated with Honours if you secrecy mark, Sir, 237
Young lambs to sell, young lambs to sell, 197

GENERAL INDEX

Abbey Church,
Dorchester-on-Thames,
78-9
Abercrombie, Lascelles,
311
Aberdeenshire, 12,16
Aboard The Man-o'-War,
255
'Abracadabra', 115
Act of Settlement, 1689,
182, 183
Adams and Liberty, 249
Agnes, St, 38-9
Ah Vous Dirai Je, 114
Aiden, St, 85
Alan-a-Dale, 109
Albany, Charlotte,
Duchess of, 223-4
Albert, Prince Consort,
260
Albert Hall, 288
Alcantara bridge, 86
Aleyn, Simon, 211
Alfonso, King of Castile,
107
Alford, Violet, 20-1
Alfred, King of England,
87
The Algier Slave's Release,
255
Alhambra Theatre, 276
'Ali Baba and the Forty
Thieves', 115
All Fools' Day, 70-1
All Hallow's Day, 117

All Saints' Day, 119
All Soul's Day, 119, 120
Almond, river, 192, 193
America, 52; buys
London Bridge, 89;
ladybirds, 28; navy,
258; pancake races, 70;
rhyming slang, 318;
slavery, 33; songs,
233-5; 249-50, 267-9,
280-1; World War II,
324, 326
American Civil War,
267-9
American War of
Independence, 222,
232-3, 234-5
Ampthill Park, 144
Andalusia, 107
Angles, 55, 64
Anglesea, 33
Anglo-Saxons, 20, 187
animals, 22-31, 67, 126,
251-3
Ann, St, 12
Anne, Queen, 181-2,
183, 207, 209, 253
Anne of Cleves, 154
Annie Laurie, 263-5
Antonio, 305
Apple Wassailing, 66-7
apples, 62-63, 66, 194,
195
April, 41
April Fools' Day, 70-1

Aqua Arnemetia, 12
Arabs, 279
Aragon, 106
Arizona, 89
Armstrong, Henry W.,
306
Arndorf, 4-5
Arne, Dr, 208, 218
Arnemeza, 12
Arthur, King, 31, 55-7
Arthur, Prince, 142
Ascension day, 16
Asgard, 20
ash trees, 61-2, 128
Ash Wednesday, 70
Asia Minor, 105
Ask a Policeman, 293-5
Askr, 61
Asquith, H. H., 310
Athens, 25
Atlantic Monthly, 268
Atlantic Ocean, 141-2
August, 41
Augustine, St, 64
Augustus Emperor, 41
Auld Lang Syne, 225-7,
280
Australia, 318
Austria, 4-5, 238
Away in a Manger, 4

Baa, baa, black sheep,
113-14
Babies, *see* children
Baby Bunting, 1

Babylon, 3-4
Baden-Powell, Colonel Robert, 286
Baldur, 19, 21
Balkern, 38
balm, 202
Balmbra, 284
Balmbra's Music Hall, 285
Balmoral, 260
Baltimore, 249
Bambridge, 214
Banbury, 136, 166-8
Bannockburn, 104-5, 107
baptism, 20
Barnes, Paul, 285
Barrow, 85
Bartholomew Fair, 129, 130-1
Bastille, 238
The Basyn, 147
Bath, 296
bats, 116
Battle, 91
The Battle Hymn of the Republic, 268-9
Beaker people, 203
Beaky Burn, 192
Beanes, William, 249
beans, 63-4, 85
The Bear Went Over The Mountain, 280-1
Beaufort Club, 279
Beauvale Priory, 110
Bede, the Venerable, 71, 77; *Ecclesiastical History of the English Nation*, 64
Bedford, 145
Bedfordshire, 43, 144, 204
The Bedgeon, It is a Delicate Trade, 101
beds, 121-2
bees, 26-7, 60, 202
beggars, 149-50, 207, 256
Belgium, 169, 245
Bell, Bessie, 192
The Bellman and Little Boney, 241-2
bells, 77, 78-9, 111, 120, 150-3
Beltanes, 40
Bennett, Richard

Rodney, 174
Benson, Arthur C., 288
Berin, St., 79
berries, 59
Berwick, 104
Bessy Bell, 191-3
Bestwood Park, 181
Bethlehem, 4
Betjeman, Sir John, *Slough*, 322-3
Beuler, Jacob, 251
Beverley, 75
Bible, 6, 24, 26, 32, 42-3, 45, 48-9
bicycles, 289-90
Bil, 11
Billingsgate Fish Market, 196
Bird, Peter, *Rockets*, 327
birds, 2, 28-31, 63, 95, 148
Birmingham, 132, 198
birth, 71-2
Bishop, 266
Black Douglas, 107
Black Sea, 262
blackbirds, 148
blackcocks, 95
Blackheath, 133
Blackpool, 305
blacksmiths, 81
Blackwell Hall, London, 114
Blaydon Races, 283-5
blood charmers, 125
Blow The Man Down, 257-8
bluebells, 19
boat racing, 269-72
Bobby Shafto, 228-9
Bodleian Library, 172
Boer War, 285-6
Boleyn, Anne, 143, 146, 148, 151, 154, 157
bonfires, 172
Bosobel, 179
Bosworth Field, battle of, 141
Boteler, Sir Henry, 165
Bothwell, James Hepburn, Earl of, 75, 161
Boulogne, 240, 241, 313
Bow bells, 111

box hedges, 188
The Boy I Love Is Up In The Gallery, 292
Boy Scouts, 286, 325
Bradford, 299-300
Bramston, James, *Time's Changes*, 213
Bratton, John W., 302
Brazil, 283
Bremen, 86-7
Bridge Pavilion, Ilkley, 308
bridges, 85-90
Brighton, 288, 296
Brighton, 284
Britain, Battle of, 321
Britannia, 207-8
British army, 178-9, 231-3, 236-8
The British Grenadiers, 231-3
Brittany, 26
Brooke, Rupert, 323; *The Soldier*, 310-11
broom, 202-3
Broom Squire's Song, 203
Broome, Rev. Arthur, 253
Broughton Castle, 166
Brown, John, 267
Brown, S., *Merchant Navy*, 324
Brussels, 244
'Bucca', 45
Buckingham, Duke of, 173
Buckinghamshire, 70, 144
Buckland Rectory, 95
Buffs, 304
Bull, John, 218
Bunker's Hill, 234
Burke, Betty, 222
Burma, 323
Burns, Robert, 224, 225, 226
Bury St Edmunds, 136-7
Bushey, 200
Butler, Ralph, 324-5
butter churning, 116-17
buttons, 203
Buxton, 12
Byron, Lord, 244

Caesar, Julius, 39, 41, 196
cakes, 167-8, 197-8
Calais, 156, 163
calendars, 39-41
Calixtus II, Pope, 85
Cambridge university, 129, 270-1
Cambridgeshire, 129
Camelot, 56
Canada, 28, 33, 313
Canary Islands, 242
Candlemas, 60, 62
candles, 119-20, 122, 144-5
Canterbury Music Hall, 275-6
Care Sunday, 44
Carlisle, 57
carols, 4-5, 68-9
cars, 288, 290
Cast-a-way Well, 17-18
castles, 99, 103
Catesby, Robert, 169
Catherine, St, 144
Catherine of Aragon, 142, 143, 144, 148, 154, 155, 204
Catholic Church, 40, 64, 81, 146, 155-6, 157, 160-2, 167, 169-71, 182, 214
cats, 117
Catterns, 144
Caucasus, 194
cauls, 71
Cavalcade, 297
Cavaliers, 176-7
Caxton, William, 56; *The Game and Playe of Chesse,* 113
Cedd, St, 85
celandine, 201
Celts, 32, 33, 40
Chad, St, 64, 85
chairs, 205
Champagne Charlie, 276, 277, 279
Chaplin, Charles, 319
Chaplin, Charlie, 319-20
Chaplin, Hannah, 319-20
Chaplin, Oona, 320
Chaplin, Sydney, 319

Charles I, King of England, 62, 174-6, 181, 209
Charles II, King of England, 97, 134, 176, 178-81, 207, 208
Charlie, Bonny Prince, 10, 215-16, 219-24
'Charlie is my darling', 215
Charlton Horn Fair, 133-4
charms, 48, 79, 116-17, 118-19, 122, 125, 127-8
Chaucer, Geoffrey, 99
cheeks, 'burning', 74-5
cherries, 195
Chesapeake Bay, 249
Cheshire, 70, 120
Chester, 100
Chester, Hugh, Earl of, 98-9, 128
Chester Fair, 128-9
Chester Hand, 128-9
children, employment, 185-6; games, 44-5, 151; names, 20; as sacrifices, 86-7; superstitions about babies, 71-2, 74; tickling rhymes, 73, 301
Chillingworth, Dr, 174-5
China, 1, 25, 31, 148, 194, 327
Chopin, Frédéric, 5
Christ, 4, 26, 39, 42, 44, 56, 71, 115
'Christ's Croft', 15
Christianity, 14, 41-2, 45, 64-5, 71, 78, 81, 84, 115
Christmas, 4-5, 51, 62, 66, 68-9, 275
Christy Minstrels, 275
Church of England, 146, 155-6, 157
churches, 150-4, 159
Churchill, Sir Winston, 311, 320-1, 324
cinquefoil, 202
Cirencester, 42
Civil War, 97, 174-6, 179
Clarence, Duke of, 279

Clark, Mary Ann, 237
Clark, Elizabeth, 264
Cleveland Vessell Cups' Song, 69
clothes, 76, 124, 204-5
clouds, 59
clover, 61, 62
Coal Hole, 273
Cobb, William, 285
Cobbler, cobbler, mend my shoe, 186-7
Cobbley, Tom, 139-40
Coburn, Charles, 277-9
Cock a doodle doo, 164-6
Cockneys, 315-19
Coel (Cole), Duke of Britain, 36-8
Colchester, 36-8, 248
Coldstream Guards, 178-9
Colechurch, Peter de, 87
Coliseum, 288, 292
Collingwood, Admiral, 243
Collins, Arthur, 300
Collins, Charlie, 290
Collop Monday, 70
Cologne, 308
colours, 76, 121
Columbus, Christopher, 141-2
Come to Peacehaven, 308-9
Commissioners of Woods and Forests, 133
Commonwealth Games, 288
Connemara, 304
Constantine, Emperor, 37
'Convivial Songster', 101
Cornhill, London, 86
Cornwall, 16, 21, 31, 57, 74, 124, 163, 189
Cornwallis, General, 241
Corocoran, Mr, 266
coronations, 83
Corsica, 242
cotton thread, 21
counting, 34-5
counting-out rhymes, 32-4, 35, 45, 326
courtship, 75, 84

Covent Garden, 233, 274
Coventry, 167, 290
Coward, Noel, 297
Cowell, Sam, 274
Crabbe, George, *The Village*, 213
cradle songs, 1-5
craftsmen, 102-3
Craigdarroch, 264
Cranbrook, Earl of, 116
Cranmer, Archbishop, 156
Crazy Gang, 325
Crediton, 139
crime, 213-14
Crimean War, 262-3
Cromwell, Oliver, 3, 177, 178
Cromwell, Richard, 178
Crouch End Hippodrome, 292
crows, 30-1, 60
Crucifixion, 42, 43-4
Cruden, 16
Cruikshank, George, 246-7
Crusades, 3-4, 105-6, 279
cuckoo, 28-30, 96-7
Culloden Day, 219-20
Culloden Moor, battle of, 218, 219-20, 226
Cumberland, 35
Cumberland, Duke of, 219
Curtius, Dr, 246
Cyder Cellars, 273
Cymric, 32, 35

Dacre, Harry, 289
daisies, 201
Daisy Bell, 289-90
Dale Abbey, 18
Damascus, 194
damsons, 194
dandelions, 202
Darnley, Lord, 161
David, St, 64, 85
David, Worton, 300
Day, Daniel, 132
days of the week, 72, 73, 75, 122, 123, 124
death, 19, 63, 71, 77, 116, 125, 186

Death and Burial of Cock Robin, 168
death rhymes, 32
December, 41
Declaration of Independence, 234
Dee, river, 12
Dee mills, 98-102
Defoe, Daniel, 188; *Street Robberies Considered*, 315
Der Deitcher's Dog, 274-5
De La Mare, Walter, 311
Dell, Anis, 164-5
Dell, George, 164-5
Denham, 126
Denmark, 1, 31, 55, 73, 87
Dent Knitters' Song, 103
Derby, 216
Derby Castle Music Hall, 305
Derbyshire, 16-17, 18
Devil, 115
Devon, 9, 129, 138-40
Diana, 22
Diana's Well, 17-18
Dichu, 81
'Diddle diddle dumpling', 274
'dimple' verses, 73-4
Diocletian, Emperor, 38, 106
Diospolis, 106
Disney, Walt, 325
Dixon, Benjamin, 89
Dixon, Reginald, 297
Domesday Book, 92
domestic rhymes, 121-5
Don't Dilly Dally On The Way, 290-2, 293
Dorchester-on-Thames, 78-9
Dorset, 188
Douglas, Sir James, 107
Douglas, William, 263-4
Douglas, Lanarkshire, 107
Dowe, Robert, 152
Down Among the Dead Men, 227
Down At The Old Bull And Bush, 305
Downtown, 229

dragons, 105-6
dragon's tongue, 202
Drake, Sir Francis, 162-3
Dronach-haugh, 192
Dropping Well, 15
Druids, 12, 19, 26, 32, 33, 81, 115
Drummond, Algernon, 270
The Drunken Sayler, 52
Drury Lane Theatre, 300
Dryden, John, 100, 179, 181
ducks and drakes, 45
Duckworth, Francis, 99
Duke William's Frolic, 256
'dumb cake', 38-9
Dumfrieshire, 290
Dunbar, 104
Duncombe, Anne, 229
Duncombe Park, 229
Dundas, Sir David, 237-8
Dunlop, J. B. 290
Dunstan, St, 78, 82-3
Durandeau, A. E., 293
Durang, Ferdinand, 249-50
Durham, 72, 229, 231
dustmen, 206
The Dutchman's Dog, 275
Dyer, John, *The Fleece*, 114
Dymock, 21

Eagle tavern, London, 272-3
ears, 'burning', 74
East Anglia, 71-2
Easter, 44, 71
Edgar, King of England, 83
Edmund, King of England, 136
Edmundsbury Fair, 137
Edward I, King of England, 99, 103-4
Edward II, King of England, 104
Edward III, King of England, 8, 105-6
Edward VI, King of England, 154-5
Edward VII, King of

England, 286-8
Edwinstowe, 110
Egbert, King of Wessex, 82
eggs, birds, 63; Easter, 44, 71
Egypt, 19, 27, 39
Eisteddfod, 33
Elgar, Edward, 288
Elizabeth I, Queen of England, 23, 149, 157-60, 162-4, 169
Elizabeth II, Queen of England, 320
Elizabeth of York, 142
Ellis, Sarah, 21
Elsie Marley, 230-1
L'Enfant, Major Pierre Charles, 235
Enfield, 132
Equity, 279
Essex, 164
Essex Review, 37-8
Ethelred, King of England, 87
Eaton Boating Song, 269-70
Ettrick Bridge, 216
Evan's Supper Rooms, 274
Everest, Sir George, 326
Everest, Mount, 326-7
Exeter, 114, 129

fables, 45
Fabyan, Robert, 104-5
fairies, 18-20, 74, 120-1
Fairlop Fair, 132-3
Fairlop Oak, 132-3
fairs, 128-40
Fairy Queen, 120
Famous History of John Gilpin, 168
farming, 27-8, 48, 58, 60, 64-7, 76
Fawkes, Guy, 169-72
Fawn, James, 293-5
Feast of All Saints, 117
February, 39, 41
Februs, 41
Feldman, Bert, 300, 303-4, 305
Ferdinand, King of

Spain, 142
Ferguson, Alexander, 264
festivals, 65, 68-71
feudalism, 92
feverfew, 201
Fiennes family, 166
finger-counting, 34-5, 45
fingernails, 72
fires, 124
fish, 196
Fisher, Kitty, 235
fishermen, 8, 34, 60-1
Fitzooth, Robin, 108
Fitzwarren, Alice, 110, 111
Fitzwarren, Hugh, 111
Flamborough, 13
Flanagan, 305
Flanagan and Allen, 305, 325
Flanders, 156, 169, 236
Flint, 99
fog, 60
football, 328
For He's A jolly Good Fellow, 279-81
Forbes, Duncan, 219
Forde, Florrie, 303, 304, 305
Fort McHenry, 249, 250
fortune games and rhymes, 63, 71-9
Foster, Doctor, 103
Fotheringay Castle, 162
Fox, William, 100
Fragson, Harry, 300-1
France, 160, 232; calendar rhymes, 39; counting-out rhymes, 32; Crimean War, 262; lullabies, 1; Napoleonic Wars, 240-2, 243, 244-5, 254, 256, 327; Norman conquest, 91; nursery rhymes, 279-80; owls, 24; proverbs, 46; sea shanties, 254; strawberries, 195
Francis & Day, 307, 308
Fraser, 107
Frederick, Prince of

Wales, 211
Frederick, Maryland, 250
Freemasons, 32
French Revolution, 238, 246
Friday, 72
Frobisher, Sir Martin, 162
Frodsham, 15
'A frog he would a-wooing go', 274
frogs, 127
frost fairs, 134-5
fruit, 62-3, 66, 67, 194-5
fruit stone chants 113

Galahad, Sir, 56
games, children's, 44-5, 151
Gay, John, *Trivia*, 214
Gay, Noel, 324-5
geese, 69
Gendarmes Duet, 293
Gentlemen's Magazine, 217
George, Prince of Denmark, 183
George, St, 105-6
George I, King of England, 9, 183, 185, 209-11, 215
George II, King of England, 214, 216
George III, King of England, 223, 224, 229, 235, 236, 256, 260
George IV, King of England, 238, 253, 260
George VI, King of England, 322
Georgey Porgey, 180
Georgia, 232
Gerard, John, 200
Germany, bees, 26; counting-out rhymes, 32; lullabies, 1, 4; moon legends and rhymes, 6, 8; patron saint, 106; teeth, 126; Saxons, 55-6; World War II, 320-2, 323-4, 325, 327-8
Gibson, Wilfred, 311
Gilbert, Fred, 277

Gilbert, Rev., 248
Gilbert and Sullivan, *The Pirates of Penzance*, 293
gingerbread, 132, 198
gipsies, 32, 135-6
Girls and boys come out to play, 185-6
Gitana, Girtie, 306-7
Glasgow, 290
Glasier, Major, 232
Glastonbury, 42, 56, 83, 146
Gloucester, 103, 175
Gloucestershire, 20-1, 95
Glover, 296, 297
gloves, 84
'God rest you merry, Gentlemen', 69
God Save Great George Our King', 217-18
Godfrey, Fred, 297
God's Croft, 15
Godiva, Lady, 166-7
goldsmiths, 83
Good Friday, 18
Good Morning To All, 281
Goodbye Dolly Gray, 285-6
Goodbye Song, 281
Goose Fair, 137-8
gooseberries, 194-5
Gotham, 29, 96
grace, 159
Grainger Music Hall, 285
Granada, 107
Grand Music Hall, Stalybridge, 302
The Grand Old Duke of York, 236-8, 242
Gray, Mary, 192
'The Great Bull of Barnbury', 117
Grecian Theatre, 273
Gredesse, Walter de, 8
Greece, 1, 11-12, 18, 22, 25, 44, 106
Green, J., 248
Greenhithe, 89
Greensleeves, 121
Gregorian calendar, 40
Gregory, Pope, 40, 64
Grenadier Guards, 179, 231-3
The Grenadier March, 232, 234

Grimaldi, 274
Grose, Francis, 198
ground ivy, 201
groundsel, 67
Gruber, Franz, 5
Gunn, Martha, 298
Gunpowder Plot, 169-72
Guttit Bell, 70
Guy Fawkes' Day, 172
Gwyn, Nell, 181, 194

haberdashers, 204
Hackney, 89
Hail Mary, 32, 118
Hail to Thee Old Apple Tree, 67
Hainault Forest, 132
hair, 73
Haiti, 141
Hall, Henry, 302
Hallowe'en, 117-19, 120
Hamilton, Lady, 242, 243
Hampshire, 129
Hampstead, 200
Hampton Court, 143
Hancock, John, 234
Handley, Tommy, 325
Hanley, 306, 307
Hanover, 236
Hanover, House of, 23
Hanoverian era, 209-58
Happy Birthday To You, 281-2
Hardy, 243
hares, 116
Hargreaves, William, 295-6
Hark, Hark, the dogs do bark, 149-50
Harlequin Everywhere, 233
Harold, King of England. 91-2
Harper's Ferry, Virginia, 267
Harrogate, 14, 16
harvest, 27-8, 48, 58, 60, 64-7, 76
Harvest Festival, 65-6
Has Anybody Here Seen Kelly?, 305
Hastings, battle of, 91-2
Hastings, Warren, *Dawn Patrol*, 321

Hatfield, 164-5
Havasu, Lake, 89
The Haverley Minstrels, 282
Hawkins, Sir John, 162
The Haymarket Spring Meeting, 273
heartsease, 202
He'd have to get under, get out and get under, 288
Heimskringla, 87
Helen (daughter of Coel), 36-7
Hello! Hello! Who's Your Lady Friend, 300-1
Helsby, 15
hempseed, 119
Henley, 270
Henrietta Maria, 174, 176
Henry I, King of England, 85, 93, 130
Henry II, King of England, 108, 203
Henry IV, King of England, 110
Henry V, King of England, 110
Henry VII, King of England, 15, 77, 141-3
Henry VIII, King of England, 130, 142, 143-4, 146-9, 151, 154, 157, 203, 204
herbs, 188, 199-203
Here We Are Again, 297
Here's a health unto his Majesty', 176-7
Herrick, Robert, 62, 68
'The Hertfordshire miracle', 166
Hey diddle diddle, the cat and the fiddle, 157-9
Heywood, Robert, 172
hiccups, 53, 127
Hicks, Seymour, 282
Highgate Hill, 153
Hill, Hamilton, 285
Hill, Mildred, 281
Hill, Patty, 281-2
Hillary, Edmund, 326-7
'Hip, hip hurrah', 66
Hiroshima, 326
Hitler, Adolf, 320, 323-4

Hjuki, 11
Hob, 20
Hogg, James, 9, 215-16, 240
Holborn Theatre, 306
holidays, 65, 144
Holy Grail, 56
Holy Land, 107
Holy Trinity, 81
Holy Wars, 105
Home Guard, 309, 321
Home Sweet Home, 265-7
Honiton, 129
hopscotch, 45
horehound, 202
'Horkey' wagon, 65
Hornby, 77
Horner family, 147
Horner, Jack, 196
Horner, John, 146-7
Horner, Thomas, 147
Horse Guards, 179
horseleek, 202
horseshoes, 78
Hot cross buns, 43, 197
Hotti, 1
Houses of Parliament, 170-1
How Many Miles to Babylon?, 3-4
Howard, Catherine, 151, 154
Howe, Julia Ward, 268-9
Hugill, Stan, 254
Humpty Dumpty, 174-5
Hunt, Sir John, 326, 327
Hurley, Alec, 292
husbands, foretelling, 62, 63, 119

I Do Like To Be Beside the Seaside, 296-7
I had a little Nut Tree, 142
I Wish I Was In Dixie, 298
If I had a Donkey, 251-3
Ilford, 132
Ilkley, 308
I'm A Lassie From Lancashire, 305
I'm Shy Mary Ellen, I'm Shy, 300
I'm Twenty-one Today, 299-300

'In and out the dusky bluebells', 19
India, 141
Indians, American, 34
Industrial Revolution, 316
Ingress Abbey, 89
insects, 26-8
The Instruction of the Deer, 81
Inverness, 219
Ireland, 55, 303; bees, 26; 'Jack be Nimble', 145; potatoes, 195-6; rhyming slang, 316; St David, 85; St Patrick, 79, 81; sayings, 20
Irish Guards, 311-12
Ironsides, 178
Isabella, Queen of Spain, 141
Isis, 27
Isle of Man, 116, 303, 305
Italy, 194, 223
itches, 74
ITMA, 325
It's A Long Way To Tipperary, 302-4, 305, 307
ivy, 62

Jack and Jill, 10-11
'Jack be Nimble', 144-5
Jackson Lads, 320
Jacobites, 9-10, 23, 183-5, 211-12, 214-24
James I, King of England, 23, 161, 169, 173, 174
James II, King of England, 180-3, 214
James IV, King of Scotland, 22
James, Anthony, 164
James, Elizabeth, 164-6
January, 40-1
Janus, 40-1
Japan, 1, 26, 31, 32, 141, 326
Jean Francois, 254
Jenny Greenteeth, 13
Jenny's Bawbee, 275
Jerusalem, 279
Jews, 26, 39

Jingle Bells, 275
John, King of England, 96, 108, 133
John Brown's Body, 267-9
Johnson, Dr, 222
Johnson, William, 270
Jones, Inigo, 154
Jonson, Ben, *Bartholomew Fair*, 131
Jordan, Herbert, *Dawn Patrol*, 321
Joseph, Adam, 316
Joseph of Arimathea, 42, 56
Josephine, Empress, 240
Juanna of Castille, 142
Judge, Jack, 302-5
Julian calendar, 39-40
Julius I, Pope, 84
July, 41
June, 41
Juno, 41

The Keel Row, 228
Keir, 290
Kendall, Alec, 299
Kennedy, Jimmy, 302
Kent, Duke of, 260
Kett, Walter, 114
Kett's Hill, 114
Key, Francis Scott, 249, 250
Keystone Cops, 320
Kimberley, 285-6
Kind, 296, 297
The King's Anthem, 218
Kingston-on-Thames, 8
Kinrosshire, 162
Kipling, Rudyard, *A Death Bed*, 311-12
Kirby-in-Ashfield, 110
Kirklees nunnery, 109
Kitchener, Lord, 286
knitting, 34, 103
Knox, John, 40, 161

lace-making, 144-5, 204
ladybirds, 27-8
Ladysmith, 286
Laguna, 283
lambs, 38
The Lament of Flora MacDonald, 222

Lammas Fair, Exeter, 129
Lammastide, 95
Lanarkshire, 107
Lancashire, 13, 195
Lancaster, House of, 110, 141
Land of Hope and Glory, 287-8
Lang, Andrew, 180
Langsyne, 226
lanterns, 119-20
Laoghaire, King, 81
Last Supper, 42
Lastingham, 85
Latimer, Bishop, 156
Laurie, Annie, 263-5
lavender, 199-200, 201
Lavenham, 248
Lawrence, Katie, 289, 290
Laxden Heath, 38
Leamington, 296
leap years, 39, 40, 76
Lednock, 192, 193
Lee, Alfred, 276-7
Lee, Bert, 300
Lee, Robert E., 267
Leeds City Varieties, 298
The Legend of King Coel, Helena and Constantine, 37
Leicester, Earl of, 159
Leicester Abbey, 144
Leigh, Egerton, 100
Leigh, Fred, 290
Lent, 43, 68, 70
Leotard, 276
Lester, Thomas, 145
Lewis, Alun, *Mahratta Ghats*, 323
Leybourne, George, 275-6 298
Lichfield, 85
Life Guards, 179
Light Brigade, 261-2
Lilliburlero, 184
Lily Marlene, 325
Lily of Laguna, 282-3
lily of the valley, 200
Lincolnshire, 34-5
lions, 21-2, 23
Lisburne, Lady, 229
Lisle, Claude Joseph de, *Chant de Guerre pour*

l'armée, 238-9
Liston, John, 274
Little Bo-Peep, 160-2
Little Boy Blue, 143-4
Little Jack Horner, 145-7
Little John, 109, 110
Little Miss Muffet, 173-4
Lizzard, 163
Lloyd, Arthur, 274
Lloyd, Marie, 290, 292, 293
Loch Leven, 162
Locket, Lucy, 235
Loki, 78
London, 92; churches, 150-4; crime, 213-14; Dick Whittington, 110-11; docks, 106; fairs, 129, 130-5; Great Fire, 153, 180, 189-91, 213, 316; growth, 213; Jacobites, 216; maypole,97; merchants, 112; plague, 189; rhyming slang, 315-19; street cries, 193-206, 274; wool trade, 114
London Bridge, 85-90, 151
London Metropolitan Police Force, 293
London Palladium, 325
Loos, 309, 311
Lord Mayors, 111-12
Louis XVI, King of France, 238
Louise, Princess of Stolberg, 223
Louisville, 281
Luftwaffe, 321
lullabies, 1-5, 240-1, 279
Lupercalia, 84
Lupus, Hugh, 98
Luther, Martin, 4
Luther's Cradle Hymn, 4
Lydda, 106
Lydia Fisher's Jig, 235

MacColl, D. S., *The Miner's Response*, 311
Macdermott, 298
MacDonald, Flora, 222-3

Mackney, 298
Macmillan, Kirkpatrick, 290
Macrea, John, *In Flanders Fields*, 313
Madison, James, 249
Mafeking, 286
Magee, Wes, *Young Poets At The Big Match*, 328
magic, 18-25, 32; black magic, 115, 118
magpies, 30
Maia, 41
The Maid of Primrose Hill, 280
Malaset, 108
Malory, Sir Thomas, *Morte d'Arthur*, 56
The Man On The Flying Trapeze, 276
The Man Who Broke The Bank At Monte Carlo, 277-8
Manchester Herald, 246
Manchester Regiment, 312
mangold lanterns, 119-20
Mani, 11
'Many haws, many snaws', 59
March, 41
Marie-Antoinette, 238, 279
marigolds, 202
Marion, Maid, 108, 110
marjoram, 201-2
Marlborough, Duke of, 280
Marley, Elsie, 229-30
Marley, Ralph, 231
marriage, 29, 38-9, 71, 75-7; *see also* weddings
Mars, 41
The Marseillaise, 238-40
Marseilles, 238
Martin, Richard, 251, 253
Martinmas, 40
Mary, Queen of Scots, 22, 23, 75, 157, 160-2, 169
Mary, Virgin, 27, 42, 56
Mary I, Queen of England, 136, 144, 155-7

Mary II, Queen of
England, 181-2, 316
Mary of Modena, 182
Masefield, John, 309
Massachusetts, 34
Maxwelton, 1st Baronet
of, 263
May, 41, 97, 124
May Fair, 131-2
May games, 109
May Queen, 97
mayors, 111-12
maypole dancing, 97, 177
meat, 196
medical lore, 21, 26, 45,
62, 125-8
Meer End, 304
Meg's Diversion, 318-19
Mells, Manor of, 146, 147
Menevia, 85
Merchant Navy, 324
merchants, 112-13, 114
*The Merry Humour of Horn
Fair*, 134
Michaelmas Fair,
Banbury, 136
Middlesex, 132
Midgard, 20
Midlands, 117, 136, 144
milk, 199
milkmaids, 177-8
The Miller of Dee, 98-102
mills and millers, 98-102
mince-pies, 69
Minerva, 25
mirrors, 20
mist, 60
mistletoe, 33
Mitcham, 199-200
Mona, 33
monarchy, 83, 90
monasteries, 146, 148,
149, 204
Monk, General, 178-80
Monmouth, Duke of, 180
Monmouthshire, 85
Monte Carlo, 277
months, 39-41, 75
moon, 6-10, 11, 22-3, 327
Moore, Arthur, 273, 305
Mordred, 56
Mortlake, 270
Morton, Charles, 275,298

Moses, 6
Mothering Sunday, 68
Mounteagle, Lord, 170
Mozart, W. A., 5
Muffet, Patience, 174
Muffet, Thomas, 173-4
muffins, 198
mugwort, 202
mummers, 3, 66, 71, 105,
106
music halls, 272-4, 275,
298, 300, 305, 306-7
My Nellie's Blue Eyes, 278

Nagasaki, 326
Nanna, 19
Napoleon, 3, 238, 240-2,
243-5, 254-5
Napoleonic Wars, 240-2,
243, 244-5, 254, 256,
327
national anthems,
217-19, 233, 238,
249-50
nature rhymes, 61-4, 71
nature riddles, 48-9
Nechum, Alexander, 7
needles, 204
Nellie Dean, 306-7
Nelson, Admiral, 78,
242-3
Nepal, 326-7
Netherlands, 236, 258,
286
nettles, 127, 202
neuritis, 26
New Forest, 93
New Model Army, 178
New Orleans, Battle of,
250
New Year's Eve, 62
Newberry, Frank, 302
Newcastle, 25, 68, 216,
229, 231, 285
Newcastle Football
Team, 285
Newcastle Magazine, 231
Newgate prison, 110,
152-3, 237
night, 115
night watchmen, 87
Nightingale, Florence,
260, 262

Nile, 39
Nile, Battle of the, 242
Nina, 141
Nixon, 15
Nolan, 262
Norfolk, 34, 62, 119, 213
Normandy, 91
Normans, 91-2, 129, 202
Norse mythology, 19, 20,
21, 61, 78
North Carolina, 222
North Esk, 13-14
Northamptonshire, 162
Northumberland, 28
Norway, 91
Norwich, 106, 114
Norwich cathedral, 24
Notre Dame, Paris, 240
Nottingham, 110, 137-8,
181, 248
Nottinghamshire, 29, 96,
108-10
November, 41
numerals, 41-2
nursery rhymes, 274-7; *et
passim*
Nutcrack Night, 117

Oak of Reformation, 114
oak trees, 33, 179
Oath Book of Colchester, 37
October, 41
Odin, 20, 21, 78, 87
Offenbach, Jaques,
Genevieve de Brabant,
293
Oh Mr Porter, 292
'Oh where, Oh where
has my little dog gone',
274
Olaf the Norseman, 87
Old Bailey, 152
Oldbury, 304
Olney, 70
omens, of good fortune,
27-8; ill omens, 31, 63,
116, 125
*On The Day King Edward
Gets His Crown On*,
286-7
*One Of The Ruins
Cromwell Knocked About
A Bit*, 292

One, two, buckle my shoe', 35
onions, 64
'open sesame', 115
Orange Free State, 286
oranges, 194
Oranges and Lemons,. 150-4
Order of the Garter, 106
Oswy, King, 85
Ottar Svarte, 87
Ouse, river, 18
Owen, Wilfred, *Dulçe et Decorum*, 312-13
owls, 24-5
Oxford, 156, 175
Oxford university, 143, 172, 270-1, 309
Oxfordshire, 62, 116, 122, 135-6
oysters, 196

'pace-eggers', 71
Pace Play, 71
Pack Up Your Troubles In Your Old Kit-bag, 307-9
Palestine, 105, 106
Pallas Athene, 25
pancake day, 69
Pankhurst, Emily, 296
pantomimes, 111
Papplewick, 110
Paragon, 278
Paris, 300, 320
Park, Air Chief Marshall Sir Keith, 321
Parker, Admiral, 243
Parr, Catherine, 154
Pascal, 71
passing bell, 77
Patrick, St, 79-82
patriotism, 83
Payne, John Howard, *Home Sweet Home*, 265-7
P.C. 49, 295-6
Peacehaven, 308-9
Peake, Mervyn, *The Rhyme of the Flying Bomb*, 322
Pearl Harbour, 326
pears, 194
peas, 44, 63-4, 85, 195

pedlars, 193-4, 203-5, 207
Peel, Sir Robert, 293
peep shows, 123
'peeping Tom', 167
penny-royal, 202
Penzance, 129
Pepys, Samuel, 179, 181, 190, 253
Percy, Thomas, 169-70
Persians, 115
Perth, 192
Peter Piper, 53
Peterborough Cathedral, 162
Pevensey, 91
Philip, 22-3
Philip II, King of Spain,. 156, 158, 163, 164
Philistines, 48-9
Picktree, 231
Picts, 55
pictures, 124-5
Pie Powder Court, 137
pies, 196-7
pilgrims, 14, 85
pilot rhymes, 257
Pindar, Peter, *An Epistle to Mrs Clark*, 237
pins, 20, 122-3
Pinta, 141
Pitt, William, 236
plague, 16-17, 180, 187-9, 192
Planché, James Robinson, 273
Plantagenets, 108, 203
plants, 61-3, 188, 199-203
Pleasants, Jack, 299-300
Pleon, Harry, 286-7
Plough Play, 66
ploughing, 118
plums, 194
police, 293-6, 315
Pomp and Circumstance, 288
Poor Laws, 149-50
Pop goes the Weasel, 272-3
Pope, Alexander, 212-13
Porteous, Crichton, 16
Portsmouth, 129
Portugal, 14, 86, 106, 141
postmen, 205-6
potatoes, 195-6

Potomac river, 235
Powell, Felix, 308-9
Powell, George, 308-9
Power, Nellie, 292
Primitive calendar, 40
prisons, 110, 152-3, 214
Promenade Concerts, 288
Protestantism, 40
proverbs, 45-8, 73, 150, 212
Prussia, 244
pubs, 280, 285, 306
Pudding Lane, London, 190, 191
Pulcinella, 207
pumpkin lanterns, 119
Punch, 24, 247, 313
Punch and Judy, 206-7
Punkie Night, 119-20
Purcell, Henry, 218
Puritans, 97, 167
Put Me Amongst The Girls, 296
Putney, 270

Quartermaster's Stores, 325

rabbits, 198-9
The Ragged Rascal, 52
Raglan, Lord, 262
Rahere, 130
rainbows, 20
Rantum, 8
ravens, 31
Red Parchment Book of Colchester, 37
Redditch, 204
Reformation, 177
Reinhold, Charles, 233
The Religious Turncoat, 210
Rennie, John, 89
Reynolds, Joshua, 229
rheumatism, 26, 187, 201
Rhodes, Cecil, 285, 286
Rhuddlan, 99
Rhymes for the Nursery, 248
rhyming slang, 315-19
Richard I, King of England, 106, 108

Richard II, King of
England, 114
Richard III, King of
England, 141
'Richard the Engineer',
99-100
Richmond, Duchess of,
244
Rickaby, J. W., 295-6
Riddles, 48-51
*Ride a cock-horse to
Banbury Cross*, 166-8
Ridley, Bishop, 156
Ridley, George, 283-5
Ring-a-ring o' roses, 187-9
ring games, 19, 101-2
The Rio Grande, 254
Ritson, Joseph, 231
Rizzio, David, 161
Robert, Duke of
Normandy, 92
Robert the Bruce, 107
Roberts, Lord, 286
Robin Hood, 107-10
Robin of Barnesdale, 108
robins, 63, 93-5
Rock-a-bye Baby, 2
Rocking Carol, 4
Roger of Doncaster, Sir,
109
Rogers, E. W., 293-5
Roll Out The Barrel, 325
Romanies, 32
Romans, 36-45, 55;
apples, 194; bridges,
86; brooches, 203;
coins, 208; and Druids,
33; fairs, 128;
mythology, 18; and
owls, 24; oysters, 196;
wells, 11-12
Rome, 40, 64, 84, 223
Roosevelt, Franklin, D.,
324
Roosevelt, Theodore, 301
rosemary, 201
Ross, Mr, 307
Rossetti, Christina, 195
Rotherham, 102
Rotherhide, 133
Roundheads, 174-5
Rouse, Bravo, 273
rowan wood, 117, 118

Roxburghe Ballads, 255
Royal Air Force (R.A.F),
321
Royal Cavalcade, 302
Royal Chelsea Hospital,
181
Royal Command
Performance, 1912, 292
Royal Eagle Coronation
Pleasure Grounds, 273
royal family, 61-2
Royal Military College,
Sandhurst, 237
Royal Navy, 162-4,
242-3, 253-8, 310, 311,
324
Royal Oak Day, 179
R.S.P.C.A., 253
rue, 201
Rumania, 18
Rule Britannia, 207-8
Run Rabbit, Run, 324-5
Runswick Bay, 20
Rusher, J. G., 168, 194,
199, 206
Russia, 25, 262

sacrifices, child, 86-7;
'sacred king', 95
sage, 201
sailors, 71, 122
St Bartholomew's,
London, 129, 130
St Bartholomew's
Hospital, 110
St Catherine's Day, 144
St Clement Danes,
London, 151
St Clement's Eastcheap,
151
St David's, 85
St George, Somerset,
119-20
St George and The Dragon,
106
St George's Day, 106
St Giles' Fair, 135-6
St Helena, 245
St Magnus Mary,
London, 88
St Martin-in-the-Fields,
151, 181
St Martin's Church,

London, 151
St Mary-le-Bow,
London, 152-4
St Mary Newchurch,
London, 153
St Mary Overy, London,
132
St Mary's, Hornby, 77
St Michael Paternoster,
London, 110
St Olav's Well, 16
St. Pancreas, London, 133
St Patrick's Breastplate,
79-81
St Patrick's Day, 82
St Paul's Cathedral, 154,
190, 191, 243, 245
St Sepulchre's, London,
152
St Swithin's Day, 82
St Valentine's Day, 84
saints, 38-9, 79-85, 105-6
Saklatvala, Beram, 55
salt, 117
Salvation Army, 273, 279
Samson, 48-9
San Salvadour, 141
sand, 205
Sanscrit, 32
Santa Claus, 1
Santa Maria, 141
Saracens, 107
Sassoon, Siegfried, 312
Saul, Ireland, 81
Savannah, Battle of,
232-3
Saxons, 55-6, 57, 58-90,
91-2, 128
*Say Brothers Will You Meet
Us On Canaan's Happy
Shore*, 268
Scandinavia, 11, 253
Scarborough Castle, 157
Schubert, Franz, 5
Scot, Michael, 40
Scotland, battle of
Bannockburn, 104-5,
107; bees, 26; Black
Douglas, 107; blood
charms, 125; calendar
reform, 40; and
Charles II, 178;
Hallowe'en, 117;

Jacobites, 214-24; King Arthur, 56-7; ladybirds, 28; lullabies, 2; and Mary Queen of Scots, 160-2; pins, 20, 123; plague, 192-3; rhymes about death, 19; ring games, 19; siege of Berwick, 104; snail superstitions, 25; sneezing, 74; songs, 225-8; unicorns, 22-3; union with England, 207; water rhymes, 12-13; weather rhymes, 59

Scots, 55

Scott, Harold, 272

Scott, Lady John, 263, 264-5

Scott, Sir Walter, 224

Scutari, 263

sea shanties, 227, 253-8

Seabrook, Mr, 133

seaside songs, 296-8

seasons, 64

Sebastopol, 262

Sellenger's Round, 97

Sennet, Stan, 320

September, 41

Serraillier, Ian, *Everest Climbed*, 326

Service, Robert, *Tipperary Days*, 314-15

Seven Years' War, 223

Severn, river, 175

Severus, Septimus, Emperor, 115

Seymour, Jane, 154

Shafto family, 228-9

Shafto, Bobby, 228-9, 230

Shafto, John, 229

Shafto, Miss, 228-9

Shafto, Robert, 229

Shafto, Thomas, 229

Shakespeare, William, 89; *Macbeth*, 24; *A Midsummer Night's Dream*, 8, 24, 121

shamrock, 81

Shaw, Mary Elizabeth, 240

sheep, 34-5, 113-14

Shelley, Percy Bysshe, 239

Shepherd's Mountain Call, 283

'shepherd's score', 34-5

Sheridan, Mark, 296-7

Sherwood Forest, 108, 109-10

Shipton, Mother, 15

shoes, 186-7, 204, 205

Shooter's Hill, 133

Shropshire, 78, 179

Shrove Tuesday, 70

Silent Night, 4-5

Simnel cake, 68

Simple Simon, 196

Sing a Song of Sixpence, 147-8, 196

Sirius, 39

Sixtus V, Pope, 163

Skinner, John S., 249

skipping chants, 90, 242, 319

Skye, Isle of, 222

Slaney, river, 81

slang, rhyming, 315-19

slavery, 33, 255, 267

Sloman, Charles, 273

Smith, John Stafford, 249

Smithfield, 130, 156

snails, 25

snakes, 62, 78-9, 81

Snap, 106

sneezing, 74

snow, 59

Snow White and The Seven Dwarfs, 325

Somerset, 19, 119-20, 146-7

Somme, Battle of the, 311

Song and Skylark, 257

Song Stories for the Kindergarten, 281

Sorley, Charles Hamilton, 309-10

'Soul cake', 120

'Souling', 120

South Africa, 285-6

Southampton, 129

space travel, 327-8

Spain, 1, 141, 142, 169, 204

Spanish Armada, 162-4

Speed Bonny Boat, 223

spiders, 127

Sprayton, 139

Spring, 70-1, 96-7

Spring equinox, 70

springs, 11-14, 16

Stafford, Thomas, 157

stairs, 124

Stalybridge, 302

Stamford Bridge, 91

The Star, 248

The Star-Spangled Banner, 249-50

Starling, J. K., 290

Stephen, King of England, 108

Stevens, V. F., *Merchant Navy*, 324

Stirling Castle, 104

Stockham, Anne, 168

Stockham, Peter, 168

Stoll Theatre, 288

storms, 59, 60

Strand, London, 97

Stratford-on-Avon, 136

Stratton, Eugene, 282-3

strawberries, 194-5

street cries, 193-207, 274

Stuart, James Francis Edward (The Old Pretender), 10, 182, 183-5, 212, 214-15, 219, 223

Stuart, Leslie, 282

Stuart, House of, 23

Stuart era, 48, 130, 169-208

Sturbridge Fair, 129-30

Suetonius, 33

Suffolk, 144, 186, 248

Suffolk Regiment, 309

suffragettes, 296

suicide, 21

Sunday, 72

Surrey, 199-200

Sussex, 66

Sweden, 11

Swithin, St, 82

Sydney, Harry, 271-2

Symons, J., 128

Syria, 194

Syros, 310

Tagus, river, 86
Tamlin, 120
Taversham family, 229
Taylor, Ann, 248
Taylor, Jane, 248
Taylor, Mr, 248
teddy bears, 301-2
The Teddy Bear's Picnic, 302
teeth, 53, 125-7
'Ten little nigger boys', 35
Tennyson, Lord, 5, 245, 259; *Break, Break, Break*, 270; *The Charge of the Light Brigade*, 260-6
Tenzing, Sherpa, 326-7
Thackeray, William Makepeace, *Vanity Fair*, 244
Thames, river, 86, 88, 134-5, 151, 196, 270-1
Thames Conservancy, 271
thatchers, 103
theatre, 130, 181
thistles, 67
Thomas, Ambroise, 238
Thompson, James, 207, 212
Thompson, John, 214
Thompson's Gipsy Choir, 306
Three blind mice, 154-6
thyme, 201
Tibet, 22-3, 326
tickling rhymes, 73, 301
Tiddy Doll, 131
The Times, 260
Tintagel, 57
Tissington Wells, 16-17
To Anacreon in Heaven, 249
toads, 127
Todd, James Henthorn, 79
Tojo, 326
Tom he was a Piper's son, 211
tom-trot, 172
tombstones, 43
tongue-twisters, 52-5
Tories, 218

Tower of London, 23, 31, 171
Trafalgar, Battle of, 243
Transvaal, 286
'trashing', 76
trees, 33, 59, 60, 61-2, 117, 128, 179
Tresham, Lord, 170
Tuck, Friar, 109
Tudor era, 48, 141-68
Turkey, 49, 262
turnip lanterns, 119
Tussaud, Madame, 245-7
Tweed, river, 12-13
Twelfth Night, 62, 66
Twinkle, twinkle little star, 247-8
Two Lovely Black Eyes, 278-9

unemployment, 113, 149
unicorns, 21-3
Union Jack, 106, 208, 327
Ursula, Abbess, 109

Vagrancy Law, 149
Valentine, St, 84, 106
valentines, 84
Vance, Alfred, 298
vegetables, 195-6
Venice, 173
Vernon, Horace, 302
Versailles, 246
The Vicar of Bray, 209-11
Victoria, Queen of England, 259-60, 286, 287
Victoria Park, Hackney, 89
Victory, 243
Vikings, 87, 91
Voltaire, 246
vultures, 31

Wade, General, 216, 218
waits, 68
Wales, castles, 96, 99, 103; counting, 35; Eisteddfod, 33; Jacobites, 216; King Arthur, 57; St David, 85; St Patrick, 81; witches, 116

Walkinshaw, Clementina, 223
Walsingham, Earl of, 159
War of 1812, 249
Wars of the Roses, 110, 141
warts, 127-8
Warwickshire, 304
washing, 123-4
Washington, 235, 266, 268
Washington, George, 235
wassailing, 66-7
water chants, 10-18
water spirits, 86
watercress, 202
Waterloo, Battle of, 244-5
Watson, *Scot's Poems*, 225
We Run Them In, 293
weather lore and rhymes, 45, 58-61, 71
weaving, 102-3
wedding cakes, 159
weddings, 49, 75-7, 122, 187; *see also* marriage
Weever, John, *Ancient Funeral Monuments*, 37
Wellington, Duke of, 236, 237, 244-5
wells, 11-18, 123
Wells, Charles, 277
Wessex, 79, 82
West Country, 66, 93, 96, 213
West Indies, 141, 243
Westminster Abbey, 92, 162
Westminster Gazette, 310
Westminster School, 70, 269
Westmorland, Lord, 157
Wetmore, W. J., 267-8
Wheatsheaf Inn, Newcastle, 284, 285
wheelwrights, 205
When Irish Eyes Are Smiling, 305
Where Did You Get That Hat?, 328
Whigs, 9, 184, 218
whistling, 124
The White Paternoster, 43

Whitehall Palace, 158
Whitelands College, 97
Whitestocking Day, 254
Whiting, Richard, 146-7
Whittaker, 302
Whittington, Dick, 110-11, 153
Whittle, Charlie, 296
Whitworth Hall, 228
Who Killed Cock Robin?, 93-5
Who Were You With Last Night?, 297
The Whole Hog Or None At All, 299
whooping cough, 20, 127
Wickham, Captain, 232
Widdecombe Fair, 138-40
Wilfred, Bishop of Northumbria, 85
Will Scarlet, 109
William I, King of England, 91-2
William II, King of England, 92-5
William III, King of England, 181-2, 316
William IV, King of England, 89, 256, 259, 260, 273

William, Harry, 304
Wilton Place, Dymock, 21
Wiltshire, 229
Winchester, 56, 82, 129
wind, 116
Winner, Septimus, 274-5
winter, 59, 64
The Wise Men of Gotham, 96
wishing rhymes, 9
wishing wells, 17-18, 123
witches and witchcraft, 20-1, 62, 95, 115-19, 122
Witton Fell, 17
Wolsey, Cardinal, 143-4
wool, 113-14
Worcester, 100
Worcestershire, 204
Worcestershire Regiment, 303
Wordsworth, William, 241
World War I, 198, 296, 297, 303, 306, 307-8, 309-15, 324
World War II, 33, 89, 240, 304, 309, 320-6, 327-8
wormwood, 202

Wren, Sir Christopher, 153-4, 190-1
Wright, Mrs, 305

Yankee Doodle, 233-5
Yes, We Have No Bananas, 328
York, 85, 144
York, Frederick Augustus, Duke of, 236-8, 260
York, Henry, Duke of, 223
York, House of, 110, 141
York Empire, 305
Yorkshire, 229; apples, 63; ash tree rhymes, 61; 'dimple' verses, 73-4; fairies, 19, 20; and Guy Fawkes, 172; harvest rhymes, 66; marriage rhymes, 75; moon chants, 9; pancakes, 70; ring games, 102; 'shepherd's score', 35; snail superstitions, 25; water spirits, 13; weather rhymes, 59, 60; wells, 14-16, 17-18
Ypres, 312, 313